Recommended Principles to Guide Academy-Industry Relationships

Purpose: To sustain and protect academic freedom, academic professionalism, research integrity, and public trust.

Dedicated to the memory of
Victor J. Stone (AAUP President, 1982–84),
University of Illinois College of Law

AMERICAN ASSOCIATION OF UNIVERSITY PROFESSORS

Distributed by the University of Illinois Press

To impart the results of their own and their fellow specialists' investigations and reflection, both to students and to the general public, without fear or favor . . . requires (among other things) that the university teacher shall be exempt from any pecuniary motive or inducement to hold, or to express, any conclusion which is not the genuine and uncolored product of his own study or that of fellow specialists. Indeed, the proper fulfillment of the work of the professoriate requires that our universities shall be so free that no fair-minded person shall find any excuse for even a suspicion that the utterances of university teachers are shaped or restricted by the judgment, not of professional scholars, but of inexpert and possibly not wholly disinterested persons outside of their own ranks. . . . To the degree that professional scholars, in the formation and promulgation of their opinions, are, or by the character of their tenure appear to be, subject to any motive other than their own scientific conscience and a desire for the respect of their fellow experts, to that degree the university teaching profession is corrupted; its proper influence upon public opinion is diminished, and vitiated; and society at large fails to get from its scholars, in an unadulterated form, the peculiar and necessary service which it is the office of the professional scholar to furnish. "1915 Declaration of Principles on Academic Freedom and Academic Tenure," *AAUP Policy Documents and Reports,* Tenth Edition (Washington, DC: AAUP, 2006), 294–95.

ISBN 978-0-252-03824-2 (hardcover)
ISBN 978-0-252-07982-5 (paperback)

aaup
FOUNDATION

This report was largely written prior to the 2013 organizational restructuring of the American Association of University Professors, but it is being published in book form by the AAUP Foundation, a legal entity that was established through the restructuring. The AAUP Foundation was organized for such charitable and educational purposes, including establishing and supporting principles of academic freedom and the quality of higher education in a free and democratic society.

Contents

Preface

The American Association of University Professors (AAUP) hereby issues this comprehensive report, *Recommended Principles to Guide Academy-Industry Relationships.* Work on this project began prior to the 2013 organizational restructuring of the AAUP and at that time was funded by a bequest from the estate of Victor J. Stone, a professor in the College of Law at the University of Illinois at Urbana-Champaign who served as AAUP general counsel and from 1982 until 1984 as AAUP president, and by grants from the Open Society Foundations, the AAUP's Academic Freedom Fund, and the Canadian Association of University Teachers (CAUT). This report is being published in book form by the AAUP Foundation, which was established through restructuring to support academic freedom and the quality of higher education in a free and democratic society. Grants to the AAUP (before restructuring) and to the AAUP Foundation (after restructuring) from a number of AAUP chapters and state conferences have made the publication of this book possible. Donors include the chapters at Connecticut State University, Michigan State University, Oakland University, the University of New Hampshire, the University of Rhode Island, Rider University, the University of Illinois at Urbana-Champaign, Utah Valley University, and Wright State University, as well as the Assembly of State Conferences, the Nevada Faculty Alliance, and the AAUP state conferences in Alabama, California, Colorado, Connecticut, Illinois, Louisiana, Minnesota, Missouri, New York, Ohio, Texas, and Washington. An updated list of donors will be published in *Academe*.

This is perhaps the longest report the AAUP has ever produced, as well as the most comprehensive in its scope and collation of empirical evidence. It addresses issues that make the news weekly and regularly affect higher education in the United States and across the world. The days when industry-funded research was concentrated in a limited number of universities have passed. Every type and size of institution now faces both the opportunities and the responsibilities associated with industry-sponsored research relationships. And such relationships occur throughout the world. As a result, faculty members both here and abroad should find the report useful.

In the Summary of Recommendations, the report first outlines the 56 principles that the AAUP recommends all colleges and universities adopt, as appropriate, in their governing and advisory documents to manage academy-industry engagement. Appendix A provides condensed versions of the 56 principles in language suitable for faculty handbooks and collective bargaining agreements. The precise language a campus chooses to employ might vary according to the nature of the destination document, but much of the sample policy language provided in Appendix A should prove directly transferable.

The lengthy Introduction to this report provides a detailed overview of the current state of engagement between industry and the academy, and discusses why the AAUP is issuing these 56 principles now. The main body of the report analyses each of the AAUP's 56 recommended principles individually, discussing its rationale, significance, and application in detail. A faculty senate involved in reviewing, adopting, and implementing the recommendations should benefit from this detailed information.

Finally, Appendix B summarizes the provenance and specific sources for each of the 56 principles, identifying whether each is drawn directly from previous recommendations issued by the AAUP and other professional associations, or whether it is new.

The report demonstrates the urgent need to give faculty governing bodies greater authority over the principles and practices that regulate outside funding, and over the disposition of inventions derived from faculty research. But the report is by no means exclusively an assertion of faculty rights. It specifies—and emphasizes—the responsibilities that must come with outside funding, including public disclosure of financial conflicts of interest. Not all will readily embrace these responsibilities, but the time has surely come when every institution must debate and consider them.

This report began with a 2010 decision by Committee A on Academic Freedom and Tenure to examine the issues surrounding industry-academy engagement. A small group met early in 2011 to draft a set of sample recommendations. The resulting discussion began to reveal the scope and challenges of the project. Jennifer Washburn, an investigative journalist and author familiar with the relevant literature, was invited to help prepare a full report in collaboration with AAUP president Cary Nelson. Valuable advice came from Ernst Benjamin, former AAUP general secretary, Cat Warren, editor of *Academe,* and from the AAUP's Department of Academic Freedom, Tenure, and Shared Governance. A draft was then sent for review and comment to three AAUP standing committees (Academic Freedom and Tenure, College and University Governance, and Professional Ethics—chaired at the time, respectively, by David Rabban, Larry Gerber, and Debra Nails) and to numerous knowledgeable faculty members, administrators, and other authorities. A substantial packet of responses included comments from Marcia Angell (Medicine, Harvard University), Gerald Barnett (Research Technologies Enterprise Initiative), Eric Campbell (Medicine, Harvard University), Michael Davis (Philosophy, Illinois Institute of Technology), John R. Fuisz (The Fuisz-Kundu Group LLP), Larry Gerber (History, Auburn University), Gregory Girolami (Chemistry, University of Illinois at Urbana-Champaign), Stanton A. Glantz (Medicine, University of California, San Francisco), Robert Gorman (Law, University of Pennsylvania), Claire Katz (Philosophy, Texas A&M University), Jonathan Knight (former head of the AAUP Department of Academic Freedom, Tenure, and Shared Governance), Sheldon Krimsky (Urban and Environmental Policy, Tufts University), Russ Lea (Vice President for Research, University of South Alabama), Risa Lieberwitz (Labor and Employment Law, Cornell University), Gerald Markowitz (Public Health and American Social History, John Jay College of Justice), Debra Nails (Philosophy, Michigan State University), Richard Nelson (International Political Economy, Columbia University), Christopher Newfield (English, University of California, Santa Barbara), David Rosner (History and Public Health, Columbia University), Donald Stein (Medicine, Emory University), Joerg Tiede (Computer Science, Illinois Wesleyan University), Paula A. Treichler (Communications Research and Medicine, University of Illinois at Urbana-Champaign), John Wilson (editor of *Illinois Academe*), and Stephen Wing (Epidemiology, North Carolina State University). Washburn and Nelson incorporated the responses as appropriate into a revised draft for the standing committees to review. The consultant readers are not, of course, responsible for the final recommendations, and providing their names here does not imply their endorsement of all our recommendations, but thanks go to them for their serious, detailed, and immensely helpful engagement with the text.

A draft of the report was published online for comment in June 2012. Among the additional responses received at that point was a detailed commentary from the Association of University Technology Managers (AUTM). Once again, the coauthors of the report, Washburn and Nelson, incorporated appropriate comments into a revised version of the report. Final responsibility for wording and editorial changes, however, rests with Cary Nelson.

Jim Turk, the executive director of the Canadian Association of University Teachers, participates in meetings of the AAUP's Committee A on Academic Freedom and Tenure. CAUT issued a much condensed (and adapted) version of our Summary of Recommendations at the time we placed our full report online for comment.

On a personal note, I would like to give special thanks to Steven Doran, a PhD candidate in Communications at the University of Illinois at Urbana–Champaign, who provided indispensable assistance with the numerous editing, formatting, and computer challenges that accompany a text of this length, and Paula A. Treichler, my lifelong partner, who brought her fearless and unequalled editing skills to the task of polishing the report's prose. Finally, with a project of this scope, I would like to take the opportunity to recognize the critical help we received from the AAUP's national staff. Greg Scholtz helped us manage the approval process and our requests from the Academic Freedom Fund. Bob Kreiser, possessing wide knowledge of AAUP history and principles, pointed us toward key documents and gave sage advice about the 56 recommended principles. Mike Ferguson found a copy editor, designer, and printer and managed their work while also obtaining cost estimates for the project. Ezra Deutsch-Feldman shepherded us through several challenges handling such a complex electronic document. Robin Burns shared the public comment version of the report with reporters, while Katherine Isaac distributed it to faculty members nationwide. Finally, I would like to thank Martin Snyder, who helped to manage this massive enterprise with flawless political and practical wisdom at every stage of the process.

Income from the sale of this book is divided equally between the University of Illinois Press and the AAUP Foundation.

Cary Nelson
AAUP President, 2006–12

Glossary of Acronyms and Abbreviations

AAMC—Association of Academic Medical Centers
AAMC—Association of American Medical Colleges
AAU—American Association of Universities
AAUP—American Association of University Professors
ABIM—American Board of Internal Medicine
ABL—Advanced Biological Laboratory
ACE—American Council on Education
ACCME—Accreditation Council for Continuing Medical Education
ACP—American College of Physicians
ADAMHA—Alcohol, Drug Abuse, and Mental Health Administration
AGB—Association of Governing Boards
AIDS—Acquired Immune Deficiency Syndrome
AIR—Academy-Industry Relationship
AMSA—American Medical Student Association
APA—American Psychiatric Association
ASIM—American Society of Internal Medicine
ATS—American Thoracic Society
AUTM—Association of University Technology Managers
BB&T—Branch Banking and Trust
BBC—British Broadcasting Corporation
BD—Bayh-Dole Act
BIP—Background Intellectual Property
BMJ—*British Medical Journal*
CAUT—Canadian Association of University Professors
CDC—Centers for Disease Control
CFR—Code of Federal Regulations
CHE—Chronicle of Higher Education
CIA—Central Intelligence Agency
CME—Continuing Medical Education
CML—chronic myelogenous leukemia
COGR—Council on Government Relations
COI—Conflict of Interest
CRADA—Cooperative Research and Development Agreement
DHHS—Department of Health and Human Services
DOD—Department of Defense
DOE—Department of Energy

DOJ—Department of Justice
DSM—Diagnostic and Statistical Manual of Mental Disorders
DSMB—Data Safety Monitoring Board
EBI—Energy Biosciences Institute
EPA—Environmental Protection Agency
EPRI—Electric Power Research Institute
ERTA—Economic Recovery Tax Act
ETS—Environmental Tobacco Smoke
FASEB—Federation of American Societies for Experimental Biology
FCOI—Financial Conflict of Interest
FDA—Food and Drug Administration
FFEL—Federal Family Education Loan
FRP—Request for Proposals
FSU—Florida State University
FTE—Full-time Faculty Equivalent
GAO—General Accounting Office
GAO—Government Accountability Office
GM—genetically modified
GSK—GlaxoSmithKline
HIV—Human Immunodeficiency Virus
IBM—International Business Machine
ICMJE—International Committee of Medical Journal Editors
IMAP—Institute of Medicine as a Profession
IND—Investigational New Drug
IOM—Institute of Medicine
IP—Intellectual Property
IRB—Institutional Review Board
IRC—Immune Response Corporation
IRC—Industrial Research Consortium
IT—Information Technology
JAMA—Journal of the American Medical Association
MCV—Medical College of Virginia
MIT—Massachusetts Institute of Technology
MOOC—Massive Open Online Course
MOU—Memorandum of Understanding
MTA—Material Transfer Agreement
NACDA—National Advisory Council on Drug Abuse
NADI—Novartis Agricultural Discovery Institute
NAS—National Academy of Sciences
NEJM—New England Journal of Medicine
NIDA—National Institute on Drug Abuse

NIH—National Institutes of Health
NRC—National Research Council
NRDA—Natural Resource Damage Assessment
NSA—National Security Agency
NSAID—Nonsteroidal Anti-Inflammatory Drug
NSB—National Science Board
NSF—National Science Foundation
NYT—New York Times
NYU—New York University
OIG—Office of the Inspector General
OTT—Office of Technology Transfer
P&G—Proctor and Gamble
PEAC—President's Engineering Advisory Council
PHS—Public Health Service
PRISP—Pat Roberts Intelligence Scholars Program
R&D—Research and Development
RFP—Request for Faculty Research Proposals
RICO—Racketeer Influenced and Corrupt Organizations Act
RIN—Research Information Network
RIRs—Recommended Institutional Regulations
SCR—Semiconductor Research Corporation
SBU—Sensitive But Unclassified
SCA—Strategic Corporate Alliance
SPLC—Student Press Law Center
SSRI—Selective Serotonin Reuptake Inhibitor
TIRC—Tobacco Industry Research Committee
UCB—University of California at Berkeley
UCB-N—University of California at Berkeley-Novartis
UCLA—University of California at Los Angeles
UCSF—University of California at San Francisco
UIDP—University-Industry Demonstration Partnership
UIRC—University-Industry Research Center
UN—United Nations
US—United States
VCU—Virginia Commonwealth University
WAME—World Association of Medical Editors
WHO—World Health Organization

Summary of Recommendations

56 Principles to Guide
Academy-Industry Engagement

The American Association of University Professors (AAUP) has drafted these principles to encourage universities and their faculties to adopt stronger, more comprehensive rules to guide sponsored research on campus and to manage individual and institutional conflicts of interest more effectively. In issuing this report, the AAUP seeks to ensure that the standards and practices it recommends are consistently applied across the university as a whole. The report contains 56 recommended principles. A majority (35) are closely drawn from previous statements issued by the AAUP or other prominent academic societies and associations (such as the Institute of Medicine, the Association of American Universities, and the Association of American Medical Colleges). The remainder are either adapted from these other associations or are new recommendations that the AAUP is issuing for the first time. (Appendix B identifies which recommendations fall into each category, along with specific sources.)

The AAUP seeks to promote deeper awareness of how commercial relationships—though often highly beneficial—may have far-reaching consequences for the university, its missions, and its constituents (students, faculty, colleagues, patients, the public) as well as for the academic profession (in areas ranging from research integrity and reliability to knowledge sharing, public health, and public trust). Although the report focuses primarily on academy-industry relationships, it addresses government- and nonprofit-sponsored research when related and appropriate. Because students, graduate assistants, postdoctoral fellows, and academic professionals often work on sponsored research, the report also addresses their working conditions.

For these 56 principles to be effective, academic senates or comparable faculty governing bodies will need to review them, adapt them as appropriate, and then recommend their adoption in faculty handbooks, university policy statements, faculty guidelines, or collective bargaining contracts. (Appendix A contains specific suggested policy language that faculty and administrators may employ or adapt in their own written policies and guidelines.) Faculty bodies will benefit from working cooperatively, whenever possible, with knowledgeable university administrators to formulate clearer campus guidelines and protocols. Many administrators will be equally interested in developing clear campus guidelines that will provide greater clarity in negotiating agreements with potential sponsors.

Contents: The 56 principles recommended by the AAUP fall into two broad categories:

> GENERAL PRINCIPLES, which may be applied university-wide, that cover core academic norms and standards, such as authenticity of authorship, publication rights, and academic autonomy; they also address broad areas of academy-industry engagement, such as student education and training, financial conflicts of interest, and intellectual property management, and

> TARGETED PRINCIPLES that address specific types of academy-industry engagement, including strategic corporate alliances (SCAs), industry-sponsored clinical trials, and academy-industry interactions at academic medical centers.

Many of the principles that the AAUP recommends in this report apply to the university generally, not just to sponsored research. A faculty body reviewing these principles might begin by making certain that all relevant campus documents incorporate the fundamental positions on shared governance and academic freedom embodied in Principles 1 and 2; the reinforcement of academic publication and research and data rights in Principles 3 and 5; the protections for recruiting, impartial academic evaluation, and access to grievance procedures in Principles 8–10; the basic intellectual property guarantees in Principles 11–13; and the commitment to conflict of interest disclosure in Principle 22. Reaching consensus about these opening principles will inevitably trigger a continuing discussion of others.

At many institutions, adoption of the full set of intellectual property principles, numbers 11–21—principles that should cover all intellectual property, not just IP generated by industry-sponsored research—would represent a significant change in recent campus culture. Indeed as universities and their campus administrations become increasingly interested in claiming the rights to faculty IP, the benefit of installing these principles in faculty handbooks and collective bargaining contracts is clear. The goal should be to include appropriate language in both institutional policy guidelines and in all university contracts for funded research.

Similarly, a comprehensive campuswide set of conflict of interest (COI) policies will require consideration of the entire COI subsection, numbers 22–31. Given that sponsored research and paid consultancies occur at all types of academic institutions, reviewing each institution's existing COI policy statements and regulations—or establishing them, if none exist—should be a high priority. At the same time, Principles 36–47 are salient only for institutions that already have, or contemplate establishing, the large-scale, multi-year research partnerships known as strategic corporate alliances (SCAs). Principles 32–35 and 49–56 (addressing clinical research and conditions in academic medical colleges) are of primary interest to institutions with faculty members or academic units engaged in biomedical research and patient care.

A first step toward implementing these recommendations might be to have an AAUP chapter or a group of concerned faculty introduce a resolution in the faculty senate, or in a comparable campus governing body, to create a committee charged with comparing campus-based policies, practices, and regulations with this report's recommendations. The committee would research and report on faculty-handbook recommendations, formal university policies, patent and licensing office protocols, and other campus guidance documents. At universities in which faculty engage in collective bargaining, some of the policies could be incorporated into union contracts. In all cases, committees would consult widely with diverse groups of faculty across disciplines and build broad-based consensus around these principles and the language recommended for the destination documents.

In formulating these principles, the AAUP inevitably recognized tensions between the ideal conditions we would like to promote and the realities of contemporary academy-industry relations. We therefore sometimes state a principle first in more ideal terms and then offer qualifications, recognizing the partial compromises that may be necessary. Some faculty, academic senates, administrators, and universities will want to strengthen certain of these 56 principles, while others may wish to weaken them or adapt them in other ways. We aim to strike a realistic balance in proposing them, one flexible enough to stand the test of changing conditions. The primary value of the principles is to reaffirm universities' core academic and public missions, uphold professional academic and research standards, and influence contract relationships yet to be written or up for renewal.

Definition of a "significant" financial interest: Throughout this report and the following principles, the AAUP defines a financial interest to be "significant" if it is valued at or above $5,000 per year, and it is not controlled and/or managed by an independent entity, such as a mutual or pension fund. This definition is consistent with the definitions and de minimis threshold for financial disclosure established by the US Department of Health and Human Services in its 2011 conflict of interest disclosure rules *(Department of Health and Human Services, DHHS, 42 CFR Part 50, 45 CFR Part 94, "Responsibility of Applicants for Promoting Objectivity in Research for which Public Health Service Funding is Sought and Responsible Prospective Contractors," Federal Register, vol. 76, no. 165, August 25, 2011, available at: http://www.gpo.gov/fdsys/pkg/ FR-2011-08-25/pdf/2011-21633.pdf).*

The relevant sections of these DHHS rules are reprinted in full at the end of the Summary of Recommendations for easy reference. See pages 23–24.

PART I—GENERAL PRINCIPLES TO GUIDE ACADEMY-INDUSTRY ENGAGEMENT UNIVERSITY-WIDE

PRINCIPLE 1—Faculty Governance: The university must preserve the primacy of shared academic governance in establishing campuswide policies for planning, developing, implementing, monitoring, and assessing all donor agreements and collaborations, whether with private industry, government, or nonprofit groups. Faculty, not outside sponsors, should retain majority control over the campus management of such agreements and collaborations.

PRINCIPLE 2—Academic Freedom, Autonomy, and Control: The university must preserve its academic autonomy—including the academic freedom rights of faculty, students, postdoctoral fellows, and academic professionals—in all its relationships with industry and other funding sources by maintaining majority academic control over joint academy-industry committees and exclusive academic control over core academic functions (such as faculty research evaluations, faculty hiring and promotion decisions, classroom teaching, curriculum development, and course content).

PRINCIPLE 3—Academic Publication Rights: Academic publication rights must be fully protected, with only limited pre-publication delays (a maximum of 30–60 days★) to remove corporate proprietary or confidential information or to file for patents and other IP protections prior to publication.

Sponsor efforts to obstruct—or sponsored research agreements that do not permit—the free, timely, and open dissemination of research data, codes, reagents, methods, and results are unacceptable. Sponsor attempts to compel a faculty member, student, postdoctoral fellow, or academic professional to edit, revise, withhold, or delete contents in an academic publication (including a master's thesis or PhD dissertation) or presentation (beyond legally justified claims to protect explicit trade secrets) must be clearly prohibited in all sponsored research contracts and university policies. A funder is of course free to make editorial suggestions, but academic researchers must be free at all times to accept or reject them.

This time limit of 30–60 days for delays on publication (for the purpose of securing proprietary protection through a provisional patent or other IP filing) is consistent with recommendations issued by the National Institutes of Health, which are discussed in further detail in the main report.

PRINCIPLE 4—The Authenticity of Academic Authorship: To protect the authenticity of academic publishing, universities and their affiliated academic medical centers should prohibit faculty, students, postdoctoral fellows, medical residents, and other academic professionals from engaging in industry-led "ghostwriting" or "ghost authorship." Ghostwriting or ghostauthorship occurs when a private firm or an industry group initiates the publication of an "academic" article in a science or medical journal in support of its commercial products or interests, without publicly disclosing that the corporate entity has initiated and also often performed the initial drafting of the article, and then recruited an academic researcher (sometimes referred to as an "academic opinion leader") to sign on as the nominal "author" (frequently in exchange for a fee). Although ghostwriting has been especially widespread in academic medicine, prohibitions on ghostwriting should be applied university-wide and should cover all faculty and researchers; the practice violates scholarly standards and is unacceptable in any academic setting.

PRINCIPLE 5—Access to Complete Study Data and Independent Academic Analysis: University codes of conduct should prohibit participation in sponsored research that restricts investigators' ability to access the complete study data related to their sponsored research or that limits investigators' ability to conduct unfettered, free, and independent analyses of complete data to verify the accuracy and validity of final reported results. Protecting access to complete study data is particularly important in the area of clinical research, where drug trials and other medical investigations are often conducted at multiple institutions simultaneously. If the sponsor grants only partial access to the study's complete data sets or withholds other relevant research codes and materials, then the academic investigators and authors will not be able to perform a truly independent analysis of the study's data and outcomes. Universities should secure these basic academic freedom rights within the legal terms of all sponsored research contracts.

PRINCIPLE 6—Confidential and Classified Research: Classified research, as well as confidential corporate, government, or nonprofit research that cannot be published, is inappropriate on a university campus. Many institutions currently have written policies that ban classified government research on campus; the policies should be reviewed to ensure that they also ban confidential corporate research. Universities employ a variety of mechanisms for moving confidential and classified research off campus, sometimes using governance structures less subject to academic oversight. Sorting through multiple categories of "national security," "classified," and "sensitive but unclassified" (SBU) information requires expert monitoring by faculty governance bodies. These faculty bodies should operate with a strong presumption against permitting any confidential, classified, or non-publishable research on campus. Academic analyses and research results should always be publishable absent a compelling case to the contrary. This university commitment to knowledge sharing and openness should govern both the determination of which research will be confidential and thus cannot be performed on campus, as well as any rare exceptions that may be granted. As historical precedent suggests, the special circumstances of a formal congressional declaration of war against a specified nation-state or states may justify exceptions to the policies for the duration of the conflict.

PRINCIPLE 7—Academic Consulting: To address the potential for conflicts of commitment★ and financial conflicts of interest, all consulting contracts worth $5,000 or more a year should be reported to the university's standing COI committee(s) charged with reviewing and managing both individual and institutional conflicts of interest (see Principle 24 for discussion of these committees). Neither faculty members nor administrators should sign a consulting contract that undercuts their professional ability to express their own independent expert opinions publicly, except when consulting with industry, government, or other parties on explicitly classified or proprietary matters. All such consulting agreements should be secured in writing.

★*A "conflict of commitment" arises whenever a faculty member's or administrator's outside consulting and other activities have the potential to interfere with their primary duties, including teaching, research, time with students, or other service and administrative obligations to the university.*

PART II—GENERAL PRINCIPLES FOR ACADEMIC EDUCATION AND TRAINING

PRINCIPLE 8—Recruiting and Advising Graduate Students, Medical Residents, and Faculty: The admission of graduate students to degree programs and the appointment of medical residents and faculty should be based on their overall qualifications, not on their potential to work under a particular donor agreement or in a particular collaborative research alliance, whether commercial, governmental, or nonprofit. A PhD student's main adviser should be free of any significant financial interest, including equity, in a company that is funding or stands to profit from the student's thesis or dissertation research. Exceptions should evaluate both conflicts of interest and potential conflicts of commitment, all of which should be disclosed to all affected parties and periodically reviewed by an appropriate faculty body.

PRINCIPLE 9—Impartial Academic Evaluation: Students, postdoctoral fellows, academic professionals, and junior colleagues should always be entitled to impartial and fair evaluations of their academic performance. Because of the risk of both real and perceived bias, faculty members with a significant personal financial interest in the outcome of their students' research should not have sole responsibility for evaluating student progress toward a degree.

PRINCIPLE 10—Grievance Procedures: Universities should establish effective, well-publicized grievance procedures for all students, postdoctoral fellows, academic professionals, and faculty members, tenured and untenured, so they may freely and safely report obstacles encountered while pursuing their research and educational objectives. Obstacles may include but are not limited to inappropriate commercial or other sponsor influence over the conduct or analysis of research, unwarranted delays to degree completion, financial conflicts of interest, conflicts of commitment, and conflicts over ownership of intellectual property. Faculty with financial conflicts related to a grievance filing should recuse themselves from its adjudication in formal proceedings. Informal resolution of grievances is often preferable when possible.

PART III—GENERAL PRINCIPLES FOR MANAGEMENT OF INTELLECTUAL PROPERTY (IP)

PRINCIPLE 11—Faculty Inventor Rights and IP Management: Faculty members' fundamental rights to direct and control their own research do not terminate with a new invention or research discovery; these rights properly extend to decisions about their intellectual property—including invention management, licensing, commercialization, dissemination, and public use. Faculty assignment of an invention to a management agent★ (including the university that hosted the underlying research) should be voluntary and negotiated rather than mandatory, unless federal statutes or previous sponsored research agreements dictate otherwise. Faculty inventors retain a vital interest in the disposition of their research inventions and discoveries and should, therefore, retain rights to negotiate the terms of their disposition. Neither the university nor its management agents should undertake intellectual property decisions or legal actions directly or indirectly affecting a faculty member's research, inventions, instruction, or public service without the faculty member's express consent. Of course, faculty members, like other campus researchers, may voluntarily undertake specific projects under "work for hire" contracts.[1] When such agreements are truly voluntary and uncoerced, their contracted terms may legitimately narrow faculty IP rights.

★*The term "invention management agent," as used in this report, covers all persons tasked with handling university generated inventions and related intellectual property, including, for example, university technology transfer offices, affiliated research foundations, contract invention management agents, and legal consultants.*

PRINCIPLE 12—Shared Governance and the Management of University Inventions: Faculty have a collective interest in how university inventions derived from academic research are managed. Through shared governance, they have a responsibility to participate in the design of university protocols that set the norms, standards, and expectations under which faculty discoveries and inventions will be controlled, distributed, licensed, and commercialized. The faculty senate or an equivalent body should play a primary role in defining the policies and public-interest commitments that will guide university-wide management of inventions and other knowledge assets stemming from campus-based research. These protocols should devote special attention to the academic and public interest obligations covered in these principles. They should also require the formation of a specially assigned faculty committee to review the university's invention management practices regularly, ensure compliance with these principles, represent the interests of faculty investigators and inventors to the campus, and make recommendations for reform when necessary.

PRINCIPLE 13—Adjudicating Disputes Involving Inventor Rights: Just as the right to control research and instruction is integral to academic freedom, so too are faculty members' rights to control the disposition of their research inventions. Inventions made in the context of university work are the result of scholarship. University policies should direct all invention management agents to represent and protect the expressed interests of faculty inventors, along with the interests of the institution and the broader public. Where the interests diverge insurmountably, the faculty senate or equivalent body should adjudicate the dispute with the aim of promoting the greatest benefit for the research in question, the broader academic community, and the public good. Student and other academic professional inventors should also have access to grievance procedures if they believe their inventor or other intellectual property rights have been violated. Students should never be urged or required to surrender their IP rights in advance to the university as a condition of participating in a degree program.

PRINCIPLE 14—IP Management and Sponsored Research Agreements: In negotiating sponsored research agreements, university administrators should make every effort to inform potentially affected faculty researchers and to involve them meaningfully in early-stage negotiations concerning invention management and intellectual property. In the case of large-scale sponsored research agreements like strategic corporate alliances (SCAs), which can affect large numbers of faculty, not all of whom may be identifiable in advance, a special faculty governance committee should be convened to participate in early-stage negotiations, represent collective faculty interests, and ensure compliance with relevant university protocols. Faculty participation in all institutionally negotiated sponsored research agreements should always be voluntary.

PRINCIPLE 15—Humanitarian Licensing, Access to Medicines: When lifesaving drugs and other critical public health technologies are developed in academic laboratories with public funding support, universities have a special obligation to license such inventions so as to ensure broad public access in both the developing and the industrialized world. Exclusive university licenses to companies for breakthrough drugs or other critical public good inventions arising in agriculture, health, environmental safety, or other fields should include humanitarian licensing provisions that will enable distribution of drugs and other inventions in developing countries at affordable prices whenever feasible.

PRINCIPLE 16—Securing Broad Research Use and Distribution Rights: All contracts and agreements covering university-generated inventions should include an express reservation of rights—often known as a "research exemption"—to allow for academic, nonprofit, and government use of academic inventions and associated IP for non-commercial research purposes. Research exemptions should be reserved and well publicized prior to assignment or licensing so faculty and other academic researchers can share protected inventions and research results (including related data, reagents, and research tools) with colleagues at the host university or at any nonprofit or government institution. The freedom to share and practice academic discoveries—whether legally protected or not—for educational and research purposes is vital for the advancement of knowledge. It also enables investigators to replicate and verify published results, a practice essential to scientific integrity.

PRINCIPLE 17—Exclusive and Nonexclusive Licensing: Universities, their contracted management agents, and faculty should avoid exclusive licensing of patentable inventions, unless such licenses are absolutely necessary to foster follow-on use or to develop an invention that would otherwise languish. Exclusive or monopolistic control of academic knowledge should be sparing, rather than a presumptive default. When exclusive licenses are granted, they should have limited terms (preferably less than eight years), include requirements that the inventions be developed, and prohibit "assert licensing" or "trolling" (aggressively enforcing patents against an alleged infringer, often with no intention of manufacturing, marketing, or making productive use of the product). Exclusive licenses issued in order to permit broad access through reasonable and nondiscriminatory sublicensing, cross-licensing, and dedication of patents to an open standard may be expected to meet public access expectations. However, the preferred methods for disseminating university research are nonexclusive licensing and open dissemination, to protect universities' public interest mission, open research culture, and commitment to advancing research and inquiry through broad knowledge sharing. To enhance compliance and public accountability, universities should require all invention management agents to promptly and publicly report any exclusive licenses issued, together with written statements detailing why an exclusive license was necessary and why a nonexclusive one would not suffice. The faculty senate or comparable governing body should periodically review exclusive licenses and corresponding statements for consistency with this principle.

PRINCIPLE 18—Upfront Exclusive Licensing Rights for Research Sponsors: Universities should refrain from signing sponsored research agreements, especially multi-year strategic corporate alliance (SCA) agreements, that grant sponsors broad title or exclusive commercial rights to future sponsored research inventions and discoveries—unless such arrangements are narrowly defined and agreed to by all faculty participating in, or foreseeably affected by, the alliance. If this is not feasible, as in the case of larger SCAs, the faculty senate should review and approve the agreement and confirm its compatibility with academic freedom, faculty independence, and the university's public interest mission. All parties should consider the impact exclusive licenses could have on future uses of technologies. When granted, exclusive rights should be defined as narrowly as possible, restricted to targeted fields of use, and designed to safeguard against abuse of the exclusive position.

PRINCIPLE 19—Research Tools and Upstream Platform Research: Universities and their contracted invention management agents should make available and broadly disseminate research tools and other upstream platform inventions in which they have acquired an ownership interest. They should avoid assessing fees, beyond those necessary to cover the costs of maintaining the tools and disseminating them, and avoid other constraints that could hamper downstream research and development. No sponsored research agreement should include contractual obligations that prevent outside investigators from accessing data, tools, inventions, and reports relating to scholarly reviews of published research, matters of public health and safety, environmental safety, and urgent public policy decisions.

PRINCIPLE 20—Diverse Licensing Models for Diverse University Inventions: Universities and their invention management agents should develop multiple licensing models appropriate to diverse categories of academic inventions, differing objectives and commitments made by faculty investigators and inventors, varying practices in the wider community and in different industries, and varied conditions present at different stages in developing a technology. Licensing models commonly used to address opportunities in biotechnology, for example, should not be established as defaults in institutional policies or used indiscriminately across other areas of innovation. Faculty investigators and inventors and their management agents should work cooperatively to identify effective licensing and distribution models for each invention to enhance public availability and use. This may include established models (exclusive or nonexclusive licensing) as well as emergent ones (patent pools, open sourcing, and public licensing offered by institutions like Creative Commons for copyright-based work).

PRINCIPLE 21—Rights to "Background Intellectual Property" (BIP): University administrators and their agents should not act unilaterally when granting sponsors' rights to university-managed background intellectual property (BIP) related to a sponsor's proposed research area but developed without the sponsor's funding support. Universities should be mindful of how BIP rights will affect faculty inventors and other investigators who are not party to the sponsored research agreement. Nor should managers obligate the BIP of one set of investigators to another's sponsored research project, unless that BIP is already being made available under nonexclusive licensing terms or the affected faculty members have consented. To do otherwise risks a chilling effect on collegiality and on faculty willingness to work with university licensing agents.

PART IV—GENERAL PRINCIPLES FOR MANAGEMENT OF CONFLICTS OF INTEREST (COI) AND FINANCIAL CONFLICTS OF INTEREST (FCOI)

A conflict of interest (COI) is broadly defined as a situation in which an individual or a corporate interest has a tendency to interfere with the proper exercise of judgment on another's behalf. Those who prefer to distinguish between individual and institutional COI often define the former as a set of circumstances creating a risk that a secondary interest, such as financial gain, may unduly influence professional judgment or actions regarding a primary interest, such as research conduct, teaching, or patient welfare. Correspondingly, an institutional COI occurs when the financial interests of an institution or institutional officials, acting within their authority on behalf of the institution, may affect or appear to affect the research, education, clinical care, business transactions, or other governing activities of the institution. A growing body of empirical research has shown that financial conflicts of interest (FCOI) are associated with decision making, as well as research, bias. (See the Introduction to this report for details.) FCOI may also introduce unreliability into the research process, undermine public trust, and erode respect for institutions of higher education. Disclosure of a COI, even full disclosure of a financial interest with informed consent, fails to resolve or eliminate such problems. However, it is critically important as a first step toward promoting transparency and awareness of the existence of COIs.

PRINCIPLE 22—Comprehensive COI Policies: Every university should have a comprehensive, written COI policy, covering both individual and institutional COI. The policy or its accompanying guidelines should specify how all conflicts of interest (COI) and financial conflicts of interest (FCOI), in particular, will be reported, reviewed, managed, or eliminated. The guidelines should identify which FCOI must be reported, which are prohibited, and what actions will be taken if faculty members do not comply with COI disclosure and management policies. Enforcement actions for noncompliance may include a faculty-led investigation leading to possible censure, federal-grant agency notification, a temporary hold on interactions with conflicted sponsors, or a temporary ban on receipt of outside research funding.

PRINCIPLE 23—Consistent COI Enforcement across Campus: University COI policies must be adopted consistently across the whole institution, including affiliated medical schools, hospitals, institutes, centers, and other facilities, and they must apply to faculty, students, administrators, and academic professionals.

PRINCIPLE 24—Standing COI Committees: Every university should have one or two standing COI committees to oversee implementation of policies addressing individual and institutional COI. At least one member should be recruited from outside the institution and approved by the faculty governing body. All committee members should be free of COI related to their oversight responsibilities. After faculty COI disclosure statements have been reviewed by an appropriate standing committee, they should be made available to the public, preferably on a readily accessible online database, as the AAUP recommends under Principle 31.

PRINCIPLE 25—Reporting Individual COI: Faculty members and academic professionals should be required to report to the standing campus COI committee all significant outside financial interests relating directly or indirectly to their professional responsibilities (research, teaching, committee work, and other activities), including the dollar amounts involved and the nature of the services compensated. The report must be made regardless of whether or not people believe their financial interests might reasonably affect their current or anticipated university activities. Faculty members should also report family member (spouse, partner, or dependent child) patent royalty income and equity holdings related to their own teaching and research areas. All administrators should report similar financial interests to both their superiors and the COI committee. Presidents and chancellors should also report to the standing committee.

PRINCIPLE 26—Inter-office Reporting and Tracking of Institutional COI: To keep track of institutional COI, every institutional COI committee should have a well-developed, campuswide reporting system that requires the technology transfer office, the office of sponsored programs, the development office, the grants office, institutional review boards (IRBs), purchasing offices, and corresponding offices at affiliated medical institutions to report to the standing COI committee at least quarterly on situations that might give rise to institutional conflicts.

PRINCIPLE 27—Strategies for Reviewing, Evaluating, and Addressing COI: Disclosure of a COI is not a sufficient management strategy. The best course of action is not to acquire COI in the first place. Strategies for addressing *individual COI* include divesting troublesome assets, terminating consulting arrangements, resigning corporate board seats, and withdrawing from affected projects. Methods for addressing *institutional* COI include the institution divesting its equity interest in companies connected with campus research, placing conflicted equity holdings in independently managed funds, establishing explicit firewalls to separate financial from academic decisions, recusing conflicted senior administrators from knowledge of, or authority over, affected research projects, and requiring outside committee review or oversight. Some university presidents decline to serve on corporate boards to avoid the appearance of COI. Because of conflicting fiduciary responsibilities, campuses should prohibit senior administrators from receiving compensation for serving on corporate boards during their time in office.

PRINCIPLE 28—Developing a Formal, Written COI Management Plan: If a university's standing COI committee finds compelling circumstances for allowing a research project or other professional activity to continue in the presence of a significant FCOI—without the elimination of the conflict—the committee should document the circumstances and write a formal management plan for each case. The plan should detail how the university will manage the FCOI and eliminate or reduce risks to its affected constituents (students, collaborating researchers, faculty, patients), its pertinent missions (research integrity, informed consent, and recruitment of research volunteers), and its reputation and public trust. This recommendation is consistent with the Department of Health and Human Services (DHHS) National Institutes of Health (NIH) rules implemented in 2011 to address financial conflicts, which require all universities that receive DHHS grants to prepare and enforce such management plans. (Those rules are partially reprinted at the end of the Summary of Recommendations.)

PRINCIPLE 29—Oversight and Enforcement of COI Rules: All university COI policies should have effective oversight procedures and sanctions for noncompliance. These are essential to ensure compliance with university rules and to sustain public trust in the university's ability to regulate itself.

PRINCIPLE 30—University-Vendor Relationships and COI: Universities should ensure that vendor evaluation, selection, and contracting for university products and services are consistent with their academic mission and do not jeopardize the best interests of students. Vendors should never be persuaded or coerced into making financial contributions to the university, either through direct university donations or recruitment of other contributing donors, in exchange for winning university contracts. All university bidding for contracts and services related to such areas as banking and student loans should be conducted through a fair, impartial, and competitive selection process. Many universities currently have ethics policies banning gifts from vendors; the policies should also clearly prohibit institutions from accepting direct remuneration, or kickbacks, from vendors doing business with the university or its students. Such profiteering can undermine public trust in the university and compromise the best interests of the students the university has pledged to serve.

PRINCIPLE 31—COI Transparency: Public Disclosure of Financial Interests and COI Management Plans: University COI policies should require faculty, administrators, students, postdoctoral fellows, and academic professionals to disclose to all journal editors all significant personal financial interests that may be directly or indirectly related to the manuscripts they are submitting for consideration. COI disclosure on publications should summarize all related funding sources received during the past five years, not simply for the project at hand. The same COI disclosure requirements should apply to oral presentations delivered in conferences, courts, and legislative chambers. After the university's standing COI committee reviews faculty conflict of interest disclosure statements, they should be posted to a publicly accessible website, and this information should remain accessible for at least ten years. This measure will help institutions address growing demands from Congress, state governments, journal editors, the media, and public interest groups for increased transparency and reporting of faculty COI. It is consistent with DHHS-NIH (2011) rules, which require universities to disclose all significant FCOI (as per the DHHS-NIH definition) related to a faculty member's DHHS-funded research on a public website or provide the information upon public request within five days. Disclosure of FCOI should also extend to affected patients and human research volunteers. (For details, see Principle 35).

PART V—TARGETED PRINCIPLES: MANAGING COI IN THE CONTEXT OF CLINICAL CARE AND HUMAN SUBJECT RESEARCH

PRINCIPLE 32—Individual and Institutional COI and Human Subject Research: To maximize patient safety and preserve public trust in the integrity of academic research, there should always be a strong presumption against permitting FCOI related to clinical medical research and experimental studies involving human subjects. A "rebuttable presumption" against permitting clinical trial research that may be compromised by FCOI should govern decisions about whether conflicted researchers or institutions are allowed to pursue a particular human subject research protocol or project, unless a compelling case can be made to justify an exception.

PRINCIPLE 33—Institutional Review Boards (IRBs) and COI Management: An IRB should review all proposed human clinical trial protocols to identify all relevant FCOI before research is allowed to proceed. First, institutions should have clear policies, compliant with applicable federal regulations, to address reporting and management of FCOI associated with IRB members themselves. Policies should require conflicted IRB members to recuse themselves from deliberations related to studies with which they have a potential conflict. Second, the policies should require the institution's standing COI committee to prepare summary information about all institutional and individual FCOI related to the research protocol under review. The summary should accompany the protocol when it is presented to the IRB. The IRB should take the COI information into account when determining whether and under what circumstances to approve a protocol. Neither the IRB nor the standing COI committee should be able to reduce the stringency of the other's management requirements. The double-protection system is consistent with the two sets of federal regulations governing clinical research and provides appropriate additional safeguards for patient volunteers. Finally, if a research protocol is allowed to proceed, university policies should require disclosure of any institutional and investigator FCOI as well as the university's management plan for addressing them to all patient volunteers (in informed consent documents) and all investigators and units involved with the research protocol.

PRINCIPLE 34—COI, Medical Purchasing, and Clinical Care: Academic medical centers should establish and implement COI policies that require all personnel to disclose financial interests in any manufacturer of pharmaceuticals, devices, or equipment or any provider of services and to recuse themselves from involvement in related purchasing decisions. If an individual's expertise is essential in evaluating a product or service, that person's financial ties must be disclosed to those responsible for purchasing decisions.

PRINCIPLE 35—COI Transparency in the Context of Medical Care: University policies should require all physicians, dentists, nurses, and other health professionals, as well as investigators, to disclose their FCOI to patients, human subject volunteers, and the broader public, unless those COI have been eliminated.

PART VI—TARGETED PRINCIPLES: STRATEGIC CORPORATE ALLIANCES (SCAs)

A strategic corporate alliance (SCA) is a formal, comprehensive, university-managed research collaboration with one or more outside company sponsors, centered around a major, multi-year financial commitment involving research, programmatic interactions, "first rights to license" intellectual property, and other services. An SCA is frequently negotiated through a central university development office in tandem with a group of faculty, an entire academic department, or many different departments in unison. In broad SCA agreements, it is customary for universities, in each new grant cycle, to issue a formal request for faculty research proposals on behalf of the outside corporate sponsor(s). In narrow SCA agreements, by contrast, all faculty members eligible for SCA funding and their projects are named and identified in advance, so a university-led RFP and research-selection process is not required.

PRINCIPLE 36—Shared Governance and Strategic Corporate Alliances (SCAs): Faculty senates should be fully involved in the planning, negotiation, approval, execution, and ongoing oversight of SCAs formed on campus. The senate should appoint a confidential committee to review a first draft of a memorandum of understanding (MOU) pertaining to newly proposed SCAs. All parties' direct and indirect financial obligations should be made clear from the outset. Before an agreement is finalized on a broad SCA, the full faculty senate should review it. Formal approval of broad SCAs should await both stages in this process. All approved SCA agreements should be made available to faculty, academic professionals, and the public. If the SCA

designates funding for new faculty appointments (FTEs), all normal university and departmental procedures for academic searches, hiring, and promotion
decisions must be followed to honor and protect academic self-governance
and academic freedom. Temporary employees should not exclusively staff,
administer, or supervise SCAs. Normal grievance procedures, under collective bargaining agreements where they exist, should govern complaints about
interference with academic freedom or other academic rights that may arise
under SCAs. In the absence of such procedures, grievances and complaints
should be reported to the SCA faculty oversight committee (see Principle
47 for details) or to relevant college or university grievance committees for
independent investigation. Standard safeguards regarding procedural fairness
and due process must be respected and followed.

PRINCIPLE 37—SCA Governance and Majority Academic Control:
The best practice in any academy-industry alliance agreement—consistent
with the principles of academic freedom, university autonomy, and faculty
self-governance—is to build clear boundaries separating corporate funders
from the university's academic work. Yet the current conditions of increasingly close university-industry relations make erecting strict walls unrealistic
on some campuses. Instead, at a minimum, universities should retain majority
academic control and voting power over internal governing bodies charged
with directing or administering SCAs in collaboration with corporate sponsors. The SCA's main governing body should also include members who are
neither direct stakeholders of the SCA nor based in academic disciplines or
units likely to benefit from the SCA. A joint university-industry SCA governing body may have a role in awarding funding, but it should have no role
in such exclusively academic functions as faculty hiring, curriculum design,
course content, and academic personnel evaluation.

**PRINCIPLE 38—Academic Control over SCA Research Selection
(for Broad SCAs):** In the case of broad SCAs, university representatives
should retain majority representation and voting power on SCA committees
charged with evaluating and selecting research proposals and making final
research awards. These committees should also employ an independent peer-
review process.

PRINCIPLE 39—Peer Review (for Broad SCAs): Using a standard
peer-review process, independent academic experts should evaluate and
award funding whenever SCAs issue a request for proposals (RFP) in a new
grant cycle. Any expert involved in the peer-review and grant-award process should be free of personal FCOI related to the area of research being

reviewed to ensure that research selection is scientifically driven, impartial, and fair. Appointees to committees charged with research selection for a given SCA should be prohibited from awarding that funding to themselves, their departments, or their labs and should not be past recipients of funding from that SCA.

PRINCIPLE 40—Transparency regarding the SCA Research Application Process (for Broad SCAs): SCA agreements must clearly and transparently detail the methods and criteria for research selection and must explain how academic researchers may apply for SCA grants.

PRINCIPLE 41—Protection of Publication Rights and Knowledge Sharing in SCA Agreements: All the provisions of Principle 3 should apply to SCAs as well.

PRINCIPLE 42—SCA Confidentiality Restrictions: To protect the university's distinctively open academic research environment, restrictions on sharing corporate confidential information and other confidentiality restrictions should be minimized to the maximum extent possible in SCA agreements. To achieve this objective, sponsors should be discouraged from sharing confidential corporate trade secrets with their academic partners except when absolutely necessary. Such confidential information should ordinarily be disclosed to the smallest number of academic investigators possible, with strict supervision from the university's legal office to prevent corruption of the academic research environment.

PRINCIPLE 43—SCA Anti-Competitor Agreements: Anti-competitor or noncompete agreements compromise the university's academic autonomy, its ability to collaborate with other outside firms, and its commitment to knowledge sharing and broad public service. Restrictions in SCA agreements on faculty, academic professionals, postdoctoral fellows, and students interacting with or sharing information and research with private-sector competitors of SCA sponsors, or receiving separate research support from outside firms, should be avoided or minimized to the greatest extent possible.

PRINCIPLE 44—Exclusive Licensing and SCA Agreements: All the provisions of Principles 17 and 18 should apply to SCAs as well.

PRINCIPLE 45—Limits on Broader Academic Disruption by SCAs: Given the size and scope of many SCAs, a vigorous effort must be made to ensure that diverse areas of research—research that pursues avenues of inquiry outside the purview of, not in conformity with, or even in opposition to the SCA's research agenda—are not crowded out and continue to enjoy institutional support, resources, and sufficient financing. SCAs should be approved only if faculty and students within all academic units will, as a practical as well as a theoretical matter, retain the freedom to pursue their chosen research topics. SCA agreements should not disrupt the financial, intellectual, or professional arrangements of other academic units, colleges, and the university as a whole, and should avoid impact on faculty, academic professionals, postdoctoral fellows, and students engaged in research and activities outside the purview of the SCA. University policies should clearly affirm that no faculty member, postdoctoral fellow, academic professional, or student will be coerced into participating in a sponsored project; all participation must be entirely voluntary.

PRINCIPLE 46—Early Termination of SCA Sponsor Funding: With any large-scale SCA, sponsors may threaten reduction or termination of funding or limits on funding in order to shape the research agenda or to express displeasure with its direction or findings. To reduce this risk, SCA contracts should include legally binding provisions to prohibit sudden, early termination of the agreement. If the negotiating process leads to inclusion of an early-termination option, it must prohibit the sponsor from arbitrarily or suddenly terminating the agreement or lowering pledged funding without at least three months advance notification. Salaries and research costs associated with the project must be continued for that period.

PRINCIPLE 47—Independent, Majority Faculty Oversight of the SCA, and Post-Agreement Evaluation: An independent, majority faculty oversight committee consisting of faculty with no direct involvement in the SCA should be established at the start of a new SCA agreement to monitor and at least annually review the SCA and its compliance with university policies and guidelines. A post-agreement evaluation plan should also be included in the SCA contract so the campus can reflect and draw on the experience in organizing future campus-based academy-industry alliances. External evaluation may be appropriate for broad SCAs. Evaluation reports should be public documents.

PRINCIPLE 48—Public Disclosure of SCA Research Contracts and Funding Transparency: No SCA or other industry-, government-, or nonprofit-sponsored contract should restrict faculty, students, postdoctoral fellows, or academic professionals from freely disclosing their funding source.

A signed copy of all final legal research contracts and MOUs formalizing the SCA and any other types of sponsored agreements formed on campus should be made freely available to the public—with discrete redactions only to protect valid commercial trade secrets, not for other reasons.

PART VII—TARGETED PRINCIPLES: CLINICAL MEDICINE, CLINICAL RESEARCH, AND INDUSTRY SPONSORSHIP

PRINCIPLE 49—Access to Complete Clinical Trial Data and the Performance of Independent Academic Analysis: All the provisions of Principle 5 should apply to clinical trial data as well.

PRINCIPLE 50—Registry of Academic-Based Clinical Trials in a National Registry: Universities and affiliated academic medical centers should adopt clear, uniform, written policies to require all clinical trials conducted by their academic investigators to be entered into ClinicalTrials.gov (http://www.clinicaltrials.gov/)—the national clinical trial registry maintained by the US National Library of Medicine (NLM) and the National Institutes of Health (NIH). The entry should be made at or before the onset of patient enrollment. Entry in the register will help ward against manipulation of study results, suppression of negative findings, and improper altering of clinical trial protocols after the research has begun.

PRINCIPLE 51—Safeguarding the Integrity and Appropriate Conduct of Clinical Trials: All clinical trials affiliated with academic institutions should be required to use independent data safety monitoring boards (DSMBs) and/or publication and analysis committees to protect the integrity and appropriate conduct of academic-based clinical trial research.

PRINCIPLE 52—Patient Notification: No industry-, government-, or nonprofit-sponsored research agreement should restrict faculty or academic professionals from notifying patients about health risks or lack of treatment efficacy when such information emerges and patients' health may be adversely affected.

PRINCIPLE 53—Undue Commercial Marketing Influence and Control at Academic Medical Centers: Educational programs, academic events, and presentations by faculty, students, postdoctoral fellows, and academic professionals must be free of industry marketing influence and control. Both academics and administrators should be prohibited from participating in industry-led "speakers bureaus" financed by pharmaceutical or other industry groups. Institutions should also establish funding mechanisms for clinical practice guidelines and high-quality accredited continuing medical education (CME) programs free of industry influence.

PRINCIPLE 54—Appropriate Use of Facilities and Classrooms at Universities and Academic Medical Centers: Universities, academic medical schools, and affiliated teaching hospitals should have clear and consistent policies and practices barring pharmaceutical, medical device, and biotechnology companies from distributing free meals, gifts, or drug samples on campus and at affiliated academic medical centers, except under the control of central administration offices for use by patients who lack access to medications. As a general principle, academic facilities and classrooms should not be used for commercial marketing and promotion purposes unless advance written permission from academic institutional authorities is explicitly granted and academic supervision ensured. (Commercial marketing of services would, for example, be appropriate at a job fair.) Campus policies should also require all marketing representatives to obtain authorization before site visits. Finally, faculty, physicians, trainees, and students should be prohibited from directly accepting travel funds from industry, other than for legitimate reimbursement of contractual academic services. Direct or indirect industry travel funding for commercial marketing junkets, which may include trips to luxury resorts and expensive dinners, should be prohibited.

PRINCIPLE 55—Marketing Projects Masquerading as Clinical Research: Faculty, students, postdoctoral fellows, and academic professionals based at academic-affiliated institutions must not participate in marketing studies that masquerade as scientifically-driven clinical trial research. Such thinly disguised marketing studies are frequently referred to as "seeding trials" because they are intended primarily to expose doctors and patients to newer, brand-name drugs, not to uncover medically valuable or scientifically important insights.

PRINCIPLE 56—Predetermined Research Results: Faculty and other academic investigators should be prohibited from soliciting research funding from outside sponsors with the implied suggestion or promise of predetermined research results.

SIGNIFICANT FINANCIAL INTEREST: Throughout this report we make use of the current Department of Health and Human Services definition. The DHHS rule defines a "significant" financial conflict of interest as follows: "Financial conflict of interest (FCOI) means a significant financial interest that could directly and significantly affect the design, conduct, or reporting of PHS-funded research. . . . Significant financial interest means:

(1) A financial interest consisting of one or more of the following interests of the Investigator (and those of the Investigator's spouse and dependent children) that reasonably appears to be related to the Investigator's institutional responsibilities:

    (i) With regard to any publicly traded entity, a significant financial interest exists if the value of any remuneration received from the entity in the twelve months preceding the disclosure and the value of any equity interest in the entity as of the date of disclosure, when aggregated, exceeds $5,000. For purposes of this definition, remuneration includes salary and any payment for services not otherwise identified as salary (e.g., consulting fees, honoraria, paid authorship); equity interest includes any stock, stock option, or other ownership interest, as determined through reference to public prices or other reasonable measures of fair market value;

    (ii) With regard to any non-publicly traded entity, a significant financial interest exists if the value of any remuneration received from the entity in the twelve months preceding the disclosure, when aggregated, exceeds $5,000, or when the Investigator (or the Investigator's spouse or dependent children) holds any equity interest (e.g., stock, stock option, or other ownership interest); or

    (iii) Intellectual property rights and interests (e.g., patents, copyrights), upon receipt of income related to such rights and interests.

(2) Investigators also must disclose the occurrence of any reimbursed or sponsored travel (i.e., that which is paid on behalf of the Investigator and not reimbursed to the Investigator so that the exact monetary value may not be readily available), related to their institutional responsibilities; provided, however, that this disclosure requirement does not apply to travel that is reimbursed or sponsored by a Federal, state, or local government agency, an Institution of higher education as

defined at 20 U.S.C. 1001(a), an academic teaching hospital, a medical center, or a research institute that is affiliated with an Institution of higher education. The Institution's FCOI policy will specify the details of this disclosure, which will include, at a minimum, the purpose of the trip, the identity of the sponsor/organizer, the destination, and the duration. In accordance with the Institution's FCOI policy, the institutional official(s) will determine if further information is needed, including a determination or disclosure of monetary value, in order to determine whether the travel constitutes an FCOI with the PHS-funded research.

(3) The term significant financial interest does not include the following types of financial interests: salary, royalties, or other remuneration paid by the Institution to the Investigator if the Investigator is currently employed or otherwise appointed by the Institution, including intellectual property rights assigned to the Institution and agreements to share in royalties related to such rights; any ownership interest in the Institution held by the Investigator, if the Institution is a commercial or for-profit organization; *income from investment vehicles, such as mutual funds and retirement accounts, as long as the Investigator does not directly control the investment decisions made in these vehicles*; income from seminars, lectures, or teaching engagements sponsored by a Federal, state, or local government agency, an Institution of higher education as defined at 20 U.S.C. 1001(a), an academic teaching hospital, a medical center, or a research institute that is affiliated with an Institution of higher education; or income from service on advisory committees or review panels for a Federal, state, or local government agency, an Institution of higher education as defined at 20 U.S.C. 1001(a), an academic teaching hospital, a medical center, or a research institute that is affiliated with an Institution of higher education." [Emphasis added] (Source: Department of Health and Human Services, 42 CFR Part 50, 45 CFR Part 94, "Responsibility of Applicants for Promoting Objectivity in Research for which Public Health Service Funding is Sought and Responsible Prospective Contractors," *Federal Register*, vol. 76, no. 165, August 25, 2011, quotes on pp. 53283–84, available at: http://www.gpo.gov/fdsys/pkg/FR-2011-08-25/pdf/2011-21633.pdf)

Introduction

An Overview of the Benefits and Risks of Heightened Academy-Industry Engagement

Why the AAUP Is Issuing This Report

In 1915, the American Association of University Professors warned of the risks to higher education from the influence of "commercial practices in which large vested interests are involved."[2] The 1915 Declaration warned of "a real danger that pressure from vested interests may, sometimes deliberately, and sometimes unconsciously, sometimes openly and sometimes subtly and in obscure ways, be brought to bear upon academic authorities."[3] Yet the Declaration's framers could never have envisioned a corporation offering a university president hundreds of thousands of dollars to serve on a corporate board, or a start-up firm offering faculty members stock options and research funding to test products in which they have a direct financial stake—situations that have become commonplace today.

By 2004, when the Association adopted its "Statement on Corporate Funding of Academic Research," contractual relationships between universities, university personnel, and corporations had become far more entangled. Nonetheless, the statement pointed out that the connection between industry and higher education "has never been free of concerns that the financial ties of researchers or their institutions to industry may exert improper pressure on the design and outcome of research."[4] That 2004 language in fact echoes the Association's 1990 "Statement on Conflicts of Interest," which stated that "faculties should ensure that any cooperative venture between members of the faculty and outside agencies, whether public or private, respects the primacy of the university's principal mission, with regard to the choice of subjects of research and the reaching and publication of results."[5] That statement goes on to say, "Faculties should make certain that the pursuit of such joint ventures does not become an end in itself and so introduce distortions into traditional university understandings and arrangements."[6]

As early as 1965, in "On Preventing Conflicts of Interest in Government-Sponsored Research at Universities," the AAUP urged "the formulation of standards to guide the individual university staff members in governing their conduct in relation to outside interests that might raise questions of conflicts of interest."[7] It is entirely appropriate that faculty play the leading role in formulating the standards. The 1966 "Statement on Government of Colleges and Universities"—formulated by the AAUP, the American Council on Education, and the Association of Governing Boards—recognizes that faculty should have "primary responsibility" for research matters.[8] The expanding relationship between industry and institutions of higher education in funding faculty research threatens not only academic freedom and academic integrity but also the faculty role in institutional governance. As noted in the AAUP's 1994 statement "On the Relationship of Faculty Governance to Academic Freedom," the concepts of academic freedom and shared governance are "inextricably linked."[9] While reasserting the faculty's primary responsibility for research may not be enough to resolve many of the issues identified in this report, faculty involvement in formulating governance procedures is crucial for success.

As we report below, many academic and professional groups—such as the Association of American Universities (AAU), the Association of American Medical Colleges (AAMC), and the Institute of Medicine (IOM)—have already formulated and endorsed stringent, well-defined standards to address financial conflicts of interest (FCOI) and other threats to research integrity, primarily within the fields of biomedicine. Many of those standards are formulated explicitly to safeguard the AAUP's 1915 directive: "the scholar must be absolutely free not only to pursue his investigations but to declare the results of his researches, no matter where they may lead."[10] However, other professional guidelines, including those put forward by the University-Industry Demonstration Partnership (UIDP), a project of the National Academies, focus too narrowly on expanding academy-industry collaboration and managing intellectual property without paying sufficient attention to academic freedom, research integrity, and conflicts of interest.[11]

This report draws together the most well articulated and effective of these prior guidelines and statements into a comprehensive set of "Recommended Principles to Guide Academy-Industry Relationships" for all US colleges and universities to consider adopting. Where necessary, the AAUP has expanded upon advice contained in existing guidelines or developed new ones, in light of the values we have promoted for 100 years.

Collaborations between industry and the academy present tremendous opportunities for advancing knowledge, applying it to real-world problems, and bringing about various social benefits. Cooperative research involving both university and industry scientists has proven critical to the development of numerous powerful methods, products, and technologies. A number of books and reports document the considerable accomplishments of academy-industry collaborations in agriculture, biotechnology, engineering, computing, and other academic fields.[12] But the increasing number, financial scope, and complexity of these collaborations call for more specific standards and principles than the AAUP and other professional academic associations have offered thus far. In putting forward these new guidelines we do not aim to curtail collaborations between business and academia. Instead, we want to help higher education faculty and administrators manage these collaborations in a manner consistent with the long-term interests of both universities and the broader public, including private industry.

This report offers numerous examples and case studies of university-industry relationships that have compromised the research standards and principles that should govern university life. We do not mean to suggest that these examples represent the norm, but they document problems that can arise from both industry and university roles and thus demonstrate the need for stronger written protocols, guides, and templates for contracts that could minimize or eliminate such difficulties. In most instances, moreover, the AAUP has drawn together substantial empirical evidence to supplement these cases, documenting the breadth and depth of the problems and the consequences of ignoring them. Because this AAUP report responds to the mounting challenges of academy-industry relationships, we make no effort to report on the entire history of such collaborations or to survey their considerable accomplishments, which have been covered elsewhere.[13]

Although we focus on academy-industry collaborations, we recognize that some of the problems and challenges we address may also arise with government and nonprofit contracts and alliances. Any number of special-interest groups, mission-directed nonprofits, and government agencies can pressure faculty for results that support their agendas. Such pressure may include offering incentives, biasing experiment design and analysis of data, discouraging contrary viewpoints, and delaying the release of research results. Some nonprofits receive substantial industry funding and can thereby mask industry's role in selecting and even managing individual academic projects. The report highlights particular principles that should apply to such collaborations.

Of course, faculty investigators also have biases—whether they arise from past scholarly debates, professional competition, personal affinities, or political and religious commitments. Faculty status does not confer independence from the activities and interests of the communities in which faculty members live and work. But the heart of the matter, which this report seeks to address, is that faculty must not be contractually obligated to represent positions at odds with their professional judgment and public commitments, or be placed in compromised situations, financial and otherwise, that are more likely to produce bias.

A number of warning signs can suggest that particular projects may require extra scrutiny and safeguards. A proposed research design or protocol for reporting and publication may indicate that university involvement is sought primarily to help a sponsor clear regulatory hurdles by supplying confirming or positive field data or analysis. The risk of compromised research also increases when future investment depends on positive results. The same issues arise when either investigators or institutions stand to benefit from additional research funding, licensing revenues, or the value of equity held in the sponsor's company. We put forward principles designed to help manage such problems.

As this report will show, existing university policies and procedures for managing academy-industry engagement and conflicts of interest remain highly variable, inconsistent, and overall too weak. As we have noted, many academic and professional societies agree with this assessment and have already issued recommendations to strengthen the management and oversight of academy-industry relationships. But with the exception of the AAU's 2001 recommendations, issued in its "Report on Individual and Institutional Financial Conflict of Interest," most of these guidelines deal only with biomedicine and human-subject research.[14] Indeed that was the domain in which ethical concerns, including COI, were first identified and began to be codified. We have drawn from these recommendations and added our own in an effort to strengthen institutional oversight and protection across the entire university. This report also documents how recent developments have eroded faculty control over research and intellectual property, as well as the faculty role in shared governance. It calls on faculty to take responsibility for strengthening the campuswide guidelines governing academy-industry relationships, thereby reaffirming the primacy of shared governance, academic freedom, research integrity, and faculty control over research.

Society traditionally has placed great trust in universities and their faculty, as well as in physicians and other professionals, and has granted them considerable leeway for self-regulation. But mounting concern from lawmakers, government agencies, and the public demonstrates the urgent need for stronger measures to protect the public trust in academic research. Evidence shows that inadequate or misguided management of academy-industry relationships threatens the very principles that universities hold most sacred: academic freedom, independent inquiry, the right to publish, research autonomy, scientific objectivity, research accuracy, broad dissemination of knowledge, unfettered analysis and research verification, and the development of reliable information and products that serve the public good.

Academic Freedom: The Relationship between Individual Faculty Rights and the Public Interest

Faculty members and administrators often cite academic freedom to justify their objections to stronger standards for regulating COI and the conduct of relations with industry. Their objections obscure the history and function of academic freedom. It evolved not only to protect individual faculty rights but to insulate the academy and safeguard the discovery process from powerful social forces, initially the church and later big government and big business. At this point we need to agree upon rules to preserve freedom of research, teaching, and inquiry.

Academic freedom does not entitle faculty members to accept outside responsibilities that jeopardize or gravely compromise their primary university responsibilities. Academic freedom does not entitle faculty members to sign away their freedom to disseminate research results. Academic freedom does not entitle faculty members to ignore financial conflicts of interest that could dangerously compromise the informed consent process and the impartiality of research. It follows, therefore, that academic freedom does not guarantee faculty members the freedom to take money regardless of the conditions attached.[15]

The institution's responsibility to protect research integrity and the university's reputation for the conduct of independent research—indeed its ability to carry out independent research—can at times dramatically conflict with an individual faculty member's wishes and perceived rights. The AAUP's 1992 statement, "An Issue of Academic Freedom in Refusing Outside Funding for Faculty Research," highlighted the friction. The statement noted that institutions have the right to decline grants offered faculty if unacceptable conditions are attached—when, for example, an "agency was imposing conditions on the research that violated academic freedom."[16]

Yet rejecting an individual sponsored-research contract that entails "unacceptable conditions" is not the same as banning a whole class of funding. When the AAUP was asked to consider prohibiting the whole category of tobacco-industry funding, the Association argued that such a wholesale ban presented "a very different situation," as when "a university objects to a funding agency because of its corporate behavior."[17] The AAUP reasoned that "the distinction between degrees of corporate misdeeds is too uncertain to sustain a clear, consistent, and principled policy for determining which research funds to accept and which to reject. . . . A university which starts down this path will find it difficult to resist demands that research bans should be imposed on other funding agencies that are seen as reckless or supportive of repellant programs."

The AAUP clarified its reasoning in 2003, after faculty governing bodies at two University of California campuses voted to refuse research awards from tobacco companies on the grounds that a growing body of evidence documented the industry's efforts to unduly influence and manipulate scientific research both on and off campus. Thus the campuses argued that they were trying to protect the broad social purpose of academic freedom and the process of scientific discovery from industry manipulation, even if individual faculty might feel their right to accept whatever funding they chose was being compromised. The AAUP's Committee A on Academic Freedom and Tenure countered that its concerns about such restraints on academic freedom were not lessened when "the initiative in calling for these bans on the funding of faculty research comes from the faculty itself."[18]

The AAUP based its reasoning on the conviction, no doubt widely shared by faculty across the United States, that the right of individual faculty members to choose what research they wish to conduct is fundamental, indeed foundational. The right is central to the AAUP's 1915 Declaration, and to numerous policy statements issued since then. If faculty members are free to choose their own research projects and agendas, the reasoning goes, they should be free to accept the funding needed to conduct their research. Even an industry that manufactures a deadly product, like tobacco, moreover, will sometimes fund useful research—if for no other reason than the positive publicity it can generate. Should that research be prohibited? For most US institutions, the argument against banning a whole class of funding predominates because such prohibitions are perceived to violate individual faculty rights. More recently, however, some medical colleges and schools of public health have dissented from this view. These schools contend that, while individuals can pursue any research they choose, that does not give them the right to accept funding from the tobacco industry in the light of its exceptionally well documented, decades-long history of collusion and willful manipulation of research on tobacco and health.

As of this writing, schools of public health at Arizona, Columbia, Harvard, Iowa, Johns Hopkins, North Carolina, South Carolina and elsewhere, along with schools of medicine at Emory, Harvard, and Johns Hopkins, all now formally decline to accept tobacco funding. A similar movement is under way overseas. The University of Geneva, the University of Hong Kong, the German Cancer Research Center, London School of Hygiene and Tropical Medicine, and seventeen Australian universities now decline to accept tobacco funding. After five University of California campuses voted to refuse tobacco funds in 2007, the UC Regents reasoned that accepting tobacco industry funding might undermine the university system's reputation and adopted a compromise policy. Rather than adopt an outright ban, they identified tobacco as a special case requiring each campus chancellor to review and approve new tobacco industry funding. The Regents also requested an annual report detailing any new grants issued, but since the policy was adopted the UC has received no new tobacco industry funding.

Action by these medical schools and public health institutions was precipitated by a variety of factors, including continuing litigation against tobacco firms over many decades, documentation of tobacco-industry collusion to distort scientific research, and the passage of global treaties to curb tobacco company influence. This litigation led to public access to immense archives of internal tobacco industry documents that detailed the companies' suppression of research linking smoking with cancer and their decades-long campaign to sow confusion in the scientific literature and manipulate public opinion. As the evidence accumulated, faculty members, health advocates, and government agencies alike began to question whether tobacco industry funding ought to be treated as a special case. Clinicians were especially sensitive to the health consequences of smoking for their patients. Some medical faculty and administrators thus perceived a growing conflict between their institutions' core public health mission and the tobacco industry's ongoing campaign to downplay the risks of smoking. Even weapons manufacturers could claim their lethal products advanced national security and thus had a social benefit; not so tobacco companies.

Scholarly research and detailed reviews of litigation documents revealed how the tobacco firms had formally colluded to manipulate scientific evidence—including academic research—to suppress the truth about the health hazards of cigarettes and stave off regulation. In 2003, the World Health Organization adopted its Framework Convention on Tobacco Control, one of the most widely embraced treaties in UN history. Within a year, 168 nations had signed the treaty, which was aimed at curtailing the "globalization of the tobacco epidemic." Guidelines for implementing the treaty, which took effect in 2005, specifically recommend that public educational institutions and other government bodies prohibit "contributions from the tobacco industry or from those working to further its interests," and direct all signatories "to protect these policies from commercial and other vested interests of the tobacco industry."[19]

In 2012, the National Institute on Drug Abuse (NIDA),[20] a division of the National Institutes of Health (NIH), officially recounted how tobacco companies had formally banded together to produce science that would bolster their business objectives while suppressing evidence of smoking's harmful effects:

> Integrity and honesty in conducting research are essential to sound science and form the basis for public confidence and trust in the results of scientific research. Recent landmark judicial rulings against the tobacco industry found that prior tobacco industry-sponsored research was biased in support of the interests and goals of the tobacco companies. In 2006, a federal court [in *US Department of Justice v. Philip Morris USA Inc. et al.*[21]] found that the cigarette industry engaged in willful racketeering and conspiracy to conceal the dangers of smoking from the American public by improperly suppressing and terminating scientific research and destroying research documents. This ruling was upheld in 2009 by the US Court of Appeals and in 2010 the US Supreme Court denied further review of the ruling. In the final opinion in that case, the presiding judge ruled that nine manufacturers of cigarettes and two tobacco-related trade organizations had violated the Racketeer Influenced and Corrupt Organizations Act (RICO) by engaging in a lengthy, unlawful conspiracy to deceive the American public about the health effects of smoking and environmental tobacco smoke, the addictiveness of nicotine, the lack of health benefits from low tar and "light" cigarettes, and their manipulating the design and composition of cigarettes in order to create and sustain nicotine addiction.[22]

The NIH website went on to warn: "The tobacco industry manufactures, markets, and distributes products that are both addictive and lethal. In fact, cigarette smoking remains the leading cause of premature death in the United States, killing approximately 440,000 people per year. Thus, it is the opinion of NACDA [the National Advisory Council on Drug Abuse] that the interests of the tobacco industry are *fundamentally incompatible* with the scientific goals and public health mission of NIDA."[23] Finally, and most significantly for university investigators, the NIH noted that a history of prior tobacco industry funding could jeopardize the success of new scientific grant applications filed with the agency.

These public health and medical school bans on tobacco industry funding are unlikely to spread to other broad categories of funding, not only because of the individual academic freedom concerns discussed above but also because of the high standard for proof of industry deception and the high degree of international consent presented by the case of tobacco. Yet these debates about the ethics of tobacco industry funding are rooted in arguments made since the AAUP's founding in 1915: that academic freedom entails responsibility not only to one's campus and one's profession but also to the public good.

The problems presented by FCOI and other forms of undue industry influence are not, of course, limited to tobacco industry funding. When corporations, or nominally nonprofit funding agencies, effectively bribe faculty members to publish articles with doubtful product claims, dubious economic assessments, or attacks on well-established science, faculty scholars betray their professional and public responsibilities. No body of rules and guidelines can guarantee professional ethics. But principles like the ones offered in this report can educate faculty members and institutions about their obligations to uphold standards of professional and personal integrity. The principles can also remind faculty of the broader social goals of their research and scholarship, a particularly important objective in disciplines that have a limited history of interrogating such issues collectively.[24]

* * *

This broad concern with professional ethics and the public good helps to explain why we believe faculty members and students across all disciplines, not only those engaged in corporate-sponsored research, will have a keen interest in this report. A campus that compromises its core academic principles risks undermining its reputation and integrity. Whenever the potential for financial gains exists, such compromises, left unchallenged, are also likely to occur again. As this report will show, the potential for abuse extends beyond those engaged in sponsored research. Historians, economists, statisticians, business faculty, and lawyers are among those who have accepted lucrative consultantships to advise companies and defend products and policies proven to be dangerous to public health or to the national economy. Everyone on campus has a stake in the institution's reputation and its success in upholding its mission.

The AAUP respects institutional autonomy. This report offers basic principles that universities and their faculty may either adopt directly or use to formulate their own policies, while leaving room for adaptation to address specific, local, campus-based needs. Some colleges on a large campus may feel the need to adopt stronger policies in certain areas, like COI disclosure, because of the challenges particular disciplines confront. If so, the faculty senate should review any college-specific regulations. Because comprehensive and rigorous national standards are urgently needed, however, the AAUP is recommending that institutions begin by considering the language and policy guidelines covering the broad range of existing commercial and non-profit interactions on campus that we offer here.

Universities have long relied on financial support from outside sources, including industry, to sustain their operations. The issue we seek to address here is not the funding source *per se* but the conditions attached to the funding and the effects that COI may have. Various forms of academy-industry engagement are emerging that impose new pressures and constraints on the historic autonomy of the university. Such arrangements have the potential to limit faculty authority over academic matters (peer review, research selection, curriculum design, and faculty hiring), and erode academic research standards (access to data, scientific objectivity, independent statistical analysis, and the ability to independently verify reported research findings).

The public trusts that universities and faculty members will remain professionally independent and maintain high standards of teaching and research. Universities cannot allow flagrant violations of professional norms and scientific standards to go unchecked lest the foundation of academic freedom—indeed the justification for its existence—become unstable and eventually collapse. Even private corporations should recognize that the extraordinary value of the academy—its ability to carry out cutting-edge science, perform reliable research, and garner public trust—rests on the independence and perceived integrity of university research culture. That, in essence, is why the AAUP has issued these recommendations: to protect universities' distinctive academic and research culture and their public knowledge missions. Industries seeking genuine partnerships with the academy will welcome proof that university labs and company labs are not interchangeable.

The AAUP urges universities—and especially faculty senates or comparable governing bodies—to promptly review, update, and strengthen their written policies and guidelines for structuring and managing academy-industry alliances and other sponsored research agreements on their campuses. We also urge faculty to work actively with their administrations to update and strengthen campuswide COI policies covering both individuals and the institution. The credibility and integrity of our nation's universities are now at stake.

★ ★ ★

Embracing Diverse Missions:
A Brief History of Academy-Industry Relationships

University-industry ties, which date back to the mid-1800s, have produced numerous important benefits across many fields, from engineering and chemistry to agriculture and public health. Collaborations between university and industry scientists have given rise to whole new academic disciplines (such as chemical and electrical engineering) as well as new medical products and devices. They have also given rise to scientific and industrial breakthroughs, such as the green revolution in agriculture and the biotechnology revolution in biology and medicine. The Internet browser Netscape, the search engine Google, and numerous successful biotechnology firms have their roots in university-based research.[25]

America's research universities, and many of its colleges and community colleges, have long embraced collaborations with industry, government, and outside public interest groups to fund university research, advance and promote practical knowledge, and deliver other important societal benefits, including expert advice, impartial analysis, new medical breakthroughs, and products. American land grant universities have a proud tradition of nurturing working relationships with industry and providing direct public service. Since their establishment well over a century ago, they have expressly sought to further local and regional economic development. Today, virtually all American universities recognize economic development and community service as a vital part of their mission. When managed wisely, efforts to foster commercial and economic development may be pursued in a manner that comports with the university's educational mission and its commitment to fundamental and ground breaking research.

Nevertheless, notable tension among these goals has always existed and persists to the present day. A two-year investigation of academy-industry partnerships led by the Business-Higher Education Forum made the following observation: "Corporations and universities are not natural partners. Their cultures and their missions differ. Companies' underlying goals—and the prime responsibilities of top management—are to make a profit and build value for shareholders by serving customers. Universities' traditional missions are to develop new knowledge and educate the next generation."[26]

Society relies on universities to carry out a public knowledge mission with many well-recognized components. It is a mission that no other private or market agent has proved capable of delivering so ably or effectively. To fulfill that mission the university takes on responsibilities to

- Deliver advanced-level graduate and professional training;

- Deliver broad-based undergraduate training, as opposed to narrow workforce training;

- Cultivate the critical thinking and civic understanding that are essential to a functioning democracy;

- Conduct fundamental, curiosity-driven, and frontier science, which generates enormous public and societal value but may not generate profit or serve business interests;

- Freely disseminate new knowledge to advance follow-on research and exploration;

- Verify new research discoveries and theories through publication, commentary, or actual testing and replication of reported research results;

- Provide space for social criticism and expression of unpopular viewpoints;

- Conduct public-good research, such as research into climate change and occupational health;

- Encourage public discussion and debate;

- Enable research and scholarly inquiry free from unwanted special-interest influence and control;

- Provide impartial expert advice for the general public, government agencies, industry, and other constituencies;

- Preserve a "public domain for knowledge" or a "knowledge commons"—the wellspring for future creativity and invention;

- Preserve and explore past intellectual and artistic achievement;

- Challenge received opinion in all domains when history or new knowledge suggests that is necessary;

- Continuously advance knowledge across all disciplines.

Protecting these unique and distinctive activities, while continuing to foster productive engagement with outside industries, interest groups, and funding sources, has never been simple. Over the last thirty years or so, legislators, the media, and university administrators have expanded the list of responsibilities by emphasizing that universities are also expected to make significant economic contributions to state and country. These include supplying professional credentialing and degrees, new products, start-up firms, job creation, and private-sector revenue generation. New state and federal laws and policies likewise encourage more active cooperation between higher education institutions and the commercial and manufacturing sectors with the goal of stimulating advanced research, innovation, and economic development.

While most interactions with industry are concentrated in distinct parts of the university—notably agriculture, business, chemistry, education, engineering, biomedicine, economics, veterinary medicine, and computer science—the institutional and cultural values associated with the emphasis on serving business and driving economic growth are now pervasive. Pressure on all units is mounting, even in the humanities and other traditional non-market disciplines, to become more commercially "relevant" and to generate private revenue. Buildings and professorships named after corporate sponsors or living donors contribute to this more commercial atmosphere. The University of Missouri features a Monsanto Auditorium; Iowa State University has a Monsanto Student Services Wing inside its main agriculture building. Purdue University's School of Food Sciences features two research labs named after Kroger and ConAgra.[27] Rice University dubbed one of its business schools the Ken Lay Center for the Study of Markets in Transition, a naming choice that became embarrassing after Enron's collapse and Lay's subsequent indictment.[28] By 1999, the trend was well under way: corporate professorships included the Boeing Company Chair in Aeronautics at the California Institute of Technology, the Coca-Cola Professors of Marketing at both the University of Arizona and the University of Georgia, the La Quinta Motor Inns Professor of Business at the University of Texas, the Taco Bell Distinguished Professor of Hotel and Restaurant Administration at Washington University, and many others.[29] As the campus becomes a site to promote corporate branding, the admirable practice of naming buildings, programs, or professorships after admired individuals from the past begins to fade.

The decline in public support for higher education is helping to drive this trend. In recent decades, state financing of higher education and federal funding of research has shrunk to a fraction of university operating costs, leading the managers of many institutions to argue that enhanced collaborations with private industry and business support are necessary to sustain institutional operations. But despite a perennial hope that corporate funding will make up university operating shortfalls, there is reason to be skeptical. Industry support for universities has stayed persistently low and regularly fails to meet the overhead costs related to the research it initiates.[30]

The considerable accomplishments of academy-industry collaborations in agriculture, medicine, biotechnology, engineering, computing, and many other academic fields are well documented.[31] As noted earlier, we will not undertake a comprehensive survey of such relationships but rather address the challenges presented by the variety, pervasiveness, and growing importance of commercial relationships on campus. The steady growth of sponsored research, along with patenting, licensing, and other commercial activity on campus, raises the risk that COI will compromise academic judgment and undermine universities' identity.

There is considerable evidence that these challenges warrant urgent attention. We conclude that commercial and other COI threaten the integrity of academic research, the objectivity of scientific investigations, the accuracy of published research results, the quality of patient care, and public confidence in higher education. Recent news stories, congressional investigations, litigation documents, reports by nonprofit activist groups, and academic analyses identify a variety of disturbing commercial conflicts. Here are a few snapshots:

- Physicians and researchers failed to disclose substantial payments from drug companies that manufacture the products they study, thus violating university, government agency, and medical journal requirements;[32]

- Agricultural industry groups sought to intimidate academic researchers and threatened to withhold university funding in an effort to undermine a report calling for reduced use of antibiotics in meat production and better waste-management practices;[33]

- Companies and academic investigators failed to publish negative results from industry-sponsored clinical trials or delayed publication for a year or more after trial completion;[34]

- Academics put their names on manuscripts after the data were collected and analyzed and after the first drafts had been ghostwritten by industry-paid authors;[35]

- Private foundations funded endowed professorships and research centers under contracts requiring advance vetting of appointees and projects by the foundation's self-appointed advisory board;[36]

- Nominally independent science organizations (established by the tobacco industry) systematically funded research designed to confuse the public about the dangers of smoking;[37]

- Corporate gifts contractually stipulated that certain books must be assigned as required university classroom reading;[38]

- Corporate grant contracts permitted company employees to design new university courses;[39]

- Industry groups routinely funded official medical clinical practice guidelines and the academics who write them.[40]

These challenges to the university's historic autonomy, academic freedom, and research integrity are profound. Most of the points in this list could be rephrased in the present tense, for they are ongoing. Many books published since 2000 warn that these commercial influences, when insufficiently regulated, may undermine teaching, scientific objectivity, and the evidentiary foundations of medicine, as well as the role of universities as arbiters of reliable public knowledge and guarantors of the public interest.[41]

We will now discuss these challenges in more detail, concentrating primarily on the risks that have precipitated this report. But before that we will review the history of recent academy-industry engagement and the congressional actions and legal struggles that have helped make fresh action necessary.

* * *

The Growth of University-Industry Engagement: 1970 to the Present

Between 1970 and 2000 alone, the share of university research funding from private industry tripled in value. This represented a tenfold increase in real research and development (R&D) dollars coming from industry at a time when total university R&D funding only increased by a factor of 3.5.[42]

Despite growth since then, industry funding represents a relatively small fraction of overall university research financing. According to 2008 statistics from the National Science Board (NSB), the federal government continues to contribute 60 percent (or $51.9 billion) of American university R&D funding—representing then and now a higher percentage for private than for public university funding. Recent (2012) statistics from NSF show the federal government providing 71 percent of R&D funding for private institutions, but only 54 percent for public institutions.[43] The 2008 figures showed private sources providing only roughly six percent (or $2.9 billion) of R&D funding overall.[44] Yet industry funds concentrate their impact, selectively facilitating expansion of research into new areas and enhancing the existing ones that meet commercial priorities. But many industry contracts, like those from government and nonprofit foundations, fail to cover the full indirect costs. In such cases, universities may actually lose money overall, while other unsponsored work is curtailed to pay for the unreimbursed costs of sponsored research. According to the journal *Nature*, "[U]niversities are increasingly subsidizing grants from their own funds. . . . Between 1969 and 2009, the proportion of research funding supported by institutional money rose from 10% to 20%, according to the US National Science Foundation. Public universities and all but the wealthiest private ones are increasingly taking that money from tuition fees."[45]

Moreover, the NSB's six percent figure can be misleading; it represents *industry*-sponsored research only. It does not include industry funding that comes in the form of academic gifts, endowments for new faculty appointments, faculty consulting, honoraria, seats on company boards, commercial licensing income, funds for new construction, or equity and options in start-ups. Many of these other commercial funding streams are not tracked nationally by category, though some—like consulting income—are immensely influential in certain disciplines. But it is impossible to gauge the magnitude of their impact or how it may have changed over time.

What we do know, according to National Science Foundation data, is that industry funding of university research varies considerably by campus. In 2009, some colleges and universities obtained anywhere from 12 to 50 percent of their R&D budgets from industry sources, percentages far higher than the six percent national average. The University of Tulsa, for example, received 48.5 percent of its R&D budget from industry, Duke University and the University at Albany got 22.8 percent each, Northeastern University 19.8 percent, MIT 14 percent, the University of Southern California 13.7, and the University of Maryland–Baltimore 12.6 percent.[46] The numbers fluctuate from year to year, particularly at less research-intensive universities, where a few large industry grants can markedly alter the share.

The impact of corporate funding is greatest in the fields where it is most concentrated, including medicine, biology, chemistry, engineering, economics, business, and agriculture. A 2010 analysis by Food & Water Watch, a research and advocacy group based in Washington, DC, reported that nearly a quarter of all agricultural research funding for land grant universities came from private sources, compared to less than 15 percent from the United States Department of Agriculture (USDA).[47] Meanwhile, at many individual agricultural schools and departments, the report found far heavier reliance on industry funding. Over the period 2006–10, for example, the University of Illinois crop sciences department and the Iowa State University agronomy department obtained 44 percent ($18.7 million) and 48 percent ($19.5

million) of their research budgets, respectively, from private industry sources, including Syngenta, the Iowa Soybean Association, Dow, and Monsanto.[48] At Iowa State alone, the study identified six professors of agriculture who drew over 90 percent of their personal research funding from industry.[49] The chart below, reproduced from the Food & Water Watch report, makes this pattern clear.

LAND GRANT UNIVERSITY	ACADEMIC YEARS	PRIVATE GRANTS	SHARE OF DEPT. GRANTS	AGRIBUSINESS DONORS INCLUDE...
University of Illinois Crop Sciences	2006–10	$18.7 million	44 percent	Monsanto, Syngenta, SmithBucklin & Associates
University of Illinois Food Sciences and Human Nutrition	2006–10	$7.7 million	46 percent	Pfizer, PepsiCo, Nestlé Nutrition
University of Illinois Animal Sciences	2006–10	$6.2 million	33 percent	Elanco, Pfizer, National Pork Board
University of Missouri Plant Sciences	2007–10	$16.4 million	42 percent	Phillip Morris, Monsanto, Dow Agroscience, SmithBucklin & Associates
University of Missouri Veterinary Medicine	2004–10	$6.1 million	63 percent	Iams, Pfizer, American Veterinary Medical Association
Purdue Agronomy	2010–11	$2.5 million	31 percent	Dow, Deere & Company
Purdue University Food Science	2010–11	$1.5 million	38 percent	Hinsdale Farms, Nestlé, BASF
University of Florida Large Animal Sciences Clinic	2006–10	$2.7 million	56 percent	Pfizer, Intervet
University of Florida Small Animal Sciences Clinic	2006–10	$5.5 million	70 percent	Alcon Research, Mars, Vistakon
University of California Viticulture and Oenology	2006–10	$5.0 million	49 percent	Nomacorc, American Vineyard Foundation
University of California Plant Sciences	2006–10	$33.6 million	28 percent	Chevron Technology Ventures, Arcadia Bioscience

LAND GRANT UNIVERSITY	ACADEMIC YEARS	PRIVATE GRANTS	SHARE OF DEPT. GRANTS	AGRIBUSINESS DONORS INCLUDE...
University of California Nutrition	2006–10	$5.0 million	49 percent	Mars, Novo Nordisk
Iowa State University Agronomy	2006–10	$19.5 million	48 percent	Dow, Monsanto, Iowa Soybean Association
Iowa State University Agricultural & Biosystems Engineering	2006–10	$9.5 million	44 percent	Deere & Company, Iowa Cattlemen's Association, National Pork Board
Iowa State University Entomology	2006–10	$3.7 million	52 percent	Syngenta, Bayer
Iowa State University Plant Pathology	2006–10	$10.7 million	38 percent	United Soybean Board, Dow, Iowa Soybean Association
Texas A&M Institute of Plant Genomics	2006–10	$1.8 million	46 percent	Cotton Inc., Chevron Technology
Texas A&M Animal Science	2006–10	$5.1 million	32 percent	National Cattlemen's Beef Association, National Pork Board, Donald Danforth Plant Science Center
Texas A&M Soil and Crop Sciences	2006–10	$13.0 million	56 percent	Monsanto, Cotton Inc., Pioneer Hi-Bred

The share of research support derived from private industry is also substantial in biomedicine. Private industry is now the largest source of funding for biomedical research in the United States. Between 1977 and 1989, the proportion of total industry funding for clinical and nonclinical research grew from 29 to 45 percent.[50] Between 1995 and 2003, the annual figures ranged from 57 to 61 percent.[51] Not surprisingly, given this level of collaboration, relationships between academic biomedicine and industry are extensive. A 2006 national survey of department chairs at medical schools and large teaching hospitals found that 67 percent of academic departments had formal administrative relationships with industry.[52] Also, 27 percent of nonclinical departments and 16 percent of clinical departments received income from commercial licensing of intellectual property developed in academic research.

At the same time, federal government support for academic biomedicine remains substantial: In 2008, projects in the life sciences received 60 percent, or $18.7 billion, of the federal R&D budget devoted to university research.[53] A 2008 study also shows industry's influence in biomedicine trending down.

Overall, from 1995 through 2006, the proportion of biomedical faculty (clinical and nonclinical) who received industry funding dropped from 28 percent to 20 percent. Faculty members getting industry support took a median of $99,000 in 2006.[54]

Academy-industry collaborations are not limited to biomedicine.[55] In other fields—ranging from engineering, chemistry, agriculture, toxicology and information technology to energy, law, and economics—academics also rely heavily on industry funding and frequently engage with outside companies in other ways as well. Many faculty in these disciplines consult for private companies and sit on their boards. However, compared to biomedicine, where the effects of industry funding and FCOI have been studied extensively, we know much less about the size or possible scope of industry influence in other academic disciplines. Public disclosure of faculty funding sources is often poor. Sometimes university scholars report their funding sources in conjunction with published academic research, but often they do not.

Compromised medical research has obvious implications for public health and safety. But unregulated—and often undisclosed—FCOI in other fields can also compromise research results, university reputations, and the public welfare. The financial meltdown that began in December 2007 affected millions of people worldwide. University economists with strong financial service industry ties helped trigger the recession by promoting or defending the very investment strategies that produced it. A 2010 study of academic financial economists, examining a small but influential cohort of university professors, found extraordinarily limited public disclosure of their ties to banking and other financial service companies. Though 70 percent of the surveyed economists worked with and received funding from private financial institutions, and some held senior positions (co-founder, managing partner, chief economist, president), few of their public presentations or publications disclosed their roles or the income they received as a result.[56]

Potential consequences of this secrecy were revealed when several prominent academic economists were interviewed about their banking and other industry ties in the Academy Award-winning 2010 documentary *Inside Job*. A series of economists at elite universities repeatedly dismissed the need to publicly disclose their FCOI, despite their role in the global economic crisis. Many of these seemingly independent academic economists, including people like Laura Tyson (Berkeley) and Martin Feldstein (Harvard), had either strenuously defended high-risk investment vehicles like collaterized debt obligations and credit default swaps or been otherwise deeply involved in the financial services industry, whether serving on a hedge fund board or working as a consultant to a private equity fund. Others, like Harvard's Larry Summers refused to be interviewed and were given partial cover by the UC

Berkeley and Harvard failure to require disclosure of outside income. But we do know that Summers helped market CDOs and that his government role encompassed resisting the regulation of over-the-counter derivatives. Tyson was an adviser to Credit Suisse. Feldstein served on the board of directors of AIG Financial Products for over two decades. Economics professors issued overwhelmingly pro-industry opinions, while the same industry they were purportedly evaluating with disinterested professional eyes paid them quite handsomely, in some cases at the multi-million-dollar level. They continued to reassure government agencies and the public that our economic and financial systems were healthy up until the stock-market collapse, the tidal wave of home foreclosures, and the resulting job losses.

The case of Frederic Mishkin, Columbia University Business School professor of banking and finance, highlights the problems accompanying nondisclosure. In 2006, Mishkin, who served as director of research at the New York Federal Reserve from 2006 to 2008, published a widely circulated paper titled "Financial Stability in Iceland." The publication praised the stability and reliability of the Icelandic banking system and recommended it as a model for the rest of the world. Just two years later, Iceland's banking system dramatically collapsed. Mishkin's paper did not disclose his funding source, but his Federal Reserve disclosure form revealed that he had been paid over $120,000 by the Icelandic Chamber of Commerce to author the report.[57] As Mishkin later confirmed during his interview for *Inside Job*, the main sources he drew upon for his confident conclusions were interviews with Iceland's bankers. Whether this funding influenced his decision to take the bankers at their word, rather than doing any confirming research with other sources, is impossible to say, though he did largely say exactly what the Icelandic Chamber of Commerce would have wanted him to say. The point about FCOI disclosure in the paper is that it would have given readers reason to be skeptical about his conclusions. The public outrage generated by the Mishkin profile and others featured in *Inside Job* helped persuade the American Economic Association, in January 2012, to adopt new standards for the disclosure of authors' FCOI in the association's economics journals. This marked the first time the association had ever required its authors to report funding sources and other research-related financial ties, though the requirement does not extend to non-AEA economics journals.

Over a period of decades—dating from the 1980s—Congress has repeatedly proven itself unable or unwilling to regulate finance capital in any meaningful way. Neoliberal faith in the primacy of the market rules, even in the wake of the 2008 recession. One may speculate that faculty who made themselves rich serving the financial services industry simply felt they were taking opportunistic advantage of the world as it was. Yet universities are uniquely positioned to be different from the wider political culture. They have sufficient relative autonomy at least to shed light on the financial activities of their faculty. The faculty collectively can mandate that sunlight shine on the discretionary income their colleagues earn in the service of industry.

Public debate over the natural-gas-extraction method known as "hydraulic fracking" also suggests the distorting influence of financial relationships on objective academic research—in this case, energy research—and on its public reception, with possibly far reaching consequences for energy and environmental policy and public decision making. Controversy over university ties to the natural gas and "fracking" industry went national in the spring and summer of 2012, with a score of stories in the *New York Times, Scientific American, Wall Street Journal, Chronicle of Higher Education, Inside Higher Education,* and *Bloomberg News,* along with local coverage in venues like the *Dallas Observer* and *Buffalo News.* These stories revealed undisclosed fracking industry ties to faculty members supposedly doing objective energy research.[58]

A May 2012 report issued by the University of Buffalo's Shale Resources and Society Institute strongly endorsed the claim that fracking—a process in which millions of gallons of toxic, carcinogenic, chemically treated water and sand are pumped underground to free natural gas deposits by shattering layers of rock in which the gas is trapped—presents no serious environmental risks. The University issued a press release stating that the report had no industry funding. Neither the press release nor the report itself acknowledged that the principal authors had received extensive industry funding for producing previous fracking advocacy reports and publications and therefore had long-standing friendly ties to the industry. News reports further disclosed that one of the report's authors, Tim Considine, served as a key researcher and contributor to a 2009 Pennsylvania State University report that helped convince state legislators not to impose state taxes on natural gas production. Community members, students, and UB faculty formed a local advocacy group, UB CLEAR, to press the university to deal with problems at the Institute. And the Buffalo-based Public Accountability Initiative, a nonprofit public interest research organization, issued a substantive analysis of flaws and deceptive claims in the Institute's report. On November 19, 2012, UB President Satish K. Tripathi wrote a public letter acknowledging inconsistencies in the management of FCOI and other problems at the Shale Resources and Society Institute, which "impacted the appearance of independence and integrity of the institute's research." Tripathi announced he was shutting the Institute down.[59]

Publicity over these undisclosed FCOI at the University of Buffalo helped to draw attention to a February 2012 University of Texas–Austin study that reported no risk of groundwater contamination from fracking.

The UT Austin report failed to disclose that its author, Charles Groat, had extensive ties to the energy industry, including a seat on the board of Plains Exploration & Production, a gas producer operating in Texas that paid him $400,000 in direct compensation the previous year. Indeed Groat had not disclosed the income to the university. The report itself once again received a detailed analysis and critique from Public Accountability Initiative. The campus launched an investigation, Groat has since retired, and the university has placed its Energy Institute under new administration.[60]

The events of 2012 created a credibility crisis surrounding industry-funded fracking research at universities that continues today. Indeed Public Accountability Initiative released a March 2013 report drawing overdue attention to an influential 2011 MIT study, "The Future of Natural Gas," that was also written by faculty members with extensive industry ties. The study was the product of the Massachusetts Institute of Technology Energy Initiative, led by Ernest Moniz, President Obama's 2013 choice for Energy Secretary. One may reasonably ask whether Moniz can be trusted to oversee the objective research on fracking that the American public needs and deserves.

Many academic fracking researchers are now leery of direct industry connections, thereby, in our view, necessitating a mechanism for the independent assignment of research dollars. Contributing to the crisis are suggestions that universities should lease some of their own land for fracking operations. Directing some of the resulting revenue toward fracking research by campus faculty raises yet another potential COI, since faculty members with research documenting health risks or environmental dangers might be hesitant to recommend that their own institutions curtail their fracking revenue streams. Of course student, faculty, and community opposition to fracking mixes concern about faculty or administration COI with health and environmental issues. Meanwhile, some state governments have exerted considerable pressure to increase their own tax revenue through more extensive drilling operations. The jobs and revenue that fracking provides are appealing to cash-strapped states. But risks and costs of the process are well established: toxic spills, faulty wells, leaky containment ponds, deteriorating air quality in regions with extensive drilling, community disruption from massive construction and trucking operations, social dislocation from dramatically increased rents and the influx of temporary workers. Potential risks that require further research verification include groundwater and aquifer contamination, potential earthquake hazards, excessive demands on plains state water supplies, and long-term environmental degradation.[61]

Such COI cases raise questions about faculty responsibilities that extend beyond the scope of this report. Disclosure is rarely a sufficient remedy for such problems, but it is the necessary starting point: readers and citizens must, at a minimum, be informed about FCOI that may justify added scrutiny and skepticism about a publication's conclusions. As this report's COI principles recommend, universities and their faculty should be required to disclose on all publications and at any public presentations a concise summary of all related financial ties going back at least five years. Universities that perform routine and comprehensive reviews of their professors' COI should also be required to post and maintain this information (including all funding sources and other research-related financial ties) on a publicly accessible website for at least ten years.

★ ★ ★

What Accounts for Rising Levels of Academy-Industry Engagement?

Several factors have contributed to increased levels of academy-industry engagement since the 1970s. During the final years of the Carter administration and into the Reagan years, several policy measures designed to stimulate R&D and innovation sparked new incentives for academy-industry collaboration. These included landmark congressional legislation sponsored by Senators Birch Bayh and Bob Dole, known as the Bayh-Dole Act (1980);[62] an R&D tax credit (1981, enhanced in 1986);[63] and relaxed antitrust rules for R&D joint ventures (1984).[64]

The Bayh-Dole Act, the *Stanford v. Roche* Decision, and Campus IP Management

The Bayh-Dole Act addresses inventions and associated patent rights, not other forms of intellectual property. It established a uniform policy across all government agencies with regard to the procurement of inventions by federal agencies in federally supported research at universities, nonprofit organizations, and small businesses. The Act did not mandate either that universities own, or have a first right to own, inventions made with federal support, or that they need to commercialize such inventions. It did require universities to honor the conditions of a standard patent rights clause to be developed by the Department of Commerce for use in all federal funding agreements. That standard rights clause instructs universities to require their research personnel to make a written agreement to protect the government's interest in any inventions they may make.

The written agreement—under the standard patent rights clause, to be required by universities of their research personnel—provides: (1) that faculty notify their university when they have made an invention with federal support; (2) that faculty (as initial owners of their inventions) sign documents allowing patent applications to be filed when the owner of the invention, which may be the government or an invention management agent, desires such an application to proceed; (3) that the inventors sign documents that establish the government's rights in their inventions, which may include assignment of ownership or granting the government a nonexclusive right to use an invention developed with federal funds. The latter requirement assures federal agencies that they have access to federally funded inventions for government purposes.

These requirements were spelled out in a patent rights clause that Bayh-Dole authorized the Commerce Department to create. It is notable that faculty have long been able to honor these requirements without assigning their IP rights to the university. Universities have tried to claim that the only way they can guarantee that faculty will honor these responsibilities is by taking ownership of all faculty inventions, but obviously there are contractual alternatives to what amounts to a wholesale institutional grab of significant developments of faculty scholarship. Bayh-Dole also carefully avoided dictating to universities and faculty alike what patent rights they might be interested in or how these rights might be used—whether dedicated to the public, licensed nonexclusively, licensed exclusively, or held so the university could develop an invention directly.

Nowhere does the Act mandate university ownership of faculty inventions. Indeed, until a university intervenes—except for the requirement of the written agreement, which confirms the delegation of personal responsibility to potential inventors—the operative relationship is between the government and the inventor. It is only when a faculty member chooses to assign rights to another agent, such as the university, that Bayh-Dole's complexities come into play.

Nevertheless, American university patent managers over the course of thirty years came to interpret the Bayh-Dole Act as granting them automatic ownership rights to all federally supported inventions generated on campus, including the right to license this IP to industry and others in exchange for royalties, equity, and other fees. The US Supreme Court, however, in a landmark 2011 decision—*Board of Trustees of Leland Stanford Junior University v. Roche Molecular Systems, Inc. (Stanford v. Roche)*—offered a different interpretation of the Bayh-Dole Act. The court firmly rejected the claims by Stanford and other institutions favoring federally sanctioned, compulsory university ownership of faculty research inventions.[65]

Stanford had sued Roche in 2005, alleging that Roche's kits for detecting the human immunodeficiency virus (HIV) infringed university patents. After years of litigation, Stanford pushed its case to the highest court, with support from other universities, including many major research universities, who saw the case as an opportunity to secure court endorsement for their interpretation of Bayh-Dole.[66] In an amicus brief filed on behalf of Stanford, the Association of University Technology Managers (a professional organization representing university licensing staff) and the Association of American Universities (an association of 62 top research universities), joined by six other research associations and five dozen universities, argued that Bayh-Dole has been "incredibly successful in stimulating innovation by giving universities certainty regarding their ownership of federally funded inventions." The brief went on to argue that Bayh-Dole vested ownership of inventions made with federal funds in the university that contracted to do the research: "Where, as here, a university elects to exercise its right under Bayh-Dole to retain title to an invention, the individual inventor cannot assign that invention to a third party because the invention is assigned, by operation of law, to the university."[67]

But the Supreme Court in its ruling refuted this interpretation of the law. For while it is true that Bayh-Dole requires universities to secure faculty agreement to protect and honor the US government's interest in federally funded inventions, the Court concluded there was nothing in the act that automatically vests title to their own inventions in their university employers.[68] Nor does the Act require faculty to assign their inventions to their universities or any other agent for management.

In its own successful amicus brief, the AAUP elaborated on this very point, arguing that Bayh-Dole does not alter the basic ownership rights granted to inventors by law. Rather it helps bring inventions forward to benefit the public good by clarifying that government agencies are to allow certain assignees of federally funded inventions to retain ownership, if and when they come to accept ownership, provided they meet various requirements to protect the government's interest, and the public interest.[69] The high court agreed, ruling that US patent law has always favored, and should continue to favor, the rights of individual inventors, and that universities need a written assignment from researchers to establish ownership of their inventions.

The AAUP considers *Stanford v. Roche* an important victory for faculty rights. The Supreme Court decision demonstrates once again that academic researchers and inventors remain, as they have traditionally been, much more than mere employees of their institutions, recognized by the respect afforded them by the federal government in its contracting with universities. Arguments underlying the compulsory assignment of faculty IP to university employers (which continue to be advanced by Stanford, AAU, AUTM, and most university administrations) begin with the assumption that faculty are no different from corporate employees who owe their employers the fruits of their labor. But the AAUP's 1915 "Declaration of Principles on Academic Freedom and Academic Tenure" anticipated and firmly disputed that claim. The declaration observed that faculty could not maintain academic freedom and the ability to serve the interests of society as truly independent experts and academic scholars unless they were recognized as "appointees," not corporate employees.[70] It is now well established, indeed few academic administrators would disagree, that academic freedom firmly secures faculty members' rights to direct and control their own scholarly research and classroom instruction. By attempting to force assignment of faculty research inventions and, more broadly, intangible assets in any form, to universities (as university administrations are doing today), the institutions are effectively arguing that faculty lose academic freedom the moment they become inventors, at which point their scholarly autonomy is lost and they become mere employees. The argument amounts to an assertion of employer control over faculty research, including the dissemination and possible future uses of academic research discoveries and results. Such a claim is as objectionable for faculty research as it is for classroom instruction. It is also objectionable to other types of investigators who may be formally recognized and named as inventors of academic discoveries, such as postdoctoral fellows and students, who should never be expected to give away such rights wholesale to their universities.

Of course professors (and other kinds of academic investigators) may choose to negotiate separate contractual agreements with their universities outside of their normal teaching, research, and scholarly responsibilities. These agreements typically involve the performance of optional tasks that may be expressly identified in advance as "works for hire," in which university ownership claims to resulting IP may be reasonably included by mutual agreement. Such a situation might arise, for example, if a professor voluntarily consents to signing a discrete "work for hire" contract to develop a new online course, which permits the university to own and distribute that course through its online education division. This is altogether different, however, from the current situation where universities are claiming automatic, broad ownership rights to all IP developed in the course of faculty's ordinary and continuing research, scholarship, and teaching. Such claims pose a direct challenge to academic freedom because they undermine faculty members' ability to control and direct the dissemination of their research.

That said, it is altogether inappropriate to *require* a faculty member to cede ownership of a course to the university merely because the course is prepared in a format suitable to online presentation. Faculty members who do so should realize they are signing away to the university their right to modify the course or control its performance. The university may modify the course or assign it to someone else to teach or change the attribution of authorship. The major national outlets for MOOCs are so far apparently not demanding ownership of university-based courses. Nor do they require universities to assert ownership. University administrators are simply exploiting this as an opportunity to take ownership of faculty instructional IP, when all that is needed is for a faculty member to grant permission to the university to host a course in an online program.

Contrary to the emerging pattern of coopting faculty instructional IP, an April 2013 memo from the California State University Long Beach administration established an interim agreement for faculty applying for 2013 internal grants to support development of online courses, using a very different approach to define a principle that could be widely adopted:

> the faculty member shall retain ownership of all works he or she produces for . . . online instruction. Thus, in the absence of a separate, written "work-for-hire agreement" which may supersede this agreement, the undersigned faculty member shall be deemed to be the sole owner of all intellectual property rights in his or her course materials, even though the faculty member is receiving a financial stipend to support the creation of online lectures, electronic presentations, podcasts, quizzes, tests, readings, simulations, including development of software, and other teaching and learning activities or material. The fact that the faculty member might use common campus resources (e.g., computers, library books, library databases, software licensed to CSULB for faculty and staff use, consultations with reference librarians, assistance from the Faculty Center for Professional Development and Instructional Technology Support Services staff) shall not alter faculty ownership of the works produced by the faculty member.

Faculty handbooks or collective bargaining agreements could embody the principle at stake—rejecting any institutional claim of ownership based on the use of university resources in course development—with the following language:

> The university shall make no claim of ownership or financial interest in course materials prepared under the direction of a faculty member, unless the university and faculty member have so agreed in a separate, voluntary agreement. Payment of a financial stipend, use of university resources, or release time to develop course materials

> shall not be construed by the university as creating a basis for a claim
> of institutional ownership of such materials, nor that a work for hire
> relationship exists between the university and the faculty member
> with regard to the preparation of any such materials.

A provision like this would be especially relevant to the creation of MOOCs, where the use of university resources—especially assistance from staff—tends to be greater. One might note, however, that universities do not typically ask for an actual accounting of resources used.

As the AAUP's 1999 "Statement on Copyright" observed regarding faculty research and inventions subject to copyright: "the faculty member rather than the institution determines the subject matter, the intellectual approach and direction, and the conclusions"; for the institution to control the "dissemination of the work" would be "deeply inconsistent with fundamental principles of academic freedom." The statement goes on to note: "it has been the prevailing academic practice to treat the faculty member as the copyright owner of works that are created independently and at the faculty member's own initiative for traditional academic purposes." And it adds, "it is unlikely that the institution will be regarded as having contributed the kind of 'authorship' that is necessary for a 'joint work' that automatically entitles it to a share in the copyright ownership."

In 1998, the AAUP established a Special Committee on Distance Education and Intellectual Property Issues, which released several documents the following year, including one recommending language for campus policies regarding IP rights and management titled "Sample Intellectual Property Policy and Contract Language." This document begins: "the copyright statement takes as its guiding assumption that the faculty member (or members) who create the intellectual property own the intellectual property," adding that "that assumption applies to the patent area as well." It went on to recommend the following language for campus adoption: "Intellectual property created, made, or originated by a faculty member shall be the sole and exclusive property of the faculty, author, or inventor, except as he or she may voluntarily choose to transfer such property, in full or in part." Drawing on a detailed discussion of "work made for hire" in the "Statement on Copyright," the Special Committee endorsed the following: "A work should not be treated as 'made for hire' merely because it is created with the use of university resources, facilities, or materials of the sort traditionally and commonly made available to faculty members." It went on to note: "Funds received by the faculty member from the sale of intellectual property owned by the faculty author or inventor shall be allocated and expended as determined solely by the faculty author or inventor." Recognizing the current trend for universities to assign IP rights to institutions involuntarily, the AAUP "Statement on Copyright" further warns: "If the faculty member is indeed the initial owner of copyright, then a unilateral institutional declaration cannot effect a transfer, nor is it likely that a valid transfer can be effected by the issuance of appointment letters to new faculty members requiring, as a condition of employment, that they abide by a faculty handbook that purports to vest in the institution the ownership of all works created by the faculty member for an indefinite future."

The AAUP's "Statement on Distance Education" is prefaced by a warning that the "vital intersection of emergent technologies and the traditional interests of faculty members in their own intellectual products requires scrutiny and the formulation of policies that address the former while preserving the latter." The statement itself emphasizes that "the faculty should have primary responsibility for determining the policies and practices of the institution in regard to distance education." That includes authority for determining whether particular courses should receive credit at a college and how much credit they should receive. The statement does not anticipate the phenomenon of a MOOC enrolling 100,000 students, but it takes a firm stand on principles that should govern online courses no matter what their size: "Provision should also be made for the original teacher-creator, the teacher-adapter, or an appropriate faculty body to exercise control over the future use and distribution of recorded instructional material and to determine whether the material should be revised or withdrawn from use."

Even when a faculty member willingly takes on a distance education course on a work for hire basis, the "Statement on Copyright" clarifies a key condition: "the faculty member should, at a minimum, retain the right to take credit for creative contributions, to reproduce the work for his or her instructional purposes, and to incorporate the work in future scholarly works authored by the faculty member."

The *Stanford v. Roche* decision challenges a number of practices university administrators have imposed on faculty since Bayh-Dole, practices which lack standing in law and equity. Soon after the Supreme Court's ruling, IP experts predicted that US universities would respond defensively by incorporating new clauses in faculty employment contracts that assign ownership of faculty inventions to the institutions automatically.[71] The University of California is acting comprehensively with a different strategy: at the end of 2011 it began demanding that current faculty sign a letter assigning upfront to the university ownership to all their future inventions.[72] Such an arrangement is called an assignment of expectant interests, or a "present assignment." The claim made for such assignments is that they become effective the moment an invention is made, without the need for notice to the university, review of circumstances, or a determination of the university's proper interest in the invention as provided by policy. We have received copies of letters from senior UC administrators informing UC faculty that the university will refuse to approve their grant applications if they have not signed the new patent/invention assignment form. Indeed the UC is withdrawing already submitted applications if faculty refuse to comply.

In requiring present assignment of all future patent rights from current faculty, the UC system is effectively violating the agreements faculty made when they were hired, for the UC had long followed a policy of evaluating inventions on a case-by-case basis. If that long-standing policy had contractual status, then the new requirement effectively modifies a contract without negotiation or consent. At the same time, institutions like the University of Illinois that have simply responded to *Stanford v. Roche* by posting a universal claim to institutional patent ownership on the university website are no better observers of academic freedom and faculty rights. They are imposing an objectionable condition of employment without a contract at all.

These deliberate strategies represent a disturbing, ongoing trend. Most of the developments in university research and invention policies over the past thirty years have significantly limited or even ended opportunities for faculty investigators and inventors to decide the disposition of their research results and instructional materials, whether prepared for their colleagues, for a sponsor of research, for industry, or for the classroom. Some universities, such as the University of Washington, invoke state ethics laws to exclude faculty investigators from participating in invention-management and IP transactions involving the state because, the universities argue, the faculty might receive pay and other financial benefits from such negotiations (such as summer salary, which would not otherwise be allocated) and might therefore have a personal interest in the research agreement. Universities also now commonly insert automatic institutional ownership clauses into standard sponsored research agreements with industry and private foundations, claiming title and management rights to all faculty inventions developed under the agreement even when the sponsor does not require such institutional interest. Faculty with little bargaining power, including PhDs in their first jobs, are particularly vulnerable to pressure to sign away their invention rights, possibly for their entire careers.

Many current university policies distinguish between faculty IP that can be protected by copyright versus IP that is patentable, with universities commonly asserting automatic institutional ownership claims only on patentable IP. We consider this distinction to be fundamentally flawed as a method for assigning ownership rights: it is not based on any rational analysis of the nature of faculty research and productivity and it violates academic freedom. Indeed, the possibility arises that universities will expand their IP ownership claims to copyrightable faculty work as well, given that the distinction in this context is arbitrary.

Since 2007 the National Association of College and University Attorneys (NACUA) has promoted university ownership of both patentable and copyrightable IP. That year, four attorneys delivered a paper, "Creating Intellectual Property Policies and Current Issues in Administering Online Courses," at NACUA's annual meeting, and NACUA posted the paper on the members-only section of its website. We obtained a copy in 2012 and *Inside Higher Education* convinced NACUA to make it public through *InsideHigherEd. com*.[73] The authors call for comprehensive university ownership of faculty IP whenever its creation has involved substantial use of university resources. "Substantial resources," they argue, "might include specialized computer resources or other equipment and significant use of student or research support."[74] A large number of income-producing activities, including textbook authorship, would readily fall under this broad definitional umbrella.

The NACUA paper also stipulates that institutions may claim a share of faculty consulting income if "the faculty member is involved with university research in the same area as the consulting" or if the consulting is in the same general area in which the faculty member teaches. Both conditions are widely applicable to faculty consulting across numerous academic disciplines. Indeed it is improbable that faculty members would be consulting in areas for which they have no demonstrated expertise as scholars and teachers. The NACUA paper further recommends that faculty members' right to make any software they have created be freely available through open-source licensing should be subject to review to determine whether "the goals of the institution would be better served through commercialization."[75]

Such positions are serious challenges to academic freedom and all the more troubling from the perspective of universities' long-standing commitments to broad public dissemination of new knowledge. If a professor judges that his or her research would be more broadly utilized in continuing research or commercial applications if it were freely disseminated through "open sourcing," why should that professor be compelled to adhere to the dictates of the university's technology transfer officers who typically have far less insight into the technology in question and its possible applications? Why, furthermore, should faculty members lose the right to open source their research if the technology transfer office's preference for control—and the imposition of licensing fees—stems principally from a desire to maximize revenue for the university rather than a desire to maximize public use of the invention? Such preferences for profit-seeking undercut claims that institutional ownership is the best route to serving the public good. Such assertions in institutional policy are essentially empty aspirational distractions.

The recommendations contained in the 2007 NACUA paper violate the fundamental principle that faculty should control their own research, and further indicate that universities may move to assert control over all potentially profitable faculty research products, regardless of whether they are subject to copyright or are patentable. Indeed, one comprehensive survey of university technology transfer offices (TTOs), conducted by researchers Jerry Thursby, Richard Jensen, and Marie Thursby, found that most TTOs assume that comprehensive institutional ownership of faculty inventions is already the norm.[76] In response to the question, "Who owns inventions and materials made or developed by faculty or other personnel in your university?," all but one TTO in the sample asserted that the university owns patentable inventions and materials. For copyrightable inventions, 66 percent stated that the university was also the owner.

In a letter submitted to the AAUP in 2012, Gerald Barnett, an expert on the management of university IP, commented on compulsory ownership: "A compulsory ownership claim changes the relationship between faculty and administration from one of administrative governance and support to one of an employer with authority over the disposition of work of employees. . . . [This] is routine in companies, but is anything but routine, or acceptable, for university faculty."

Interestingly, it was not always so. The history of IP management at universities makes it clear that some institutions once strongly respected faculty IP rights.[77] Whereas Stanford, MIT, and the University of Illinois sought comprehensive control over faculty IP as early as the 1930s or 1940s, the University of California's 1943 policy went a different route: "Assignment to the Regents of whatever rights the inventor or discoverer may possess in the patent or appointment of the Board as the agent of the inventor or discoverer shall be optional on the part of the faculty member or employee." Rutgers was even more concise in 1946: "the University claims no interest in any invention by members of its staff." That same year the University of Cincinnati affirmed "the right of absolute ownership by a faculty member or student or other person connected with the teaching or research staff of the University of his own inventions, discoveries, writings, creations, and/or developments, whether or not made while using the regular facility of the University." Columbia included an exception typical of a number of institutions: "While it is the policy of the Faculty of Medicine to discourage the patenting of any medical discovery or invention . . . the right of staff members in other divisions of the University to secure patents on their own inventions is well recognized."

The policy for the University of Texas, adopted in 1945, similarly assert-ed that "the title to a patent for any discovery or invention made by an employee of the University of Texas belongs to the said employee and he is free to develop or handle it in any manner he sees fit." The University of Arizona in 1939 also declared that "no inventor shall be compelled to submit an invention to the Patent Committee." Princeton adopted its policy in 1938: "If a member of the University desires to obtain a patent on his own responsibility he may do so." All three institutions did mandate modest profit sharing, which remains an appropriate and reasonable practice today. These university policies demonstrate that faculty research ownership and IP rights do not have to be invented; they merely need to be revived, publicized, and reinforced.

The *Stanford v. Roche* decision opens the door for faculty and their gov-erning bodies to press for a return to the far stronger faculty inventor rights that led the development of new research technology in the years prior to the passage of the Bayh-Dole Act, and for more visionary shared governance systems around IP and invention management. The Supreme Court's ruling strongly bolsters the AAUP position that faculty should be free to control the disposition of their scholarship without interference by profit-seeking university IP administrators. It logically follows from this that faculty should be free to choose how their inventions are managed, including how best to disseminate, license, or develop their discoveries, as well as which manage-ment agent is best equipped to work with them to handle the patenting and license negotiations. As a university makes disposition of these rights a condi-tion of employment, these rights could be secured for faculty in collective bargaining agreements.

Under such a system, professors might very well choose to grant inven-tion rights to their own institutions. But those institutions would have to compete for faculty business on a level playing field; they could not simply claim automatic, monopoly control over faculty research. Instead, they would have to offer services consistent with faculty investigator objectives, and be held accountable for the commitments made to support licensing of the invention. The institutions would also, then, have to show how their program of invention deployment better served the public than comparable services offered by private invention management agents. Faculty could choose instead to work with an outside IP expert or management agency (unless they have previously agreed otherwise).

Faculty members' ability to retain title to their inventive scholarship not only protects academic freedom and inventors' rights, it requires universities to work much more collaboratively with faculty, both in negotiations over individual faculty inventions and in the development of shared protocols to guide invention management practices university-wide. The establishment of such shared governing protocols for the management of university IP is critically important. In a 2011 report titled "Managing University Intellectual Property in the Public Interest," the National Research Council and the National Academies made a similar recommendation, calling on faculty, administrators, and other constituencies with an interest in campus-based inventions and IP management practices to develop such protocols. The NRC explained: "It is essential that universities give a clear policy mandate to their technology transfer offices and acknowledge the tensions among frequently stated goals: knowledge dissemination, regional economic development, service to faculty, generation of revenue for the institution, and, more recently, addressing humanitarian needs."[78]

Most universities currently operate without clear shared governance protocols to guide their invention management and technology transfer operations. The result is widespread complaints from faculty, industry, private foundations, legal experts, government agencies, and public interest groups that universities are unaccountable, overly focused on maximizing profits and ineffective in managing inventions in the public interest. In 2007, officials from the Ewing Marion Kauffman Foundation, the leading US foundation dedicated to entrepreneurship research, wrote that university-based "Technology Transfer Offices (TTOs) were envisioned as gateways to facilitate the flow of innovation but have instead become gatekeepers that often constrain the flow of inventions and frustrate faculty, entrepreneurs, and industry."[79] Many in industry are quite vocal about poor university management of research inventions, lack of sufficient expertise in university TTOs, and the imposition of excessive licensing restrictions and fees that impede industry use.[80]

The AAUP agrees with the US Supreme Court that universities have a legal obligation to honor faculty inventor rights and to respect faculty's central role in the disposition of IP deriving from their own research. The strongest opposition to this position is likely to emanate from the TTOs themselves, which have a vested interest in the status quo. In a written public comment submitted to the AAUP on July 17, 2012—after the Supreme Court's *Stanford v. Roche* ruling—the Board of Directors of the Association of University Technology Managers (AUTM), representing TTO officers, continued to proclaim that as "employees of a university, faculty members are subject to employment contracts like any other profession" and should not be granted "free agency" when it comes to the ownership and management of their research discoveries and inventions.

According to AUTM's letter, compulsory assignment of invention rights is justified because TTOs are best equipped to fulfill the public objectives of technology transfer, which the Association defines as: "1. to give taxpayers a return on their invested research dollars, and 2. to benefit the public by transferring new technologies for public use expeditiously and effectively." In AUTM's view, this is because university TTOs (also known as Technology Licensing Offices or TLOs) are the most experienced managers of these inventions, and also the least biased:

> University TLOs, experienced in dealing with multiple inventors and multiple institutions, are in the best position to be neutral, objective and unbiased advocates of federally funded inventions. Further, the benefit of this expertise extends to the transfer of technologies that have other sources of funding.

AUTM provided no evidence to support its assertions, but most data on the management of campus-based research and inventions would counter the claim that TTOs are neutral and unbiased guardians of the public interest. Most universities expect their TTOs to be financially self-sustaining, which, given their operating costs, creates a strong incentive for their officers to put institutional revenue generation ahead of other competing public interest goals. The Thursby et al. survey found that university TTOs rank revenue generation (from licensing royalties and fees) as their number one priority—not widespread use of faculty inventions or even effective commercialization.[81]

Yet there is one general caveat that applies to all invention-management negotiations: no party to a contract is inherently immune to disabling motivations and biases. Faculty investigators and inventors, as well as administrators, may be biased by the apparent opportunity for substantial wealth when negotiating IP and research contracts. The reality of such influences strengthens the argument for collectively defined university IP protocols, such as the ones we recommend. The development of such IP protocols could benefit the public by clarifying institutional support for procedures by which creative workers hosted by a university may transfer academic knowledge to society. When universities assume monopoly ownership over research inventions (and therefore need not negotiate with faculty inventors nor face competition from independent IP management agencies and professionals), it gives them a powerful incentive to pursue more restrictive and thus what they take to be potentially more profitable licensing arrangements. In actual practice, such behaviors tend to rely on a very few licensing deals generating a disproportionate amount of licensing income, while the vast majority of inventions claimed by a university languish: the extra licensing income serves to file patents—that is, to claim formal institutional ownership of inventions—but is not used to transfer these inventions to the public. In fact, the institutionally created patents become barriers to access and serve to undermine the value of the research that led to the discoveries and inventions in the first place.

In its written comments, AUTM argued that in order to foster successful technology transfer it was necessary to give universities the power to patent government-funded inventions and license them exclusively to private companies. Otherwise, it stated, those companies would be unwilling to invest the capital required to bring embryonic academic inventions into commercial development. This may be true for some inventions, but it is by no means applicable to all or even most university discoveries. As recent cases involving stem cells, breast cancer genes, disease patents, and software demonstrate, this more aggressive university focus on patents and exclusive licensing is often not in the public interest and poorly serves innovation and economic vitality. AUTM and the university technology licensing community routinely disparage all alternatives to their adopted policy model: using specialized invention management agents, allowing investigators and inventors to work with the IP attorneys and management agents of their choice, using nonexclusive licensing to promote competition and free enterprise, dedication of inventions to the public domain, using open innovation strategies, and licensing for quality control without requiring payment. But studies show such alternative methods of technology transfer remain the most common channels by which industry gains access to academic knowledge and inventions. One survey of firms in the manufacturing sector reported that the four highest-ranked channels for accessing university knowledge were traditional, open academic channels: publications, conferences, informal information exchange, and consulting.[82] Patents and licensing ranked far lower on the list. Even in pharmaceuticals, where patents and licenses are considered important to facilitate commercialization, firms still rely heavily on traditional open channels.[83]

The notion that stronger IP control accelerates commercialization of federally funded research runs contrary to important economic principles. When publicly funded knowledge is "non-rivalrous," as academic science frequently is, its use in additional applications poses no real economic cost. By contrast, when any one party is denied access to a discovery, it can stifle the potential for continuing research and commercial application.[84]

Ironically, the way most academic inventions reach the attention of strategically located people in industry is through their existing contacts with faculty inventors. When Thursby et al. asked TTOs to describe the procedures used to market scholarly work, the role of faculty inventors was paramount. Fifty-eight percent of the respondents listed faculty inventor contacts as useful for marketing academic technology to industry. "It is also likely," noted the survey's authors, "that some of the 75% of TTOs who listed personal contacts as important were referring to the personal contacts of faculty."[85] A companion Thursby et al. survey of businesses who license university technologies generated similar results: 46 percent of industry respondents said that personal contacts between their R&D staff and university faculty were extremely important in identifying new technologies to license.[86] These results accord with a 1999 study finding that 56 percent of the primary leads for university license adoptions, in the 1100 licenses examined, originated from faculty.[87] These surveys suggest that TTOs could not operate effectively without help from faculty inventors, through their contacts in industry and their deep knowledge of invention technologies and applications. According to Thursby et al.: "[t]he importance of the faculty in finding licensees follows, we believe, from the generally early stage of university technologies since, for such technologies, it is the faculty who are able best to articulate the value and nature of such technologies."[88]

It thus seems particularly short sighted for AUTM and university administrations to insist on the compulsory assignment of faculty research inventions to the university—a process that necessarily distances faculty from the management and marketing of their own inventions. Given that faculty inventors have the deepest knowledge of their own inventions, and often are sole sources of the expertise that surrounds their scholarly work (which is often experiential and cannot be patented), it is simply sound policy for faculty to control the dissemination of their own scholarship and research.

In seeking to strengthen these rights, faculty will likely face considerable opposition from university technology licensing officers and their legal counsel, who have grown accustomed to asserting monopoly positions on faculty scholarship and all of whom have a powerful interest in maintaining the status quo that funds their salaries. Propelled by Bayh-Dole and other legislative reforms, universities have invested heavily in their technology ownership and licensing operations over the last three decades, expending large sums on licensing staff, legal experts, patenting and licensing fees, and IP-related litigation.

This expenditure has certainly brought some returns for a handful of institutions, but it has also generated everywhere substantial infrastructure overhead and expense. From 1983 to 2003, the number of patents issued directly to American universities grew from 434 to 3,259.[89] The overwhelming majority of these patents were concentrated in biomedicine, but patents also came from engineering, computer science, agriculture, and numerous other fields. Universities, however, refuse to disclose how many of these patents have not been licensed, and of those that have been licensed, which of these licenses have resulted in new products made available to the public at a reasonable cost. Total annual revenues from the licensing of university inventions increased from roughly $200 million in 1991 to $1.85 billion in 2006.[90] In 2007, AUTM reported a total of 3,148 cumulative, operational startup firms associated with US university patenting and licensing activities.

But it does not report how many of these firms are still in business or which of them has ever produced a new product offered for sale.[91]

The figures are intended to look impressive. But they are not. Contrary to widespread assumptions, most universities have not actually generated substantial income from their patenting and licensing activities, nor has their licensing activity resulted in a significant number of new products coming into commercial use. Only roughly two dozen US universities with "blockbuster" inventions generate sizable revenue from their licensing activities.[92] A 2006 econometric analysis found that, after subtracting the costs of patent management, universities netted "on average, quite modest" revenues from 1998 until 2002, two decades after Bayh-Dole took effect. This study concluded: "universities should form a more realistic perspective of the possible economic returns from patenting and licensing activities."[93] Lita Nelsen, director of the technology licensing office at MIT, made similar observations: "the direct economic impact of technology licensing on the universities themselves has been relatively small (a surprise to many who believed that royalties could compensate for declining federal support of research) . . . [M]ost university licensing offices barely break even."[94] Difficulty breaking even is especially true for licensing offices less than twenty years old and for institutions with annual research budgets of less than $100 million. Especially those universities with research budgets under $100 million should, for financial reasons as well as those of academic freedom and support for innovation, adopt policies that restore faculty control of their inventive scholarship. The "big hit" invention that a member of their faculty might make is more likely to benefit the institution through a voluntary collaboration than through a compulsory ownership policy that demands to manage all inventions for fear of losing out on one lucrative invention every two or three decades.

Supporters of Bayh-Dole may have hoped the legislation would create opportunities for universities to manage academic inventions made with federal support and thus speed the pace of technological innovation in the United States. But here too the legislation's economic legacy has been mixed. Though university patents soared after Bayh-Dole, studies find that academic patenting does not correlate well with increased industrial use or commercial development of academic discoveries.[95] A 2002 study of the patent portfolios of Stanford and Columbia found that, of eleven major inventions, seven would have been commercialized without any assertion of patent rights or TTO licensing, because "strategically located people in industry were well aware of the university research projects even before the universities' [TTOs] began to market the inventions."[96]

Other Factors Driving Academy–Industry Engagement

The Bayh-Dole Act and subsequent tax incentives were not the only forces stimulating university patenting and commercial activity. Changes in US patent law provided another stimulus by vastly expanding the types of academic knowledge eligible for patent protection to include genetic code, human genes, medical processes, and algorithms in computer code.[97] Some have expressed concern that the vast growth in US patenting, including increased patenting and other types of IP controls in academia, could shrink the public commons for basic scientific knowledge, long considered a wellspring for invention and discovery.

The emergence of a knowledge-driven economy has also spurred greater industry engagement with academia. In one 2004 study, industry representatives reported that universities had become more important as the locus of technical change shifted toward basic science in such fields as biotechnology and information technology. Business representatives also credit enhanced outsourcing to academic labs to the decline in direct industry spending on basic research and the closing of industry-based R&D labs following the wave of corporate restructuring in the 1980s.[98]

The 2004 study identified reductions in federal research support levels as universities' primary motivation for industry partnerships. According to Bronwyn H. Hall, a UC Berkeley economist, the "real growth in federal R&D funding for universities was 16% between 1953 and 1968 and 1% between 1969 and 1983, followed by an upturn to 5% between 1984 and 2000, but with substantial declines in non-biomedical areas."[99] According to more recent federal data, inflation-adjusted obligations for academic R&D peaked in 2004 at $22.1 billion (in constant 2000 dollars) and has since declined to an estimated $20.7 billion in 2009.[100] The federal decline, combined with declines in state funding as a share of overall expenditures, have left universities increasingly reliant on tuition, alumni giving, endowment interest, private fundraising, research licensing, and funding from industry sources.[101]

The evolution of science itself is another force driving academy–industry engagement. Both the biotechnology and information technology revolutions were born in academic laboratories, leading to greater faculty entrepreneurship and a desire to engage with venture capital firms and outside industry groups. Moreover, the practice of science has become a more complex, collaborative, and multidisciplinary enterprise. As the Business–Higher Education Forum observed in a two-year study of academy-industry partnerships, "the increasing volume and accelerating pace of knowledge creation has transformed the research process to the point where no one scientist, institution, or even nation can conduct wholly independent research programs;

rising costs, driven by increasingly complex research, make resource-sharing an imperative. Changes in the nature of innovation largely depend on multidisciplinary approaches and use tools from a range of seemingly unrelated fields."[102]

The US government has also been encouraging academy-industry-government engagement through its grant allocation system.[103] Government-academy-industry partnerships now span a wide range of sectors: electronic storage, flat-panel displays, turbine technologies, new textile manufacturing techniques, new materials, magnetic storage, next-generation vehicles, batteries, biotechnology, optoelectronics, and ship construction. According to one estimate, because of the federal government's growing preference for allocating R&D funds through corporate "matching grants" and other industrial cost-sharing research arrangements, private industry now influences 20 to 25 percent of overall university research funding.[104]

In a 2007 interview with the Center for American Progress, Jilda D. Garton, the associate vice provost for research at Georgia Institute of Technology—a top US engineering school—stated that roughly half the industry money that now pays for academic research at Georgia Tech comes from federal grants originally issued to corporations through various cost-sharing arrangements.[105] After corporations receive these matched federal research grants, they frequently contract with universities to perform the actual research, with only minimal government oversight or control. A growing share of taxpayer funding that began as public in character effectively turns private by the time the money reaches academic investigators.

Public-private partnerships are now actively encouraged through a variety of federal grant programs, including the National Manufacturing Initiative; the National Science Foundation's "engineering research centers" and "science and technology centers"; the National Institute of Standards and Technology's Manufacturing Extension and Advanced Technology Program (dual-use programs run by the Department of Defense); and the popular Small Business Innovation Research (SBIR) and Cooperative Research and Development Agreements (CRADA) programs. The National Institutes of Health and the Department of Energy have also expanded their commitment to public-private partnering.[106]

In 2008, an official at the DOE told the Center for American Progress that the agency distributed roughly 80 to 90 percent of its federal funds for efficient and renewable energy R&D through some form of public-private cost sharing. Corporate beneficiaries are typically asked to contribute matching grants of 20 to 50 percent, depending on the project and its potential commercial application.[107]

★ ★ ★

Types of Academy-Industry Research Collaboration

Industry support of university research takes a variety of forms, from smaller, more casual grants to individual researchers to larger, more institutionalized research grants and consortia involving dozens of firms paying fees to support a quasi-permanent research facility. As Bronwyn Hall observed: "The implication of this variety is that no one data source provides information on university–industry partnering, so that it is hard to get a picture of the system as a whole."[108] Below is a box summarizing the main types of academy-industry relationships:

Common Types of Academy-Industry Relationships

1. **Research Contracts:** Industry support of university-based research usually takes the form of a grant or a contract. These may be initiated by academic scientists, industrial sponsors, or company scientists. Institutions can benefit financially when research grants support salaries and facilities which otherwise would have to be supported by the institution, fund raising, or other grants.[109] Unfortunately, while research contracts, like federal and foundation grants, can help expand investigations into new areas or enhance existing ones, they often fail to cover full indirect costs. Universities may actually lose money on them.

2. **Consulting:** A faculty member provides advice, service, or information to a commercial firm or organization. Individual faculty earn consulting fees over and above their institutional salaries. Institutions can benefit financially when faculty use the money to support professional activities they would otherwise charge to the institution.[110]

3. **Industrial Consortia:** Large laboratories funded through a consortia agreement involving multiple firms, such as the Stanford Center for Integrated Systems. Companies usually pay annual membership fees to participate in consortia, with academic research results and discoveries shared among all the consortia members under nonexclusive licensing terms.

---

4. **Quasi-permanent University-Industry Research Centers (UIRCs) and Engineering Research Centers:** UIRCs are partially funded by the federal government and partially by industry.[111]

5. **Strategic Corporate Alliances (SCAs):** SCAs are multi-year, multi-million-dollar sponsored research alliances, commonly negotiated with just one corporation, set up to fund many campus-based labs and faculty research projects at once. Because SCAs often permit corporate sponsors to influence the university's research portfolio, resources, and internal governance systems, SCAs can raise institutional COI concerns. SCAs may not cover full indirect costs, and they may reshape core departmental teaching and research missions.

6. **Clinical Research Trials:** Pharmaceutical, biotechnology, and medical device manufacturers often finance academic investigators to test the safety and efficacy of their products. Clinical research trials are also addressed in the AAUP's recommended principles because research has shown that corporate sponsors frequently exert undue influence over the conduct and reporting of university-based clinical trials, and faculty investigators also frequently have personal financial interests in their research.

7. **Licensing:** Licensing grants industry the rights to commercialize university-owned or co-owned technologies in exchange for royalties or other profit-sharing arrangements. Most universities now have dedicated TTOs that handle all university-generated IP and related patenting, copyright, and licensing. Most universities share financial benefits with faculty inventors.

8. **Equity:** Academic faculty and academic institutions participate in the founding or ownership of new companies commercializing university-based research. Often these cash-poor companies provide equity or options to purchase equity as compensation for relationships, such as consulting and licensing. Equity relationships are especially common in biotechnology, but occur in other fields as well.[112]

9. **Training:** Companies provide support for graduate students or post-doctoral fellows, or contract with academic institutions to provide various educational experiences, such as seminars or fellowships, to industrial employees.

10. **Gifts:** The transfer of funding or resources (scientific or nonscientific), independent of an institutionally negotiated research grant or contract, between an industry group and an academic institution or an individual faculty member. Gifts may include discretionary funding, equipment, biomaterials, support for travel to professional meetings, and entertainment (tickets to sporting events, cultural events, dinners, resort travel).[113]

Strategic Corporate Alliances (SCAs)

Several university committees have studied the emergence of large-scale, multi-year strategic corporate alliances on campus.[114] SCAs now span disciplines ranging from medicine to agriculture to energy research; they need more oversight because of their size, scope and structure and their tendency to grant industry sponsors an unusual degree of research influence and administrative control. After the conclusion of the UC Berkeley-Novartis alliance, an independent Michigan State University review emphasized the need to "reassess in a comprehensive fashion the implications of non-financial and institutional conflicts of interest" at large-scale SCAs.[115] Cornell University's faculty senate reached a similar conclusion: "The essential quality of academic independence from the sponsor is more difficult to maintain at an institutional, as well as individual, level" with SCAs, the panel wrote.[116] See the discussion of SCAs under Part VI in the main report for more detail.

The Benefits and Compromises of Academy-Industry Engagement

From the emergence of the modern research university, interactions between private industry and university professors have been critically important. As a 1995 Industrial Research Institute report points out, in addition to providing financial support for education and research, academy-industry collaborations enhance the following institutional goals: fulfilling the university's service mission and demonstrating the value of academic research and expertise; broadening student and faculty experience; identifying interesting problems and relevant applications for university research inquiry; stimulating regional economic development; increasing post-graduation employment opportunities for students.[117] This list remains equally relevant today and can certainly be expanded.

Industry also brings new technology to university campuses, and can help promote public support for university research. Academic investigators find that knowledge flows not only from the university to industry but also from industry to the university. Innovation is by definition a learning process that continuously tests existing knowledge and practices against proposals for technological and social change. Knowledge and interaction that flow between faculty and industry can improve the quality of research by testing its results in practice. Indeed, companies spend millions of dollars trying to replicate published claims of university research, sometimes without success. Such industry efforts to evaluate and validate university research contribute to the advancement of knowledge.

According to a 2002 Business Higher Education Forum survey of university researchers, corporate sponsorship often exacts a lesser administrative burden than the federal government's voluminous and fiercely competitive grant application process. Researchers point out that additional visibility from academy-industry research collaborations can lead to greater peer recognition and, in some cases, enhanced consulting opportunities.[118] Many entrepreneurial faculty report that they enjoy research with real-world applications and direct public benefits. These faculty relish their involvement with exciting new businesses, rapidly developing technology, commercial scale production, and practical research. Some evidence suggests that industry partnerships may also enhance faculty members' competitive edge for winning federal research awards.[119] Federal funding is increasingly awarded in conjunction with corporate matching grants for research that has already demonstrated commercial application.

Collaborations also facilitate faster commercial adoption of academic knowledge. One study found that faculty with industrial research relationships were significantly more likely than faculty without to be involved with a start-up company (14 percent versus 6 percent), apply for a patent (42 percent versus 24 percent), have a patent granted (25 percent versus 13 percent), have a patent licensed (18 percent versus 9 percent), have a product under review (27 percent versus 5 percent), or have a product on the market (26 percent versus 11 percent).[120] Collaboration with industry is not necessarily causal: industry may fund more productive scientists or those whose research already has greater likelihood of commercial application. Nevertheless, industry funding encourages scientists to be more commercially successful.[121]

Yet important caveats accompany these benefits: (1) Declines in federal funding for research (in constant dollars) and state funding for basic operations often leave untenured faculty feeling strong pressure to seek out and accept available industry money; (2) Monetary pressures can lead faculty members to seek larger grants from industry, rather than smaller available grants from the government or nonprofits; (3) Industry funding may lead faculty to pursue topics based on market demands rather than academic merit; (4) The pressure to raise research funds in academia long predates the intensified pursuit of corporate dollars. Market forces can generate valuable research and serve public interests, but academic freedom and innovation require flexibility and freedom of choice in the selection of research questions, avenues of research, and methods of inquiry.

Pressure also increases when faculty are expected to use grants to fund a portion of their own salaries. This practice is commonplace in schools of medicine, but it affects other academic disciplines as well. These faculty may feel extreme pressure to "serve the market," which may, in turn, introduce unconscious bias into research selection and professional judgment. University faculty should not be reduced to evaluating research solely or even primarily based on its potential short-term commercial value. They should be free to work on fundamental science, neglected areas of inquiry, and research for the public good. They should also feel free to contribute to the public body of knowledge (such as through the development of open source software or the free transmission of research tools and materials), rather than feel compelled to pursue proprietary dissemination of the fruits of their research.

For students and junior faculty members, however, industry collaborations may be a significant recruitment draw, given that an increasing proportion of university graduates now move into private sector careers. Commercial research collaborations may provide students with valuable corporate research experience that leads to early job offers. Still, as the Business-Higher Education Forum survey cautions, "sponsored research also may pose risks" for students and junior faculty. "Universities should not divert graduate students toward efforts that will not advance their education or their thesis research," the survey cautions. "If students' work is hemmed in by corporate confidentiality requirements, they may find themselves barred from presenting their work at scientific meetings—or, even worse, unable to publish a Ph.D. thesis."[122]

Significantly, research has found that faculty with industry research relationships are more productive (even when measured in traditional academic terms) than faculty without such relationships. A 2009 survey of more than 3,000 faculty in the life sciences found that, across all measures, those with industry relationships were more academically productive.[123] They published significantly more and at a greater rate (in the past three years) than respondents unconnected to industry. The average journal impact factor of the most recent five articles was also higher for respondents with at least one industry relationship. This corroborated earlier evidence that articles with joint academy-industry authorship have higher citation rates than publications with single- or multiple-university authorships.[124] Researchers with at least one industry relationship conducted more service activities in their institutions or disciplines than respondents without industry relationships. Finally, academics with industry relationships spent significantly more weekly hours performing outside professional activities, such as giving external lectures and working with professional societies and advisory groups. The findings remained constant over time when the authors compared 1995 with 2006 survey data.[125]

A 2007 study, the first longitudinal analysis of medical school faculty patenting, found that, despite public concern that Bayh-Dole would transform the ethos of medical schools by making them more proprietary, patenting activities are concentrated among a small number of departments and faculty, and the most prolific academic patenters remain active in traditional scientific activities.[126] More subtle is the question of how sponsored research is designed or selected for funding. Might these industrial collaborations unduly influence the research agenda of the university or medical school as a whole, as well as individual researchers, pushing the focus from more fundamental to more applied research? Or might the collaborations steer research toward more commercially profitable areas and away from public good research (such as research on environmental toxins, third world diseases, or global climate change)? The latter question has not been examined empirically, but the former has, and studies have generally failed to document a sizable shift in the balance between basic and applied university research.[127] In part, this may stem from the fact that most experts now agree distinctions between purely basic and applied research are largely artificial, since so much academic research is focused on real-world applications (a cure for cancer, a cleaner energy source, a lighter material for manufacturing) but the nature of the research itself is still quite fundamental and far from immediate use or application.[128]

Finally, it is important to note that benefits and risks are often two sides of the same coin. Many of the benefits highlighted above—including opportunities for service learning, applied or translational research, enhanced student job opportunities, contributions to economic development, increased research opportunities, and demonstration of the practical value of academic research—are the same forces that can generate COI and threaten the free inquiry and open culture of the university.

Six Risks of Academy-Industry Engagement

Risk 1: Violations of Academic Freedom and Researcher Autonomy

The proprietary nature of some sponsored research may entail confidentiality restrictions, publication delays, or industry requests for editorial changes. Such restraints can jeopardize free and open inquiry. Most university sponsored research contracts try to include provisions securing faculty's right to publish, but contracts that failed to secure basic publication rights have sometimes slipped through. And many more university contracts fail to secure faculty rights adequately; instead they allow industry sponsors to control data access, draft manuscripts, insert their own statistical analyses, and make final editorial revisions.

Industry sponsors sometimes try to interfere directly with faculty members' academic freedom by blocking or impeding their ability to carry out their research and publish independent findings. Numerous disputes have emerged over professors' rights to publish or speak about what they believe to be true. The more well-publicized cases came to light because faculty members, at great cost to their own careers and reputations, refused to tolerate industry interference with their professional work. We review a number of these cases and sketch the issues they involve.

Thalassemia: The Case of Nancy Olivieri
In 1996, Nancy Olivieri MD, a University of Toronto professor and hematologist, and her research colleagues, found that deferiprone, a drug used to treat thalassemia, an inherited, potentially fatal blood disorder, could worsen hepatic fibrosis. When she moved to inform patients, the drug's manufacturer,

Apotex Inc., prematurely terminated the clinical trials. Simultaneously, the company threatened legal action against Olivieri if she attempted to disclose the risk to her patients or the medical community. Several months later, after a thorough review of patients' charts, Olivieri identified a second, more serious risk. Again, Apotex issued legal warnings against disclosure.

The academic contract Olivieri and her hospital signed with Apotex was poorly drafted and forbade disclosure of results for up to three years without the company's consent. The prohibition violated Olivieri's professional medical, ethical, and academic obligations to care for and do no harm to her patients. Despite the threat of a lawsuit from the company and ineffective assistance from her university and its affiliated hospital, Olivieri informed her patients and the scientific community of the risks she had identified. The dispute became public in 1998, when Olivieri published her findings in a leading scientific journal.

Olivieri then faced work restrictions and public criticism. Her hospital, Apotex, and some colleagues tried to discredit her. However, an independent investigation by the Canadian Association of University Teachers (CAUT) found that Olivieri's academic freedom rights were violated.[129] The investigators also found other serious violations of her professional rights and responsibilities.[130] The whole case would later inspire John le Carré's 2001 novel *The Constant Gardener.*

As of this writing, Dr. Olivieri is a Senior Scientist with the Toronto General Research Institute; she continues to hold an appointment at the University of Toronto, where she teaches a course on Health and Pharmaceuticals which explores the industry's role in society as well as its influence on research and clinical practice. Her research program continues, now linked to her interests in international and community health; she and her collaborators have documented the range, severity, and complications of thalassemia in Sri Lanka, Bangladesh, and elsewhere in Asia.

Thyroid Conditions: The Case of Betty Dong

In 1987, the manufacturer of Synthroid (levothyroxine) contracted with Betty Dong, Pharm D, a clinical pharmacist at UC San Francisco, to study whether its drug was more effective than competing preparations for treating thyroid conditions. In 1990, Dong found Synthroid no more effective than other preparations, including cheaper generics. The sponsoring company, Boots Pharmaceuticals and later Knoll Pharmaceuticals, refused to allow the findings to be published. The pharmaceutical company's contract with UCSF required the manufacturer's consent before releasing information. The prohibition violated the university's own written policies.

Over the next four years, Boots/Knoll waged a vigorous campaign to discredit the study and prevent publication, claiming the research was flawed. Two university investigations found only the most minor and easily correctable problems in Dong's research and concluded that the company's attacks amounted to "harassment" designed to prevent publication. Eventually, the study passed the *Journal of the American Medical Association's* peer review process and was scheduled for publication on January 25, 1995. Shortly before publication, however, the company threatened a lawsuit.

At that point, it seemed unlikely that Dong's research would see the light of day. Then a *Wall Street Journal* reporter learned about the study and exposed what had happened.[131] Soon, pressure from the Food and Drug Administration forced Knoll to back off, and the study finally appeared in *JAMA* in April 1997.[132] The lengthy delay was a victory for Boots/Knoll because it enabled the company to sustain Synthroid's dominant market position.[133] For the general public, it was not good. Dong and her colleagues estimated that if an equally effective generic or brand-name preparation were substituted for Synthroid, patients would have saved $356 million annually in lower drug prices.[134]

Dong is now Professor of Clinical Pharmacy at UCSF and a Clinical Professor in the Department of Family and Community Medicine. She continues to conduct research on thyroid drugs as well as their interaction with HIV medications among HIV patients in the United States and in sub-Saharan Africa.

HIV/AIDS: The Case of James Kahn

In September 2000, Immune Response Corporation, a biopharmaceutical company, sued the University of California at San Francisco for $7 million, after Dr. James Kahn and his clinical research team sought to publish findings from a clinical trial of the company's experimental acquired immunodeficiency syndrome (AIDS) vaccine, Remune, which they found to be ineffective. The team had terminated the study when these findings emerged.

The investigators refused to allow the company to insert its own statistical analyses into the manuscript.[135] The sponsor, IRC, claimed that a subset of the patients did better, demanded that the researchers not publish the article, and withdrew part of the study data in an effort to dampen publication prospects.[136] Kahn responded that those patients were included in his findings, but IRC was not satisfied; nevertheless, the investigators persuaded *JAMA* to proceed with publication, with an explanation of the circumstances.[137] After publication, IRC sued, and the legal battle ended only after the university countersued, alleging that the contract did grant the researchers permission to publish, and the legal battle came to an end.[138] It is notable that UCSF supported Dr. Kahn, who now directs the university's Center for AIDS Research (CFAR).

Several well-publicized academic freedom cases have also arisen in fields outside of clinical research, including occupational health, environmental toxicology, and agricultural research.

Environmental Toxicology: The Case of Tyrone Hayes[139]

In 1998, the same year that UC Berkeley signed a $25 million research alliance with Novartis, later renamed Syngenta, Tyrone Hayes, a biologist at UC Berkeley, accepted a $100,000 grant from Pacific EcoRisk, a consulting firm hired by Novartis-Syngenta to study the effects of its most popular weed killer, atrazine, on frogs. One of the most heavily applied herbicides in the United States, atrazine is widely used on agricultural croplands, golf courses, and lawns; it leaves chemical traces in streams, waterways, and rainwater, especially after the planting season.

Not long after Hayes's research began, he turned up disturbing results. Exposure to atrazine appeared to disrupt male frogs' sexual development. Their voice boxes shrank, and they developed ovaries. The research suggested that atrazine was part of a family of chemicals known as endocrine disrupters. Even in minute traces, they can significantly interfere with hormones that regulate key biological activities in both wildlife and humans. Hayes wondered if atrazine use might explain why 58 amphibian species had disappeared or become extinct and another 91 had been listed as endangered in the past twenty years.[140]

Although Hayes was eager to publish his research, he soon learned that his contract gave EcoRisk and Syngenta ultimate control over publication. As in the Betty Dong case, the UC grants office had overlooked this glaring breach of its own policy on publication. EcoRisk called in its own consulting group, the Atrazine Endocrine Risk Assessment Panel, chaired by Texas Tech University Professor Ronald J. Kendall, to analyze and evaluate Hayes's results. Hayes suspected that the panel's true purpose was to forestall publication, and he quit.[141] Soon after, Hayes acquired enough new funding from W. Alton Jones, the World Wildlife Fund, and the National Science Foundation to continue his research, the first part of which he published in the April 2002 *Proceedings of the National Academy of Science.*

The study's impact was immediate: the US Environmental Protection Agency was, at that moment, reviewing atrazine's safety to determine whether to reauthorize it for use as an herbicide. The EPA's scientific panel had been leaning in favor of reapproval until it saw Hayes's results. They showed that atrazine levels as low as 1 part per 10 billion in water could cause tadpoles to develop into frogs with both male and female sexual organs. If Hayes's results were accurate, serious hormone disruption was occurring at concentrations thirty times lower than the EPA's then-approved levels.[142] By 2002, much of Europe had already banned atrazine, and the European Union would ban it in 2004 because of its persistent groundwater contamination.

Alert to the financial and political stakes involved, Syngenta and EcoRisk quickly tried to discredit Hayes's study. On June 20, 2002, they issued a press release announcing that "three separate studies by university scientists have failed to replicate" Hayes's findings.[143] None of those studies had been published in peer-reviewed journals; Syngenta had underwritten them all. One study, written by Texas Tech's James A. Carr, EcoRisk's Kendall, and others, later appeared in the journal *Environmental Toxicology and Chemistry* (ET&C)—where Kendall was an editor. Prior to publication, Kendall was quoted in a press release: "As research on this issue continues, one thing is certain. No conclusions can be drawn at this time on atrazine and its purported effect on frogs."

How independent were the studies? Syngenta informed the EPA that the Texas Tech study published in ET&C "was conducted under the direction and auspices of an independent scientific panel." But Goldie Blumenstyk, an investigative reporter with the *Chronicle of Higher Education,* revealed that under the $600,000 contract between Texas Tech and EcoRisk all research data and analyses belonged to EcoRisk "and/or its client." Furthermore, any publication of the research required "appropriate review and written permission by EcoRisk."[144]

In October 2002, Hayes published a second study in *Environmental Health Perspectives* and a shorter piece in *Nature* based on field research examining native populations of frogs at eight sites, seven with detectable traces of atrazine.[145] At one site in Wyoming, 92 percent of the male frogs actually had immature eggs inside of them. At six of the other sites, the researchers found that 10 to 40 percent of the frogs were hermaphrodites. The only site where they found no abnormal males was the one where they found no traces of atrazine.

The EcoRisk panel, the Kansas Corn Growers Association, and the Triazine Network, an association of 1,000 growers and herbicide manufacturers, challenged the validity of Hayes's research. Under a law known as the Data Safety Quality Act of 2001, they petitioned the EPA to disregard all Hayes's findings. Nevertheless, in June 2003, an EPA scientific advisory panel found "sufficient evidence" to suggest that one of the country's most widely used herbicides, atrazine, causes sexual abnormalities in frogs. Additional studies showed a variety of defects, including the development of multiple testes and multiple ovaries. The panel judged the data persuasive and significant.[146] But four months later, the EPA reversed course in its final ruling and reapproved atrazine's use as a weed killer. Critics cried foul, noting that Kendall, who oversaw the $600,000 Syngenta-EcoRisk grant at Texas Tech, also sat on the board of the EPA's scientific advisory panel on atrazine and its endocrine-disruptor screening committee, both of which would have had a say in a final decision on atrazine's reapproval.[147]

The controversy surrounding atrazine has not abated. More recent studies have questioned Hayes's results, though a 2007 study found tadpole resistance to infection impaired, but only at a higher concentration of atrazine, and a 2008 study reported that tadpoles exposed to atrazine developed deformed hearts, impaired kidneys, and damaged digestive systems. Nonetheless, the Australian Pesticides and Veterinary Medicines Authority ruled atrazine safe to use in 2010, arguing Hayes's results were not definitive. That same year a US Geological Survey reported considerable reproductive system damage to fish exposed to atrazine at levels below EPA standards.

Meanwhile, although the EPA ruled in 2000 that atrazine presents no cancer risk to humans, that issue remains contentious as well. A 2009 *New York Times* article provocatively titled "Debating How Much Weed Killer Is Safe in Your Water Glass" (documented, along with other recent studies, in note 137) raised questions about potential birth defects at atrazine exposure below EPA standards. A 2009 *Natural Resources Defense Council* report echoed that concern. On the other hand, the 2011 US National Cancer Institute Agricultural Health Study judged there to be no conclusive evidence linking atrazine use and any cancer sites.

The atrazine story is thus partly about researcher intimidation but also about government policy. When do possible health and environmental risks outweigh economic benefits? What level of evidence should trigger government restrictions on a product? Atrazine use is not alone in confronting such dilemmas.

Occupational Health: The Case of David Kern

Dr. David Kern, a specialist in occupational medicine, served as a faculty member at Brown University's School of Medicine for fifteen years, starting in 1984; during his last five years, he was an associate professor. He also worked as a clinician at Brown's affiliated Memorial Hospital, where he directed an environmental and occupational health clinic. The following account—drawn from a 2011 article in *Academe*[148]—is based upon primary documents that Kern provided to the AAUP,[149] an official Brown University investigation of Kern's case,[150] and Kern's own account published in the *International Journal of Occupational and Environmental Health*.[151]

In the mid-1990s, Kern saw two patients suffering from a rare lung condition; both happened to work at the same factory run by Microfibres, Inc., a Rhode Island manufacturer of nylon-flocked fabrics. Microfibres was a Memorial Hospital donor, and its owner and two family members sat on its board. With the company's permission, Kern and his students made one preliminary visit to Microfibres's factory to conduct air tests but turned up little. Fifteen months later, in March 1996, Kern proposed that Microfibres hire him as a consultant to conduct a more thorough health investigation, and the company agreed.[152]

Records show that Memorial Hospital processed Kern's consulting payments but did not negotiate a formal research contract with Microfibres. Kern states that he separately pressed Microfibres to sign his own clinic contract, but when the company refused, he pressed ahead with his investigation seeking to uncover the cause of his patients' illnesses.

Soon Kern identified 10 workers out of 165 at the Microfibres plant who were suffering from variations of the same rare condition, known as interstitial lung disease. He also identified a similar lung outbreak in a Canadian nylon-flocking factory and soon determined that he had sufficient evidence to publish an article about what he believed to be a new lung disease. Kern informed Microfibres of his plan to publish and present his findings at an American Thoracic Society meeting in May 1997. The company responded by threatening to sue, citing a confidentiality agreement Kern had signed fifteen months earlier, during his initial air-testing visit. Kern turned to Brown University for support, but Brown officials told him not to publish or present his findings. In a letter dated November 18, 1996, Peter R. Shank, Brown's associate dean of medicine and research, informed Kern that, based on the earlier confidentiality agreement, "I see no way in which you can publish results of your studies at the company without their written approval. . . . [Y]ou should immediately withdraw your abstract [from] the national meeting."[153]

Kern said he was shocked. Patients' lives were at stake. One had already died; two others were seriously ill. In Kern's view, Brown had a moral and medical obligation to make his research public and to ensure that workers under his care, as well as workers at other nylon-flocking plants, received appropriate preventive treatment and care. Besides, it was Kern's opinion—and that of his legal advisers—that the confidentiality agreement Kern had signed during his prior air-testing visit referenced only "trade secrets," which Kern's health investigation would not touch upon or disclose.

Then, in a December 23, 1996, memorandum, Memorial's president instructed Kern to "withdraw [his] abstract from publication or presentation before the deadline of Jan. 15, 1997." The hospital, he stated, was shutting down Kern's entire occupational health program "effective immediately."[154] Brown's medical school dean, Donald J. Marsh, initially stated publicly that he was never consulted about the closure of Kern's program, but in an April 30, 1997 letter to the hospital's president, he wrote that he was notified and "raised no objection."[155]

Over the course of the spring and summer of 1997, Kern's case attracted the attention of high-profile public health professors, resulting in more than one hundred letters addressed to Brown University protesting Kern's treatment. Kern also sought help from Brown's faculty senate and the AAUP, but an organized defense never materialized.

Kern proceeded with his publication and presented evidence at the thoracic society conference of what he considered to be a new lung disease.[156] Brown issued a statement at the time noting that "many questions remain unresolved" about the case but expressing support for Kern "in his right to conduct research and in his academic freedom to publish results."[157] Less than a week after the conference, however, Kern received letters from Brown's president, Vartan Gregorian, and from the president of Memorial Hospital, Francis Dietz. They said that, as a result of the closure of the occupational-health program, Kern's teaching and research were being eliminated. Kern would remain at the hospital until his five-year contract ended in 1999, but the closure of his program left him unable to seek research contracts within his field of occupational and environmental medicine. Memorial Hospital also barred him from treating his former Microfibres patients. Later that fall, Kern received a letter from the Centers for Disease Control and Prevention officially recognizing the new disease he had identified: flock worker's lung.

In 2011, more than thirteen years after his first publication exposing the dangers of flock worker's lung,[158] Kern published a follow-up study in the *Journal of Occupational and Environmental Health*.[159] The article examined a longer-range set of public health records for the original cohort of male Microfibres workers. The study uncovered a threefold increase in lung cancer incidence. Kern completed the study without the benefits of an academic research appointment, while working as a clinician providing inpatient hospital services at Togus Veterans Administration Medical Center in Augusta, Maine. If Brown-Memorial had allowed Kern to retain his faculty position and not barred him seeing his Microfibres patients, this potentially grave cancer risk would almost certainly have been uncovered far sooner, potentially saving workers' lives.

Agricultural Research: The Case of Ignacio Chapela

In November 2003, Ignacio Chapela, a UC Berkeley microbial biology professor and an outspoken critic of its $25 million research alliance with Novartis-Syngenta, was formally denied tenure. Almost immediately, large numbers of faculty protested the decision and questioned whether an objective assessment of his scholarship or politics drove Chapela's tenure review.

When Michigan State University researchers were invited to the Berkeley campus to conduct a review of the UC Berkeley-Novartis deal, they devoted an entire section of their report to Chapela's tenure case: "Regardless of whether Chapela's denial of tenure was justified, there is little doubt that the UCB-N agreement played a role in it. First, the very existence of UCB-N changed the rules of the game. Certain faculty were denied participation in the process because of the agreement. Second, while the administration saw fit to avoid conflicts of interest (COI) among faculty, they ignored the potential for COI among administrators. Thus, regardless of its validity, the decision of top administrators to accept the decision of the Budget Committee was seen by many as a COI."[160]

The backstory to the tenure decision helps explain the strong response and the need for an external review. In 1998, when UC Berkeley's College of Natural Resources first planned to sign a five-year, $25 million research alliance with Novartis, Chapela served as the elected chair of the College's executive committee, the faculty governing body. The position put him at the center of a vibrant faculty debate about the proposed Novartis alliance, the single largest academy-industry alliance ever negotiated on the campus. Although not yet tenured, Chapela orchestrated a campus survey to gather faculty viewpoints on the alliance and candidly voiced his own reservations about the deal, creating rifts with other scientists, including other microbiologists in the Department of Plant and Microbial Biology, the department slated to receive the Novartis funding.

In the fall of 2001, Chapela and his graduate student, David Quist, reported in the journal *Nature* that foreign DNA material from genetically modified (GM) plants appeared to be migrating into native varieties of corn in southern Mexico, although Mexico had banned the planting of modified corn as early as 1998.[161] Corn was first cultivated in Mexico 10,000 years ago and remains the center of corn genetic diversity around the world, which is why both the Mexican government and the environmental community reacted with great concern to the study's findings.[162] Like all *Nature* papers, the Chapela-Quist study was rigorously peer-reviewed prior to publication. The moment it was released, it became the subject of unusual scientific debate. A petition calling on *Nature* and Chapela to retract the study appeared on AgBioWorld, a biotechnology LISTSERV to which more than 3,000 scientists subscribe.[163] This type of backlash is not unprecedented in the agriculture-biotech sector, where a number of scientists who have published research critical of GM agriculture have had both their research and their personal integrity attacked, often by large agricultural interests with profits riding on the research.[164]

Many of the harshest scientific critics who wrote letters to *Nature* and posted comments on AgBioWorld were directly tied to UC Berkeley's Plant and Microbial Biology Department, the beneficiary of the $25 million in Novartis funding. Numerous current and former researchers in the department, for example, signed two group letters to *Nature* challenging the validity of Chapela's study.[165] Michael Freeling, a plant and microbial biology professor, signed the petition calling for a full retraction of the paper.[166] With each side accusing the other of impure motives, and the Novartis-alliance controversy lurking, judging the Chapel-Quist study on purely scientific grounds became increasingly difficult.[167]

Few disputed Chapela and Quist's main finding that genetically modified plants had contaminated native Mexican maize, but they disagreed over its significance. Biotech supporters maintained the contamination posed no threat, while critics worried that genetic contamination could erode plant genetic diversity and create other long-term ecological problems. Chapela and Quist's second conclusion, concerning the movement of foreign DNA around the corn plant, sparked more controversy, with critics attacking their testing method as unreliable. In the end, *Nature* did not retract the peer-reviewed paper, but it did do something unparalleled in its 133-year history: The journal printed an editorial note stating that the "evidence available is not sufficient to justify" the original publication and calling upon readers to judge the science for themselves.[168]

Not surprisingly, the controversy became a central issue in Chapela's tenure review. At first, the College of Natural Resources voted thirty-two to one (with three abstentions) in favor of tenure. Then an ad hoc tenure committee with five experts chosen for their ability to evaluate Chapela's research voted unanimously in his favor again. But the final arbiter, the Budget Committee—with members from across the college—denied tenure. Immediately, Wayne Getz, an insect biology professor and a member of the ad hoc tenure committee, charged that the process had "gone awry." Then the chair of the ad hoc committee, who originally voted in favor of tenure, rescinded his recommendation.

As it turned out, a member of the campuswide budget committee, genetics Professor Jasper Rine, had ties to the biotech industry, which raised COI concerns.[169] In the past, universities only had to monitor their professors' potential COI, wrote the Michigan State reviewers. But the Berkeley-Novartis agreement "raised issues of a different sort. In this case, it is the *institution's* potential for conflict of interest relative to the funds it receives that is at issue."[170] After Chapela was formally denied tenure, he filed a lawsuit challenging the fairness and impartiality of his tenure review. In May 2005, the university reversed its decision and granted him tenure.[171]

As of this writing, Chapela, in addition to his faculty position, collaborates with indigenous communities in Mexico, Costa Rica, and Ecuador on issues of their right to genetic resources. He has appeared in several films on genetically modified organisms and food systems including *The World According to Monsanto* (2008 documentary film directed by Marie-Monique Robin) and *The Future of Food* (2004 documentary film written and directed by Deborah Koons Garcia).

All of these cases are troubling. Except for the James O. Kahn case, they represent instances in which universities themselves have compromised a faculty member's academic freedom in deference to an industrial partner's economic interests. However, as Patricia Baird commented in the *Canadian Medical Association Journal,* such well publicized cases "are likely only the visible tip of a bigger iceberg" because many academic investigators probably are reticent to speak out when threatened. "For many academic researchers," Baird explains, "the future prospects of their laboratories and careers depend on renewed industry funding. They also may be understandably reluctant to speak out: if they trigger a legal action, it is time consuming and expensive, and it disrupts work and harms reputations."[172]

Overreliance on industry funding can lead both professors and universities to distort their research priorities to favor their sponsors' commercial interests, while simultaneously shying away from controversial topics that might alienate those firms. Consider academic agriculture where, as noted above, industry funding is now pervasive. Food & Water Watch's 2012 report—based on extensive data obtained through Freedom of Information Act filings and other public documents—concluded that, since the early 1990s, sharp increases in private funding have had a "chilling effect" on the public research mission of agricultural colleges, discouraging professors from researching environmental, public health, and food safety risks associated with industrial-scale agriculture, and leading schools to pursue far more aggressive proprietary and pro-industry forms of research inquiry, knowledge protection, and dissemination.[173]

At the University of Arkansas, the school's largest research facility within the School of Poultry Science is housed in the John W. Tyson building. The Tyson family has also endowed six of the agricultural colleges' 15 chairs. In 2005, after the company confronted allegations of inhumane poultry slaughtering practices that had been caught on video, Tyson Foods conducted its own animal welfare study that denied any inhumane practices. Tyson then supplied a $1.5 million grant and hired one of its endowed professors at the U. of Arkansas to confirm its own findings.[174]

In 2009, meanwhile, the *New York Times* reported that 26 professors, most of them based at land grant universities, had submitted an anonymous letter to the EPA complaining that restrictive industry licensing agreements and contracts with universities were barring academic scientists from conducting the objective research on genetically modified corn plants necessary to provide impartial guidance to the public and government regulators.[175] "These agreements inhibit public scientists from pursuing their mandated role on behalf of the public good unless the research is approved by industry," the letter's authors asserted. "As a result of restricted access, no truly independent research can be legally conducted on many critical questions regarding the technology."[176] All the letter's authors withheld their names for fear of being blacklisted and losing private sector research funding.[177]

Anecdotal accounts like these have become increasingly common. In 2002, *Nature* reported that, after a professor at Ohio State University produced research questioning the biological safety of genetically modified sunflowers, Dow Agro Sciences and Pioneer Hi-Bred shut down her research by blocking her use of their seeds.[178] In 2009, *Nature Biotechnology* reported a similar case in which professors funded by Pioneer Hi-Bred had found a new GE corn variety to be deadly to beneficial beetles, only to see the company subsequently bar them from publishing their findings. Pioneer Hi-Bred then hired a different cohort of scientists, who produced the necessary results to secure regulatory approval.[179]

The effects of this agriculture industry influence are not easy to quantify. One 2005 University of Wisconsin survey of land grant scientists found that private-sector funding arrangements restrict open communication among scientists and create publication delays. The study further found that the amount of money that professors generate from research grants and contracts has a significant influence over tenure and salary levels, thus creating pressure for faculty to pursue industry funding. Nearly a third of those surveyed also consult for private industry.[180]

According to the Food & Water Watch report, much of this industry support "diverts" precious university resources away from projects "that challenge corporate control of food systems" and buys direct academic influence. Sometimes this influence is explicit: At the University of Georgia's Center for Food Safety companies are invited to purchase seats (for $20,000 apiece) on its board of advisers, enabling them to help direct the Center's research efforts.[181] Purdue University openly solicits industry support by permitting donors to influence curricula and direct research programs.[182] Meanwhile, in 2009, Monsanto appointed South Dakota State University president David Chicoine to its board of directors with a first-year salary of $390,000, an amount substantially larger than his academic salary.[183] After this appointment, SDSU formally joined a Monsanto subsidary, WestBred, in a public-private program called the Farmers Yield Initiative, which sues farmers for seed patent infringement. According to Food & Water Watch, SDSU's wheat seeds, which were the subject of some of these lawsuits, were developed with farmer and taxpayer dollars.[184]

Risk 2: Restricted Access to Data and Suppression of Negative Results

Especially with industry-supported clinical trial research, which often involves multiple trial sites, academic investigators frequently lack access to complete study data; that leaves them almost entirely reliant on company sponsors and company statisticians for data analysis. This well-documented phenomenon can cripple academic scholarship.[185]

In one review, six academic investigators reported cases in which corporate sponsors stopped publication of articles or altered their content. In many instances, the suppression was not publicly acknowledged at the time.[186] Dr. Curt Furberg, a professor of public health sciences at Wake Forest University School of Medicine, reported that he refused to place his name on the published results of a study in which he was the principal investigator because the sponsor was "attempting to wield undue influence on the nature of the final paper. This effort was so oppressive that we felt it inhibited academic freedom."[187]

In another case, a pivotal trial of Celebrex for treatment of arthritis, the manufacturer Pharmacia Corporation selectively published only six months of clinical trial data,[188] even though the original protocol called for a longer trial, and the twelve-month outcomes were available when the manuscript was submitted.[189] At six months, the outcomes seemed to favor Celebrex over competing drugs, but at twelve months most of Celebrex's advantages disappeared because of ulcer complications that arose in patients taking the drug.[190] When Dr. M. Michael Wolfe, a gastroenterologist at Boston University who had written a favorable review of the six-month study, learned of the deception, he told the *Washington Post:* "I am furious. I looked like a fool. But . . . all I had available to me was the data presented in the article."[191] None of the original study's sixteen authors, including eight university professors, spoke out publicly about the suppression of data. All the authors were either Pharmacia employees or paid company consultants.[192]

In 2001, concerns about the integrity of clinical trial research and access to data grew so serious that leading medical journal editors, together with the International Committee of Medical Journal Editors (ICMJE), condemned intrusive industry influence and, in an effort to curb such abuses, revised their collective requirements for manuscript submissions.[193] The revisions call for full disclosure of an industry sponsor's role in the clinical trial research, as well as assurances that investigators are independent of the sponsor, are fully accountable for the trial's design and conduct, have independent access to all trial data, and control all editorial and publication decisions.[194]

Universities have nonetheless generally been slow to affirm these principles in their own industry-sponsored contracts and sponsored research agreements. One 2002 survey of contracting practices at 108 medical schools found that only 1 percent would guarantee academic investigators access to complete trial data associated with a multi-site clinical trial; 50 percent would allow the industry sponsor to write the final manuscript and only allow the investigators to review it and suggest revisions; 35 percent would permit a corporate sponsor to store the study data, and release portions to the investigators; 41 percent would allow a sponsor to prohibit investigators from sharing raw research data with third parties after the trial was over.[195] (For further discussion of this topic please see Risk 6 below.)

Some experts suggest universities and their academic medical schools are afraid of losing pharmaceutical industry funding for clinical trials due to increased competition from for-profit contract research firms, which have garnered a growing share of the clinical trial research market. Today an estimated 70 percent of all clinical research is funded by private industry, not the federal government.[196] However, most medical experts agree these battles over data ownership and control must be resolved if the university research mission is to be preserved. Aubrey Blumsohn, a pathologist and osteoporosis specialist who documented the fact that Procter and Gamble denied both himself and other academic investigators access to their own clinical trial data, argued as follows in a 2006 article:

> If the industry wishes to sell its products under the banner of science, it has to accept the rules of science. Most importantly, as academics we need to reassert the importance of data and the meaning of authorship. We also need to assert "old fashioned" ideas of academic freedom, our right to speak the truth as we see it, and to allow that truth to be subjected to open debate. In the words of George Orwell (1984), "Freedom is the freedom to say that two plus two make four. If that is granted, all else follows."[197]

Dr. Robert Steinbrook, who has reported on contractual "gag clauses" that block researcher data access, wholly agrees:

> A basic tenet of research ethics is that the data from clinical trials should be fully analyzed and published. If the knowledge gained

from trials is not shared, subjects have been exposed to risk needless-
ly. Moreover, participants in future studies may be harmed because
earlier results were not available. These principles are reflected in federal regulations regarding the protection of human subjects, which
define research as "a systematic investigation designed to develop or
contribute to generalizable knowledge."[198]

*When professors are denied access to data and cannot perform independent academic
analyses, it compromises the evidentiary foundation of medicine, the treatment of disease, and academic freedom.*

The Case of SSRI (Selective Serotonin Reuptake Inhibitor) Antidepressant Drugs

One striking case involves clinical trials assessing the safety and effectiveness
of a broad class of drugs known as selective serotonin reuptake inhibitors
(SSRIs) used to treat depression in children and teens.[199] SSRIs, including
top-sellers such as Zoloft, Paxil, and Prozac, are widely prescribed to adults
as well.

In a 2004 letter to the FDA, David Healy MD, an Irish psychiatrist
and professor of Psychological Medicine at Cardiff University School of
Medicine in Wales who published early research findings linking SSRI drugs
and suicide, wrote that there "is probably no other area of medicine in which
the academic literature is so at odds with the raw data."[200] Indeed, that same
year, one meta-analysis of the published medical literature[201] concluded that
SSRI antidepressant drugs were safe and effective, but a more comprehensive
meta-analysis,[202] examining both published and unpublished data, reached
precisely the opposite conclusion: that elevated risks of suicide outweigh the
benefits for all but one drug in the entire class of antidepressants.[203]

After doubts grew about the validity of the published SSRI studies on
children, several academic authors reported that they were denied access to
unpublished suicide data from their own clinical studies. The explanation,
they told the *New York Times,* was that US medical schools, in agreeing to
run the tests, had also consented to permit the manufacturers to keep the
underlying data confidential.[204]

In October 2004, the FDA announced that the entire class of SSRI
antidepressants was associated with an increased risk of suicidal thoughts and
actions in children and teens. The FDA also raised similar concerns for adults
and issued new patient warning labels. Nearly one year earlier, the British
equivalent of the FDA had effectively banned the use of SSRIs, except for
Prozac, in children and adolescents under eighteen.[205]

The editors of *The Lancet* summed up the antidepressant debacle as follows: "Confusion, manipulation, and institutional failure."[206] It is unknown how many patients may have been harmed or committed suicide as a result of taking SSRIs. According to one source, GlaxoSmithKline paid nearly $1 billion to settle Paxil lawsuits in 2010, including $390 million for suicides and attempted suicides thought to be related to the drug. Meanwhile, several lawsuits charge that the use of SSRIs during pregnancy may cause birth defects that require emergency treatment at birth and lifelong medical issues as well. Again, the charge is that manufacturers withheld knowledge of these potentially harmful effects from patients and consumers.

Yet dispute about this widely used class of drugs continues. The intellectual and economic stakes are high, creating considerable difficulty in separating interested claims from objective scholarly findings.[207]

The Vioxx Case

Suppression of negative research findings in clinical research is far from an isolated problem. Consider the case of Vioxx, a widely prescribed painkiller. According to numerous independent analyses of Vioxx clinical trials and detailed reviews of litigation documents, the drug's manufacturer, Merck, repeatedly suppressed data showing that Vioxx was associated with serious cardiovascular risks, including heart attacks.[208] In 2004, after a public outcry triggered by previously undisclosed heart risks, Merck agreed to remove Vioxx from the market. According to one estimate, at least 50,000 people died due to the health risks associated with Vioxx that were obscured from doctors, authoring academics, patients, and regulators.[209]

In one 2008 analysis, researchers found that, in addition to suppressing negative data, Merck marketed and promoted Vioxx through extensive use of industry-paid ghostwriters. Based upon a detailed review of court documents, the authors described how "review manuscripts were often prepared by unacknowledged authors and subsequently attributed authorship to academically affiliated investigators who often did not disclose industry financial support."[210]

According to litigation documents obtained by the *New York Times*, a major Vioxx trial known as the "Advantage Trial" was also riddled with research problems. The trial was completed in 2000, but results were not published until 2003 in the *Annals of Internal Medicine*. The article's lead author was listed as Dr. Jeffrey R. Lisse, a University of Arizona rheumatologist. But the newspaper reported that Lisse later admitted he had not written the article, and was only peripherally involved in the study. "Merck designed the trial, paid for the trial, ran the trial," Lisse acknowledged. "Merck came to me after the study was completed and said, 'We want your help to work on the paper.' The initial paper was written at Merck, and then it was sent to me for editing."[211]

The Advantage Trial's final published article also reported false results: it stated that five patients taking Vioxx, compared with one patient taking naproxen, a competing painkiller, suffered heart attacks during the trial—a difference that, the authors stated, failed to reach statistical significance. In actuality, however, three additional trial participants taking Vioxx had suffered cardiac deaths, a statistically significant—and deadly—finding not reported at the time.

In March 2010, an Australian class-action lawsuit against Merck came to the conclusion that Vioxx doubled the risk of heart attacks and that Merck had breached the Trade Practices Act by selling a drug that was unfit for sale. The following year Merck announced a civil settlement with the US Attorney's Office for the District of Massachusetts, along with individual settlements with 43 states and the District of Columbia. It resolved civil claims over Vioxx with a settlement of over $600 million. Litigation with seven additional states remains to be resolved. Merck also pled guilty to a federal misdemeanor charge of marketing of the drug across state lines and was fined $321.6 million. Merck's sales revenue the year before the drug was withdrawn was $2.5 billion.

The Avandia Case

In many ways, the story of Avandia is the story of Vioxx all over again, as Robert Steinbrook and Jerome P. Kassirer, former editors at the *New England Journal of Medicine,* commented in 2010.[212] Once again, the published research on Avandia—a top-selling diabetes drug—proved to be dangerously at odds with the true, raw, scientific data. And once again, the manufacturer—GlaxoSmithKline in the case of Avandia—actively suppressed the data and manipulated the reported results.

In July 2010, FDA medical officer Thomas Marciniak reported that a GlaxoSmithKline trial designed to study Avandia's cardiovascular risks was riddled with errors that biased its conclusions. When reviewing the company's complete study data, Marciniak uncovered a dozen instances in which patients taking Avandia appeared to suffer serious heart problems, some requiring hospitalization, which the study's final tally of adverse events failed to count. Such mistakes "should not be found even as single occurrences" and "suggest serious flaws with trial conduct," Marciniak wrote.[213] In September 2010 the FDA announced it would restrict sales of Avandia due to serious, previously unreported heart risks associated with the drug.[214]

To many in the medical community who had watched the Avandia case closely, the FDA's actions came too late. As early as 2007, Steven Nissen,

MD, a cardiologist at the Cleveland Clinic, uncovered and carefully analyzed 42 Avandia clinical trials—only fifteen of which had ever been published. Although Nissen was unaware of the origins of the data he had unearthed at the time, Glaxo posted the 42 unpublished Avandia studies online in response to a 2004 lawsuit against them filed by New York attorney general Eliot Spitzer. The suit alleged Glaxo had concealed negative trial data associated with its popular antidepressant drug Paxil, and as part of the settlement Glaxo agreed to post its unpublished drug trial data on a publicly accessible web-site.[215] Nissen's paper examining these data, which he published in *NEJM*, found that Avandia raised the risk of heart attacks in patients by 43 percent.[216] The news shocked the medical world and instantly made front-page head-lines. Two days later, the FDA, which had already started to question Avandia's health risks, announced that it would impose its toughest "black box" warn-ing label on the drug.

During a hearing chaired by Congressman Henry Waxman, it came to light that the FDA had considered a black-box warning label for Avandia years earlier because of its increased cardiovascular risks. Rosemary Johann-Liang, a former FDA drug safety supervisor, testified that she had recommended a warning label for Avandia one year before Nissen's publication. Glaxo's own meta-analysis, presented internally to the FDA in 2006, showed Avandia increased heart attack risk by 31 percent. But, according to Johann-Liang, "my recommending a heart failure box warning was not well received by my superiors, and I was told that I would not be overseeing that project."[217]

Internal company documents obtained by the *New York Times* in July 2010 also revealed that GlaxoSmithKline "had data hinting at Avandia's extensive heart problems almost as soon as the drug was introduced in 1999, and sought intensively to keep those risks from becoming public." In one document, the company calculated the potential lost sales revenue if Avandia's cardiovascular safety risk "intensifies": $600 million from 2002 to 2004 alone.[218]

After this hearing, the Avandia case continued to interest Waxman as well as Senators Charles Grassley, Max Baucus and others who were pressing for stronger federal regulation of clinical trials.[219] According to one investigative report from the Senate Committee on Finance, GlaxoSmithKline tried to intimidate university physicians who were critical of Avandia and its safety profile. The Committee summarized the evidence as follows:

> In November 2007, the Committee reported on the intimida-
> tion of Dr. John Buse, a professor of medicine at the University of
> North Carolina (UNC) who specializes in diabetes. Based partly on
> internal documents from GSK, the Committee reported on what
> appeared to be an orchestrated plan by GSK to stifle the opinion

of Dr. Buse in 1999. At that time, Dr. Buse argued at several medical conferences and in letters to the FDA that GSK's diabetes drug Avandia may cause cardiovascular problems.

According to GSK emails made available to the Committee, GSK executives labeled Dr. Buse a "renegade" and silenced his concerns about Avandia by complaining to his superiors at UNC and threatening a lawsuit. The call to Dr. Buse's superiors was made by Dr. Tachi Yamada, then GSK's head of research. In discussions with Committee investigators, Dr. Yamada denied that his call was meant to intimidate Dr. Buse. Instead, Dr. Yamada argued that he had made the call to determine if Dr. Buse was making legitimate statements or if he was possibly on the payroll of a GSK rival.

Dr. Yamada also made a call to the University of Pennsylvania (Penn) regarding two physicians who were about to publish a case study that Avandia may have caused liver problems in one of their patients . . . Both physicians also said that the calls placed by GSK officials, including Dr. Yamada, were highly unprofessional and had a chilling effect on their professional activity.[220]

In 2006, Avandia was one of the largest-grossing drugs in the world, with sales of $3.2 billion. According to a 2010 *JAMA* analysis of Medicare records, from 1999 to 2009 an estimated 47,000 people taking Avandia suffered heart attacks, strokes, heart failure, or died, most probably as a direct consequence of taking the diabetes medication.[221]

As of the present writing, Steven Nissen is chair of the Department of Cardiovascular Medicine at the Cleveland Clinic. In 2007 *Time Magazine* named him as one of the 100 most influential people in the world.

Risk 3: Threats to Open Science, Knowledge Sharing, and Timely Publication

Over many decades the academic community has developed distinctive open knowledge science systems built on reputational rewards, priority of discovery, timely publication, and broad dissemination of research results. This system was ably described by Robert Merton in 1957 and in later work by Paul David and others.[222] A fundamental academic tenet is that research should be published as efficiently as researchers and peer reviewers deem prudent so it can be broadly shared, utilized, and independently verified or disproven. The academic community's traditions stand in contrast to the knowledge systems prevailing in private industry, which place a premium on secrecy and confidentiality to prevent leaks to competitors and facilitate commercial investment and development.

With the expansion of commercial activities on campus, many observers are concerned about how to protect university culture. Numerous case studies describe how industry sponsors have delayed reporting clinical trial results and adverse-event reports, sometimes for years.[223] In one case involving the antidepressant drug Paxil, negative clinical trial data were released only after a lawsuit was filed against the manufacturer.[224]

Evidence suggests industry intrusion on academic culture is systemic:

- Empirical work has consistently found that industry funding is associated with publication delays.[225]

- A 2008 study conducted by Wesley Cohen and John Walsh found that the effects of increased academic patenting on knowledge sharing have not been as onerous as some anticipated. But other empirical research by the same authors and others has found that increased campus commercial engagement is consistently associated with longer publication delays, greater information withholding, heightened secrecy, and other serious threats to open science.[226]

- A 1996 survey of 210 life science companies found that nearly 60 percent of the agreements these firms sign require university investigators to keep research results confidential for more than six months—considerably longer than the 30-to-60-day delay that NIH recommends to file for provisional patent protection. One-third of the 210 companies also reported disputes with academic collaborators over intellectual property, and 30 percent noted that COI emerged when university researchers became involved with other companies.[227]

Industry-imposed interference with publication is not limited to medicine. A 1994 study of engineering conducted by researchers at Carnegie Mellon University found pervasive delays at US university-industry research centers with more than $100,000 in funding and at least one active industry partner. The study found that half the 1,056 university-industry centers surveyed could force publication delays; more than one-third could also delete information from academic papers prior to publication.[228]

Although the primary concern is that research results be accurate and truthful, prompt publication can have social value and facilitate the advancement of knowledge. The benefit of quickly disseminating medical knowledge that has direct impact on public health research and treatments is readily apparent. The advantage of efficient publication is also notable in biology, where the biotechnology revolution would have been considerably delayed had a single company or set of researchers hoarded the major scientific break-throughs that led to the discovery of gene splicing. Publication ensures that valuable knowledge is shared with others who can use it productively and creatively in their own research. Some research results also have notable social impact, so their delay or suppression can damage the public welfare. The freedom to publish promptly when appropriate, without sponsor constraint or prohibition, is fundamental to academic freedom and the vibrancy of national research innovation.

Industry and government have both sometimes delayed publication of academic research they funded. Widely publicized cases occurred after two of the biggest US environmental disasters: the 1989 Exxon Valdez oil spill in Alaska's Prince William Sound and the 2010 BP-America oil spill in the Gulf of Mexico. Exxon and BP each sought to delay release of industry-funded academic research examining the respective oil spills and their broader environmental and economic impacts. After the Deepwater Horizon explosion, BP initially asked university faculty and their departments to sign research contracts that gave the company's lawyers the right to delay any communication or publication of results for up to three years.[229] Similarly—in accordance with the US Natural Resource Damage Assessment (NRDA) procedures, which prescribe how the federal government will assess restoration needs, possible legal liability, and the scope of environmental and economic damages following a major disaster—various government agencies also sought to use their contractual authority to impose publication delays on academic investigators. Knowing they would eventually face one another in court, both the oil industry and the government pressured academics to keep sponsored academic research results confidential to avoid giving advantage to their opponent. Such constraints can be hugely detrimental after natural disasters, where timely publication of research results may be critical in designing effective follow-on research investigations, cleanup efforts, wildlife preservation, public health initiatives, and litigation efforts by directly affected localities, individuals, and small businesses.

Another threat to academic culture comes from both direct and indirect industry intimidation. Faculty members who criticize powerful industries may find those industries vigorously defending their interests and working to silence critique. Such intimidation is as likely to occur in the social sciences as in the hard sciences. As *The Nation* reported in 2005:

> Twenty of the biggest chemical companies in the United States have launched a campaign to discredit two historians who have studied the industry's efforts to conceal links between their products and cancer. In an unprecedented move, attorneys for Dow, Monsanto,

Goodrich, Goodyear, Union Carbide and others have subpoenaed and deposed five academics who recommended that the University of California Press publish the book *Deceit and Denial: The Deadly Politics of Industrial Pollution* by Gerald Markowitz and David Rosner.[230] The companies have also recruited their own historian to argue that Markowitz and Rosner engaged in unethical conduct.[231]

Markowitz and Rosner based their book *Deceit and Denial* in part on an archive of company and trade association documents that a Louisiana attorney had obtained through discovery. The documents demonstrated that, as early as 1973, the chemical industry had learned that vinyl chloride—used in numerous consumer products—caused cancer in animals, but the industry failed to disclose the findings. After the UC Press obtained eight reviews of the manuscript, the book's copublisher, the Milbank Memorial Fund, sponsored a two-day conference to bring together the reviewers and authors to discuss the manuscript. However, when a worker exposed to vinyl chloride sued for damages after being diagnosed with liver cancer, the chemical companies sought to discredit the book. Their paid historian, a Rutgers University–Camden business professor who had also testified for the asbestos industry, alleged that the Milbank conference was unethical because it allowed the authors to know who reviewed their book, a standard practice if reviewers agree. He also charged it was inappropriate for the authors to recommend reviewers, also a common academic practice. The accusations against Markowitz and Rosner were dismissed, but only after the authors and the book's reviewers were subjected to days of cross-examination in court. Had the Milbank foundation not provided representation, they all would have faced significant legal costs. Although it is difficult to quantify the full effect of such intimidation, it can certainly have a chilling effect on scholars whose research challenges industry practices.

In 2009, a similar situation arose when the tobacco industry threatened Stanford University historian Robert Proctor. After Proctor emailed a colleague to confirm that a University of Texas–San Antonio faculty member had hired University of Florida graduate students to perform research for an upcoming Florida trial in which the faculty member was scheduled to testify, tobacco industry attorneys argued that Proctor's email constituted an "improper" effort to "influence, interfere, or intimidate" a defense witness.[232] The judge ordered Proctor to submit his emails to the court, after which the tobacco lawyers dropped their accusations because the emails were ruled harmless. Still, Proctor was forced to undergo sixteen hours of depositions under oath by twelve lawyers. The attorneys for R.J. Reynolds then subpoenaed Proctor's unfinished book manuscript on the history of the tobacco industry, a move the *Chronicle of Higher Education* characterized as highly intimidating and having "major implications for scholars and publishers."[233] A judge eventually held "that an author has a constitutional right to choose when and where his writings are published."[234] Academic freedom thus survived, but only after considerable intimidation, time, and expense.

The Proctor and Markowitz and Rosner cases are far from isolated. Some industry campaigns, however, like the one tobacco firms waged against UC San Francisco professor of medicine Stanton A. Glantz, are more secretive and only come to light if litigation forces disclosure of internal company documents. Glantz was certainly aware of tobacco industry opposition to his scholarship, but he was not aware of the scope of their campaign against him. On March 14, 1995, a large display ad personally attacking him appeared in the *Washington Times*. The ad stated it was financed by "the 130/10 Club, a group of citizens who chip in $10 a month to expose government waste." Yet the president of the Philip Morris–funded American Smokers Alliance actually managed the 130/10 group, and the "waste" the ad decried centered around a National Cancer Institute grant awarded to Glantz in part so he could track tobacco industry campaign contributions and correlate them with state legislators' votes on tobacco-related issues. Seven months after the attack ad appeared, former US Surgeon General C. Everett Koop and others signed a *New York Times* opinion-page ad defending Glantz's research. However, when Glantz typed his name into the Legacy Tobacco Documents Archive, an online textual database containing nationwide tobacco industry documents, he was surprised to encounter 500 pages of internal documents showing that the tobacco industry's campaign to derail his research and reputation went far deeper than he had realized. For example, after Glantz and a colleague presented a paper summarizing research on the dangers of second-hand smoke, and the *New York Times* published a full-page story in May 1990 discussing their presentation, the tobacco companies' public relations arm kicked into gear and orchestrated an elaborate plan to have Glantz's National Cancer Institute funding withdrawn. This included an effort to recruit pro-tobacco legislators to the cause, as well as a more covert campaign to recruit seemingly independent university faculty and others to write letters to academic journals and newspapers discrediting Glantz's scholarship. The professors who participated billed the tobacco companies roughly $3,000 for each letter.[235]

Other threats to academic knowledge sharing involve restrictions on data, research materials, research tools, and other scientific input and output. A central tenet of academic science is that information, data, reagents, and materials should be freely shared with other academic investigators, especially when they are associated with an academic publication. Once again, studies find that industry relationships are associated with greater restrictions on such practices. Yet threats to sharing data and other basic research outputs and discoveries stem from many sources. Sometimes they originate with an industry sponsor who wishes to restrict access to research tools that might be advantageous to competitors. Other times they originate with universities and academic investigators themselves.

As we noted earlier, after passage of the 1980 Bayh–Dole Act, universities became more enthusiastic about patenting academic discoveries and imposing exclusive licenses and other IP restrictions on the use of research reagents, tools, and other discoveries. Increased commercializing of academic research was fueled by a desire to generate new income streams for the university and its investigators. Many legal scholars, economists, and historians of scientific and industrial innovation have expressed concern that Bayh–Dole may be fostering a significant, if somewhat harder to detect, sea change in the norms and customs that govern the dissemination of basic academic knowledge.[236] Industrial historian Richard Nelson and others have warned that increased patenting and other proprietary restrictions on knowledge sharing could lead to a "privatization of the scientific commons"—an important wellspring for future research and discovery.[237]

Whenever universities seek IP protection through patents, copyright, exclusive licenses, and other legal mechanisms known as Material Transfer Agreements—which are frequently imposed on basic research materials—it has the potential to impose burdensome costs on and impede downstream research, invention, and product development.[238] Some controversial university MTA licenses require that royalties be paid to the institution on all future products developed using its research tools or reagents. These more aggressive intellectual property claims are often referred to as "reach-through" royalties.

According to a 2001 study in which the authors obtained rare access to university invention portfolios, 90 percent of all UC discoveries and 59 percent of all Stanford discoveries were licensed under reasonably "exclusive" terms.[239] "Exclusive" was defined as either global exclusivity or restrictive as to market or field of use. Increases in academic patenting and licensing have been particularly evident in the biomedical, biotechnology, and information technology sectors.[240] Some have expressed concern that Bayh–Dole may have created new incentives for US universities to put licensing income ahead of other important academic goals.

When a University of Utah professor patented two human breast cancer genes, the university licensed them exclusively to the professor's own start-up company, Myriad Genetics, Inc. The company soon began to hoard the genes, using legal threats and other tactics to block other academic scientists and physicians in the United States and abroad from using them in their own research and diagnostic testing. The case drew international attention and outrage; it also led to protracted litigation. In March 2012 the US Supreme Court ruled that a diagnostic test developed by Myriad was ineligible for patent protection because it was a simple application of a law of nature. The court ordered a lower appeals court to reconsider its decision to uphold the patents on the genes, which are associated with a high risk of breast and ovarian cancer.[241] It is important to note that Myriad's patents increased the cost of testing to determine whether a patient had the gene and thus made the test unaffordable for some women. That came to an end when the Supreme Court decided *Association for Molecular Pathology v. Myriad Genetics* in June 2013 in a decisive 9–0 decision, invalidating the patents and ruling that unmodified human genes are not eligible for patent protection.

A set of controversial patents filed by the University of Wisconsin claimed broad rights to valuable embryonic stem cell lines.[242] Both academics and biotechnology firms eager to do research on stem cells have complained about Wisconsin's licensing fees and about reach through provisions that call for royalties on any future products developed from use of Wisconsin's stem cells, with additional restrictions imposed on use.[243] According to some outside observers, rather than promote commercialization, patents on basic research platforms, such as the breast cancer genes and stem cells, constitute a "veritable tax on commercialization."[244]

NIH shares the concern. In 1999 it issued guidelines urging universities to avoid seeking patents and other restrictive licenses on data, materials, and other research tools unless they were necessary to attract investors for commercial use and development.[245] In 2005 NIH issued guidelines to protect genomic inventions from excessive proprietary controls.[246] NIH also argued against reach-through royalties, and encouraged universities to license research tools with few encumbrances and at reasonable fees. But the NIH guidelines lack the force of law. In 2000, one year after the first guidance, Maria Freire, then director of NIH's Office of Technology Transfer, reported that scientists were still having problems accessing research tools, particularly in negotiations between academia and industry.[247]

Risk 4: Financial Conflicts of Interest (FCOI)

A number of recent scholarly books—beginning with Stanton Glantz's collaborative *The Cigarette Papers,* and including Allan Brandt's *The Cigarette Century,* David Michaels's *Doubt is Their Product,* and Robert Proctor's *The Golden Holocaust*—credit the tobacco industry with inventing the modern corporate strategy of manufacturing scientific controversy and manipulating science to advance corporate interests, shape public opinion, and forestall industry regulation.[248] Because financial payments and consequent FCOI have been a central tool in the strategy, the tobacco industry may also be credited with mounting one of the most sophisticated and extensive campaigns to manipulate academic science by buying university faculty.

As early as the 1930s and 1940s, epidemiological and laboratory evidence linked cigarette smoking and lung cancer. But it was not until the early 1950s that more sophisticated and reliable laboratory experiments with animals decisively demonstrated nicotine's addictive power and the carcinogenicity of the tars in cigarette smoke. In the early twentieth century, smoking rose dramatically in the United States, and, two to three decades later, lung cancer diagnoses climbed at comparable rates. Connections with coronary heart disease and other conditions would gradually be established as well.

As early as 1911, tobacco companies had been accused of collusion. But when the US Department of Justice filed a successful Racketeer Influenced and Corrupt Organizations Act (RICO) case against the tobacco industry in 2006, it built its case around a set of internal memos documenting an infamous meeting of tobacco company executives held in December 1953 at the New York Plaza Hotel.[249] There executives from six tobacco companies hammered out a public relations strategy—one they would vigorously pursue over the next half century—based largely on the advice of John W. Hill, the president of Hill & Knowlton, the country's most influential public relations firm. Hill argued—at that meeting, and in a written proposal he drew up afterward—that advertising alone could not counter the mounting scientific consensus that tobacco was harmful to public health. Rather than contest the science from the sidelines, the tobacco companies should start funding and controlling science themselves.[250]

Shortly after this meeting, the tobacco companies pooled their funding to set up the Tobacco Industry Research Committee, which was headquartered inside Hill and Knowlton's offices. In January 1954 TIRC trumpeted its pursuit of scientific truth and its commitment to public health in 400 newspaper ads, and soon it was issuing grants to academic investigators. University scientists, including many who were already skeptical of the link between smoking and cancer—a sizable number of whom smoked themselves—proved key allies in the tobacco industry campaign to manipulate scientific evidence.

Much of TIRC's funded research had no bearing on the actual link between smoking and cancer; instead it was cleverly designed to distract and confuse. TIRC promoted genetic predispositions to cancer. It even occasionally publicized the benefits of smoking, promoting nicotine's value as a "tranquilizer," and, in one study, suggesting that secondhand smoke increased airline pilot alertness. Above all, as the scientific consensus about the hazards of smoking became decisive, the industry employed seemingly independent and objective faculty allies to create the fiction of an ongoing scientific controversy over whether smoking caused lung cancer. Although the number of university skeptics financed by the tobacco industry remained small overall, tobacco companies could rely on newspapers and other media, eager to report on controversy and demonstrate "journalistic balance," to spread the perception of scientific doubt and trump the overwhelming scientific consensus that tobacco smoking was, indeed, hazardous. As a now famous 1969 internal tobacco industry memo bluntly explained, "Doubt is our product, since it is the best means of competing with the 'body of fact' that exists in the minds of the general public. It is also the means of establishing a controversy."[251]

This lesson was repeated when tobacco companies turned their attention to sowing doubts about research demonstrating the dangers of secondhand or environmental tobacco smoke. As David Michaels, a scholar of the tobacco industry, wrote, "No industry has employed the strategy of promoting doubt and uncertainty more effectively, or for a longer period, and with more serious consequences."[252] In time, other major industry groups adopted the "tobacco strategy" of manipulating scientific research and manufacturing scientific controversy in order to cast doubts on the dangers of asbestos, power plant emissions, mercury in fish, lead in paint and gasoline, as well as the impact of fluorocarbons on the ozone layer, and, of course, the environmental and economic threats posed by global warming.

Interestingly, academic scientists were not the only university faculty compromised by tobacco industry funding. We now know—based on more than 80 million pages of tobacco industry documents contained in the Legacy Tobacco Documents Library (http://legacy.library.ucsf.edu), which became fully digital and text searchable in 2007—that literally thousands of university faculty across a wide range of disciplines received undisclosed funding from tobacco companies, including scientists, statisticians, legal experts, and historians.[253] Working as paid researchers and consultants, they performed research, provided analysis, and advised the companies on advertising, litigation strategies, and other matters. Some of the tobacco industry's funding relationships with universities were public, but many remained confidential. Such confidentiality reminds us of the need to adopt policies to promote transparency, disclosure, and management of FCOI.

Although Proctor details the early history of faculty member collusion with the tobacco industry, his more surprising evidence concerns the assistance the industry received from university faculty over the last generation. That includes the more than fifty historians who have testified in court on the industry's behalf since 1990. But other historians worked quietly as consultants, some signing confidentiality agreements not to publish on topics under investigation. A few faculty names and dates of those testifying or providing affidavits, depositions, or reports since 2000 give graphic demonstration of the pattern: Jonathan J. Bean, Southern Illinois University (*St. Louis v. American Tobacco,* 2004); Michael B. Chesson, University of Massachusetts, Boston (*Longden v. Philip Morris,* 2003); Elizabeth Cobbs-Hoffman, San Diego State University (*Boeken v. Philip Morris,* 2001); Thomas V. Dibacco, American University (*Katz v. Reynolds,* 2010); Peter Calvin English, Duke University (*Bullock v. Philip Morris,* 2002); Lacy K. Ford, Jr., University of South Carolina (multiple *Engle Progeny* cases, 2008–11); Jon M. Harkness, University of Minnesota (*Boerner v. Brown,* 2003); James Hilty, Temple University (*Carter v. Philip Morris,* 2003); Jacob Judd, Lehman College (*Standish v. American Tobacco,* 2003); Kenneth M. Ludmerer, Washington University (*Harvey v. ABB Lummus Global,* 2002); Gregg L. Michel, University of Texas at San Antonio (*Webb v. Reynolds,* 2010); Robert Jefferson Norrell III, University of Tennessee (*Martin v. Philip Morris,* 2009); Michael Schaller, University of Arizona (multiple *Engle Progeny* cases, 2009–11); William Stueck, University of Georgia (*Alexander v. Philip Morris,* 2010). The list of historians who have served as expert consultants for the tobacco industry without testifying includes Richard M. Abrams (UC Berkeley), Richard Harp (English, University of Kansas), Ernest B. Hook (UC Berkeley), Robert H. Kargon (Johns Hopkins University), Herbert Klein (Stanford University), Howard I. Kushner (Emory University), James Muldoon (Rutgers University), David F. Musto (Yale University), Morton Sosna (Cornell University), and Irwin Unger (New York University). Proctor's list of university statisticians is comparable.

Over the past three decades, changes in the academic landscape—especially in biomedicine but also in many other academic disciplines—have dramatically increased the possibility of FCOI like those that emerged from tobacco's extensive campus engagements. Increased industry funding, more varied forms of university-industry engagement, and more explicit university and faculty involvement in commercial pursuits have all contributed to this trend. So has the presence of dedicated patenting, licensing, and technology-transfer offices on virtually every research university campus. Through equity, options, royalties, and licensing fees, these TTOs have vastly expanded the opportunities for faculty members and universities to acquire financial interests in campus-based research.

University owned and operated research parks, incubator programs, and venture capital funds as well as faculty participation in start-ups and other businesses may help the university transfer technology to the private sector. Yet these activities can also lead to serious institutional FCOI. In 2005, for example, reporters revealed that an academic medical center, the Cleveland

Clinic, and its chief executive officer had undisclosed financial interests in a medical device firm. The medical center used the firm's heart surgery device, and hospital surgeons promoted it, but the center's patients remained uninformed about these serious FCOI. The medical center's board subsequently enacted tough policies to reign in such financial conflicts.[254]

Experts on ethics and professionalism have largely reached a consensus on the broad definition of a FCOI: it may be broadly defined as a situation in which an individual or a corporate financial interest has a tendency to interfere with the proper exercise of judgment. (For more detailed COI definitions, and the principles we are recommending to manage them, see Part IV of this report or consult the key sources for definitions, among them an IOM Statement[255] and a report by the AAU.[256]) It is worth emphasizing again that a FCOI describes a circumstantial situation; it does not imply confirmed wrongdoing. As the IOM stated in a lengthy 2009 report: "A conflict of interest is not an actual occurrence of bias or a corrupt decision but, rather, a set of circumstances that past experience and other evidence have shown poses a risk that primary interests may be compromised by secondary interests. The existence of a conflict of interest does not imply that any individual is improperly motivated."[257] Because financial conflicts are a function of a situation, rather than a function of whether someone is actually biased, they are either present, or they are not. Thus a FCOI should rarely be termed "potential," a qualifier one hears all too frequently in popular discourse, because that implies the conflict is only a future possibility, thereby seeming to downgrade the current risks it presents.

COI policies in corporations, government, the legal profession, and the judicial system are designed to be preventative. The purpose of a university COI policy as well should be to prevent or manage situations that might compromise, or appear to compromise, the ability of a university administrator or faculty member to make unbiased decisions about contract negotiations, evaluations, teaching, research, academic promotions, new faculty hires, or patient care. A university COI policy should also address institutional relationships that might weaken public trust in the university, a concern for both public and private institutions receiving taxpayer support.

Obviously, FCOI are not the only types of conflicts or competing interests that may play a role in distorting academic decision making or research. As the AAMC wrote, other competing interests—such as the desire for "priority of discovery," reputational or career advancement, and scientific competition—are "an inescapable fact of academic life," but most of these "are managed through institutional policies and practices, and through the constraints imposed by the scientific method."[258] Experts on ethics and professionalism tend to distinguish FCOI from these other competing interests:

first, financial conflicts are discernible, measurable, discretionary, and manageable; and second, research has found that even token financial benefits may affect peoples' judgment.

While the AAUP endorses full disclosure of FCOI on a publicly accessible website, we recognize that disclosure alone is not enough. Indeed, in some contexts disclosure can be entirely inadequate. For medicine, the risks are particularly notable in patient care. A 2012 editorial in *PLoS Medicine,* building on research by Lisa Cosgrove and Sheldon Krimsky, expresses concern over the number of financial conflicts among psychiatrists contributing to the fifth and most recent edition of the *Diagnostic and Statistical Manual of Mental Disorders* (DSM), the so-called "bible of psychiatry."[259] Based on faculty self-disclosure, which may understate reality, nearly 70 percent of DSM-5 Task Force and Work Group members had or have had financial ties with the pharmaceutical industry, up from 57 percent for the manual's fourth edition. The rate is still higher for contributors to the psychotic disorders section—83 percent. The editorial asks whether physicians who disclose may feel impervious to bias or, even worse, that disclosure absolves them of personal responsibility for managing their FCOI. What's more, patients may not be knowledgeable enough to assess the relative merits of differing professional advice in the light of FCOI disclosure. Academics are relatively well versed in professional skepticism, though perhaps mostly in their own disciplines. The same cannot be said of all members of the public, especially with regard to professional advice. While disclosure is essential, therefore, it is clearly only a first step in ameliorating the problems created by FCOI.

Risk 5: Research Bias and Unreliability Associated with Corporate Funding

Below, we summarize the empirical research in psychology, neurobiology, and other social sciences demonstrating that COI are associated with bias and unreliability in the academy, although investigators frequently fail to perceive their own limitations.

Industry Sponsorship and Pro-Industry Findings

A large number of systematic reviews or meta-analyses, as well as individual studies, have found that industry-sponsored clinical trials, and trials where industry ties are present, are significantly more likely to report results favoring the sponsors' products or interests.

- One meta-analysis found that clinical trials in which either the drug manufacturer funded the trial or the investigators had financial relationships with the manufacturer were 3.6 times more likely to find that the drug tested was effective compared to studies without such ties (Bekelman et al. 2003).

- Another meta-analysis (which included non-English language research not included in the Bekelman study) found that clinical studies favoring a drug were four times more likely to be funded by the drug maker than any other type of funder (Lexchin et al. 2003).

- A 2008 literature review found that seventeen of nineteen studies, published since the preceding two meta-analyses, reported "an association, typically a strong one, between industry support and published pro-industry results" (Sismondo, 2008, p. 112).

- Another 2008 review found that industry-funded studies were more likely than other studies to conclude that a drug was safe, even when the studies found statistically significant increases in adverse events for the experimental drug (Golder and Loke, 2008).

These studies do not prove industry funding caused research bias. Companies, for example, fund trials only when they predict a strong likelihood of success for their product. But the documented association between funding source and research bias, carried out now across diverse areas of clinical drug and tobacco research, raises serious concerns about possible undue influence on research results.[260]

Gifts, Financial Inducements, and Biased Decision Making

Extensive research in psychology and other social sciences demonstrates that financial inducements can introduce bias and distort decision making.[261] Much of this research has been carried out in biomedicine, but the results have ramifications for any academic discipline with outside funding relationships with industry, such as energy, economics, toxicology, and agriculture. These studies confirm that pharmaceutical and biomedical firm gifts and other small financial inducements—including free meals, travel expenses, and drug samples—have a powerful effect on physician behavior even without any explicit contract or "strings" attached.[262]

These studies identify the following effects:

- Physicians who request additions to hospital drug formularies are far more likely to have accepted free meals or travel funds from drug manufacturers.[263]

- The rate of prescriptions physicians write for given drugs increases substantially after they see sales representatives,[264] attend company-supported symposia,[265] or accept free drug samples.[266]

- Receiving gifts is associated with positive physician attitudes toward pharmaceutical representatives.[267]

- A systematic review of the 2000 medical literature on gifting found that an overwhelming majority of industry interactions negatively influenced clinical care.[268]

- A 2010 AAMC task force report suggests that "inherent biological processes cause individuals to respond reciprocally—and typically unconsciously—to relationships that involve even simple gifts, sponsorships, or the development of personal relationships."[269] Neurobiology is still an emerging science, but the AAMC report points out that research "suggests that the neurobiological processes that engage the brain's reward and decision-making circuitry can operate below the detection and overt control of higher cognition." A 2009 IOM panel report sums up the influence on investigator objectivity of industry funding and gift giving with the following quote from Jason Dana, a University of Pennsylvania psychology professor:

> This research shows that when individuals stand to gain by reaching a particular conclusion, they tend to unconsciously and unintentionally weigh evidence in a biased fashion that favors that conclusion. Furthermore, the process of weighing evidence can happen beneath the individual's level of awareness, such that a biased individual will sincerely claim objectivity. Application of this research to medical conflicts of interest suggests that physicians who strive to maintain objectivity and policy makers who seek to limit the negative effects of physician-industry interaction face a number of challenges. This research explains how even well-intentioned individuals can succumb to conflicts of interest and why the effects of conflicts of interest are so insidious and difficult to combat.[270]

Much of the initial impetus to address COI in universities focused on biomedical research and aimed to protect human subjects. Beginning in the late 1990s, however, DHHS and NSF passed federal COI rules covering all university grantees; the explicit purpose was to protect research objectivity, reliability, and integrity—a much broader mission that acknowledged the potential for COI to undermine publicly funded research itself.[271] A historical overview of both government and university efforts to address COI at academic medical centers and universities follows.

A Brief History of Efforts to Address COI at US Universities and Academic Medical Centers

California was the first state to address COI within universities by requiring public universities and their faculty to comply with the same state COI laws that apply to public officials and state agencies. Today, all state universities in California must comply with the COI reporting and regulatory requirements contained in the Political Reform Act of 1974, a law managed by the California Fair Political Practices Commission (FPPC)—a state agency similar to the Federal Election Commission. In 1983, the FPPC ordered an investigation of the UC's enforcement of rules on disclosure of corporate support of faculty research—after finding that more than fifty faculty members had financial interests in companies that were also funding their research.[272]

It was not until 1995, more than ten years later, that the US Public Health Service (PHS) implemented the first comprehensive federal rules designed to address COI at universities receiving DHHS research funding, which included all NIH grantees.[273] Interestingly, however, this was not the first time the US government had voiced serious concerns about COI growth inside universities and had pressed for greater federal regulation. Its first attempt to establish COI rules for university grantees was in 1989, after a series of Congressional investigations sponsored by then-Senator Albert Gore uncovered major COI concerns and potential research abuses at prominent academic institutions. But this federal effort failed after strenuous opposition from universities, medical schools, and academic societies. The Federation of American Societies for Experimental Biology, to cite one example, asserted the proposed rules would "devastate productive relationships between university researchers and industry, deny scientists outlets for their discoveries at the bench and interfere with the technology transfer."[274]

In June 1990, the AAUP approved its own "Statement on Conflicts of Interest," which strongly echoed widespread academic opposition to federal mandates for COI disclosure:

> Government proposals for policing possible conflicts of interest have been overwhelmingly rejected by the academic community as involving a massive, unneeded enlargement of the government's role on the campus. Faculties must be careful, however, to ensure that they do not defensively propose a similar bureaucratic burden differing only in the locus of administration. Any requirements for disclosure of potential conflicts of interests should be carefully focused on legitimate areas of concern and not improperly interfere with the privacy rights of faculty members and their families.[275]

The AAUP's 1990 statement reflected widespread faculty views at the time; it also embodied the Association's long-standing commitment to protecting faculty rights and autonomy. But many of these concerns are now moot. Federal proposals to address COI in academia have since become federal rules. In part, this shift was a direct result of the failure of universities to regulate their own COI, and in part it resulted from the steady exposure of new COI problems inside academia by Congressional agencies, the media, and independent researchers. Finally, it stemmed from growing recognition that COI pose real dangers to research integrity and the academy's reputation.

While the AAUP's insistence on limiting COI disclosure to "legitimate areas of concern" remains valid, these areas have multiplied dramatically since 1990 and now pose a significant threat to the university's educational, research, and public knowledge missions. Thus it is now clear that a family member's stock holdings or patent income also need to be reported if they overlap with a faculty member's teaching or research areas; a generation ago that requirement would have seemed an invasion of privacy. The AAUP is thus clarifying its position on regulation and disclosure of individual and institutional COI; the present report is an outcome of that process.

The 1995 PHS rules required all DHHS grantees to ensure that their federally funded research was not "biased by any conflicting financial interest of an Investigator."[276] The rules also required faculty members with related FCOI (greater than $10,000 or five percent ownership in a single entity) to report their interests to their university employers for internal review, reduction, elimination, or management, with some modest reporting back to the federal granting agency. But the 1995 PHS rules provided little guidance on how universities should manage such financial conflicts, leaving the institutions considerable discretion to formulate their own regulatory policies and procedures. The same was true of the COI rules NSF issued in 1995 and the FDA adopted in 1998, though both sets of rules were even more limited than those of the PHS.[277] Most universities used the new federal rules as a baseline for developing their own COI policies. By early 2000, however, a series of independent assessments revealed that university COI policies varied markedly from one institution to the next and remained weak overall.[278]

One notable feature of these university policies was that information about faculty FCOI was kept strictly confidential. Faculty reported their FCOI to the university, which in turn provided minimal information to the federal funding agencies, but public disclosure was strictly limited. But such conflicts were not always easy to contain. Over the next two decades, class-action lawsuits filed against tobacco and pharmaceutical firms, combined with heightened scrutiny by Congress, science journalists, journal editors, and the mainstream media pushed these faculty and institutional FCOI into the open, generating widespread public concern.

A major wave of negative public scrutiny occurred in 1999 after a young man, Jesse Gelsinger, died in a University of Pennsylvania gene therapy experiment. Evidence soon emerged that the experiment was riddled with financial conflicts and grave breaches of federal safety rules designed to protect human research volunteers. A 2009 IOM review of the case documented widespread problems with the university's oversight and conduct of the study. It also highlighted the extensive financial conflicts surrounding the trial. Both the university itself and several past and present faculty and administrative officials had direct financial interests in the biotechnology company that developed the experimental medical intervention being tested. The biotechnology company had also contributed $25 million to the annual budget of the Penn research institute conducting the study and held exclusive rights to develop products emerging from the trial and related research. Meanwhile, the institute's director, who also served as the trial's lead investigator, maintained a significant financial interest in the same biotech firm, a company he had earlier helped to found.[279]

Gelsinger's tragic death in a university-administered clinical trial riddled with research abuses and financial conflicts led to a lawsuit, congressional inquiries, and probing investigations by both the media and federal agencies. This, in turn, generated widespread calls for strengthened federal rules governing university financial conflicts.[280] Yet when the DHHS proposed new COI rules in January 2001,[281] once again most major academic institutions and medical groups strongly objected, just as they had in 1989, citing the academic community's preference for self-regulation.[282] Soon the proposed federal rules were tabled.

Following Gelsinger's death, various academic and medical groups tried to reassure the public and outside critics that universities would do a much better job of managing FCOI. To advance this goal, a series of consensus reports aimed at providing more detailed guidance were issued by the AAMC (2001, 2002, 2008c), the AAU (2001), the AAMC and AAU jointly (AAMC-AAU, 2008), and the Council on Government Relations (COGR, 2002). Adoption of these stricter rules was voluntary and once again highly variable.

In 2001, just two years after the Gelsinger tragedy, medical journal editors also began to issue statements and editorials expressing grave concerns about the prevalence of FCOI and the growing evidence of undue commercial influence on clinical research. That year thirteen medical journal editors published a high-profile editorial in NEJM. It argued that industry sponsors were exerting excessive control over clinical-trial design, data access, and final analysis of reported research results—based on evidence that had come to their attention in reviewing and vetting academic research. They concluded by announcing that the International Committee of Medical Journal Editors (ICMJE) would soon require all manuscript submissions to include full disclosure of FCOI.[283] These new mandates also called for full disclosure of the industry sponsors' roles in the conduct of research and required the study's lead authors to provide written assurances that they remained independent from sponsors, were fully accountable for trial design and conduct, had independent access to all trial data, and controlled all editorial and publication decisions. The journal editors also urged the medical community and universities to restore traditional academic and scientific standards to academic contract research. They noted that academic "contracts [with private sponsors] should give the researchers a substantial say in trial design, access to the raw data, responsibility for data analysis and interpretation, and the right to publish—the hallmarks of scholarly independence and, ultimately, academic freedom."[284]

Yet public exposure of serious university FCOI problems continued. In 2005, Senator Chuck Grassley, R-Iowa, spearheaded a new series of investigations into industry relationships with academic researchers and continuing medical education programs, which uncovered persistent financial and other commercial COI in federally funded research.[285] Grassley obtained documents covering research at more than two dozen medical schools and found that several high-ranking academic physicians had accepted substantial funds from private companies with direct financial interests in their research but had neglected to report this income to their own universities or the NIH accurately, as campus and federal rules require.[286] Grassley's staff discovered these widespread disparities by making separate inquiries of drug companies and universities and comparing the data provided. In some cases, it appeared that the disclosures omitted from university documents involved companies whose products the researchers were investigating.[287] The list reads like a who's who of leading psychiatrists:

- Dr. Charles Nemeroff, an influential psychiatrist then chair of the Emory University Psychiatry Department, reportedly earned more than $2.8 million in consulting arrangements with drug makers between 2000 and 2007, yet failed to disclose much of this outside income to Emory in violation of federal research rules, according to documents provided to congressional investigators. In one telling example recounted in the *New York Times,* Nemeroff signed a letter dated July 15, 2004, promising Emory administrators that he would comply with federal rules and would earn less than $10,000 a year from GlaxoSmithKline (GSK). But that very day he was at the Four Seasons Resort in Jackson Hole, Wyoming earning $3,000 of what would become $170,000 in GSK income that year.[288] Confronted with these unreported COI and negative media reports, the NIH forced Nemeroff to step down from NIH-funded university research projects and froze funding for a $9.3 million investigation of depression he was then leading. Emory subsequently removed Nemeroff as department chair and restricted his outside activities. He soon moved to the University of Miami.[289] As of this writing he is Chair of the Department of Psychiatry and Behavioral Sciences in the University of Miami Health System.

- Dr. Alan Schatzberg, then chair of the Stanford University Psychiatry Department, received an NIH grant to study the drug mifepristone for use as an antidepressant while owning millions of shares of founders stock in the drug's developer, Corcept Therapeutics, which was then seeking FDA approval to market the drug.[290] Grassley's investigation questioned Stanford's oversight of the conflict. In comments and a letter to Stanford published in the *Congressional Record,* Grassley noted that Stanford had required Schatzberg to disclose stock valued at more than $100,000, but Stanford did not require the psychiatry chair to report profits of $109,000 from the sale of some of his Corcept shares in 2005, or the fact that his 2 million remaining shares were worth more than an estimated $6 million. "Obviously, $6 million is a dramatically higher number than $100,000 and I am concerned that Stanford may not have been able to adequately monitor the degree of Dr. Schatzberg's conflicts of interest with its current disclosure policies," Grassley wrote in a letter to Stanford University President John Hennessy.[291] An NIH oversight group later stepped in and recommended that Stanford's clinical trial on mifepristone be "terminated immediately and permanently," due to concerns over FCOI and patient safety, according to internal emails obtained by an outside public interest group. Later, Stanford also asked Schatzberg to step down as chair of the Psychiatry Department temporarily.[292] The recommendation reflected concerns over COI and patient safety, among other issues. As of this writing he remains a professor in Stanford's Department of Psychiatry and Behavioral Sciences. He chaired the department until 2010.

- Another leading Harvard child psychiatrist, Dr. Joseph Biederman— whose work helped fuel an explosion in the use of antipsychotic medicines in children—earned an estimated $1.6 million in consulting fees from drug makers between 2000 and 2007. Grassley's investigators discovered that for years he failed to report much of this outside income to university officials. According to a *New York Times* report, two of Biederman's colleagues also violated federal and university disclosure rules: "Dr. [Timothy E.] Wilens belatedly reported earning at least $1.6 million from 2000 to 2007, and another Harvard colleague, Dr. Thomas Spencer, reported earning at least $1 million after being pressed by Mr. Grassley's investigators."[293] Harvard later disciplined the three physicians by requiring them to refrain from "all industry-sponsored outside activities" for one year, and afterward only with permission. But some commentators questioned whether the punishment was sufficient,[294] especially after court documents later suggested that Biederman may have breached his research protocol[295] and solicited drug company funding by suggesting that his clinical trials would yield outcomes benefiting the company's products and interests.[296] As of this writing, he is Chief of Clinical and Research Programs in Pediatric Psychopharmacology and Adult ADHD at Massachusetts General Hospital and Professor of Psychiatry at Harvard Medical School.

This latest round of high-profile Congressional exposés and media attention renewed calls for greater federal oversight over both individual and institutional COI, as well as greater public transparency. A 2008 report from the Office of the Inspector General at the DHHS, for example, criticized the NIH for inadequately overseeing grantee institutions and their management of faculty COI and urged DHHS to implement institutional COI regulations as well.[297]

The following year, in 2009, Grassley and other senators passed the Physician Payment Sunshine Act.[298] The landmark law mandates that drug, biologic, and medical device manufacturers disclose all gifts and other payments, including all "transfers of value," to physicians inside and outside of academia and publicly post the payments on a national online database. Under the law, companies that fail to report face financial penalties. Several states, and some private companies, have since adopted similar medical industry payment disclosure policies, making pharmaceutical industry payments, at least, somewhat easier to research.[299]

Finally, on August 23, 2011, after a lengthy comment period, the US DHHS issued new rules for regulating FCOI at universities and other external grantee institutions. The rules include the following provisions:

- New requirements for investigators to disclose to university employers all significant financial interests related to their "institutional responsibilities," not just those connected to specific research projects.

- A lowering of the threshold required for COI disclosure, generally dropping the minimum from $10,000 to $5,000.

- More extensive university reporting to federal grant agencies of the scope of their faculty investigators' FCOI, along with written management plans explaining how the university plans to address them.

- New requirements that universities make some information about faculty COI and university management plans accessible to the public, either on a public website or within five days of any written request.[300]

It is too soon to gauge the effect on academia of the 2011 DHHS COI rules and the 2009 Sunshine Act. It is clear, however, that public scrutiny of university and faculty COI will likely intensify due to these changes: more stringent financial disclosure requirements at leading science journals, new federal rules covering public disclosure of significant financial conflicts related to federal grants, and Sunshine Act laws requiring public reporting of all industry payments to physicians.

Yet just as in 1995, the 2011 federal rules do not provide specific guidance on how universities can or should review, reduce, eliminate, or manage their COI internally. Each university is left to implement the policies at its discretion. If the past is any indication, that could mean COI regulation and enforcement remain insufficient. According to a 2009 IOM panel review, "extensive variations" in university COI policies and procedures "raise concerns that some institutions may not have sufficient data to make determinations about the extent and the nature of an individual's financial relationships or to judge the severity of a conflict of interest. . . . Absent outside pressures and oversight, variation in conflict of interest policies may encourage an unhealthy competition among institutions to adopt weak policies and shirk enforcement."[301]

Some universities have chosen to adopt more comprehensive COI policies; they should be emulated. But most have been slow to heed the various academic and medical associations' calls to tighten COI policies and their enforcement, even in the wake of the Gelsinger tragedy and other investigations and reports. Independent surveys find that academic COI policies—even at medical centers, which have borne the brunt of recent public criticism—generally remain inadequate:

- In 2001 the AAMC called on universities to strengthen COI policies governing human subject research, urging specifically that policy language establish a strong "rebuttable presumption" against conducting research on human volunteers whenever investigators have a related FCOI, except in exceptional circumstances. But a 2003 AAMC survey found that only 61 percent of medical schools had incorporated a "rebuttable presumption" into their human subject research policies; of those, only a minority had defined the compelling circumstances that would support an exception.[302]

- A later 2006 analysis found that only 48 percent of medical schools had policies to inform research participants about investigators' FCOI. The policies also varied considerably regarding what information must be disclosed.[303]

- In 2008, yet another AAMC survey found that despite a 2002 joint recommendation from the AAMC and AAU that all universities implement institutional COI policies, only 38 percent of academic medical schools reported having such a policy in place. Another 37 percent reported they were still in the process of developing one.[304]

- In 2009, as noted earlier, the DHHS's Office of the Inspector General reported serious deficiencies in how universities managed FCOI and carried out enforcement. After reviewing 184 separate FCOI reports that 41 grantee institutions submitted to the NIH in 2006, the OIG found that serious "vulnerabilities exist in grantee institutions' identification, management, and oversight of financial conflicts of interest."[305] Here are the main findings:

How NIH Grantees Manage Financial Conflicts of Interest

Office of the Inspector General, Department of Health and Human Services

November 2009[306]

Of the forty-one grantee institutions, 90 percent rely solely on researcher discretion to determine which of their significant financial interests are related to their research and therefore need to be reported.

Grantee institutions routinely fail to verify the information researchers submit. Thirty of the forty-one institutions reported verifying information researchers disclosed, but only nineteen of the institutions documented how they did so.

To manage FCOI, grantee institutions often require researchers to disclose conflicts in research publications; however, grantee institutions rarely reduce or eliminate financial conflicts of interest. (Grantee institutions reported that they managed 136 researcher conflicts, reduced 6 researcher conflicts, and eliminated 6 researcher conflicts. Another 17 researcher conflicts were handled using a combination of management, reduction, and elimination.) Other studies have corroborated the finding.[307]

Because nearly half of the grantee institutions do not require researchers to disclose specific dollar amounts of equity or other compensation on their financial disclosure forms, the specific financial interests of NIH-funded researchers are often unknown. Equity, including stocks and options, was the most common FCOI disclosed to the NIH on external grantee disclosure forms.[308]

Grantee institutions did not uniformly report conflicts to the federal government.

Grantee institutions fail to document their oversight of conflicts.

"Given the complex nature of researchers' conflicts and the vulnerabilities that exist regarding their identification and management," concluded the

OIG, "[i]ncreased oversight is needed to ensure that (1) these conflicts are managed appropriately, (2) the research conducted using Federal funds is not biased by any conflicting financial interests of researchers, and (3) human subjects are not subjected to unnecessary risks."[309]

Much less is known about COI management practices outside biomedicine. The NSF's COI rules governing multiple science disciplines are less strong than the DHHS rules. And no other federal grant-making agencies have COI policies covering their university grantees. In November 2003, the GAO issued a report tellingly titled "Most Federal Agencies Need to Better Protect against Financial Conflicts of Interest."[310] In 2010, Francis Collins and Sally Rockey, then NIH director and deputy director of extramural research, respectively, published a piece calling for new efforts to address FCOI:

> Clearly, investigators, institutions, and NIH need to redouble collaborative efforts to uphold the integrity of federally funded biomedical and behavioral research. If NIH-supported researchers fail to disclose the full extent of their financial interests, universities fail to comprehensively manage FCOI, or NIH fails to diligently oversee the entire system, public trust will be jeopardized in ways that may have far-reaching implications for the future of science. . . . Consequently, for the good of the research enterprise and for our nation as a whole, it is imperative to take collective steps now to usher in a new era of clarity and transparency in the management of FCOI.[311]

Risk 6: The Absence of Legal Protections to Safeguard Research Integrity and Academic Freedom in Industry-Sponsored Research Contracts

University policies and procedures to address COI are not the only, nor necessarily the most important, mechanisms for managing academy-industry relationships. It is also critical to negotiate legal contracts for industry-university partnerships that protect research integrity and faculty academic freedom.

Most cooperative activities in higher education—from industry-funded research to a large portion of academic consulting—are governed by contracts. The contracts set out terms and conditions for the university and its faculty to perform a certain scope of work under a specified budget over a specified time frame. These legal contracts usually spell out deliverables for each project and address critical details about IP ownership and the responsibilities of all parties. But these contracts too often fail to include language that would better protect research integrity and secure core academic principles, including the freedom rights of faculty members.

In 2002 Kevin Schulman, a Duke University researcher, surveyed senior administrators at the sponsored research offices of 108 medical schools to evaluate how well their contracts with industry sponsors conformed to long-accepted standards of academic authorship and research integrity. In 2001, before Shulman embarked on his research, the International Committee of Medical Journal Editors had reaffirmed the standards scholarly institutions should follow, and 500 scientific journals had adopted them.[312] In summarizing his findings, Shulman wrote:

> Our findings suggest that academic institutions routinely participate in clinical research that does not adhere to ICMJE standards of accountability, access to data, and control of publication. . . .We found that academic institutions rarely ensure that their investigators have full participation in the design of the trials, unimpeded access to trial data, and the right to publish their findings.[313]

Here are the main problems he found:

Data Control: Only one percent of the site agreements between medical schools and industry sponsors required academic investigators to be given access to all the trial data in multi-site clinical trials. Interestingly, this figure rose to 50 percent for "coordinating center agreements," where one institution, department, or center agrees to be responsible for the conduct or administrative/coordinating functions of a multi-center study.

Data Analysis: Only one percent of the site agreements required the use of independent executive committees or data-and-safety-monitoring boards (DSMBs) to provide independent oversight of the trial.

Publication: None of the site agreements required publication of trial results. Only 40 percent of the site agreements addressed the issue of editorial control over reported trial results.

Public Disclosure/Transparency: Only 17 percent of institutions in the site survey (and 36 percent in the coordinating-center survey) had a policy dictating limits on the duration of confidentiality. The median duration of confidentiality was five years, in both site and coordinating-center agreements.[314]

After the Schulman study was published, Jeffrey Drazen, *NEJM* editor in chief, commented as follows:

This survey paints a bleak picture of the state of academic-industrial contracting. According to the results, very few centers included standard language in their contracts that guaranteed the investigators at a given center access to the primary data from the entire study. Without such a guarantee, the entities sponsoring the research can effectively implement a "divide and conquer" strategy that allows each group of investigators access to their own data, but makes analysis of all the data in a multicenter trial a virtual impossibility.

He added that universities would do well to adopt standard contract language: "If universally adopted, such language would help safeguard the integrity of the research process."[315]

Yet further studies have found a persistent lack of academic research protections in university contracts with industry. A 2005 study led by Michelle Mello at the Harvard School of Public Health surveyed research administrators responsible for negotiating clinical-trial agreements with industry at 107 US medical schools.[316] The study found that standards "for certain restrictive provisions in clinical-trial agreements with industry sponsors vary considerably among academic medical centers." Although 85 percent of administrators surveyed reported that their offices would not approve contract provisions giving industry sponsors authority to revise manuscripts or decide whether results should be published, more detailed survey questions revealed the following disconcerting gaps:

- 62 percent permitted sponsors to alter study design after agreements are executed;

- 50 percent allowed industry sponsors to draft final manuscripts, with academic investigators' roles limited to review and suggestions for revision (40 percent prohibited industry sponsors from drafting final manuscripts);

- 24 percent permitted industry sponsors to insert their own statistical analyses into final manuscripts, another 29 percent were unsure whether to allow it, and 47 percent disallowed it;

- 41 percent allowed industry sponsors to bar academic investigators from sharing data with third parties after trials were complete, another 24 percent were unsure whether to allow this, and 34 percent disallowed it;

- 80 percent of the agreements allowed sponsors to own research data;

- 35 percent permitted sponsors to store the data, and release only portions to investigators;

- 62 percent of medical schools kept the terms of clinical-trial agreements confidential;

- After trials end, 21 percent of agreements prohibited investigators from discussing research results, including presentations at scientific meetings, until sponsors consented to dissemination;

- After the legal research agreements had been signed, disputes with industry sponsors were common. Disagreement most frequently centered on payment (75 percent reported at least one payment dispute in the previous year), intellectual property (30 percent), and control of or access to data (17 percent).

- 69 percent of administrators perceived that competition for research funds created pressure on administrators to compromise on the language in their industry contracts, with 24 percent of those describing the pressure as great.

A final study of policies and contract relationships that bears mention is a 2011 survey of clinical care policies governing US universities' interactions with industry, led by Susan Chimonas at Columbia University's Institute on Medicine as a Profession. The study examined US medical school policies and procedures addressing a broad range of academy-industry relationships, sometimes described as "marketing relationships"—e.g., receipt of industry gifts, free drug samples, free meals, and positions on industry-led "speakers bureaus"—which empirical research (already discussed) has shown to be associated with bias in both research and professional decision making. Many professional medical groups—including the IMAP and the American Board of Internal Medicine (ABIM) Foundation, publishing in the *JAMA*,[317] the AAMC,[318] and the IOM[319]—have already issued strong consensus recommendations urging university medical schools to restrict biomedical industry gifts, meals, ghostwriting, and speakers bureaus. These same associations have also urged universities and their medical schools to establish central repositories for free drug and product samples, and have called for full transparency in university consulting and research contracts. The differences among the groups' recommendations are minor. However, the Chimonas study found that, as of December 2008, US medical schools' adoption of these policy recommendations covering physician-industry interactions was "notably incomplete."[320] Here are the major findings:

- The absence of any policy governing industry marketing relationships was the most prevalent finding in seven of eleven areas examined.

- Even the most frequently regulated areas—industry gifts and industry consulting—had "no policy" rates of 25 percent and 23 percent, respectively.

- Faculty involvement in industry-led ghostwriting—which is both widespread and controversial—was the most neglected policy area: 70 percent of medical schools had no explicit policies to address ghostwriting. However, at nineteen institutions where policies did address ghostwriting, it was usually strongly prohibited.

- The study also considered the "stringency" of the policies and found "very low adoption of stringent policies (less than 5 percent)" addressing consulting, honoraria, and faculty participation in industry speakers bureaus.

- Medical school policies had higher rates of stringency for gifts (30 percent), meals (26 percent), industry-vendor site access (19 percent), free drug samples (17 percent), and continuing medical education (16 percent).

Detailed Discussion
of the 56 Recommended Principles

The AAUP recommendations include:

GENERAL PRINCIPLES, which may be applied university-wide, that cover core academic norms and standards, such as authenticity of authorship, publication rights, and academic autonomy; they also address broad areas of academy-industry engagement, such as student education and training, financial conflicts of interest, and intellectual property management.

TARGETED PRINCIPLES that address specific types of academy-industry engagement, including strategic corporate alliances, industry-sponsored clinical trials, and academy-industry interactions at academic medical centers.

Some repetition has been necessary to ensure adequate explanation of the individual principles.

Definition of a "significant" financial interest

As noted in the Summary of Recommendations, throughout this report the AAUP defines a financial interest to be "significant" if it is valued at or above $5,000 per year and it is not controlled or managed by an independent entity such as a mutual or pension fund. This definition is consistent with the definitions and de minimis threshold for financial disclosure established by the US Department of Health and Human Services in its 2011 conflict of interest disclosure rules *(Department of Health and Human Services, 42 CFR Part 50, 45 CFR Part 94, "Responsibility of Applicants for Promoting Objectivity in Research for which Public Health Service Funding is Sought and Responsible Prospective Contractors," Federal Register, vol. 76, no. 165, August 25, 2011, available at: http://www.gpo.gov/fdsys/pkg/FR-2011-08-25/pdf/2011-21633.pdf). The relevant sections of these DHHS rules are reprinted in full at the end of the Summary of Recommendations for easy reference.*

PART I.

General Principles to Guide Academy-Industry Relationships University-Wide (1–7)

PRINCIPLE 1: Faculty Governance

The university must preserve the primacy of shared academic governance in establishing campuswide policies for planning, developing, implementing, monitoring, and assessing all donor agreements and collaborations, whether with private industry, government, or nonprofit groups. Faculty, not outside sponsors, should retain majority control over the campus management of such agreements and collaborations.

Threats to faculty control over research and teaching as well as violations of good shared governance practices run through many of the case studies and risk categories associated with academy-industry engagement we have reviewed. Academy-industry partnerships play a vital role in funding research and bring many additional benefits. Yet in the face of mounting COI and commercial threats to academic freedom and research integrity, the time has come for stronger faculty input and guidance in this broad arena. Establishing the standards we recommend will strengthen university policymaking in this growing area of outside donor collaborations, safeguard academic freedom and professionalism, and engender greater campuswide support and public trust.

The AAUP recommends the following corrective and preventative measures:

- The faculty collectively through the academic senate should have a direct role in formulating the campuswide policies, principles, and standards that will guide all donor agreements and collaborations, including those forged with private industry, government, and nonprofit groups. We mean "assessment" above to refer not only to negotiation of a contract's content but also to the ongoing evaluation of a project and the review of a project after it has concluded.

- University policies should draw and build on these recommendations.

- To ensure that all forms of academy-industry engagement are addressed in an effective and comprehensive manner across campus, these policies should cover the university proper as well as any affiliated medical schools, hospitals, institutes, foundations, associations, and centers.

- No external relationships, donor agreements, or university-industry collaborations should be allowed to intrude on academic governance, or contravene existing academic policies or collective bargaining agreements.

- Most donor agreements can be formulated to comply with these campuswide standards and protocols without advance senate approval. But because of their potential to exert disproportionate influence, the senate should be explicitly involved in the development and final approval of any large-scale, multi-year strategic corporate alliances. Large-scale SCAs are covered in detail in Part VI of this report.

Too often faculty governing bodies are shut out of policy making and other negotiations surrounding the formation of academy-industry partnerships, even when these partnerships have a direct bearing on research and other academic matters traditionally considered faculty responsibilities. This is particularly true with SCAs, which often emerge from one department or institute without supervision, oversight, input, or evaluation by collective faculty governing bodies.[321] Because of complex negotiations and confidentiality concerns, SCAs are often presented to faculty senates largely as faits accompli, thus permitting minimal collective faculty input.[322] Such end runs around shared governance are unacceptable.

Simply keeping track of academy-industry engagements can be tricky, for they can take place under the auspices of several different offices (the Office of Sponsored Programs, the Office of Research Administration, the Office of Technology Transfer) and may be negotiated by a handful of university and company representatives.

At many state universities, moreover, a sizable portion of this private- and corporate-sector gift and grant administration has been transferred to legally separate, university-affiliated, nonprofit foundations, which are highly opaque because they frequently claim exemption from both normal academic governance and state open record laws.[323] As the private assets of university-affiliated foundations have grown, so too has their influence and potential for abuse. Allegations of misuse of university foundation assets have already led to civil suits, as well as state and federal criminal investigations. Here is a summary of a few of these cases, prepared by the Student Press

Law Center, which tracks these university-affiliated foundations and their handling of donor funds:[324]

Misuse of University-Affiliated, Nonprofit Foundation Funding

• At the University of Idaho a former university vice president pleaded guilty to misuse of state funds and was sentenced to probation for his role in secretly diverting foundation money to prop up a financially troubled $136 million project.[325]

• In 2005, the *Atlanta Journal-Constitution* reported that University System of Georgia Foundation donor lists—which were disclosed only after a legal battle—revealed that colleges within the system awarded companies lucrative contracts after they had made large donations to a special fund that supplemented the university chancellor's salary.[326]

• At Iowa State University, an independent audit in 1999–2000 revealed that the ISU Foundation was still paying a former football coach, who resigned in 1994, over half-a-million dollars a year as part of a deferred compensation contract payable over 20 years. (While actually employed by the university, the coach's annual salary was $111,197.)[327]

• At Florida Atlantic University, a 2003 investigation revealed that its foundation had set aside $42,000 to purchase a red Corvette for the school's outgoing president.[328]

Given such examples, it is imperative for faculty to protect academic governance by drawing up stronger consensus policies to guide academy-industry relationships—so all academy-industry engagement (whether advanced by an administrator, a handful of faculty investigators, the Office of Sponsored Research, or a university-affiliated foundation) is governed by a common set of standards.

Principle 1 on Faculty Governance helps clarify the recommendations already issued in the AAUP's "Statement on Government of Colleges and Universities" and the "Statement on Corporate Funding of Academic Research."[329]

PRINCIPLE 2: Academic Freedom, Autonomy, and Control

The university must preserve its academic autonomy—including the academic freedom rights of faculty, students, postdoctoral fellows, and academic professionals—in all its relationships with industry and other funding sources by maintaining majority academic control over joint academy-industry committees and exclusive academic control over core academic functions (such as faculty research evaluations, faculty hiring and promotion decisions, classroom teaching, curriculum development, and course content).

- No academic institution should accept financial support that is either explicitly or implicitly conditional on a donor's right to influence or control core academic functions.

- Principle 2 builds on the AAUP's 1990 "Statement on Conflicts of Interest," which reads in part as follows:

    Because the central business of the university remains teaching and research unfettered by extra-university dictates, faculties should ensure that any cooperative venture between members of the faculty and outside agencies, whether public or private, respects the primacy of the university's principal mission, with regard to the choice of subjects of research and the reaching and publication of results.[330]

- Principle 2 also draws on a 2007 statement issued by the AAUP's Committee A on Academic Freedom and Tenure, warning that academic institutions surrender their autonomy and authority—and break with the principles of academic freedom—when they accept outside funding that is "conditioned on a requirement to assign specific course material that the faculty would not otherwise assign."[331]

- As part of their academic freedom and professional autonomy faculty have a collective responsibility to uphold the highest standards of scholarly integrity. This pillar of academic freedom and professional responsibility is elaborated on in many of these principles.

In the last decade, a number of corporate- and private-foundation partnerships that impinge on core areas of faculty autonomy—including faculty hiring, research direction, and curriculum design—have been described in the media. Recent cases have involved IBM, BB&T, and the Charles G. Koch Foundation in the United States; in Germany a prominent case arose involving Deutsche Bank.[332] In the box below is a summary of US cases:

Donor Intrusions on Academic Autonomy

• As of 2013, the Charles G. Koch Foundation (a libertarian foundation founded by one of the heirs to Koch Industries, a major US oil, gas, and chemical conglomerate with annual revenues of $110 billion) reported issuing grants to more than 220 colleges and universities.[333] Many of the Koch agreements contained highly controversial restrictions on academic freedom and autonomy, which became public only after the underlying contracts were disclosed by faculty members and the news media. From 2007 to 2009, for example, Utah State University received more than $700,000 from the Koch Foundation to supplement the salaries of five business school faculty members. After stating these appointments would be subject to standard hiring procedures, the actual contract required the Koch Foundation to approve all faculty members hired. A 2008 agreement between the Koch Foundation and Florida State University, which became public in 2011, also cedes control over faculty hiring. Under the FSU contract, an advisory committee composed of faculty members selected by the Koch Foundation is charged with vetting and approving (or disapproving) prospective faculty appointments. This Koch-selected advisory committee is also charged with evaluating overall ideological conformity with the Foundation's libertarian economic and political goals.[334]

• In 2006, North Carolina State University inaugurated a new academic concentration, "Services Management," open to graduate students pursuing either a Masters in Business Administration or a Masters of Sciences in Computer Networking, whose coursework was co-developed by IBM. According to the *Wall Street Journal,* in exchange for IBM granting the university five faculty awards of $30,000 each, plus the time of its employees, IBM was permitted to co-create the curriculum and co-teach five university courses.[335]

• At the University of North Carolina–Charlotte and more than two dozen other colleges across the nation, BB&T, a southern banking giant, made donations to humanities and business programs contingent on Ayn Rand's free market theories being incorporated into the curriculum and her books assigned as required reading.[336]

Academic independence has historically been rooted in the university's belief that it must be able to control its own internal academic affairs. This is referred to as academic self-governance or academic autonomy. Since the birth of the academic freedom movement in the early 1900s, US universities and their faculty have worked vigorously to prevent outside donors (whether a wealthy benefactor, a commercial sponsor, or a federal grant-making agency) from exercising undue influence and control over academic decisions. The rationale for this is straightforward: If universities allow themselves to be guided by the dictates and interests of their outside financial supporters, they cannot credibly carry out their core academic and public interest missions.

PRINCIPLE 3: Academic Publication Rights

Academic publication rights must be fully protected, with only limited pre-publication delays (a maximum of 30–60 days) to remove corporate proprietary or confidential information or to file for patents and other IP protections prior to publication. Sponsor efforts to obstruct—or sponsored research agreements that do not permit—the free, timely, and open dissemination of research data, codes, reagents, methods, and results are unacceptable. Sponsor attempts to compel a faculty member, student, postdoctoral fellow, or academic professional to edit, revise, withhold, or delete contents in an academic publication (including a master's thesis or PhD dissertation) or presentation (beyond legally justified claims to protect explicit trade secrets) must be clearly prohibited in all sponsored research contracts and university policies. A funder is of course free to make editorial suggestions, but academic researchers must be free at all times to accept or reject them.

As a condition of research sponsorship, it is common for a corporate sponsor to insist on "first look" rights to ensure that academic publications or public presentations of the research do not disclose proprietary information that has not yet been secured through intellectual property protection. The National Institutes of Health generally recommends granting sponsors no more than a 30-to-60-day window for pre-publication review, which it considers sufficient time for the corporate sponsor, or the university, to file a provisional patent claim or remove any sensitive proprietary information.[337]

Publication is the lifeblood of the university; it guarantees the diffusion of new knowledge and ensures that it will be independently scrutinized and verified for accuracy. In some research fields, an enforced delay of even thirty days is hugely significant. These "first look" rights should be restricted to 30 days wherever possible (60 days maximum). They should also clearly specify that delays can be invoked only for the purposes noted above, not to suppress undesirable results, even temporarily, or to otherwise amend or edit the content, substance, or conclusions of the research. Corporate sponsors should also be encouraged to agree to "rapid clearance procedures" for time-sensitive materials to enable expedited reviews of two weeks or less. Research results that bear on natural disasters, industrial accidents, product safety, or immediate medical needs are examples of work that may require rapid clearance.

PRINCIPLE 4: The Authenticity of Academic Authorship

To protect the authenticity of academic publishing, universities and their affiliated academic medical centers should prohibit faculty, students, postdoctoral fellows, medical residents, and other academic professionals from engaging in industry-led "ghostwriting" or "ghost authorship." Ghostwriting or ghostauthorship occurs when a private firm or an industry group initiates the publication of an "academic" article in a science or medical journal in support of its commercial products or interests, without publicly disclosing that the corporate entity has initiated and also often performed the initial drafting of the article, and then recruited an academic researcher (sometimes referred to as an "academic opinion leader") to sign on as the nominal "author" (frequently in exchange for a fee). Although ghostwriting has been especially widespread in academic medicine, prohibitions on ghostwriting should be applied university-wide and should cover all faculty and researchers; the practice violates scholarly standards and is unacceptable in any academic setting.

- Numerous academic societies and journals have issued similar recommendations. In the field of medicine, the IOM (2009),[338] AAMC (2006);[339] and the AAU 2008[340] have called for the unambiguous prohibition of faculty participation in ghostwriting. Starting in 2001, medical journal editors collectively took steps to detect and prohibit ghostwriting through the International Committee of Medical Journal Editors (ICMJE) and the World Association of Medical Editors (WAME).[341] Concerned about threats to the integrity of clinical trials in a research environment increasingly controlled by private interests, the ICMJE revised its "Uniform Requirements for Manuscripts Submitted to Biomedical Journals" to call for full disclosure of the sponsor's role in the research, as well as assurances that the investigators are independent of the sponsor, are fully accountable for the design and conduct of the trial, have independent access to all trial data, and control all editorial and publication decisions. These ICMJE-WAME principles are now widely seen as the gold standard for research and authorship. All universities should hold their faculty members responsible for upholding these standards, just as they would prohibit fraud, plagiarism, and other serious violations of accepted scholarly practice. Indeed it is not sufficient to require faculty to honor the standards of their fields, the view taken in Harvard University's COI policy.[342] These standards need to be required of faculty whether or not their academic disciplines have adopted such safeguards.

- Despite the prevalence of ghostwriting documented in the academic literature (see the discussion below for details), university and medical school policymaking in this area remains remarkably weak. A 2010 study published in *PLoS Medicine* found that only 13 of the top 50 US medical schools have policies that specifically prohibit ghostwriting.[343]

- Two hallmarks of academic integrity are intellectual independence and accountability; both are violated when a faculty member assumes credit as the "author" of a manuscript prepared by an unacknowledged, or inadequately acknowledged, industry-paid writer.[344] Adequate acknowledgment would have to specify the role played by these industry-paid writers, for example as the preparers of the first draft, as well as the specific roles of all major authors. Faculty have a special obligation to demonstrate and protect their intellectual independence, uphold the highest standards of scholarship, and act as role models for their students. Any faculty member who is proven to have engaged in ghostwriting should be appropriately disciplined.

Studies have documented prevalent industry-led ghostwriting in academia, especially within the field of medicine.[345] Investigations based on litigation documents and other sources have documented how pharmaceutical companies used behind-the-scenes ghostwriting techniques to market sertraline,[346] olanzapine,[347] gabapentin,[348] estrogen replacement therapy,[349] rofecoxib,[350] paroxetine,[351] methylphenidate,[352] milnacipran,[353] venlafaxine,[354] and dexfenfluramine.[355] One survey of major biomedical journals found that 13 percent of all research articles had unacknowledged ghost authors.[356] Other estimates of ghostwriting prevalence run higher.[357] Ghostwriting has not been investigated thoroughly beyond medicine, however, so its true scope is unknown.

Another variant on ghostwriting has been pervasive in the field of tobacco research. Numerous studies have shown how the tobacco industry influences academic authors by carefully vetting who will receive its funding, shaping study design, and making suggestions about what investigators should and shouldn't say in their papers.[358]

Industry efforts to manipulate and influence academic authors have drawn ire from public officials and the media. A 2009 *New York Times* article characterized medical ghostwriting as "an academic crime akin to plagiarism."[359] Senator Chuck Grassley (R-IA), a longtime ranking member of the Senate Committee on Finance, reported in 2010 on a series of investigations into financial relationships between drug and device companies and academic physicians, with an especially critical eye trained on ghostwriting.[360]

In addition to compromising the authenticity of authorship and undermining peer review for faculty appointments and promotions, ghostwritten articles and reviews can introduce commercial bias and distortion into scientific literature. Drs. Jeffrey Lacasse and Jonathan Leo, the authors of a 2010 survey of ghostwriting, argue that the practice may be "dangerous to public health." Quoting from various studies (cited in the endnote) they conclude that:

> [G]hostwritten articles on [the pain killer, Vioxx] rofecoxib probably contributed to . . . "lasting injury and even deaths as a result of prescribers and patients being misinformed about risks." Study 329, a randomized controlled trial of [the antidepressant drug, Paxil] paroxetine in adolescents, was ghostwritten to claim that paroxetine is "generally well tolerated and effective for major depression in adolescents," although data made available through legal proceedings show that "Study 329 was negative for efficacy on all 8 protocol specified outcomes and positive for harm." Even beyond frank misrepresentation of data, commercially driven ghostwritten articles shape the medical literature in subtler but important ways, affecting how health conditions and treatments are perceived by clinicians.[361]

PRINCIPLE 5: Access to Complete Study Data and Independent Academic Analysis

University codes of conduct should prohibit participation in sponsored research that restricts investigators' ability to access the complete study data related to their sponsored research or that limits investigators' ability to conduct unfettered, free, and independent analyses of complete data to verify the accuracy and validity of final reported results. Protecting access to complete study data is particularly important in the area of clinical research, where drug trials and other medical investigations are often conducted at multiple institutions simultaneously. If the sponsor grants only partial access to the study's complete data sets or withholds other relevant research codes and materials, then the academic investigators and authors will not be able to perform a truly independent analysis of the study's data and outcomes. Universities should secure these basic academic freedom rights within the legal terms of all sponsored research contracts.

- This principle is in keeping with recommendations already issued by the AAMC (2001[362] and 2006[363]), the ICMJE (2001),[364] and WAME.[365] This principle is reaffirmed under Principle 49, which addresses "Access to Complete Clinical Trial Data and the Performance of Independent Academic Analysis" within the context of academic medicine and clinical research.

- In 2001, the AAMC issued conflict of interest recommendations that emphasized the need for academic investigators to retain control over both data access and data analysis:

  The [conflict of interest] policy should affirm an investigator's accountability for the integrity of any publication that bears his or her name. The policy should also affirm the right of a principal investigator to receive, analyze, and interpret all data generated in the research, and to publish the results, independent of the outcome of the research. Institutions should not enter, nor permit a covered individual to enter, research agreements that permit a sponsor or other financially interested company to require more than a reasonable period of pre-publication review, or that interfere with an investigator's access to the data or ability to analyze the data independently.[366]

- In 2002, a *NJEM* survey of 108 medical schools found that only one percent of university-industry contracts to multi-site clinical trials required the academic authors to have independent access to the complete study data. As we noted above, *NEJM* editor Jeffrey Drazen responded by urging universal contract language requiring that academic investigators have complete data access.[367]

- A 2005 analysis of 107 medical schools found that industry sponsor control over data access and analysis remains widespread. The survey concluded that 50 percent of medical schools would allow their industry sponsors to draft the final manuscript, with the academic investigators' role limited to review and suggestions for revision; 24 percent would permit the industry sponsors to insert their own statistical analyses into the final manuscript (another 29 percent were not sure whether to permit this or not); 41 percent would allow industry sponsors to prohibit academic investigators from sharing data with third parties after the study was concluded (another 24 percent were not sure whether they should allow this practice, and 34 percent disallowed it).[368] In addition to the problem of bias, the delegation of statistical analysis to industry employees removes it from the supervision expected of independent scholarly inquiry.

It has become common for pharmaceutical and other biomedical companies to assert "proprietary control" over the complete study data associated with a particular clinical research trial (which is often conducted at multiple testing sites simultaneously) as well as the corresponding statistical codes used to "blind" the study's investigators from any possible bias. Both data and codes are required to interpret research findings. Industry sponsors may assert that data and related codes must be guarded on company computers and only be analyzed by company chosen statisticians.[369] One academic physician has dubbed such industry-controlled drug trials "ghost science" because they effectively permit the sponsor to control both the analysis and final interpretation of all study results, making independent academic authorship meaningless.[370] Attaching one's name to industry-generated analyses raises serious issues of misconduct, since the academic researcher can claim no genuine intellectual responsibility for the reported results. When Procter and Gamble Pharmaceuticals (P&G) blocked researchers at Sheffield University in the United Kingdom from analyzing data related to an osteoporosis drug trial, the company told the media that it was "standard industry practice" to deny authors access to raw data in drug studies.[371]

As noted in the discussion of Principle 4, clear indication of these problems came in 2001 when the ICMJE announced it was revising its manuscript submission standards to try to curb industry influence over trial design, data access and analysis, and reporting of study results.[372] These requirements have been adopted by 500 science journals, but compliance is voluntary, and not all journals have well defined FCOI disclosure policies.[373] Moreover, many universities and their medical schools do not include these standards in their own research contracts with industry. It is not sufficient for journals alone to adopt these standards; universities must do so as well.

PRINCIPLE 6: Confidential and Classified Research

Classified research, as well as confidential corporate, government, or non-profit research that cannot be published, is inappropriate on a university campus. Many institutions currently have written policies that ban classified government research on campus; the policies should be reviewed to ensure that they also ban confidential corporate research. Universities employ a variety of mechanisms for moving confidential and classified research off campus, sometimes using governance structures less subject to academic oversight. Sorting through multiple categories of "national security," "classified," and "sensitive but unclassified" (SBU) information requires expert monitoring by faculty governance bodies. These faculty bodies should operate with a strong presumption against permitting any confidential, classified, or non-publishable research on campus. Academic analyses and research results should always be publishable absent a compelling case to the contrary. This university commitment to knowledge sharing and openness should govern both the determination of which research will be confidential and thus cannot be performed on campus, as well as any rare exceptions that may be granted. As historical precedent suggests, the special circumstances of a formal congressional declaration of war against a specified nation-state or states may justify exceptions to the policies for the duration of the conflict.

- Given the university's open culture and long-standing commitment to the broad dissemination of new knowledge, any sponsored research project that would restrict free and open publication, presentation, and discussion of results is not acceptable.

- Universities will need to pay close attention to the US government's multiple categories of "sensitive but unclassified" (SBU) information in order to determine what research will be confidential and cannot be conducted on campus. In line with this principle, the AAUP recommends against establishing secure buildings or facilities within buildings on campus to conduct secret sponsored research.

- This is a general principle with broad academic endorsement. The AAUP has addressed this issue on numerous occasions. In 1967 the national AAUP's annual meeting resolved that

    all secret arrangements entered into by academic institutions or individuals in an academic capacity threaten the integrity of the academic community. The agreements between academic individuals and organizations and the Central Intelligence Agency constituted such a threat. Accordingly, the Annual Meeting calls upon all elements of the academic community to scrutinize any and all arrangements with public and private organizations and individuals to make certain that such arrangements are consistent with the basic principles upon which higher education in this country rests.[374]

The following year the Association reaffirmed its concern

about secrecy in research. Any arrangement with an outside agency that places restrictions on the open publication of results of research raises serious questions of academic integrity. Accordingly, the Annual Meeting calls upon the academic community to examine with great care the nature and consequences of research relationships with all outside agencies to make certain that such activities are consistent with the basic principles upon which higher education in this country rests.

The AAUP took up the matter again in a 2003 statement titled "Academic Freedom and National Security in a Time of Crisis." Addressing the sweeping legal changes Congress adopted following the September 11, 2001, terrorist attacks, the Association sought to balance security needs with the principles of civil and academic liberties:

There may be points where some of our freedoms will have to yield to the manifest imperatives of security. What we should not accept is that we must yield those freedoms whenever the alarm of security is sounded. Given the extensive historical record of governmental overreaching and abuse in the name of security, we are right to be skeptical. Even at the height of the Cold War, when we faced the prospect of nuclear annihilation, the government did not institute security measures as far reaching as some now proposed. . . . Accordingly, when the government invokes claims of security to justify an infringement of our civil or academic liberties, the burden of persuasion must be on the government to satisfy three essential criteria: 1. The government must demonstrate the particular threat to which the measure is intended to respond, not as a matter of fear, conjecture, or supposition, but as a matter of fact. . . . 2. The government must demonstrate how any proposed measure will effectively deal with a particular threat. . . . 3. The government must show why the desired result could not be reached by means having a less significant impact on the exercise of our civil or academic liberties. . . . Under certain circumstances, academic research can directly affect national security, and in those circumstances, a system of classification may be necessary, as it has been in the past. The hazards of a dangerous world cannot be ignored. At the same time, secrecy, an inescapable element of classified research, is fundamentally incompatible with freedom of inquiry and freedom of expression. . . . Not only are fewer restrictions better than more, but restrictions on research, to the extent that any are required, must be precise, narrowly defined, and applied only in exceptional circumstances. These seem to be the lessons the academic community has drawn from its past experiences with classified research.[375]

- An earlier AAUP report raises arguments against classified research that are also relevant to confidential corporate research. A 1983 Committee A report, "The Enlargement of the Classified Information System," asserts that the Reagan administration's Executive Order 12356 (April 2, 1982) "significantly abridges academic freedom beyond the needs of national security." The report adds that "insofar as academic freedom is improperly curtailed, the nation's security is ill-served," for "open and free scientific communication is essential for ensuring national security."[376] The 1983 statement observes that the "freedom to engage in academic research and to publish the results is essential to advance knowledge and to sustain our democratic society" while secrecy "defeats its own purpose . . . if it imperils the freedoms it is meant to protect." Secrecy not only curtails public knowledge; it also produces "the bleak prospect of academic researchers who are walled-off from each other . . . thus forestalling mutual enrichment through the exchange of ideas and constructive criticism."[377] The problems associated with national security restrictions are equally characteristic of confidential corporate research.

- Many universities have policies in place banning confidential or classified research from their campuses, including Cornell, MIT, and UC Berkeley, but not all address commercially funded research.

- Cornell's policy seeks to ensure public access to new knowledge by explicitly prohibiting classified research on campus:

  Given the open nature of Cornell University, research projects which do not permit the free and open publication, presentation, or discussion of results are not acceptable. . . . In particular, research which is confidential to the sponsor or which is classified for security purposes is not permitted at Cornell University.[378]

- MIT also has a written policy that strongly discourages the conduct of classified or unpublishable research on campus. There are some exceptions, but these are rare.[379] In 2002, a special MIT faculty committee, mindful of national security needs following 9/11 and of MIT's history of national service, recommended that the university provide off-campus facilities to help faculty perform classified public service or other research. The committee also reaffirmed MIT's long-standing policy of intellectual openness:

  > We recommend that no classified research should be carried out on campus; that no student, graduate or undergraduate, should be required to have a security clearance to perform thesis research; and that no thesis research should be carried out in [intellectual] areas requiring access to classified materials.[380]

- UC Berkeley's policy bans the performance of classified or non-publishable research, stating that "classified projects are not consistent with the teaching, research, and public service missions of the Berkeley campus."[381] The policy notes the institution's commitment "to maintaining a teaching and research environment that is open for the free exchange of ideas among faculty and students in all forums—classrooms, laboratories, seminars, meetings, and elsewhere . . . There can be no fundamental limitation on the freedom to publish as the result of accepting extramural research support."[382] But the Energy Biosciences Institute (EBI)—a ten-year research alliance between UC Berkeley, Lawrence Berkeley National Laboratory, the University of Illinois at Urbana-Champaign, and the oil giant BP—appears to circumvent this policy. The EBI contract expressly permits BP employees to carry out "private, confidential, and proprietary research" and to keep that research secret, despite their physical presence inside a university-owned academic building.[383] UC Berkeley has stated that, because this policy only applies to BP employees working at the EBI's academic labs, it does not violate the UC ban on confidential research. Yet because those same BP scientists have extensive collaborations with UC Berkeley professors and students, some critics remain skeptical.[384] A similar confidentiality provision in the 2006 draft EBI proposal prompted an editorial from the *San Francisco Chronicle:* "On the face of it, this arrangement conflicts not only with the 'open' nature of a university, especially a public one, but also with Berkeley's prohibition against classified research on campus."[385]

PRINCIPLE 7: Academic Consulting

To address the potential for conflicts of commitment and financial conflicts of interest, all consulting contracts worth $5,000 or more a year should be reported to the university's standing COI committee(s) charged with reviewing and managing both individual and institutional conflicts of interest (see Principle 24 for discussion of these committees). Neither faculty members nor administrators should sign a consulting contract that undercuts their professional ability to express their own independent expert opinions publicly, except when consulting with industry, government, or other parties on explicitly classified or proprietary matters. All such consulting agreements should be secured in writing.

Consulting is a vital part of university life, but neither consulting contracts nor financial remuneration should interfere with the recipient's primary institutional, academic, and professional obligations and commitments. Outside consulting enables faculty to improve their understanding of social, industrial, health, and other real-world problems and processes, to develop more interesting and relevant research questions, and to apply their academic expertise and knowledge to real world needs. Yet current codes of conduct and COI policies at many leading universities do not prohibit faculty members from signing consulting agreements that explicitly conflict with their ability to engage in free expression and free inquiry—the pillars of academic freedom. The advantages of outside consulting can outweigh the risks if COI rules are in place and enforced, if the freedom to publish and express independent opinions is guaranteed, if the consulting work itself remains a small proportion of an individual's overall time, and if any single consulting responsibility represents a small proportion of his or her total income.

A "conflict of commitment" arises whenever a faculty member's or administrator's outside consulting has the potential to interfere with their primary duties, including teaching, research, time with students, or service and administrative obligations to the university. Today it is common for both faculty and administrators to accept outside consulting positions with a variety of groups, including industry.

- In accordance with a joint statement issued by AAU-AAMC (2008),[386] the AAUP recommends that an institution consider exempting certain clearly defined types of consulting and fees from their definitions of reportable financial interests: fees for serving on grant review committees (study sections) and fees given as honoraria by another academic institution for an academic activity, public lecture, seminar, or grand rounds presentation.

- This principle accords with recommendations issued by the IOM in 2009: "Faculty should engage only in bona fide consulting arrangements that require their expertise, that are based on written contracts with specific tasks and deliverables, and that are paid for at fair market value. As part of their administration of conflict of interest policies, university review of faculty consulting and other contracts is prudent and desirable."[387]

- Certain types of outside corporate consulting—i.e., board of director seats, seats on corporate scientific advisory boards, faculty participation in corporate "speakers bureaus"—raise FCOI concerns because irreconcilable conflicts may exist between the recipients' academic duties and the commercial and fiduciary obligations required by these outside positions.[388] Such consulting arrangements may warrant oversight and possible prohibition by the university's standing COI committee.

- Both administrators and faculty should be held to the same standards of disclosure with respect to outside consulting, though campuses may want to consider a more restrictive policy for senior administrators to avoid the potential for institutional COI.

- At a minimum, senior administrators should be prohibited from sitting on the boards of corporations that are seeking or already have research contracts with campus faculty. The responsibility for administrative oversight can be seriously compromised by such arrangements.

Consulting arrangements that infringe on basic academic principles are cropping up in different fields:

- In July 2010, shortly after BP's massive Deepwater Horizon oil spill, the *Press-Register* of Mobile, Alabama, reported that BP was racing to sign research and consulting contracts with university departments in the Gulf of Mexico region. Some scientists complained that the terms of these lucrative contracts violated their academic freedom. At the University of South Alabama in Mobile, for example, Russ Lea, the university's vice-president for research, reported that data collected by academic scientists would be held confidential under BP's proposed contract and could not be published for up to three years without BP's permission.[389] The contract also contained onerous restrictions on scientists' freedom to work with other companies or public agencies engaged in similar research.[390] *Nature News* later reported that a number of scientists felt ensnared by a larger legal scramble by BP and the federal government (then preparing its own official assessment of the oil spill, known as the Natural Resource Damage Assessment, NRDA) as they both sought to round up expert witnesses, sequester data, and impose gag orders on scientists.[391]

- According to a professor at Harvard's School of Public Health, writing in the *Chronicle of Higher Education,* similar industry restrictions on academic consulting have emerged in the field of epidemiology. This professor reported that his proposed contract with a large pharmaceutical company to assist in the design of a clinical trial "seemed to require that I sign away my right to criticize the product."[392] He explained:

> One provision would prohibit me from entering into "any agreement or relationship to render services as . . . adviser or consultant to, any other individual, firm, or corporation that would be inimical to or in conflict with" the aspects of the company's business covered by the agreement. Another would forbid me to engage, in any capacity, directly or indirectly, in "any business," with or without compensation, relating to the class of products under discussion—not just for the term of the contract, but for the year after as well. Those provisions could restrain me from providing candid advice to a regulator, a government official, or the editor of a peer-reviewed journal about the class of products on which I was consulting, even if the advice were based on publicly available information. I objected to those terms, as did a colleague who was offered the same arrangement.[393]

Part II.

General Principles for Academic Education and Training (8–10)

Students, postdoctoral fellows, adjuncts, and junior researchers participate in a variety of industry-sponsored activities, both on and off campus. Such collaborations—working in an industry-sponsored lab on campus, a professor's start-up company off site, or a corporate lab—offer attractive professional opportunities, especially as a growing proportion of science and technical careers are now in the private sector. These experiences can enhance exposure to the commercial research environment and can foster relationships that will lead to full employment.

Yet such collaborations present serious risks. Faculty mentors involved with an outside company may divert graduate students toward efforts that will benefit the company but not necessarily advance a student's education or thesis research. If students' work is constrained by proprietary restrictions (confidentiality requirements, non-compete agreements, non-disclosure terms, secrecy restrictions), they may find themselves blocked from presenting their work at scientific meetings—or, worse, from completing their degrees in a timely manner.

Disputes can and do also arise over the ownership of new ideas, resulting in difficult, complex, and often damaging IP battles that undermine mentor-student relationships. A senior faculty member with a significant FCOI may be unable to give truly impartial advice or appropriately supervise younger investigators' research.[394] A 2009 IOM panel on COI observed that exploitation of students and untenured investigators by conflicted senior advisers "is unethical and also has the potential to bias research design, conduct, or findings. Areas that may raise problems with undue influence include decisions about an individual's inclusion or exclusion from a research project; the focus, design, and conduct of a study; the publication of research findings (including the suppression of publication); and the treatment of intellectual property interests."[395]

These men and women are, first and foremost, students, trainees, and young scholars. The university has a responsibility to ensure that their primary academic interests are not compromised by participation in sponsored research collaborations. The following principles are intended, therefore, to safeguard the interests of students, postdoctoral fellows, and other untenured and junior investigators while simultaneously protecting the university's vital commitment to education.

PRINCIPLE 8: Recruiting and Advising Graduate Students, Medical Residents, and Faculty

The admission of graduate students to degree programs and the appointment of medical residents and faculty should be based on their overall qualifications, not on their potential to work under a particular donor agreement or in a particular collaborative research alliance, whether commercial, governmental, or nonprofit. A PhD student's main adviser should be free of any significant financial interest, including equity, in a company that is funding or stands to profit from the student's thesis or dissertation research. Exceptions should evaluate both conflicts of interest and potential conflicts of commitment, all of which should be disclosed to all affected parties and periodically reviewed by an appropriate faculty body.

- As noted above, in accordance with the DHHS-NIH 2011 disclosure rules, the AAUP defines a financial interest as "significant" if it is valued at or above $5,000 per year and it is not controlled or managed by an independent entity, such as a mutual or pension fund.[396]

- This principle is drawn from recommendations issued by the University of California at San Diego Academic Senate, Administration Committee on University Interaction with Industry[397] and by the AAMC (2001)[398] and the AAMC (2008),[399] the latter noting that advisers should "recognize the possibility of conflicts between the interests of externally funded research programs and those of the graduate student."

- Faculty advisers should not pressure students to take on thesis topics that reflect the priorities of a faculty start-up company or corporate research sponsor, rather than advancing students' best educational and personal interests.

- Faculty mentors and advisers should avoid any situation that makes MA or PhD thesis research unpublishable because of corporate non-disclosure agreements or other secrecy constraints.[400]

- This principle is not meant to bar an adviser who receives modest benefits like an honorarium for discussing research at an industry meeting or public conference.

- Faculty members should not accept employment in an entity substantially controlled by a student advisee or one enrolled in one of his or her departmental degree programs. "Control" refers not only to administrative authority but also major equity positions.

- Faculty members must ensure that students are not assigned work that exploits them in the service of a family member's financial interests.

Surprisingly little scholarly attention has focused on COIs that arise in mentor or supervisor relationships, even though anecdotal evidence and scholarly discussion of such problems are numerous.[401] According to a two-year analysis of university-industry partnerships conducted by the University-Industry Research Collaboration Initiative,[402] it is not unusual for a student involved in an industry-sponsored project to take six months longer to earn a PhD than would be the case with purely academic research. If such delays are likely, students must be fully informed and willing to make this additional time commitment.[403]

PRINCIPLE 9: Impartial Academic Evaluation

Students, postdoctoral fellows, academic professionals, and junior colleagues should always be entitled to impartial and fair evaluations of their academic performance. Because of the risk of both real and perceived bias, faculty members with a significant personal financial interest in the outcome of their students' research should not have sole responsibility for evaluating student progress toward a degree.[404]

- Because of the risk of both real and perceived bias, faculty members with a personal financial interest in the outcome of their students' or junior colleagues' research should never be given primary responsibility for evaluating student progress toward a degree or faculty progress toward tenure. Whenever a faculty adviser has an FCOI, any students, postdoctoral fellows, and untenured faculty colleagues working on a compromised project should be assigned a different adviser, someone with suitable expertise, no financial interest in the work, and qualified to provide impartial oversight of academic evaluations.

- This principle is adapted from 2001[405] and 2008[406] AAMC recommendations, and from a 2009 IOM proposal. In 2008, the AAMC cautioned that when a faculty adviser has a related FCOI, the university should carefully assess whether "the roles of students, trainees, and junior faculty and staff [are] appropriate and free from exploitation," and whether special protections are needed for "vulnerable members" of the research team.[407] In such circumstances, the Institute of Medicine proposed, "one protection might be to provide such individuals with access to independent senior faculty members for independent review and guidance when questions and concerns arise."[408]

PRINCIPLE 10: Grievance Procedures

Universities should establish effective, well-publicized grievance procedures for all students, postdoctoral fellows, academic professionals, and faculty members, tenured and untenured, so they may freely and safely report obstacles encountered while pursuing their research and educational objectives. Obstacles may include but are not limited to inappropriate commercial or other sponsor influence over the conduct or analysis of research, unwarranted delays to degree completion, financial conflicts of interest, conflicts of commitment, and conflicts over ownership of intellectual property. Faculty with financial conflicts related to a grievance filing should recuse themselves from its adjudication in formal proceedings. Informal resolution of grievances is often preferable when possible.

Students and others depend on their faculty mentors' or supervisors' guidance, support, and goodwill to advance their own academic careers. This arrangement works well under normal circumstances, but mentoring relationships are fragile and may be disrupted by outside commercial conflicts. This is one reason why universities need to implement clear and effective channels for graduate students, postdoctoral fellows, and untenured faculty to report problems and seek help from objective third parties should the need arise. Confidential complaints about contract provisions, COI, and inappropriate commercial consequences should be given full consideration. Complaints by individuals claiming a violation of their rights, however, need to be signed and communicated to the accused party, as the right to confront an accuser is fundamental to due process.

Several principles should be incorporated into all grievance procedures:

- A grievant should have the right to have an observer at all meetings arranged to discuss a grievance and to have counsel present during formal proceedings.

- Neither faculty nor administrators may harass, retaliate, or discriminate against a grievant, witness, or other participant in a grievance process.

- With the exception of grievances involving disciplinary action against the grievant, the grievant bears the burden of proof. With grievances involving disciplinary action, the burden of proof is on the administration.

- At a grievance hearing, the grievant has the right to present any evidence in support of the grievance.

- The grievant must be provided with a written decision that includes reasons for the decision. No documents can be referenced in the decision unless they have been provided to the grievant or the grievant's legal counsel. Copies of relevant documents should accompany the decision, unless they are posted online and can simply be referenced with a URL.

Part III.
General Principles for Management of Intellectual Property (IP) (11–21)

The management of inventions, patents, and other forms of intellectual property (IP) in a university setting warrants special guidance because it bears directly on the university's core values, including principles of academic freedom, scholarship, research, and the transmission of knowledge to the public. These core values distinguish university activity from that of government and industry, and provide the argument for public support of research and the role of the university as an independent contributor to and commentator on both policy and commerce. The negotiation and management of university-generated IP can be complex and carry significant consequences for those directly involved in negotiations (faculty inventors, companies, university administrators, attorneys, invention management agents) as well as others who may be less directly affected (competing companies, the public, patients, and the wider research community).

Intellectual property refers broadly to patents, copyrights, trademarks, and (according to some definitions) trade secrets.[409] In common usage the term also refers to the underlying subject matter that is controlled by the owner of these property rights (inventions, works of authorship, and identifiers that distinguish goods and services in the marketplace). Patents provide the owner with the right to exclude others from "practicing" (making, using, and selling) an invention. A patent, unlike a copyright, goes beyond the protection of written expression to accord an exclusive right to the operational principles that underlie the invention. Unlike the case of copyright, where exclusions are triggered by unauthorized copying or modification of particular instances of expression, a patent permits the exclusion of work created independently, is not limited to precise "expression," and has no "fair use" exception, even for nonprofit purposes. Thus patents may have a substantial impact on university research, may affect the value and role of scholarly publication, and may interfere with collaborations and the transfer of technology developed or improved in other research settings. Recognizing the potential for harm, the faculty of a number of medical schools for years prohibited the patenting of inventions pertaining to public health.

Patents may cover new, useful, and non-obvious inventions, which are distinguished by patent law as processes, machines, manufacture, and composition of matter. As such, patentable inventions may span a wide range of results of academic work, including devices, chemical compounds, biological materials, research methods and tools, production processes, software, and other new products. Design patents cover new designs. Plant patents and related plant variety protection laws cover reproducing, selling, or using patented plants. Patents are acquired by an application that is reviewed by a patent examiner; the process may take up to three years. A patent has a term of twenty years from the date of application.

Trademarks distinguish goods and services in the marketplace and are classed as trademarks, service marks, certification marks (showing testing by an independent laboratory, for instance), and collective marks (identifying membership in an organization, such as real estate agents). Trademarks may be common law, that is, acquired by use in commerce, or registered at the state or federal level. A trademark remains in existence as long as it is being used. In academic settings, names, logos, and tag lines for assests such as software programs, research laboratories, new techniques, services offered by departments, web sites, and programs of research may all come to have trademark status.

Copyright encompasses original works of authorship fixed in any tangible medium of expression. Copyright vests in a work when it meets the requirements of the law; no application or registration process is now required. Classes of copyright eligible subject matter include printed matter, architectural or engineering drawings, circuit diagrams, lectures, musical or dramatic compositions, motion pictures, sound recordings, choreography, computer software or databases, pictorial works, sculpture, and instructional materials. Copyright now has a term of the life of the author plus 70 years, or in the case of work made for hire, 95 years from the date of first publication or 120 years from the date of creation of the work, whichever is shorter.

These lists are not exhaustive. The scope of work subject to IP claims has expanded considerably over the past thirty years, both as a matter of changes in law as well as changes in university policy. As well, the term of copyright has been extended and registration formalities removed. Thus, even where university IP policies have not changed, the range of faculty-led work subject to these policies has expanded significantly, changing and complicating the landscape for discussions of the appropriate role for institutional controls on scholarship and the responsibilities to the public of faculty authors, inventors, and entrepreneurs.

Whether ownership of a particular invention resides with the inventor, or is assigned by the inventor to an organization for management (such as a university TTO, an affiliated foundation, or an independent invention management agency), all those involved need to recognize the distinctive role played by inventions emerging from scholarly research. Faculty investigators and inventors, together with university administrators, must recognize this role and shape their policies and practices in the development and deployment of patent rights accordingly.

One fundamental principle is clear: Inventions are owned initially by their own inventors. That principle is established in both the US Constitution and federal patent law. As the US Supreme Court affirmed in its 2011 decision in *Stanford v. Roche*, federal funding of faculty-led research does not change this principle: inventors in a university setting using federal funds are also owners of their inventions. Universities as hosts of federally supported research have neither an obligation nor a mandate under federal law to take ownership of faculty inventions made in such research. Ownership of patent rights attached to an invention, however, may be transferred to another party by a written instrument signed by the inventor. Control of patent rights can be distinguished from ownership. A patent owner may contract (grant a license) to another entity to manage those patent rights on the owner's behalf. Furthermore, a patent owner's invention may include elements that are subject to the patent claims of others, and therefore the owner and any of the owner's licensees may not be able to practice the invention without a license from other patent holders. A university may become the owner of patent rights via voluntary assignment by a faculty inventor, as was the case at most universities prior to the Bayh-Dole Act of 1980.

Unfortunately, universities are increasingly making their ownership of all faculty patent rights a general condition of employment, which implies that the university controls faculty scholarship as an employer, and that faculty are expressly hired to invent. Some universities cite use of university facilities as a justification for asserting their ownership or claim that participation in externally funded research requires that the university must own the resulting IP. Though these strategies are increasingly preferred by many universities, there is little to indicate that such ownership claims advance university interests, whether taken narrowly as the pursuit of income from patent licenses or broadly in terms of the social value of research and broad access to its results.

One fundamental problem with university ownership of patent rights to faculty inventions is that it creates institutional COI between the university's governance role and its own financial and competitive interests in exploiting patented inventions. This institutional COI is particularly challenging to manage because it is easy for universities to conflate royalty income from the use or manufacture of patented inventions with their public service mission to enhance economic growth—thus failing to perceive or acknowledge the conflict that arises with other institutional responsibilities and the university's long-standing commitment to the broad dissemination of knowledge.

When faculty inventors and university administrators agree to use patents only for defensive purposes, and to allow general access to technology platforms and make them readily available for adoption, there is generally minimal institutional COI. But when an invention is used to seek financial gain by exploiting monopoly marketplace positions—as necessary as this may be at times—faculty inventors and administrators alike find themselves institutionally in a far more conflicted position. Then it may be beneficial for the university and the faculty inventor to use an external invention management agent to promote development of the underlying invention while simultaneously protecting continued use of the invention in ongoing research and education.

Despite distinctions often drawn in university policy statements, inventions are a natural outgrowth of scholarly activities, and have enjoyed a symbiotic role in faculty research for over a century. As patent law has expanded what is patentable to include software, business methods, and biological materials, results of scholarly activity have become more exposed to ownership claims based on patents. The scholarly nature of university-based inventions does not simply disappear with the addition of a potential patent or other IP rights. A patent is simply a specialized way of transmitting knowledge to society, teaching a new invention to the world in exchange for limited rights to exclude others from practice, in order to promote investment, development, and exploitation of the invention. Thus patented inventions and other discoveries subject to IP protection should properly be viewed as extensions of scholarship subject to the principles of academic freedom and faculty rights, just as are copyrights in manuscripts prepared by faculty. Patents are regularly used in industry to exclude others from using inventions. But faculty members should often be focused instead on creating conditions that give the public access to inventions, regardless of the possibility that a monopoly position might attract more payment to the university for granting an exclusive license. It is a rare university-hosted invention that absolutely must enjoy a monopoly in order to attract investment necessary to be used and developed by those learning of the invention.

Commercial development of university knowledge to stimulate economic growth and bring public benefits is unquestionably good. But some university practices associated with patenting and licensing operations may negatively affect economic growth as well as scholarship, the public interest, and the university's educational mission.[410] These include narrow exclusive licensing, speculative reselling and relicensing of patent rights, assert licensing, (in which an offer to license is preceded by a claim of possible infringement), trolling activities (in which litigation is considered the primary means to realize the value of a patent), and aggressive reach through provisions (which claim an interest—ownership or license—in inventions and other developments made with the use of a licensed invention). Other activities associated with commercialization may be consistent with scholarship and academic norms, particularly when broad access to university inventions and research is protected through fair, reasonable, nonexclusive licensing, especially where practice of the invention does not require any product to be developed, as is the case with many inventions that are methods. In any case, it is important that the university or other licensing agent make an express dedication of rights for research and experimental practice. Faculty investigators and inventors must have a strong voice in decisions involving patent management. A university administration and its faculty collectively also have an obligation to ensure that both institutional and individual interests in using patents to seek financial and logistic advantages are conducted within the context of (and remain subordinate to) the university's broader scholarly and public research missions.

Both IP contracting and licensing may be managed directly by the university or through one or more outside agents (such as a research foundation working under contract with the university, or a private invention management agency). Licensing is also regularly undertaken by inventors acting privately, as with open source software. When negotiating sponsored research agreements, a university administration and its invention management agents must address the management of IP and proprietary matter that may be provided by the sponsor, as well as the disposition of any inventions or discoveries that may arise in the course of the sponsored project (including intended deliverables, unexpected discoveries, or findings entirely unrelated to the sponsor's commercial goals).

University administrators and faculty can also make research funded by the federal government and other sources available and managed for public benefit. This might occur through broad dissemination of the research (as happened with the Cohen-Boyer gene splicing technique developed at UC San Francisco and Stanford that launched the biotechnology revolution) or through more targeted exclusive licensing, which gives one firm—say, a pharmaceutical company—monopoly rights to a discovery provided that the company invests the substantial resources required to develop the discovery into a viable new drug.

Finally, a university's nonprofit status and its reliance on public funding mean that its management agents are responsible for upholding high academic, educational, and research standards and obligations. These obligations necessarily shape the opportunities that may be considered by faculty and administrators in their choice of licensing models, invention management agents, and acceptable licensing terms and practices.

The keys to proper IP management are consultation, collaboration, and consent. That does not guarantee that invention licensing and management negotiations will be easy, but it does promote a system of checks and balances that can potentially produce better overall results. Any of the parties to such negotiations can exercise bad judgment. Faculty may have a sound understanding of the science and technology underlying their inventions but be unable to gauge their usefulness to industry or marketability. University technology transfer offices, on the other hand, may understand the legal and technical logistics but not the underlying science with its uncertainties and thus may also overstate an invention's commercial value and misjudge how to disseminate it most effectively. Each party in these negotiations (a university technology transfer office, a sponsoring company, or a faculty member) can be motivated by the narrower goal of maximizing profits and fail to consider the best interests of the public. That is one reason why faculty collectively, through their governing bodies, need to be involved in setting policy, and why Principles 11 through 13 are interdependent and equally necessary.

The dangers in having institutions or their agents exercise unilateral authority over patenting and other IP negotiations are illustrated by a cautionary tale summarized by Siddhartha Mukherjee in his 2010 book *The Emperor of all Maladies: A Biography of Cancer.* In the late 1980s, Brian Drucker, a young faculty member at Boston's Harvard-allied Dana-Farber Cancer Institute, was investigating chronic myelogenous leukemia (CML), a disease that affected only a few thousand people annually but was incurable and had only a three to five year life expectancy after diagnosis. Drucker wanted to determine whether drugs might intervene in the cancer's genetics. Ciba–Geigy scientists had synthesized a number of promising compounds now held in the firm's freezer in Basel, Switzerland. Drucker proposed a collaboration between Ciba–Geigy and the Dana-Farber Cancer Institute to test those compounds in patients but, according to Mukherjee's account, "the agreement fell apart; the legal teams in Basel and Boston could not reach agreeable terms . . . scientists and lawyers could not partner with each other to bring these drugs to patients."[411] It was not until Drucker moved to Portland's Oregon Health and Science University in 1993 that he was able to get independent authority from an academic institution to move his research forward.

One of the Ciba–Geigy compounds showed dramatic results in the lab, but because CML afflicts only a few thousand patients a year in the United States, the company questioned whether it was worth the investment. Ciba–Geigy had meanwhile fused with Sandoz to form Novartis, and eventually the new company agreed to synthesize the experimental drug—Gleevac—for patient testing. The results were dramatic: Drucker witnessed dozens of deep remissions. Today the drug is so effective that the cumulative number of surviving patients is significant: "As of 2009, CML patients treated with Gleevac are expected to survive an average of thirty years after their diagnosis . . . within the next decade, 250,000 people will be living with CML in America."[412]

As this account reminds us, faculty and administrators can fulfill an important shared governance role by collaboratively establishing the university-wide protocols that will manage faculty inventions so they simultaneously protect the best interests of the faculty, the university, and the national science and research communities, while promoting technological innovation, public health, economic development, and the public good. The AAUP recommends that faculty senates, together with their university administration, consider adoption of Principles 11–21 to ensure that academic inventions and IP management advance all these goals.

PRINCIPLE 11: Faculty Inventor Rights and IP Management

Faculty members' fundamental rights to direct and control their own research do not terminate with a new invention or research discovery; these rights properly extend to decisions about their intellectual property—including invention management, licensing, commercialization, dissemination, and public use. Faculty assignment of an invention to a management agent (including the university that hosted the underlying research) should be voluntary and negotiated rather than mandatory, unless federal statutes or previous sponsored research agreements dictate otherwise. Faculty inventors retain a vital interest in the disposition of their research inventions and discoveries and should, therefore, retain rights to negotiate the terms of their disposition. Neither the university nor its management agents should undertake intellectual property decisions or legal actions directly or indirectly affecting a faculty member's research, inventions, instruction, or public service without the faculty member's express consent. Of course, faculty members, like other campus researchers, may voluntarily undertake specific projects under "work for hire" contracts. When such agreements are truly voluntary and uncoerced, their contracted terms may legitimately narrow faculty IP rights.

- Principle 11 is designed to protect the professoriate's academic freedom rights, including the fundamental right to control academic research and instruction, which should logically encompass the faculty's right to control how their inventions are managed, licensed, commercialized, and otherwise transferred to society.

- If faculty are to have genuine control over their own research, they must not be asked to sign university employment contracts or comply with university regulations that require them to give away that control. Employment contracts or rules that make the assignment of faculty inventions to the university and its IP management agents compulsory rather than voluntary abrogate the faculty's academic freedom by compelling them to divest themselves of their property and submit to decisions that may be at odds with their professional judgment or their assessment of the public interest.

PRINCIPLE 12: Shared Governance and the Management of University Inventions

Faculty have a collective interest in how university inventions derived from academic research are managed. Through shared governance, they have a responsibility to participate in the design of university protocols that set the norms, standards, and expectations under which faculty discoveries and inventions will be controlled, distributed, licensed, and commercialized. The faculty senate or an equivalent body should play a primary role in defining the policies and public-interest commitments that will guide university-wide management of inventions and other knowledge assets stemming from campus-based research. These protocols should devote special attention to the academic and public interest obligations covered in these principles. They should also require the formation of a specially assigned faculty committee to review the university's invention management practices regularly, ensure compliance with these principles, represent the interests of faculty investigators and inventors to the campus, and make recommendations for reform when necessary.

PRINCIPLE 13: Adjudicating Disputes Involving Inventor Rights

Just as the right to control research and instruction is integral to academic freedom, so too are faculty members' rights to control the disposition of their research inventions. Inventions made in the context of university work are the result of scholarship. University policies should direct all invention management agents to represent and protect the expressed interests of faculty inventors, along with the interests of the institution and the broader public. Where the interests diverge insurmountably, the faculty senate or equivalent body should adjudicate the dispute with the aim of promoting the greatest benefit for the research in question, the broader academic community, and the public good. Student and other academic professional inventors should also have access to grievance procedures if they believe their inventor or other intellectual property rights have been violated. Students should never be urged or required to surrender their IP rights in advance to the university as a condition of participating in a degree program.

Professors in many fields report that their academic freedom was infringed upon when university technology transfer officers made managerial decisions or took legal actions that impeded their research or inhibited its use and dissemination. In 2002, the online magazine *Salon.com* reported several such cases involving professors in computing and information technology. Cynthia Gibas, for example, a bioinformatics professor at Virginia Tech, said she was concerned that her university and others were using the Bayh-Dole Act to prevent professors from contributing to open-source software projects. Steven Brenner, a computational biologist at UC Berkeley, reported that it took several months and significant legal fees to reach an agreement with his own TTO that would allow him to disseminate his software inventions on an open source basis.[413]

In June 2009, Dr. Robert Shafer, a bioinformatics and HIV expert, filed a formal grievance with Stanford University's faculty Advisory Board charging that the university's invention management/IP agents had violated his academic freedom.[414] As part of his HIV research, Shafer maintains a continually updated online database used by researchers, drug companies, and clinicians throughout the world. It tracks the latest mutations of the virus and current drug options. Doctors can enter individual patient data and obtain treatment recommendations. The database is especially vital in developing countries.

When a patent infringement dispute between Stanford and a French company, Advanced Biological Laboratory, included claims about Shafer's database, Stanford's chief counsel publicly asserted that the university, not Shafer, owned the project. Stanford then privately negotiated a settlement with ABL without notifying or involving Shafer. Shafer meanwhile argued that ABL's patent claims were spurious, and indeed ABL's patents were later invalidated. The settlement led the university to compel Shafer to place a warning on the database that, in effect, suggested that use of the resource might entail payments to ABL or spur new claims of patent infringement. Shafer argued that the warning would mislead and possibly intimidate database users and impair his own ability to fund, maintain, and operate it. ABL's claim eventually collapsed, and Shafer was able to remove the offending language from the database; meanwhile, however, he accumulated several hundred thousand dollars in legal costs defending his rights.

In April 2010, Stanford's Faculty Advisory Board ruled that the university had indeed taken IP actions that "imposed a burden" on Dr. Shafer's academic freedom rights:

> The board concluded that actions taken in connection with the agreement with ABL were not consistent with the general principles set forth in the preamble of Statement on Academic Freedom which provide that: "Stanford University's central functions of teaching, learning, research, and scholarship depend upon an atmosphere in which freedom of inquiry, thought, expression, publication and peaceable assembly are given the fullest protection. Expression of the widest range of viewpoints should be encouraged, free from institutional orthodoxy and from internal or external coercion." The board concluded it was a mistake to enter into the binding agreement with ABL without consulting Professor Shafer and expressed deep concerns about some of the subsequent actions taken by the university to comply with the binding agreement. The board concluded that these actions were inconsistent with the general principles of academic freedom.[415]

Despite the Advisory Board ruling and a strong letter condemning the university's actions from the AAUP, Stanford has made no offer to assist Shafer with his legal costs.

PRINCIPLE 14: IP Management and Sponsored Research Agreements

In negotiating sponsored research agreements, university administrators should make every effort to inform potentially affected faculty researchers and to involve them meaningfully in early-stage negotiations concerning invention management and intellectual property. In the case of large-scale sponsored research agreements like strategic corporate alliances (SCAs), which can affect large numbers of faculty, not all of whom may be identifiable in advance, a special faculty governance committee should be convened to participate in early-stage negotiations, represent collective faculty interests, and ensure compliance with relevant university protocols. Faculty participation in all institutionally negotiated sponsored research agreements should always be voluntary.

PRINCIPLE 15: Humanitarian Licensing—Access to Medicines

When lifesaving drugs and other critical public health technologies are developed in academic laboratories with public funding support, universities have a special obligation to license such inventions so as to ensure broad public access in both the developing and the industrialized world. Exclusive university licenses to companies for breakthrough drugs or other critical public good inventions arising in agriculture, health, environmental safety, or other fields should include humanitarian licensing provisions that will enable distribution of drugs and other inventions in developing countries at affordable prices whenever feasible.

- Humanitarian licensing has been endorsed by the Association of University Technology Managers (AUTM), the Association of American Medical Colleges (AAMC), and fifty universities in a consensus statement titled, "In the Public Interest: Nine Points to Consider in Licensing University Technology." The document urges universities to address developing nations' needs for lifesaving medicines and other critical technologies:

  > **Point 9:** Consider including provisions that address unmet needs, such as those of neglected patient populations or geographic areas, giving particular attention to improved therapeutics, diagnostics and agricultural technologies for the developing world.[416]

- If a university includes a humanitarian licensing provision in a contract with a commercial entity, it usually has little impact on company profits, since most companies see no viable commercial markets for their products in low-income developing countries. But the effect of a humanitarian license is huge, because it makes it possible for generic manufacturers, nonprofits, and international and government agencies to find innovative ways of producing drugs or products at substantially discounted prices. That broadens access, potentially saving millions of lives.

- In 2009, AUTM and its university members further elaborated on this critical public health goal in their "Statement of Principles and Strategies for the Equitable Dissemination of Medical Technologies" (SPS),[417] endorsed by many universities as well as the NIH and the CDC.

In a detailed 2011 analysis of patenting, citation, and other data, Frank Lichtenberg (Columbia Business School) and Bhaven Sampat (Columbia University Mailman School of Public Health) examined both the direct and indirect role of government in funding new drug development. They found that government-funded research, much of it performed at US universities, played a powerful indirect role (i.e., generating the underlying basic research required) in developing almost half the drugs approved by the FDA between 1988 and 2005 and close to two-thirds of the drugs deemed most innovative (using the FDA's definition).[418]

Universities currently hold key patent rights on drugs to treat HIV/ AIDS, cancer, hepatitis B, and other major diseases. Stavudine (sold under the brand name Zerit)—a critical drug in the treatment of HIV/AIDS—was originally developed at Yale University; it later became the centerpiece of a major student-led, human-rights campaign to broaden access to medicines in developing countries.[419] Many drug compounds licensed by universities nonetheless remain largely out of reach for millions of patients in the developing world.[420] The practice of including humanitarian licensing rights in the contracts universities sign needs to become routine.

The federal Uniform Administrative Requirements for Grants and Contracts with Institutions of Higher Education, Hospitals, and Other Non-Profit Organizations (2 CFR 215) require universities to act as a trustee for the beneficiaries of the project or program under which property was acquired or improved. As a trustee, a university may consider dedicating its share of the proceeds from licensing to advance the welfare of patients affected by the disorder the invention is intended to treat.[421]

PRINCIPLE 16: Securing Broad Research Use and Distribution Rights

All contracts and agreements covering university-generated inventions should include an express reservation of rights—often known as a "research exemption"—to allow for academic, nonprofit, and government use of academic inventions and associated IP for non-commercial research purposes. Research exemptions should be reserved and well publicized prior to assignment or licensing so faculty and other academic researchers can share protected inventions and research results (including related data, reagents, and research tools) with colleagues at the host university or at any nonprofit or government institution. The freedom to share and practice academic discoveries—whether legally protected or not—for educational and research purposes is vital for the advancement of knowledge. It also enables investigators to replicate and verify published results, a practice essential to scientific integrity.

- Protecting this "research use exemption" is important for the verification and replication of research results. Without this check on the accuracy of published research, the university's ability to advance reliable public knowledge is dangerously impeded.

- University-issued research use exemptions should cover three distinct categories of research: "Evaluation of," which refers to the practice (use) of an invention or research tool to evaluate the claims made and replicate the procedures used in published findings; "Research on," which covers efforts to study how the invention or tools work and make improvements or modifications; and "Research with," which covers the use of such inventions/tools in conducting one's own research, which may involve similar or entirely different subjects and uses from the ones under which the invention was created.

- A similar recommendation to endorse these principles for research use exemption has been endorsed by more than fifty universities (as well as the AAMC and AUTM) in the 2007 consensus statement "In the Public Interest: Nine Points to Consider in Licensing University Technology."[422] This provision reads as follows:

> **Point 1:** Universities should reserve the right to practice licensed inventions and to allow other non-profit and governmental organizations to do so. In the spirit of preserving the ability of all universities to perform research, ensuring that researchers are able to publish the results of their research in dissertations and peer-reviewed journals and that other scholars are able to verify published results without concern for patents, universities should consider reserving rights in all fields of use, even if the invention is licensed exclusively to a commercial entity, for themselves and other non-profit and governmental organizations:
>
> > • to practice inventions and to use associated information and data for research and educational purposes, including research sponsored by commercial entities; and
> >
> > • to transfer tangible research materials (e.g., biological materials and chemical compounds) and intangible materials (e.g.,

computer software, databases and know-how) to others in the non-profit and governmental sectors.

Unfortunately, these academic research and use exemptions have not been widely utilized, even by universities that were the original signatories to this Nine Points statement. Faculty members and their governing bodies can thus play a critical role in developing such polices and assuring their implementation.[423]

After the 2002 US Supreme Court decision in *John M. F. Madey v. Duke University,* university and government researchers could no longer take it for granted that they would automatically enjoy a "research or experimental use exemption" allowing use of patented inventions for academic and research purposes without threat of a lawsuit.[424] This ruling put universities, nonprofits, and government agencies on notice that a patent ownership position could now place their researchers and their institutions at risk of an infringement action if they practiced a claimed invention. Universities and their faculty must reaffirm and secure these research exemption rights by requiring all sponsored research agreements and IP management contracts to include this exemption from infringement suits. Since universities themselves over the last several decades have vastly expanded their own IP claims, it is incumbent on them to protect knowledge sharing to the greatest extent possible.

PRINCIPLE 17: Exclusive and Nonexclusive Licensing

Universities, their contracted management agents, and faculty should avoid exclusive licensing of patentable inventions, unless such licenses are absolutely necessary to foster follow-on use or to develop an invention that would otherwise languish. Exclusive or monopolistic control of academic knowledge should be sparing, rather than a presumptive default. When exclusive licenses are granted, they should have limited terms (preferably less than eight years), include requirements that the inventions be developed, and prohibit "assert licensing" or "trolling" (aggressively enforcing patents against an alleged infringer, often with no intention of manufacturing, marketing, or making productive use of the product). Exclusive licenses issued in order to permit broad access through reasonable and nondiscriminatory sublicensing, cross-licensing, and dedication of patents to an open standard may be expected to meet public access expectations. However, the preferred methods for disseminating university research are nonexclusive licensing and open dissemination, to protect universities' public interest mission, open research culture, and commitment to advancing research and inquiry through broad knowledge sharing. To enhance compliance and public accountability, universities should require all invention management agents to promptly and publicly report any exclusive licenses issued, together with written statements detailing why an exclusive license was necessary and why a nonexclusive one would not suffice. The faculty senate or comparable governing body should periodically review exclusive licenses and corresponding statements for consistency with this principle.

- A comparable recommendation, favoring nonexclusive licensing, is contained in a 2011 NAS committee report addressing the management of university IP, which reads as follows:

  Universities should pursue patenting and licensing practices that, to the greatest extent practicable, maximize the further development, use, and beneficial social impact of their technologies. Exclusive licenses generally should be reserved for technologies that require significant follow-on investment to achieve commercialization, or where exclusivity is needed to confer a competitive advantage (so-called rival-in-use technologies). For technologies that are not rival-in-use or require little or no follow-on investment, nonexclusive licenses are generally warranted.[425]

- The AAMC, AUTM, and over fifty universities have endorsed the warning against an overreliance on exclusive licensing in the Nine Points statement (discussed above):

  When significant investment of time and resources in a technology are needed in order to achieve its broad implementation, an exclusive license often is necessary and appropriate. However, it is important that technology transfer offices be aware of the potential impact that the exclusive license might have on further research, unanticipated uses, future commercialization efforts and markets. Universities need to be mindful of the impact of granting overly broad exclusive rights and should strive to grant just those rights necessary to encourage development of the technology.[426]

PRINCIPLE 18: Upfront Exclusive Licensing Rights for Research Sponsors

Universities should refrain from signing sponsored research agreements, especially multi-year strategic corporate alliance (SCA) agreements, that grant sponsors broad title or exclusive commercial rights to future sponsored research inventions and discoveries—unless such arrangements are narrowly defined and agreed to by all faculty participating in, or foreseeably affected by, the alliance. If this is not feasible, as in the case of larger SCAs, the faculty senate should review and approve the agreement and confirm its compatibility with academic freedom, faculty independence, and the university's public interest mission. All parties should consider the impact exclusive licenses could have on future uses of technologies. When granted, exclusive rights should be defined as narrowly as possible, restricted to targeted fields of use, and designed to safeguard against abuse of the exclusive position.

- Similar recommendations are contained in the Cornell University faculty senate statement on large-scale strategic corporate alliances.[427] Those points are also affirmed in the Nine Points referenced earlier:[428]

  > Special consideration should be given to the impact of an exclusive license on uses of a technology that may not be appreciated at the time of initial licensing. A license grant that encompasses all fields of use for the life of the licensed patent(s) may have negative consequences if the subject technology is found to have unanticipated utility. This possibility is particularly troublesome if the licensee is not able or willing to develop the technology in fields outside of its core business. Universities are encouraged to use approaches that balance a licensee's legitimate commercial needs against the university's goal (based on its educational and charitable mission and the public interest) of ensuring broad practical application of the fruits of its research programs. There are many alternatives to strict exclusive licensing, several of which are described in the Appendix.

- Principle 18 is also consistent with the objectives of the Bayh–Dole Act (35 USC 200), which expects universities and other nonprofit organizations to use inventions to promote free competition and enterprise.

- Agreements involving title or exclusive rights must further conform to applicable tax laws regarding private use of facilities constructed with tax-free bonds.[429]

PRINCIPLE 19: Research Tools and Upstream Platform Research

Universities and their contracted invention management agents should make available and broadly disseminate research tools and other upstream platform inventions in which they have acquired an ownership interest. They should avoid assessing fees, beyond those necessary to cover the costs of maintaining the tools and disseminating them, and avoid other constraints that could hamper downstream research and development. No sponsored research agreement should include contractual obligations that prevent outside investigators from accessing data, tools, inventions, and reports relating to scholarly reviews of published research, matters of public health and safety, environmental safety, and urgent public policy decisions.

- In December 1999, NIH issued guidelines covering research tools developed in whole, or in part, with federal funding, which are consistent with this principle. The NIH guidelines discourage the patenting of research tools and urge that they be licensed with as few encumbrances and as broadly as possible.[430] NIH thus cautions against the use of commercially aggressive reach-through rights, a legal provision that enables a university to claim royalties for any future product developed through use of its research tools. NIH also discourages use of restrictive material transfer agreements (MTAs) for the exchange of basic research materials, which can slow the pace of research progress and significantly raise its cost.

- The Nine Points statement referenced above recommends as follows:

  > Consistent with the NIH Guidelines on Research Tools, principles set forth by various charitable foundations that sponsor academic research programs and by the mission of the typical university to advance scientific research, universities are expected to make research tools as broadly available as possible . . . . Through a blend of field-exclusive and non-exclusive licenses, research tools may be licensed appropriately, depending on the resources needed to develop each particular invention, the licensee's needs and the public good.[431]

- The goals articulated in Principle 19 are also consistent with the Bayh-Dole Act, which warns against use of patent rights that unduly encumber future research and discovery, and with the federal Uniform Administrative Requirements for Grants and Contracts with Institutions of Higher

Education, Hospitals, and Other Non-Profit Organizations (2 CFR 215), which requires universities to act as a trustee for the beneficiaries of the project or program under which the intangible property was acquired or improved (2 CFR 215.37) and also requires public access to research data relating to published research findings produced under a federal award that were used in certain federal agency rule-making (2 CFR 215.36(d)).[432]

Access to publicly funded research tools has become one of the more contentious areas of university IP management. At issue is whether these tools should be exclusively licensed to one company (often a faculty start-up firm), or licensed nonexclusively, so they can be utilized more broadly in a variety of applications, or not be subject to IP ownership claims at all. Research tools are also sometimes withheld by faculty investigators or administrators to advance their competitive position, perhaps in anticipation of future grant funding.

Many academic researchers, of course, still choose to share and distribute new research tools freely, including software, laboratory reagents, and animal disease models. Yet because many universities are now more focused on patenting, licensing, and revenue generation, research tools and other basic platform inventions often become tied up by IP considerations that prioritize financial benefits to the university.

Critics in academia, government, and industry contend these restrictions on tool sharing not only lead researchers to forgo otherwise promising lines of research, but also hamper the evaluation and replication of published research claims.[433] Yet research tools can be highly complex entities that require significant follow-on research to develop. As the University-Industry Research Collaboration Initiative, a project of the Business Higher Education Forum, explained in a 2002 report: "At the heart of the research-tool problem . . . is the fact that one person's research tool can be another person's key strategic product. Tool developers, which often later emerge as biotechnology firms, claim that without exclusive licenses, they cannot secure venture capital funding, thus stifling innovation."[434]

Nonetheless, many experts on innovation, along with companies in the information technology sector and other industries, complain that increasingly restrictive university IP practices undermine the open academic research culture and dangerously inhibit broader commercial use and development of academic research.[435] Some of the most lucrative revenue-generating patents licensed by universities notably have involved research tools; thus it may be expected that university administrators and some faculty inventors will balk at fully implementing Principle 19. Yet most of these famous "big hit" university licenses, including the Cohen-Boyer,[436] Axel,[437] and Hall[438] inventions, also involved the use of nonexclusive licenses which generally safeguarded broad access and use.

PRINCIPLE 20: Diverse Licensing Models for Diverse University Inventions

Universities and their invention management agents should develop multiple licensing models appropriate to diverse categories of academic inventions, differing objectives and commitments made by faculty investigators and inventors, varying practices in the wider community and in different industries, and varied conditions present at different stages in developing a technology. Licensing models commonly used to address opportunities in biotechnology, for example, should not be established as defaults in institutional policies or used indiscriminately across other areas of innovation. Faculty investigators and inventors and their management agents should work cooperatively to identify effective licensing and distribution models for each invention to enhance public availability and use. This may include established models (exclusive or nonexclusive licensing) as well as emergent ones (patent pools, open sourcing, and public licensing offered by institutions like Creative Commons for copyright-based work).

- To cite but one illustration of this problem, there is robust evidence that exclusive licensing plays a more limited role in the development and commercialization of information technology than it does in certain pharmaceutical and biotechnology sectors, though according to experts many universities fail to draw adequate distinctions.[439] In August 2000, the Office of the President of the UC system recognized this fact when it announced a program to exempt Computer Science as well as Electrical and Computer Engineering IP from the standard UC system-wide licensing policies and authorized giving licensing officers greater flexibility when licensing IT discoveries. The President's Engineering Advisory Council reviewed the matter:

  [T]he rapid rate of technological change in the engineering fields of electronics, communications technology, [and] computer hardware and software results in new products with a typical lifetime of a few years or less. Competitive success rarely is based upon the statutory protection of intellectual property as requirements for conformance with industry wide standards reduce the value of proprietary technology. Rapid product development and early market entry with innovative products are the keys to market leadership and successful products.[440]

PRINCIPLE 21: Rights to "Background Intellectual Property" (BIP)

University administrators and their agents should not act unilaterally when granting sponsors' rights to university-managed background intellectual property (BIP) related to a sponsor's proposed research area but developed without the sponsor's funding support. Universities should be mindful of how BIP rights will affect faculty inventors and other investigators who are not party to the sponsored research agreement. Nor should managers obligate the BIP of one set of investigators to another's sponsored research project, unless that BIP is already being made available under nonexclusive licensing terms or the affected faculty members have consented. To do otherwise risks a chilling effect on collegiality and on faculty willingness to work with university licensing agents.

- This recommendation draws on the "Background Rights" section of *Working Together, Creating Knowledge: The University-Industry Research Collaboration Initiative,* a report based on a two-year study of academy-industry partnerships published by the Business-Higher Education Forum in 2001.[441] The Research Collaboration Initiative's members included 37 university presidents, senior officers at major corporations, and heads of business and educational associations.

"Background rights" are the licensing rights that universities may provide to an industry sponsor to cover "background intellectual property" (BIP) related to a proposed research project the sponsor plans to undertake. By definition, BIP consists of research inventions created by university employees outside the current project, using funding from other sources, often including federal government funds. Companies often seek BIP rights before signing a contract, so as to complete their IP portfolios and secure all the licensing rights they anticipate needing to commercialize the results of their sponsored research.

Yet universities face numerous problems in offering them. Many faculty members feel strongly that IP belonging to one faculty member should not be mortgaged for the benefit of another or be leveraged to help the institution secure research funding. Merely identifying IP that might be relevant is both time-consuming and expensive. Agreements on BIP rights usually say that the parties will make a "good faith effort" or use "reasonable efforts to disclose in the field of use" in order to identify potential background conflicts. These are legal terms whose interpretation will require counsel; the university could be liable for any oversight. "The only way you should even begin down that path [of offering BIP rights] is to have a full-blown infringement opinion done looking at your entire portfolio within a certain area of technology," noted NC State's W. Mark Crowell in an interview for the Research Collaboration Initiative, and "if anybody here has ever paid the cost to have an infringement opinion done, you're talking about a pretty scary proposition."[442] There are thus multiple reasons for universities to be cautious about signing binding BIP rights agreements.

Moreover, providing background rights to an outside sponsor, even to license technology at commercially reasonable rates, can complicate or limit academic researchers' ability to pursue their own lines of inquiry; it can also limit the university's ability to license related technology inventions to another firm. This can affect the university's ability to attract future sponsored research support, and it can complicate incentives for start-up companies to participate in regional economic development plans involving the university. According to the Research Collaboration Initiative, requests to provide background rights began with research consortia alliances such as the Semiconductor Research Corporation (SRC/SEMATECH), a government-industry manufacturing technology collaboration in the semiconductor industry, and the Electric Power Research Institute (EPRI). These agreements require the university to license back to the consortia any background rights deemed necessary on a nonexclusive basis. There is growing demand from companies, particularly in information technology, for background rights to the university research they sponsor."[443]

In 2007, the British-based oil giant BP successfully secured BIP rights for the Energy Biosciences Institute (EBI), the ten-year, $500-million research collaboration with UC Berkeley and two other public institutions.[444] According to a UC Berkeley faculty senate committee, the BIP terms were extensive and unusual, though they did include a positive effort to obtain informed consent by faculty inventors and other personnel:

> The usual practice . . . has been to defer such negotiations about BIP to subsequent licensing negotiations. This contract, however, contains a general provision (App. 2, Sec. 8.12), which permits BP's right to license the BIP related to a discovery developed in a specific funded project in the EBI. Any such BIP has to have been included in a list prepared by the Project Investigator in advance in

the application for funding. . . . In addition, all participants in an EBI project must agree to these BIP provisions as a condition of funding . . . . The issue came up only in the contract negotiations, and both we and the administration would have preferred to treat BIP in the standard manner, relegating the issue to subsequent licensing negotiations. The resulting position reflects a compromise between UC and BP.[445]

Part IV.
General Principles for Management of Conflicts of Interest (COI) and Financial Conflicts of Interest (FCOI) (22–31)

We have already discussed conflicts of interest at many points in this book, most thoroughly in "A Brief History of Efforts to Address Financial Conflicts of Interest at US Universities and Academic Medical Centers" under Risk 5 in the Introduction. This section will necessarily repeat some points in order to emphasize the reasons why COI and FCOI remain among the most serious threats to the freedom, autonomy, and integrity of academic work, and to the public's support for and confidence in that work. They also remain among the most challenging problems on university campuses: and never more so than in the context of expanding academy-industry collaborations. It is also important to keep in mind that research misconduct—such as intentionally falsifying or distorting data—is a separate issue, and universities and the federal government have established separate regulations and procedures to investigate misconduct charges and to punish proven misconduct.

As we point out, a growing body of empirical research shows that COI are associated with decision-making and research bias. COI tend to introduce unreliability into the research process, undermine public trust, and erode respect for universities. COI also undercut a university's ability to perform research and teaching free of the influence of special interest groups. Disclosure of a COI, even full disclosure with informed consent, does not resolve these problems. Disclosure is an important mechanism for addressing FCOI related to academic research, but simply disclosing such conflicts is not sufficient to instill public confidence or protect the integrity of academic scholarship. Experience has clearly shown that, just as COI disclosure is inadequate, so too are policies that rely heavily, or even exclusively, on case-by-case management of individual faculty and institutional COI.

As early as 1965, in "On Preventing Conflicts of Interest in Government-Sponsored Research at Universities," the AAUP and ACE pressed for "the formulation of standards to guide the individual university staff members in governing their conduct in relation to outside interests that might raise questions of conflicts of interest."[446] Now the AAUP is returning to this issue in the context of heightened academy-industry engagement in order to provide a set of COI principles that can be adopted campuswide. The goal of these COI principles should be to encourage research integrity and the practice of objective science; preserve an institutional environment committed to openness and trust; guard against unintentional bias and error; and punish misbehavior when it is uncovered.

Starting in 2000, many professional and academic groups took note of rising commercial engagement and issued a series of consensus statements calling for stronger, more comprehensive university and academic medical center FCOI policies. The AAUP agrees with the consensus reached by numerous professional groups—including the AAU, IOM, AAMC, and, most recently, DHHS/NIH, which issued a new set of COI rules in August 2011—that the purpose of these COI regulations is to be preventative.[447] As the DHHS/NIH explains, COI rules are "intended to be proactive rather than reactive to specific evidence of bias."[448] Rather than trying to remedy possible bias or respond to damage after it has occurred or has been unearthed by the media, COI rules are needed to reduce the risk of bias and the loss of credibility that may be associated with the mere existence of these financial conflicts.

In 2009, an IOM panel on COI in biomedicine observed that "a range of supporting organizations—public and private—can promote the adoption and implementation of conflict of interest policies and help create a culture of accountability that sustains professional norms and public confidence in professional judgments."[449] The AAUP thus adds its own voice to the chorus of those calling for universities to strengthen and harmonize their COI policies. If universities do not voluntarily implement more rigorous, comprehensive, and uniform COI policies and procedures, then pressure for external regulation is likely to grow more strenuous.

The AAUP wholeheartedly agrees with the AAU's assessment that university COI policies need to be comprehensive, and must cover research "across all academic fields, not just biomedical ones."[450] This recommendation for comprehensive, campuswide COI policies has been endorsed by the AAU-AAMC (2008)[451] and by an IOM panel (2009).[452] The AAUP further agrees with the emerging consensus that these policies must encompass both individual faculty as well as institutional COI. This recommendation, too, has been explicitly endorsed by the AAU (2001); AAMC (2002); AAU-AAMC 2008;[453] COGR (2003); DHHS (2004);[454] NIH, OIG;[455] and the IOM (2009).[456]

Finally, the AAUP agrees with the AAU and others that university COI policies should "treat research consistently, regardless of the funding source—All research projects at an institution, whether federally funded, funded by a non-federal entity, or funded by the institution itself, should be managed by the same conflict of interest process."[457] Again, this is consistent with recommendations issued by the AAU-AAMC (2008)[458] and with the COI rules issued by the DHHS (2011), which require university faculty to report FCOI related to all of their "institutional responsibilities," not only their DHHS-funded research.[459] The rationale for implementing a comprehensive COI policy is clear: monitoring FCOI across the entire institution, regardless of funding source, ensures that all conflicts will be identified and handled similarly, instead of having effective procedures in place to handle some COI, while others go unidentified and potentially do serious damage.

In 2001, the AAU's Task Force on Research Accountability called on all universities to redouble their efforts to implement comprehensive COI policies:

> [A]lthough definitive data about the prevalence of conflicts of interest is lacking, academy-industry relationships are clearly increasing, and with them, the risk of conflicts of interest compromising the integrity of research conducted in academia continues to rise. Journal articles make clear that the stringency of financial conflict of interest polices varies substantially among institutions, as does the diligence of enforcement . . . [S]ince the risk to the integrity of the academic enterprise from individual conflicts of interest is substantial, research universities should re-double their efforts to ensure objectivity in research.[460]

Repeated rounds of Congressional and other federal investigations have served to expose how inadequate management of FCOI can compromise public confidence in the academy.[461] Yet most US universities have been slow to heed calls from Congress, federal agencies, and a range of professional associations to strengthen their FCOI policies and procedures.[462] As the Introduction details, we have since amassed far more evidence, especially in biomedicine, of the prevalence and consequences of FCOI. While areas of research outside biomedicine have received less scrutiny, there is no reason to expect that biomedicine is unique (witness industry influence in areas ranging from tobacco research and agriculture to economics). The operating assumption should be that such problems exist in all fields where financial temptation exists, thus requiring appropriate preventative safeguards.

As we reported earlier, DHHS issued good new FCOI disclosure rules in 2011 but once again failed to provide guidance on how to carry them out. The 2009 IOM panel's warning that "variation in conflict of interest policies may encourage an unhealthy competition among institutions to adopt weak policies and shirk enforcement."[463] Thus the AAUP is now urging all universities and their faculty to review their COI policies and bring them into compliance with the recommendations offered here, nearly all of which are drawn from recommendations issued by the AAU, AAMC, IOM, COGR, and most recently DHHS/NIH. The 2011 DHHS/NIH rules make this reexamination of university COI policies both timely and necessary.

PRINCIPLE 22: Comprehensive COI Policies

Every university should have a comprehensive, written COI policy, covering both individual and institutional COI. The policy or its accompanying guidelines should specify how all conflicts of interest (COI) and financial conflicts of interest (FCOI), in particular, will be reported, reviewed, managed, or eliminated. The guidelines should identify which FCOI must be reported, which are prohibited, and what actions will be taken if faculty members do not comply with COI disclosure and management policies. Enforcement actions for noncompliance may include a faculty-led investigation leading to possible censure, federal-grant agency notification, a temporary hold on interactions with conflicted sponsors, or a temporary ban on receipt of outside research funding.

Below are concise definitions of types of COI adapted from the IOM, from the AAU's Task Force on Research Accountability, and from the AAMC and the AAU. A proven FCOI is a function of a set of factual circumstances that identify a problem, not a function of whether someone is actually biased; COI are either present or they are not. Thus, a FCOI should not be termed "potential" because this implies that the COI only exists as a future possibility, which diminishes both its present risk and its significance:

General Definition of a COI

A conflict of interest is a set of circumstances that creates a risk that professional judgment or actions regarding a primary interest will be unduly influenced by a secondary interest.[464]

Two Definitions of an Individual FCOI

An individual FCOI describes a situation in which financial considerations may compromise or appear to compromise an investigator's professional judgment in conducting, interpreting, or reporting research. Such FCOI may also influence the hiring of staff, procurement of materials, sharing of results, involvement of human participants, and choice of protocols and statistical methods.

An individual FCOI is a set of circumstances that reasonable observers would believe creates an undue risk that an individual's judgment or actions regarding a primary interest of the university will be inappropriately influenced by a secondary financial interest.[465]

Definition of an Institutional COI

An institutional COI describes a situation in which the financial interests of an institution or an official acting on behalf of the institution may compromise or appear to compromise research, education, clinical care, business transactions, or other institutional activities. Institutional COIs are significant when financial interests create the possibility of exerting inappropriate influence over the institution's activities. The risks are particularly acute in the context of human subjects research, when the protection of human subjects may be threatened.[466]

A Checklist of What Comprehensive COI Policies Should Contain

Each campus's comprehensive COI policy should include the following elements (adapted from the AAMC, 2001 and AAU, 2001):[467]

- Clear procedures for gathering FCOI information from faculty, senior officials, and university departments. (For details on how comprehensive university-wide COI reporting should be carried out, see Principle 26, "Inter-office Reporting and Tracking of Institutional COI");

- COI disclosure forms that are standardized, easy to use, and preferably electronic; electronic forms facilitate operation of an integrated university-wide COI management system;

- Required annual FCOI reporting, with updating whenever financial interests change. Requirement of thorough reporting by all covered individuals. Failure to report is unacceptable; when people are in doubt about a situation, they should report;

- Clear procedures should be in place to verify the accuracy of reported COI information. (The 2009 federal "Physician Payment Sunshine Act"[468] and various state laws[469] now mandate that pharmaceutical and other medical companies disclose their gifts and other financial payments to physicians, thus facilitating verification of medical faculty self-reporting);[470]

- Clear explanation of how FCOI will be reviewed, reduced, eliminated, or managed;

- Faculty disclosure forms that include questions (connected with grant applications) about whether students are working on research projects that may involve FCOI;

- Clear de minimis reporting requirements, preferably $5,000, the same threshold required by the 2011 DHHS-NIH COI rule;

- Clear indication of how personal financial information will be handled internally and how confidentiality will be maintained until COI have been confirmed, an opportunity to eliminate them provided, and management plans to handle remaining ones devised;

- Clear procedures for sharing FCOI information and conflict-management information, as needed, with relevant internal offices and constituencies;

- Policies for disclosure of reported information to academic journals and the public;

- Clear time frame for required disclosure of confirmed COI to the university and to the public;

- Articulation of how COI management decisions and disputes will be adjudicated, implemented, and enforced by the university's standing COI committee;

- Articulation of how the appeals process will work and how due process will be ensured;

- Clear mechanisms to ensure compliance with COI policies and punish noncompliance.

The policy should enumerate the list of internal offices, COI committees, and affected parties who should see certain COI and FCOI information.

These would include IRBs, sponsored research offices, and TTOs; and for affected parties—research volunteers, patients, COI management staff, department chairs, deans, patients, students, and research colleagues, using safeguards to maintain the privacy of the information until it has been reviewed by the university's standing COI Committee for internal management. The policy should also detail where, when, and in what form this information may be released to patients, colleagues, and the public. Under the 2011 DHHS-NIH COI rules, universities are required to disclose all significant FCOI related to DHHS funded research on a public website, or respond to any public request within five days. To promote transparency, the AAUP, under Principle 31, recommends that faculty COI disclosure statements be posted on a readily accessible and regularly updated public website immediately after internal reviews are complete. According to the IOM (2009), some COI disclosure policies ask about relationships that are pending, in negotiation, or expected in the next 12 months. Some organizations also require disclosure for longer periods of time: for example, the American Thoracic Society requires disclosure for the previous three years, and *JAMA* requires disclosure for the previous five years.[471]

Managing institutional COI involves somewhat different issues. An institutional COI may arise when a university is conducting research on campus that could affect the value of that institution's own patents or its equity positions or options in the same company. An institutional COI may also arise if a senior official, say a department chair or dean, has a major equity holding in a medical device company, which could bias that person's decisions (about faculty appointments and promotions, assignment of office or laboratory space, or other administration matters) to favor that company's interests. It may arise again when a hospital official who selects a company's products for patient care has a personal financial interest in the manufacturer of those products. In situations such as these, secondary financial interests may bias the conduct of research or distort administrative decisions that affect the university's educational, research, and public health missions. Such institutional FCOI can erode public trust in the university or faculty trust in the fairness and impartiality of the institution's internal decision making systems. Because institutional conflicts of interest strike at the heart of the university's integrity, they must be addressed. As the AAMC and AAU wrote in a joint 2008 report on FCOI:

> Beyond compliance with policies and procedures, institutional officials must foster what has been described as a "culture of conscience" in the research enterprise. Exercising their authority within the institution, officials should insist upon rigorous enforcement of

conflict-of-interest policies. Leading by personal example, officers and administrators should demonstrate to the academic community and to the public that compliance with these policies, including full disclosure of financial conflicts of interest, is an imperative reflecting core institutional values.[472]

Of course some external relationships that may give rise to an institutional COI can also generate significant financial benefits for a university. Thus gifts to endow new professorships or fund construction of a new laboratory provide support for teaching and research at the same time as they can entail compromising relationships. As a 2009 IOM panel noted: "The question for institutions as well as individuals is whether a relationship with industry can be maintained in a way that achieves the desired benefits but avoids the risks of undue influence on decision making and the loss of public trust."[473] If strong COI policies are effectively implemented, the answer to this question is more likely to be affirmative.

PRINCIPLE 23: Consistent COI Enforcement across Campus

University COI policies must be adopted consistently across the whole institution, including affiliated medical schools, hospitals, institutes, centers, and other facilities, and they must apply to faculty, students, administrators, and academic professionals.

This recommendation is drawn from both the AAU and AAMC (2008).[474]

PRINCIPLE 24: Standing COI Committees

Every university should have one or two standing COI committees to oversee implementation of policies addressing individual and institutional COI. At least one member should be recruited from outside the institution and approved by the faculty governing body. All committee members should be free of COI related to their oversight responsibilities. After faculty COI disclosure statements have been reviewed by an appropriate standing committee, they should be made available to the public, preferably on a readily accessible online database, as the AAUP recommends under Principle 31.

This principle is drawn from recommendations issued by the Institute of Medicine (IOM, 2009) and other professional groups.[475]

- The goal of standing COI committee(s) is to bring university-wide experience, professionalism, fairness, and consistency to COI oversight.[476]

- These committee(s) should seek members who know the types and distribution of COI cases occurring in different colleges across campus.[477]

- As the IOM (2009) recommends, final responsibility for oversight of institutional COI should be lodged with an institution's governing body. But when a senior administrator receives significant income from outside corporations doing business with the institution (such as when a university president earns significant income from compensation for serving on a corporate board), a board of trustees dominated by business executives may itself risk an appearance of a conflict when evaluating whether the FCOI is serious. Organizing of a special standing faculty COI oversight committee to review administrators' consulting activities is a possible corrective.

- If the standing faculty COI oversight committee itself appears to have a related COI, then the faculty senate might seek review by an extramural committee consisting of faculty and administrators from other schools not directly involved in the matter at issue.

A 2009 IOM panel observed that managing institutional COI may, in many respects, be more challenging than managing individual COI. The panel wrote that "In the case of individual conflicts in large institutions such as universities, medical schools, and major teaching hospitals, opportunities for review usually exist at multiple levels of the institution and involve authorities who are relatively independent and do not stand to gain personally from the secondary interests in question." In contrast, the IOM panel noted, an objective or impartial review "for institutional conflicts of interest may be difficult because the institutional officers themselves may stand to benefit indirectly from the COI and may be reluctant to question current or potential relationships with companies that seem likely to improve the institution's financial welfare. . . . Because the potential financial gain from a secondary institution-level interest may not be personal for institutional officials, their decisions may be more easily rationalized as serving the institution rather than themselves—even when officials also stand to gain in personal reputation."[478]

Because of the challenges in managing institutional COI, the AAUP recommends that universities consider lodging final responsibility for oversight of institutional COI with a standing faculty COI committee capable of impartially reviewing administrative level consulting activities, with one or more independent members—not affiliated with the institution—to foster greater credibility and impartiality.

PRINCIPLE 25: Reporting Individual COI

Faculty members and academic professionals should be required to report to the standing campus COI committee all significant outside financial interests relating directly or indirectly to their professional responsibilities (research, teaching, committee work, and other activities), including the dollar amounts involved and the nature of the services compensated. The report must be made regardless of whether or not people believe their financial interests might reasonably affect their current or anticipated university activities. Faculty members should also report family member (spouse, partner, or dependent child) patent royalty income and equity holdings related to their own teaching and research areas. All administrators should report similar financial interests to both their superiors and the COI committee. Presidents and chancellors should also report to the standing committee.

- This recommendation is adapted from one issued jointly by the AAU and AAMC in 2008.[479] It is also in line with 2011 COI rules issued by DHHS-NIH expanding the definition of what financial relationships investigators must report to the university. The new rules state that grant recipients must report not just how their financial interests in a company or other entity might affect a particular federal project or grant, but how they might affect all their other "institutional responsibilities," including research, consulting, teaching, and membership on university committees—a change designed, in the words of DHHS, to "provide institutions with a better understanding of the totality of an investigator's interests."[480]

- Under this DHHS-NIH rule, universities must now determine which financial interests constitute a COI that could compromise the objectivity and integrity of DHHS-NIH-funded research and how these conflicts will be reduced, eliminated, or managed. The new rules also require the university to draw up a written COI Management Plan for submission to the federal grant agency, and the plan must be publicly accessible.

The AAUP recommends that the following types of financial relationships be disclosed to the university for internal review by a standing COI committee and made public:

Recommended List of Financial Ties to Be Disclosed to the University

- Research grants and contracts

- Consulting agreements valued at or above $5,000

- Participation in "speakers bureaus"

- Honoraria valued at or above $5,000

- Patents, licensing fees, royalties derived from inventions—either earned by either the employee or a family member if they are in areas in which a faculty member does teaching or research or in areas matching an employee's administrative responsibilities. Harvard's COI policy, notably, is among those requiring reporting of relevant family member income. It includes the observation that "a faculty member must affirmatively make inquiry into, and shall be presumed to know of, the financial interests of family members as herein defined," which means a spouse, partner, or dependent children.[481]

- Stock, options, warrants, and other equity holdings, entitlements to equity holdings, or ownership (excepting general mutual funds or other diversified financial holdings), again with the same family member provisions, including stock held in a company that is a university vendor or potential vendor that markets products or services the university seeks

- Positions with a company

- Membership on Company governing boards

- Technical advisory committees, scientific advisory boards, and marketing panels

- Company employee or officer, full or part time

- Fees for authorship of publications prepared by others, no de minimus value

(Reporting fees for authorship is required under the 2011 DHHS-NIH rules for managing FCOI, due to the federal government's growing concerns about industry-led ghostwriting of scholarly work)[482]

- Fees to serve as an expert witness for a plaintiff or a defendant

- Other significant payments (valued at or above $5,000) received from nonprofits—including professional societies, disease patient advocacy groups, research foundations, etc.—which may receive a significant amount of their funding from industry groups★

★The 2011 DHHS-NIH rules for managing financial COI also require reporting of nonprofit income, because a growing number of these nonprofit organizations now derive a sizable share of their funding from industry sources.[483] According to one recent survey, many medical specialty societies and associations rely heavily on medical industry funding.[484] The IOM (2009) noted that most professional societies and disease-focused or patient advocacy groups do not make public the details of their funding from industry, however their reliance on industry funding is well known. During one Congressional inquiry, the American Psychiatric Association (APA) reported that medical companies supplied about 28 percent of its annual income. An Associated Press story in 2009 reported that 40 percent of the annual budget of the National Fibromyalgia Association comes from industry groups.[485] Many industry-trade groups (tobacco, oil, chemical) also fund nonprofit front groups to distribute academic research grants on their behalf, making the source of this funding harder to detect.[486]

Recommendations Adapted from IOM (2009)

Outside Entities Whose Relationships with Employees Warrant Special Concern about COI

Harvard University's Faculty FCOI policy includes a useful list of the outside entities that warrant careful monitoring if any university employee maintains a relationship with them:

1. entities whose products, services, or activities are related to the areas of a faculty member's or an investigator's teaching or research;

2. entities that fund research in a faculty member's or an investigator's area of academic interest;

3. entities that own or have rights to develop intellectual property that is the subject of research in which a faculty member or an investigator participates;

4. entities that compete commercially with such an entity as described in (3)

5. entities that make or propose to make a gift to the university that would support a faculty member's or an investigator's teaching or research activities;

6. entities that furnish products or services to the university through a contractual process in which a faculty member or an investigator participates in any way;

7. entities that propose to enter a licensing agreement with the university with respect to technology invented by the faculty member or investigator

8. entities that act as a legal or defacto agent for any outside entity engaged in any of the above activities.[487]

PRINCIPLE 26: Inter-office Reporting and Tracking of Institutional COI

To keep track of institutional COI, every institutional COI committee should have a well-developed, campuswide reporting system that requires the technology transfer office, the office of sponsored programs, the development office, the grants office, institutional review boards (IRBs), purchasing operations, and corresponding offices at affiliated medical institutions to report to the standing COI committee at least quarterly on situations that might give rise to institutional conflicts.

- The purpose of this institutional COI inter-office reporting system is to ensure that all university decision making processes—and agents charged with addressing institutional financial matters—are clearly and credibly separated from the institution's academic research activities.

- This recommendation has been endorsed in similar form by the IOM (2009)[488] and by the AAMC/AAU (2008).[489]

- This campuswide reporting system should encompass the following offices, which could give rise to the following possible institutional COI situations: (1) Technology transfer office (for licensing arrangements, patents, invention disclosures); (2) Office of sponsored programs, research administration, or corporate research relations (for sponsored research agreements and products that are the subject of research); (3) Development office (for gifts); (4) Grants office (for federal and state grants); (5) Institutional review boards (IRBs) (for monitoring and approving human subjects research protocols); (6) Medical institution purchasing offices (for separation of financial interests from purchasing decisions).

Most universities have long-standing firewall arrangements governing the management of their endowment-related investment portfolios and gift funds, which separate the management of these funds from the campus's research and teaching. Such firewalls aim to ensure that the management of these funds complies with standard institutional investment policies, with no special restrictions or considerations, and with oversight by an external body or board of trustee committee that exercises no control over university operations. But many universities do not yet have firewalls in place separating the university's academic and research operations from newer types of financial instruments related to the university's technology transfer operations. Such financial arrangements can include stock options and other equity-type holdings, royalty income from commercialized inventions, milestone payments, and legal actions to protect these financial interests.[490]

At the highest levels of the institution, all streams of finance and research oversight converge. But it is important for the university to erect firewalls so any institutional financial relationships with commercial research sponsors—and all technology transfer-related decisions connected with the university's own financial holdings—are separated to the greatest extent possible from the university's academic and research operations. In 2001, Hamilton Moses and Joseph B. Martin, writing in the *Journal of the American Medical Association,* suggested that institutions create a separate entity to manage individual and institutional equity interests in companies supporting campus research. The authors recommended that this investment company be overseen by a board with wide representation and include members from outside the university.[491]

Meaningful separation is critical. Nevertheless, the AAUP agrees with the AAMC, AAU, IOM and others that even when separation has been achieved, certain financial relationships with commercial research sponsors should be examined closely for the presence of any serious COI that could compromise the institution and its research operations. With human subject research in particular there should always be a strong presumption against permitting research to go forward under the auspices of a conflicted investigator or institution.

PRINCIPLE 27: Strategies for Reviewing, Evaluating, and Addressing COI

Disclosure of a COI is not a sufficient management strategy. The best course of action is not to acquire COI in the first place. Strategies for addressing *individual COI* include divesting troublesome assets, terminating consulting arrangements, resigning corporate board seats, and withdrawing from affected projects. Methods for addressing *institutional COI* include the institution divesting its equity interest in companies connected with campus research, placing conflicted equity holdings in independently managed funds, establishing explicit firewalls to separate financial from academic decisions, recusing conflicted senior administrators from knowledge of or authority over affected research projects, and requiring outside committee review or oversight. Some university presidents decline to serve on corporate boards to avoid the appearance of COI. Because of conflicting fiduciary responsibilities, campuses should prohibit senior administrators from receiving compensation for serving on corporate boards during their time in office.

The IOM (2009) developed the following two charts, which the AAUP endorses, for evaluating the risks and benefits associated with a reported COI and for determining management strategies for responding.

BOX 3-1

Model of Steps to Identify and Respond to a COI

Step 1. Obtain the disclosure of information about financial and other relationships that could constitute a conflict of interest.
No relationships reported: stop.
Relationships disclosed: go to Step 2

Step 2. Evaluate the disclosures—in light of the individual's responsibilities or specific activities (e.g., research, teaching, and patient care)—to determine whether a conflict of interest exists. If necessary, collect additional information to assess the likelihood of undue influence and the seriousness of possible harms.
No conflict exists: stop.
Conflict exists: go to Step 3.

Step 3. Determine whether the relationship is one prohibited under institutional or other policies or whether the risks of the relationship are so serious that the individual should either eliminate it or forgo participation in the activity put at risk by the relationship.
Conflict elimination necessary: go to step 5.
Elimination not necessary: go to Step 4.

Step 4. If management is appropriate, devise and implement a plan to manage the conflict.
Go to Step 5.

Step 5. Monitor conflict elimination or management plan and assess compliance.
Plan followed.
Plan not followed: go to Step 6.

Step 6. Determine the nature of the noncompliance and the appropriate response (e.g., education, penalty, or revision of the plan) and implement the response.

BOX 3-2
Risks and Benefits to Consider in Assessing the Severity of a Researcher's COI

- Risks to human subjects: to what extent could the conflict of interest increase the risk (considering the role specified for the researcher with the conflict of interest in recruiting or treating research participants)?

- Risks of bias in data collection, analysis, and reporting: to what extent could the researcher with the conflict of interest compromise the integrity of the data?

- Risks to reputation: to what extent could the reputation of the researcher with the conflict of interest or the researcher's institution be damaged, even if the institution establishes a plan to manage the conflict?

- Expected benefits to medicine, science, and public health: how do the expected benefits of allowing the research to proceed compare with the risks?

SOURCE: Adapted from AAMC-AAU, 2008.

Strategies for eliminating, reducing, or managing FCOI could include any of the following:

For a *faculty member with a FCOI,* remedial strategies might include

- Divestiture of troublesome assets;

- Termination of consulting arrangements or seats on company boards;

- Withdrawal of the conflicted researcher from an affected project;

- Disclosure of significant financial assets in published reports and public presentations related to the affected research;

- Use of a formal external Data Safety Monitoring Board (DSMB) or similar review board to evaluate the design, analytical protocols, and primary and secondary endpoint assessments, and to provide ongoing evaluation of the study for safety, performance issues, and the reporting of results;

For an *institutional COI* involving the university or any senior officials representing it, remedial strategies might include

- Divesting the institution of an equity interest in a company performing research on campus;

- Increasing the separation between financial decision making and any research or campus activities;

- Placing conflicted equity holdings in an independently managed fund, with explicit firewalls to strictly separate financial from academic decisions;

- Isolating or recusing a conflicted senior official from decision making authority over an affected research project;

- Declining to perform externally funded research in which the institution has a significant financial stake in the outcome (as opposed to the cost of the research itself);

- Disqualifying a senior officer from activities associated with the COI;

- Recusing conflicted individuals from decision making that might potentially be affected by the COI;

- Transferring professional responsibilities or decision making authority within a proscribed area to someone who is conflict free;

- Obtaining independent review or oversight by an outside committee;

- Recusing the conflicted official from the chain of authority over the project and possibly also from authority over salary, promotion, and space allocation decisions affecting the investigator.[492]

PRINCIPLE 28: Developing a Formal, Written COI Management Plan

If a university's standing COI committee finds compelling circumstances for allowing a research project or other professional activity to continue in the presence of a significant FCOI—without the elimination of the conflict—the committee should document the circumstances and write a formal management plan for each case. The plan should detail how the university will manage the FCOI and eliminate or reduce risks to its affected constituents (students, collaborating researchers, faculty, patients), its pertinent missions (research integrity, informed consent, and recruitment of research volunteers), and its reputation and public trust. This recommendation is consistent with the Department of Health and Human Services (DHHS) National Institutes of Health (NIH) rules implemented in 2011 to address financial conflicts, which require all universities that receive DHHS grants to prepare and enforce such management plans.

- The DHHS-NIH (2011) COI rule requires universities to prepare a written Management Plan whenever a Public Health Service (PHS) grant recipient has a significant FCOI related to his or her research that has not been eliminated. The PHS encompasses DHHS, NIH, and all the other federal public health agencies. Under the 2011 COI rule, these management plans must be provided to the federal grant making agency "prior to the Institution's expenditure of any funds under a PHS-funded research project." They must also be made readily accessible to the public, either on a website or by responding to any request "within five business days."[493]

The AAUP believes these written management plans—addressing both individual and institutional COI—should encompass

1. the nature of the conflict;

2. risks to human subject research or clinical-care decisions involving research volunteers or patients;

3. issues affecting the interests of students;

4. risks to the integrity of the research (recruitment of research volunteers, informed consent, study design, protocol changes, study oversight, data analysis, statistical analysis, final reporting); and

5. any perceived risks to the reputation of the institution.

PRINCIPLE 29: Oversight and Enforcement of COI Rules

All university COI policies should have effective oversight procedures and sanctions for noncompliance. These are essential to ensure compliance with university rules and to sustain public trust in the university's ability to regulate itself.

Adequate COI compliance and enforcement policies are missing on many campuses:

- A 2002 report by the Council on Government Relations, an association of research universities, reported that "while virtually all research universities and organizations have written policies governing individual financial conflicts of interest in research-related areas, most institutions are still developing formal and informal education programs to assure that the policies are well understood and that compliance by affected faculty and researchers is fully in place."[494]

- Investigations led by Sen. Charles Grassley (R–IA) in 2008 and 2009 uncovered numerous cases where senior university faculty members failed to report millions of dollars in outside commercial income from pharmaceutical firms.[495]

- In 2008, the American Medical Student Association (AMSA) evaluated academic medical school policies and noted a strong absence of oversight and enforcement mechanisms. Of the 58 schools that initially responded to the AMSA survey and supplied policies for review, 55 percent were characterized by trained external reviewers as having oversight policies, 45 percent were as having enforcement policies, and only 34 percent as having both.[496]

- A 2009 IOM panel examining COI in biomedicine found no peer-reviewed studies on the monitoring of institutional COI policies or on the enforcement of COI disclosure requirements at academic and medical institutions.[497]

PRINCIPLE 30: University-Vendor Relationships and COI

Universities should ensure that vendor evaluation, selection, and contracting for university products and services are consistent with their academic mission and do not jeopardize the best interests of students. Vendors should never be persuaded or coerced into making financial contributions to the university, either through direct university donations or recruitment of other contributing donors, in exchange for winning university contracts. All university bidding for contracts and services related to such areas as banking and student loans should be conducted through a fair, impartial, and competitive selection process. Many universities currently have ethics policies banning gifts from vendors; the policies should also clearly prohibit institutions from accepting direct remuneration, or kickbacks, from vendors doing business with the university or its students. Such profiteering can undermine public trust in the university and compromise the best interests of the students the university has pledged to serve.

Principle 30 applies to an array of vendor relationships, from the provision of student loans and the issuance of credit cards to the purchase of medical supplies and the provision of food and beverages on campus. As public funding for higher education has declined, colleges and universities have sought new revenue sources in the form of lucrative vendor contracts with corporations eager to market products and services to student audiences. Some of these deals—including stadium naming rights and athletic and event sponsorships—tend to be less objectionable. But others may have serious consequences, such as making it easier for students to acquire credit card and other bank lending debt while universities reap profits from these vendors. A description of several categories of vending relationships that have generated serious financial conflicts and harm to students follows, along with recommendations in each area.

Student Loans for Higher Education

This principle is drawn partly from recommendations issued by the AAU in its 2007 "Statement of Guiding Principles Regarding Institutional Relationships with Student Loan Providers."[498] The AAUP endorses the following AAU recommendations:

- College and university decisions about student lenders should be based on an assessment of student borrowers' best interests.

- Institutional integrity and the appearance of integrity are essential in processes that identify and recommend student-loan providers.

- Colleges and universities should inform students and parents that they may select the lender of their choice and must not penalize students and parents for selecting a lender not on a preferred lender list.

- Colleges and universities should disclose the criteria for recommending lenders.

- Institutional personnel involved in or responsible for administration of student financial aid programs should not accept any personal benefit from a lender.

- Colleges and universities should take steps to ensure that (a) lender representatives dealing with students and parents disclose their affiliation and not assert or imply that they are employees of the institution, and (b) no lender representative promotes a particular lender's loan product in the course of permissibly serving the institution.

Universities seeking to establish appropriate vendor relationships with student loan companies should also consult the "Student Loan Code of Conduct" developed by New York Attorney General Andrew Cuomo in 2007.[499] Also helpful are November 2007 US Department of Education regulations pertaining to federal student loans.[500] Various state-level consumer protection laws for students and parents also address financial aid assistance for higher education.[501]

Credit Card Vendors and Other Banking Vendors on Campus

Outside scrutiny of college and university financial relationships with banks and credit card companies has been growing. The Board of Governors of the Federal Reserve System has started submitting annual reports to Congress covering agreements between credit card issuers and institutions of higher education, as well as such affiliated organizations as alumni associations and foundations that help market credit cards to college students.[502] This information is readily available to the public.[503]

An Overview of the 2007 National Student Loan Scandal

In 2007 a series of investigations into the campus student loan business were carried out by the New America Foundation.[504] These were joined by then New York State Attorney General Andrew Cuomo, who subpoenaed loan records from hundreds of universities either located in, or enrolling students from, New York.[505] Various Congressional and government office investigations followed. These investigations produced a series of disclosures that generated considerable public alarm and outrage:

- Top financial aid administrators at leading universities across the country—whose job it is to advise cash-strapped students—had pervasive financial ties to the loan companies they were recommending to students, and in some cases were personally profiting off their students' debt load. Numerous college financial aid directors had significant personal financial conflicts at the University of Texas at Austin (stock holdings), Columbia University (stock holdings), University of Southern California (stock holdings), and Johns Hopkins (consulting fees as well as additional payments from lenders to pay for the director's graduate education). All of them were fired from their jobs.[506]

- Several university financial aid call centers were staffed by bank employees.[507]

- Financial aid officials nationwide accepted cash, gifts, trips to exotic destinations, and sponsorships of events like awards dinners and association conferences from the same "preferred" private banking lenders they routinely recommended to students. (These "preferred" lenders' names appeared on each school's "recommended lenders list" handed out to students). Some of the preferred lenders made cash payments to universities as well.

- Some preferred lenders charged interest as much as four times as high as the rates on government subsidized loans.[508]

- Many universities had explicit revenue-sharing agreements with their "preferred lenders," which meant that they received a financial payment, or "kickback," for every new student who took out a bank loan. Colleges were thus pursuing profits in exchange for student debt that constrains how students can later use the very education the colleges are providing, for excessive debt can limit student career choices. "A preferred lender ought to mean that the lender is preferred by students for its low rates, not by schools for its kickbacks," Cuomo told *The Times Higher Education*.[509]

- Before these inquiries were over, at least 35 universities had agreed to Cuomo's demand that they pay restitution to their students equal to the amount of money they took in as kickbacks. The University of Pennsylvania was compelled to distribute $1.6 million back to students; New York University $1.4 million.[510]

- Thanks in part to privileged vending arrangements with universities like the ones discussed here, private lenders have faced little campus competition. Some schools have even accepted payments from private lenders in exchange for pulling out of the federal direct loan program.[511] One US Department of Education investigation found that out of 55 colleges surveyed, 48 held more than 95 percent of their loan volume with a single lender and seven had at least 80 percent of their volume with a single lender. The Department expressed concern that this level of concentration might signal violations of federal law, such as having financial-aid websites that automatically direct students to a particular lender.[512]

- Studies show that 90 percent of students choose from the loan companies that their university aid offices recommend.

- In the last 12 years, national student loan debt has nearly doubled, with very high interest rates charged by many private lenders (some private lenders charge as much as 19 percent).

- In June and September of 2007, Senator Edward M. Kennedy (D-MA) released two reports proving that abuses in the student loan program were widespread; numerous colleges had accepted or even solicited inducements from lenders—often with the expectation or explicit agreement that the institution would grant the said lender preferential treatment.[513] "Given the breadth of the evidence presented in this report it is clear that the problem is systemic and cannot be isolated to a few 'problem' lenders or schools," the first report concluded. "[M]any lenders in the FFEL [Federal Family Education Loan] program routinely engage in marketing practices that," according to the report, "violate the letter and spirit of the inducement prohibition of the Higher Education Act," which, the report noted, bars not only "a consummated quid pro quo deal, but the mere offer of such a deal."[514]

- Investigations by the Government Accountability Office found that "some student loan lenders were paying schools to promote their loans, and some schools were limiting students' choice of lenders."[515] The GAO and the Inspector General of the US Department of Education further found that the Department's oversight of the federal student loan program had been inadequate.

Other Banking and Credit Card Vending Relationships on Campus
Student lending is not the only area where vending relationships can generate FCOI and damage students' best interests. Universities frequently have exclusive relationships with credit card companies. Some convert their campus ID

card into a joint student ID/ATM/debit card by outsourcing the production of the card to a private bank.[516] The bank then produces the campus ID cards at no cost to the university. Students can use this ID card both to access their checking or savings accounts and as a debit card, provided they invest their personal money in that bank. In exchange, the banks will often pay a share of the money they earn off the students' purchases and debts back to the institution issuing the card, their alumni associations, or their athletics departments—enabling these colleges and universities once again to profit off of their students.[517]

In all these deals the host university or college provides financial firms with detailed student personal information. The companies then use this data—which may include permanent addresses, e-mail addresses, and local telephone numbers—to market credit cards and other financial services directly to the students. Some schools also provide companies with face-to-face access to students, allowing salespeople to set up marketing tents in central campus locations. According to Higher Ed Watch, a project of the New America Foundation, such deals are often quite profitable: "An ID card deal between the University of Minnesota and TCF Financial has yielded an estimated $40 million over 30 years for the school, while the bank's deposits have increased by $50 million."[518] When Iowa lawmakers conducted an investigation in 2007 they found that "credit card contracts generated millions of dollars a year for the institutions' privately-run alumni organizations." Bank of America had marketing arrangements with about 700 US campuses, mostly with alumni associations, athletics departments, and foundations, which typically collect 20 to 50 cents for every $100 of credit card purchases.[519]

The benefits to students are far less clear. As a blog posting from Higher Ed Watch noted, the "deals that public universities are making with banks and other finance companies for credit cards and ID cards bear a striking resemblance to the deals that were uncovered last year as part of the investigation into the 'pay-for-play' student loan scandal. Just as exclusive deals between lenders and colleges drew Congressional ire, policymakers need to take a closer look at schools' revenue machinations and their implications for students."[520]

In its October 2010 annual report to Congress, the Board of Governors of the Federal Reserve System reported receiving a total of 1,044 college credit card agreements between universities and their affiliated alumni associations and foundations and seventeen credit card issuers.[521] In 2009, these credit card issuers made total payments of $83,462,712 to higher education institutions and their affiliated organizations. The total number of college credit card accounts opened as part of these agreements was 2,008,714.

Legislation in California known as the Student Financial Responsibility Act (AB 262, Coto, Chapter 679, Statutes of 2007) requires the California State University system and California Community Colleges—and requests the Regents of the University of California and the governing bodies of private or independent colleges in the state—to adopt policies that regulate credit card companies' campus marketing practices. Each campus is directed to disclose all exclusive arrangements with banks or other entities that engage in on-campus credit card marketing activities annually. The law prohibits gifts to students who complete on-campus credit card applications for those lending entities. The bill also urges the Regents to revise the UC Policy on on-campus marketing of credit cards to students.[522]

Nellie Mae, one of the nation's largest student loan companies (fully owned by Sallie Mae), reported that 92 percent of graduate students had a credit card with an average balance of $8,612 in 2006 (15 percent had an average balance of more than $15,000). Undergraduate students averaged about $2,169 in credit card debt.[523]

PRINCIPLE 31: COI Transparency: Public Disclosure of Financial Interests and COI Management Plans

University COI policies should require faculty, administrators, students, postdoctoral fellows, and academic professionals to disclose to all journal editors all significant personal financial interests that may be directly or indirectly related to the manuscripts they are submitting for consideration. COI disclosure on publications should summarize all related funding sources received during the past five years, not simply for the project at hand. The same COI disclosure requirements should apply to oral presentations delivered in conferences, courts, and legislative chambers. After the university's standing COI committee reviews faculty conflict of interest disclosure statements, they should be posted to a public website, and this information should remain accessible for at least ten years. This measure will help institutions address growing demands from Congress, state governments, journal editors, the media, and public interest groups for increased transparency and reporting of faculty COI. It is consistent with DHHS-NIH (2011) rules, which require universities to disclose all significant FCOI (as per the DHHS-NIH definition) related to a faculty member's DHHS-funded research on a public website or provide the information upon public request within five days.524 Disclosure of FCOI should also extend to affected patients and human research volunteers. (For details, see Principle 35.)

The AAUP recommends stronger COI disclosure policies in the following four areas:

Disclosure in Academic Journals:

This principle is consistent with the standards on author disclosure of financial interests adopted by the International Committee of Medical Journal Editors and the World Association of Medical Editors, which all universities and academic medical centers should embody in their own campus policies.[525]

Disclosure in Oral Presentations:

This principle is consistent with the journal recommendation above, since oral presentations (including public lectures, Grand Rounds at medical schools, and legislative testimony) represent other common forums where faculty transmit their expertise, and thus financial COI disclosure should be required.

Disclosure of Faculty FCOI and Corresponding University Management Plans on a Public Website:

This recommendation goes further than those issued by other professional groups. However, it is fully compatible with the DHHS-NIH COI rules (2011), cited above, which require disclosure of all significant FCOI, related to DHHS-NIH funded research on a public website or release of that information within five days of any public request, as well as the development of a detailed written COI Management Plan.[526] If such disclosure is warranted in the case of DHHS-NIH funded research, why should it not be extended to all faculty research? The AAUP believes it is time for universities to make this information routinely available to promote transparency and enhance public accountability.

Disclosure of FCOI to Patients and Research Subjects:

(See Principles 32 and 35.)

Part V.
Targeted Principles: Managing COI in the Context of Clinical Care and Human Subject Research (32–35)

With the welfare of patients and research subjects always of utmost concern, academic institutions should give COI in the areas of clinical care, pre-clinical research,[527] human subject research, and animal research close scrutiny, regulation, and oversight.[528] The integrity of science and the moral imperative of medicine to "do no harm" intensify the importance of such vigilance. This principle is codified in the Charter on Medical Professionalism issued by the American Board of Internal Medicine (ABIM).[529] Adopted by more than a hundred professional groups worldwide, the Charter lays out ten essential responsibilities of medical professionals; one is to maintain patient trust by managing COI. The IOM,[530] AAU, and the AAMC (2008)[531] likewise recommend heightened attention to FCOI involving direct patient care and human subject research. Harvard University is among the institutions that require FCOI management in animal subject research as well.[532]

The AAUP agrees with these assessments. A 2010 AAMC report on clinical care observed that the "entire medical profession shares the responsibility for upholding the values of medical professionalism. The medical profession is the public face of medicine, and the degree to which all of its components accept responsibility for addressing potential conflicts that may result from its relationships with industry is directly related to the maintenance of public trust in the integrity of medical decision making."[533]

Human subject research is an acutely sensitive area. Harvard professor Eric Campbell, a 2009 IOM panel member, testified to Congress about COI regulation:

> It is critical for public trust that research institutions protect the integrity of the medical research that is the foundation of clinical practice and education. Bias in the design and conduct of clinical trials may expose research participants to risks without the prospect that the trials will generate valid, generalizable knowledge. Moreover, such bias—and bias in reporting research—may result in compromised findings being submitted to the Food and Drug Administration for approval of drugs or devices. Further, it may also expose much larger numbers of patients to ineffective or unsafe clinical care.[534]

What follows are our recommendations for clinical research and patient care.

PRINCIPLE 32: Individual and Institutional COI and Human Subject Research

To maximize patient safety and preserve public trust in the integrity of academic research, there should always be a strong presumption against permitting FCOI related to clinical medical research and experimental studies involving human subjects. A "rebuttable presumption" against permitting clinical trial research that may be compromised by FCOI should govern decisions about whether conflicted researchers or institutions are allowed to pursue a particular human subject research protocol or project, unless a compelling case can be made to justify an exception.

- This principle has been endorsed in similar form by the IOM (2009),[535] AAMC (2001, 2002), and the AAMC-AAU (2008).[536] All favor a "rebuttable presumption" against the presence of individual or institutional FCOI in human subject research.

- The IOM explains the origin and meaning of rebuttable presumption: "The 'rebuttable presumption' concept is taken from the law and refers to assumptions that are taken to be true unless they are explicitly and successfully challenged in a particular case . . . A compelling circumstance would exist, for example, if a researcher with a conflict of interest has unique expertise or skill with implanting and adjusting a complex new medical device and this expertise is needed to carry out an early-stage clinical trial safely and competently. Generally, some kind of management plan would then be devised."[537]

- A detailed discussion of the institutional financial and fiduciary interests that can affect human subject research can be found in the 2008 AAMC/AAU 2008 report *Protecting Patients, Preserving Integrity, Advancing Health*.[538]

The AAUP understands that in exceptional cases it may be necessary to allow a university investigator with a FCOI to participate in human subject research—if the testing and development of a potential new drug, therapy, or procedure would be unable to proceed without that person's participation. An example would be a surgeon who may be the only skilled expert capable of testing a new surgical technique. Such waivers of the normal prohibition against FCOI in human subject research should be rare, and the waiver should be made public, together with a copy of the university's complete COI Management Plan. As a 2009 IOM panel observed, "In most cases of a conflict of interest [related to human subject research], no compelling argument that the investigator's participation is essential can be made. Even if the investigator's participation is essential, the elimination of the conflict of interest (e.g., through the sale of stock) is the preferred step. If an exception is granted, it should be made public."[539]

PRINCIPLE 33: Institutional Review Boards (IRBs) and COI Management

An IRB should review all proposed human clinical trial protocols to identify all relevant FCOI before research is allowed to proceed. First, institutions should have clear policies, compliant with applicable federal regulations, to address reporting and management of FCOI associated with IRB members themselves. Policies should require conflicted IRB members to recuse themselves from deliberations related to studies with which they have a potential conflict. Second, the policies should require the institution's standing COI committee to prepare summary information about all institutional and individual FCOI related to the research protocol under review. The summary should accompany the protocol when it is presented to the IRB. The IRB should take the COI information into account when determining whether and under what circumstances to approve a protocol. Neither the IRB nor the standing COI committee should be able to reduce the stringency of the other's management requirements. The double-protection system is consistent with the two sets of federal regulations governing clinical research and provides appropriate additional safeguards for patient volunteers. Finally, if a research protocol is allowed to proceed, university policies should require disclosure of any institutional and investigator FCOI as well as the university's management plan for addressing them to all patient volunteers (in informed consent documents) and all investigators and units involved with the research protocol.

- This principle is drawn directly from recommendations endorsed by the AAMC/AAU in 2008,[540] along with a 2001 AAU report.[541] It addresses well-documented problems with sitting IRB members who themselves have significant FCOIs, as well as widespread evidence that IRB members often lack full knowledge of the institutional and investigator FCOI related to the research protocols under their review.[542] Such ignorance may result from inadequate communication of FCOI disclosures between the IRB and the university's COI committees.[543] The AAU (2001) thus recommends more effective integration between IRBs and the university's COI committees.[544]

- Disclosure of FCOI to patients and human subject volunteers is necessary to safeguard public confidence in medical research. Numerous media reports and public investigations, including a 2012 "60 Minutes" segment on research misconduct at Duke University, have focused attention on both university and investigator FCOI that were not disclosed to patient volunteers.[545] A 2006 study by Weinfurt et al. reported that only 48 percent of medical schools had policies that mentioned the disclosure of researchers' FCOI to research participants. The policies also varied in what information was to be disclosed.[546]

- Given the strong imperative for integrity in human subject research, one might expect such research to be largely free of institutional or individual COI, but reports like those above make it clear that better policies on disclosure and effective enforcement are needed.

PRINCIPLE 34: COI, Medical Purchasing, and Clinical Care

Academic medical centers should establish and implement COI policies that require all personnel to disclose financial interests in any manufacturer of pharmaceuticals, devices, or equipment or any provider of services and to recuse themselves from involvement in related purchasing decisions. If an individual's expertise is essential in evaluating a product or service, that person's financial ties must be disclosed to those responsible for purchasing decisions.

- This principle is drawn directly from AAMC recommendations from 2008[547] and 2010[548] about FCOI management in medical purchasing and clinical care.

PRINCIPLE 35: COI Transparency in the Context of Medical Care

University policies should require all physicians, dentists, nurses, and other health professionals, as well as investigators, to disclose their FCOI to patients, human subject volunteers, and the broader public, unless those COI have been eliminated.

- This principle is drawn from the AAMC's 2010 recommendation that FCOI be disclosed to all patients.[549] The AAUP agrees that disclosure is "one method, though not the exclusive method, of managing actual and perceived conflicts of interest in clinical care."

- The AAMC does not specify any preferred method for delivering this information to patients, but as stated in Principle 31, the AAUP believes this information should be posted on the institution's public website, together with information about the value of these outside financial relationships and the institution's management plans for reducing any potential bias.

Part VI.
Targeted Principles: Strategic Corporate Alliances (SCAs) (36–48)

What Is an SCA?

A strategic corporate alliance (SCA) is a formal, comprehensive, university-managed research collaboration with an outside company sponsor (or several company sponsors) centered around a major, multi-year financial commitment involving research, programmatic interactions, "first rights to license" intellectual property, and other services. This definition is adapted from one developed by Cornell University.[550]

An SCA is distinct from an Industrial Research Consortium (IRC), in which it is customary for a group of some ten or more companies to pay yearly membership fees to jointly fund a broad research goal or technology development objective that all the subscribers have a common interest in supporting. Research results developed within the IRC are usually shared among the sponsoring members under nonexclusive licensing terms. Research results in an SCA, by contrast, are commonly licensed exclusively to the sponsor.

The structure of an SCA is different from most industry-sponsored research agreements. Traditional industry sponsored grants involve smaller dollar amounts (usually under a million dollars); they also tend to be episodic and grow out of an individual faculty member's direct relationship with a company. An SCA, by contrast, is larger in scale, may last longer, and has greater scope and influence. SCAs are often negotiated to last three to five years in the $1 million-to-$25 million range; others may run ten years or longer in the $50 million-to-$250 million range. SCAs are usually negotiated through a central university development office in tandem with a group of faculty, an entire academic department, or many academic departments. Unlike most industry-sponsored grants, SCAs frequently require new governing structures for management and oversight.

Yet SCAs are not new. Some campuses, like MIT, have been administering them since the 1950s; MIT reports receiving roughly 45 percent of its total corporate research support in this form.[551] Though most US universities have less experience with SCAs, they are growing more common, and many universities are now actively pursuing such alliances, especially with pharmaceutical, agricultural, and energy research companies.

In the pharmaceutical sector, companies and universities are experimenting with new types of SCA collaborations in which academic researchers are more commercially engaged, participating not only in early-stage drug discovery, but also in more "translational" work—turning a drug into a marketable product. Translational work was traditionally performed in industry, not academia. The *Financial Times* reported it in this way in 2008:

> Colleges and universities have become the next generation research and development labs for drug makers at a time when they are battling increased generic competition for top-selling medicines, and a dearth of drugs in the pipeline. . . . Pharmaceutical companies have a long history of partnering with universities for drugs research and technology, but these new entrepreneurial arrangements represent a departure from the traditional model. In previous industry-academic partnerships, pharmaceutical companies engaged university researchers for a certain line of research that benefited their projects, and that research was carried out exclusively by the university scientist. New ventures, however, tend to involve teams of university and industry scientists working together on wide-ranging experiments to advance new drug discovery and stimulate basic research.[552]

Examples of SCAs in the Energy and Pharmaceutical Sectors

- In August 2006, Chevron signed a five-year, $25 million alliance with UC Davis to develop low-cost biofuels for transportation.

- In April 2007, ConocoPhillips signed an eight-year, $22.5 million research collaboration with Iowa State University to study and develop biofuels.

- In March 2007, the University of Colorado at Boulder launched an alliance with 27 large firms (including Archer Daniels Midland, Chevron, ConocoPhillips, Dow Chemical, E.I. du Pont de Nemours, and Royal Dutch Shell) to finance the Colorado Center for Biorefining and Biofuels (C2B2), a consortium to develop biofuels that has brought in $6 million over three years. This collaboration appears to be a hybrid that melds an Industrial Research Consortium with an SCA.

- In 2007, BP, the U.K.-based oil giant, signed the largest SCA to date, a 10-year, $500 million SCA, known as the Energy Biosciences Institute, with three public institutions: UC Berkeley, University of Illinois at Urbana-Champaign, and Lawrence Berkeley National Laboratory. The EBI is primarily targeting next-generation biofuels research and oil discovery work.

- In July 2008, Harvard signed a five-year, $25 million alliance with GlaxoSmithKline to support stem-cell research, particularly in the areas of heart disease and cancer. According to news reports, joint projects will take place either on campus or in Glaxo's labs. Glaxo will get the rights to any patents generated in its own labs, including those generated by university scientists, and first rights to a non-exclusive license for any discoveries made on campus. A Harvard spokesman also said the research consortium "will be overseen by a steering committee made up of equal numbers of Harvard and GSK personnel."[553]

- In 2008, *BusinessWeek* reported on two SCA agreements between Harvard and Merck: one targets treatments for the bone disease osteoporosis; the other, negotiated with the Dana-Farber Cancer Institute, a Harvard affiliate, targets cancer therapies. According to *BusinessWeek*, the agreements are "nothing like past partnerships between industry and academia, in which drug makers helped fund discoveries at the university but relied on their own teams to come up with commercial products. In this case, Merck expects its Harvard allies to stay involved throughout the drug development process." Dr. Ronald DePinho, a professor of medicine at Harvard, told the magazine that Harvard recently hired about 40 scientists from large pharmaceutical companies so they can coach the academics on drug development. "We're creating a larger discovery enterprise," he explained.[554]

- In 2008, UC San Francisco and Pfizer signed a novel, broad-ranging research alliance that will provide up to $9.5 million over three years. According to the *San Francisco Chronicle,* the agreement is "part of Pfizer's attempt to break the traditional mold of pharmaceutical development and embrace the nimble work style of biotechnology companies that build on cutting-edge research."[555]

- Pfizer also operates a three-year, $14 million SCA to study diabetes, involving four research universities: UC Santa Barbara, Caltech, MIT, and University of Massachusetts.[556]

What Distinguishes a "Broad SCA" from a "Narrow SCA"?

In broad SCA agreements, the university typically issues a formal "request for faculty research proposals" (RFP) on behalf of the outside corporate sponsor(s) in each new grant cycle. After research proposals have been received, the university (often in collaboration with the sponsor) oversees a research evaluation and selection process to choose which faculty projects will receive SCA funding. In narrow SCA agreements, by contrast, all the faculty members eligible to receive SCA funding and their projects have been named and identified in advance, so this university-led RFP and research-selection process is not required. This feature of a narrow SCA limits some, but not all, of the institutional COI concerns raised by broad SCAs. (This discussion is drawn from the detailed analysis of SCAs conducted by Cornell University's faculty senate that we cite frequently).[557]

Why Do SCAs Raise Distinctive Academic and Oversight Challenges?

SCAs raise distinct challenges for academic governance, academic freedom, and research integrity. This stems partly from the size and structure of the SCA and partly from the host of institutional COI they enable. This creates increased campus and public scrutiny that must be addressed with care by faculty governing bodies.

This overview of challenges posed by SCAs is drawn from faculty senate reviews of SCAs at both Cornell[558] and UC Berkeley,[559] a commissioned review of the UC Berkeley-Novartis SCA by researchers at Michigan State University,[560] legislative hearings in the California state senate addressing the Berkeley-Novartis deal,[561] and a detailed 2010 analysis by the Center for American Progress of the terms and conditions spelled out in ten SCA contracts between US universities and energy-related firms during the 2002–08 period.[562]

This latter analysis of SCA agreements found that a majority granted the industrial sponsor joint control over both the alliance's central steering committee and its final research-selection committee. Eight of the ten agreements permitted the corporate sponsor(s) to control the evaluation and selection of faculty research proposals.[563] None of the SCA contracts required independent peer review in awarding research grants. Two institutions stated that they did use peer review procedures in practice, though those procedures were not secured in their legal contracts. UC Berkeley's contract allows independent peer review only at the discretion of the industry sponsors; at the other institution, most of the faculty members on the SCA's research-selection committee had either personal financial interests related to biofuels research or were themselves beneficiaries of the SCA's sponsored research grants, raising serious questions about the committee's impartiality.[564] The study's major findings are discussed in the Introduction; its methodology is described in this endnote.[565]

As a consequence of these hybrid academy-industry governing structures, SCAs may challenge the university's shared governance traditions. What role should faculty governance bodies play in the design and approval of a newly proposed SCA? What role in subsequent oversight? The joint governing structure also threatens long-standing traditions of independent expert peer review and the assumption that all faculty appointments and advancement should be based on high quality scholarship and science, not on a corporate sponsor's commercial or strategic business objectives. As we pointed out in the account of the Chapela case in the Introduction, the UC Berkeley-Novartis alliance may have affected one faculty member's tenure review.[566]

SCAs may also encroach on collective faculty control over academic hiring—if, for example, new funding for full-time equivalent (FTE) faculty appointments is part of the SCA or if corporate employees are offered adjunct faculty positions. When UC Berkeley negotiated major SCA deals, first with Novartis/Syngenta and later with BP, the faculty senate expressed concern about perceived attempts to bypass established faculty procedures for academic hiring and resource allocation.[567] SCAs may also influence allocations of lab space, equipment, and graduate student recruitment and support.

In addition, SCAs may present a greater risk of distorting faculty research agendas. Faculty working at institutions with large SCAs may be more inclined to steer their research toward topics and approaches attractive to the SCA sponsor's commercial interests in order to build positive relationships with the sponsor and its employees, to bring funding into their own labs, or to ensure the sponsor remains satisfied with the partnership and continues to renew its funding. Some institutions may end up diverting additional funds to the project in an effort to produce usable results more quickly and please the corporate partner.

SCA's may also bias reported research outcomes. As noted in the Introduction, research has shown that research funded by industry sponsors is far more likely to report outcomes that favor the sponsor's products and interests when compared with nonprofit or government funded research. The Cornell faculty senate SCA committee summarized some of these challenges: "[The SCA] may result in a re-focusing of laboratory space, faculty effort and graduate student research within the department, as well as the need to limit communications between participating and non-participating faculty and graduate students to protect proprietary knowledge, and a stronger-than-usual preference for obtaining positive results in order to secure future funding (as compared, for example, with NIH funding)."[568]

SCAs can thus foster or exacerbate internal tensions and divisions within the larger university community. Tensions may arise between faculty who operate largely inside versus outside the SCA over IP, heightened secrecy, and other issues. The SCA may exacerbate perceived inequalities over which faculty research is more attractive to commercial sponsors, regardless of its scholarly value or ability to generate public good benefits. Genuine intellectual divisions and debates may arise over the university's public purpose and mission, institutional priorities, and ability to sustain support for a variety of academic disciplines.[569]

Finally, the influence of SCAs on researchers, labs, academic departments, and university governing structures tends to formalize and institutionalize the university's relationship with its corporate partner or partners. This in turn ties the university as an institution—as well as its public reputation—far more closely to its SCA sponsor(s), raising additional potential for institutional COI.[570]

After the 1998–2003 Berkeley-Novartis SCA concluded, the Michigan State University reviewers highlighted the need to address the growing problem of institutional conflicts: "This case study suggests that the boundaries of current COI policy and codes of conduct are unrealistically narrow in several respects. . . . Given the growing role of the institution in the management of [IP] and economic development, institutional COI policies (or conflicts of mission) need heightened scrutiny."[571] Cornell's faculty senate committee reached a similar conclusion: In the case of an SCA, "the essential quality of academic independence from the sponsor is more difficult to maintain at an institutional, as well as individual, level. . . . Therefore more formal decisional processes and oversight mechanisms are appropriate as continual self-checking and self-correcting mechanisms."[572] The Cornell committee added that "Academic freedom brings with it the responsibility of disinterested integrity in the conduct of research and the publication of results. . . . Although this responsibility attends all research, sponsored or not, the comprehensiveness and scale of an SCA and the pervasive influence of the corporate partner may make it particularly difficult to maintain the conditions in which faculty are able, and motivated, to fulfill their responsibility."[573]

Few reliable data or rigorous assessments of SCAs exist, though the Center for American Progress analysis of ten SCA agreements in the energy sector found significant variation in their contract terms and few academic protections overall.[574] The Cornell faculty statement represents one of the few, detailed faculty-led assessments of SCAs that the AAUP was able to identify. The senate committee that researched and wrote the statement included members from a wide cross section of academic disciplines.[575] There were points of disagreement, but the committee's consensus statement provides a well-developed set of "Principles & Best Practices" to guide the future development of "Strategic Corporate Alliances."[576] We drew upon them below.

Proprietary considerations and other negotiating issues discourage the disclosure of most SCAs to the full faculty until after university negotiations with the sponsor are nearly concluded. Many SCA contracts at both public and private universities are never reviewed by the faculty senate and never disclosed to the public. Even public institutions now contend these university-industry research agreements are "corporate proprietary information" and that their confidential nature thus does not violate state open record act laws. The Center for American Progress study reported making 35 requests for university-industry collaboration agreements, including 24 filed as formal "public record act" (PRA) requests under applicable state open record laws. Universities rejected or ignored more than half the requests. Often, when they did release the documents, it was only after lengthy delays.[577]

These facts make it clear why the AAUP is recommending that faculty senates develop written standards, principles, and procedures to guide the formation of new SCAs and require the contracts to be public documents subject to ongoing senate review, so wherever these alliances originate within the university, they will conform to standards developed by the faculty that protect the university's values. What follows are the specific principles the AAUP is recommending universities incorporate into their written policies to better address circumstances that have arisen from the rapid growth of SCAs.

PRINCIPLE 36: Shared Governance and Strategic Corporate Alliances (SCAs)

Faculty senates should be fully involved in the planning, negotiation, approval, execution, and ongoing oversight of SCAs formed on campus. The senate should appoint a confidential committee to review a first draft of a memorandum of understanding (MOU) pertaining to newly proposed SCAs. All parties' direct and indirect financial obligations should be made clear from the outset. Before an agreement is finalized on a broad SCA, the full faculty senate should review it. Formal approval of broad SCAs should await both stages in this process. All approved SCA agreements should be made available to faculty, academic professionals, and the public. If the SCA designates funding for new faculty appointments (FTEs), all normal university and departmental procedures for searches, hiring, and promotion decisions must be followed to honor and protect academic self-governance and academic freedom. Temporary employees should not exclusively staff, administer, or supervise SCAs. Normal grievance procedures, under collective bargaining agreements where they exist, should govern complaints about interference with academic freedom or other academic rights that may arise under SCAs. In the absence of such procedures, grievances and complaints should be reported to the SCA faculty oversight committee (see Principle 47) or to relevant college or university grievance committees for independent investigation. Standard safeguards regarding procedural fairness and due process must be respected and followed.

Because large-scale SCA agreements tend to have a broader impact on the university, they warrant faculty involvement from their initial design to their subsequent oversight. Faculty oversight encourages quality, greater campus support, and public trust. Support and trust can only be credibly secured if SCA agreements are made public, as the AAUP recommends under Principle 48. No SCA contract should be accepted if it is explicitly or implicitly conditional on the sponsor's opportunity to influence the selection of new faculty hires. To ensure the security of all permanent faculty, universities should have mechanisms in place to cover new SCA faculty salaries from university funds after the SCA contract ends, or in case of premature termination of the grant.

- The AAUP recognizes that this principle may not be rapidly applied in schools of medicine, where tenure of position is often not accompanied by tenure of salary. Medical faculty are often required to generate 100 percent of their salaries from clinical revenue, research grants, or both. Nonetheless, the creation of such a special group of faculty at medical schools, who lack true job security and financial autonomy, has far-reaching implications for campus standards of fairness and the ability of faculty to retain their academic freedom and professional ethics.

- This principle draws on long-standing AAUP positions, as articulated in the 1966–67 "Statement on Government of Colleges and Universities" endorsed by the ACE and the AGB—and in the 2004 AAUP "Statement on Corporate Funding of Academic Research."[578] The latter document reads in part: "Consistent with the principles of sound academic governance, the faculty should have a major role not only in formulating the institution's policy with respect to research undertaken in collaboration with industry, but also in developing the institution's plan for assessing the effectiveness of the policy."[579]

PRINCIPLE 37: SCA Governance and Majority Academic Control

The best practice in any academy-industry alliance agreement—consistent with the principles of academic freedom, university autonomy, and faculty self-governance—is to build clear boundaries separating corporate funders from the university's academic work. Yet the current conditions of increasingly close university-industry relations make erecting strict walls unrealistic on some campuses. Instead, at a minimum, universities should retain majority academic control and voting power over internal governing bodies charged with directing or administering SCAs in collaboration with corporate sponsors. The SCA's main governing body should also include members who are neither direct stakeholders of the SCA nor based in academic disciplines or units likely to benefit from the SCA. A joint university-industry SCA governing body may have a role in awarding funding, but it should have no role in such exclusively academic functions as faculty hiring, curriculum design, course content, and academic personnel evaluation.

- This principle reflects values integral to a series of AAUP documents and policy statements, beginning with the historic definition of the faculty's role in the 1915 "Declaration of Principles on Academic Freedom and Tenure" and following through to "The Role of the Faculty in Budgetary and Salary Matters" (1972, 1990), "On the Relationship of Faculty Governance to Academic Freedom" (1994) and "Statement on Corporate Funding of Academic Research" (2004). It also draws on Cornell University's "Faculty Statement of Principles & Best Practices Concerning Strategic Corporate Alliances," (2005), which reads in part: "Day-To-Day Management of the SCA should be predominantly by Cornell Faculty, not corporate representatives. One fundamental touchstone can never be lost: This is academic research, not corporate research. If there is a Director of the alliance . . . that Director needs to be a Cornell faculty member. If all management is to be done by the [Joint Steering Committee] JSC as a committee of the whole, then Cornell representation has to predominate. The corporate sponsor appropriately has a voice in management decisions, but may not have a representative with Co-Director status."[580]

PRINCIPLE 38: Academic Control over SCA Research Selection (for Broad SCAs)

In the case of broad SCAs, university representatives should retain majority representation and voting power on SCA committees charged with evaluating and selecting research proposals and making final research awards. These committees should also employ an independent peer-review process.

- This recommendation is also drawn in part from Cornell's 2005 "Faculty Statement of Principles & Best Practices Concerning Strategic Corporate Alliances." The statement firmly declares that "Selection of faculty proposals for funding should not be dictated by corporate representatives. The distribution of alliance funds to Cornell faculty, staff and students should be primarily in the hands of Cornell, not the sponsor. In keeping with the purposes of the alliance . . . representatives of the corporate sponsor may participate in the selection of proposals to be funded, but this process should be led by Cornell faculty."[581]

PRINCIPLE 39: Peer Review (for Broad SCAs)

Using a standard peer-review process, independent academic experts should evaluate and award funding whenever SCAs issue a request for proposals (RFP) in a new grant cycle. Any expert involved in the peer-review and grant-award process should be free of personal FCOI related to the area of research being reviewed to ensure that research selection is scientifically driven, impartial, and fair. Appointees to committees charged with research selection for a given SCA should be prohibited from awarding that funding to themselves, their departments, or their labs and should not be past recipients of funding from that SCA.

Peer review has long been considered the most widely accepted standard for evaluating the quality and worthiness of academic research. When faculty research proposals are evaluated by independent experts it helps ensure that corporate-research funding is awarded on the basis of scientific and academic merit, rather than the sponsor's short-term business needs or narrow strategic goals. The Cornell review of SCAs emphasized the centrality of impartial peer review: "The important point—vital to honoring the principle that we are engaged in academic, not corporate research—is that genuine, disinterested peer review occur."[582]

Anyone involved in the peer review and SCA grant awarding process should be free of personal FCOI and not be in a position to derive any financial benefit from the agreement or its corporate donors/partners. This is standard procedure at NIH and other government agencies that use peer review to award federal research grants. As noted in the Part VI overview above, this type of COI arose as a significant problem at the BP-funded Energy Biosciences Institute administered by UC Berkeley, where the vast majority of the faculty appointed to sit on the EBI's principal research-selection committee were also recipients of BP-EBI research funding.[583] To address this problem, all faculty proposals should be evaluated by non-participating faculty who are competent to assess their academic and technical merit.

The AAUP recognizes that peer review can be an imperfect process. It can, for example, reinforce biases against unconventional research. Moreover, some COI are ideological, or motivated by personal advancement or competitiveness, rather than financial gain. Heavy institutional involvement in collaborations with industry or government can also create a climate in which peer review committees are inclined to overlook problems. As David Michaels points out, the nature of peer review is also widely misunderstood: "Even rigorous peer review by honest scientists does not guarantee a study's accuracy or quality. Peer review is just one component of a larger quality control process that never ends."[584] Nonetheless, well administered peer review can help guard against many of the risks identified in this report.

PRINCIPLE 40: Transparency regarding the SCA Research Application Process (for Broad SCAs)

SCA agreements must clearly and transparently detail the methods and criteria for research selection and must explain how academic researchers may apply for SCA grants.

- In the case of many broad SCAs, the host university assumes responsibility for administering and overseeing the research selection process on behalf of the university-industry alliance. Given that university responsibility, it is essential that every SCA contract spell out how faculty may apply for SCA funding and what the methods and criteria for research selection will be. If such procedures are not specified, the university could confront accusations that it values the commercial and business interests of its corporate sponsors over its commitment to high quality, impartial evaluation of academic research—and such accusations would be difficult to refute.

PRINCIPLE 41: Protection of Publication Rights and Knowledge Sharing in SCA Agreements

All the provisions of Principle 3 should apply to SCAs as well.

- Insulating faculty and students from the pressures of self-censorship is very difficult, especially when the SCA sponsor has pledged large amounts of funding over several years. As the 2005 Cornell review of SCAs observed, "[such] difficulties are multiplied when the faculty member has been working side by side with employees of the corporate partner, who understandably share their employer's interests."[585]

- However, adhering to the principles above at least puts faculty, students, the sponsor, and sponsor employees on notice that publication rights and decisions are governed by academic judgment and guided by academic and scholarly norms, not by commercial interests.

PRINCIPLE 42: SCA Confidentiality Restrictions

To protect the university's distinctively open academic research environment, restrictions on sharing corporate confidential information and other confidentiality restrictions should be minimized to the maximum extent possible in SCA agreements. To achieve this objective, sponsors should be discouraged from sharing confidential corporate trade secrets with their academic partners except when absolutely necessary. Such confidential information should ordinarily be disclosed to the smallest number of academic investigators possible, with strict supervision from the university's legal office to prevent corruption of the academic research environment.

The University-Industry Research Collaboration Initiative addressed this issue in its 2001 report: "The ability of faculty researchers to discuss their work with colleagues and to publish their results is a cornerstone of the academic enterprise and supports the creation of new scientific knowledge. Nothing should be done to put this at risk. At the same time, companies have a legitimate need—and fiduciary responsibility to their shareholders—to protect the value of their investments. Companies recognize that universities are not the best places to try to keep secrets. The challenges and consequences of maintaining confidentiality are particularly acute in the case of students, and universities differ in their ability to manage this process."[586] Of course the most straightforward way to solve this problem is not to do trade-secret related work at universities.

Karen Hersey, former senior counsel for IP at MIT, informed the Research Collaboration that she "is leery of allowing individual faculty members to sign nondisclosure agreements." She said she preferred the institution to sign, so that the faculty would not have to put personal assets at risk. "Researchers should not be encouraged to sign unless they have been made very aware of the risks they are assuming, and unless they understand what it is they are signing," she said. "These are legal documents and enforceable against the individual. They can also be misused by industry to muzzle individual investigators." [587] That said, it is far preferable that institutions not sign them either.

PRINCIPLE 43: SCA Anti-Competitor Agreements

Anti-competitor or noncompete agreements compromise the university's academic autonomy, its ability to collaborate with other outside firms, and its commitment to knowledge sharing and broad public service. Restrictions in SCA agreements on faculty, academic professionals, postdoctoral fellows, and students interacting with or sharing information and research with private-sector competitors of SCA sponsors, or receiving separate research support from outside firms, should be avoided or minimized to the greatest extent possible.

- In an SCA agreement, it is reasonable for the university to recognize and seek to protect the sponsor's trade secrets and other confidential information, but the scope of this claimed protected material should be clearly defined in advance in writing, and any sharing of proprietary data from the company should be as limited as possible.

- Trade secret and anti-compete clauses associated with an SCA agreement should be minimized and be subject to careful review and approval by an independent faculty committee (made up of faculty who stand to gain no benefit from the deal) to make sure they are not overly broad and will not unduly interfere with campuswide research and the university's academic mission.

- The AAUP endorses the Cornell Faculty Senate statement on this issue, which reads in part as follows:

    Restrictions on relationships between faculty or students and "competitors" of the corporate partner should be minimized. Agreeing to restrict faculty or student relationships with "competitors" of the corporate partner both shrinks the sphere of potential alternative research support and inhibits the public dissemination of knowledge that is a central part of the university's traditional mission. Therefore, such promises should be made only sparingly, and should be very narrowly drawn.[588]

The Cornell report also warns that

it is important that commitments in an SCA to "facilitate" access by the corporate partner to Cornell faculty and students not become the effective equivalent of discouraging such access to the partner's competitors. A properly conceptualized SCA is a collaboration supporting academic research of interest to the corporate sponsor— it is not a joint venture in which a Cornell department/program becomes a remote research facility "belonging" to the sponsor.[589]

PRINCIPLE 44: Exclusive Licensing and SCA Agreements

All the provisions of Principles 17 and 18 should apply to strategic corporate alliances as well.

PRINCIPLE 45: Limits on Broader Academic Disruption by SCAs

Given the size and scope of many SCAs, a vigorous effort must be made to ensure that diverse areas of research—research that pursues avenues of inquiry outside the purview of, not in conformity with, or even in opposition to the SCA's research agenda—are not crowded out and continue to enjoy institutional support, resources, and sufficient financing. SCAs should be approved only if faculty and students within all academic units will, as a practical as well as a theoretical matter, retain the freedom to pursue their chosen research topics. SCA agreements should not disrupt the financial, intellectual, or professional arrangements of other academic units, colleges, or the university as a whole and should avoid impact on faculty, academic professionals, postdoctoral fellows, and students engaged in research and activities outside the purview of the SCA. University policies should clearly affirm that no faculty member, postdoctoral fellow, academic professional, or student will

be coerced into participating in a sponsored project; all participation must be entirely voluntary.

- This principle is drawn from the 2005 Cornell faculty senate recommendation:

  > [C]onstriction of research freedom by the pressure of donor preferences is not unique to SCAs. Unless a gift is unrestricted, sponsored research (public and private) always forces the researcher to choose a project of interest to the sponsor. However, the potential magnitude and comprehensiveness of SCAs substantially enhances the threat. Therefore, the key question is whether the SCA occupies so much of the department's/program's potential research capacity that it crowds out non-conforming research agendas.[590]

- This principle also draws on the 1990 AAUP "Statement on Conflicts of Interest":

  > Faculties should make certain that the pursuit of such joint [research] ventures [whether public or private] does not become an end in itself and so introduce distortions into traditional university understandings and arrangements. Private and public agencies have a direct interest in only a few fields of research and in only certain questions within those fields. Accordingly, external interests should not be allowed to shift the balance of academic priorities in a university without thorough debate about the consequences and without the considered judgment of appropriate faculty bodies. So, too, care must be taken to avoid contravening a commitment to fairness by widening disparities—in teaching loads, student supervision, or budgetary allocation—between departments engaged in such outside activity and those not less central to the nature of a university, which have, or can have, no such engagement.[591]

- To address these "research crowding" concerns, the AAUP endorses the following Cornell recommendation:

  > An SCA should be approved only if faculty within the department/program will, as a practical as well as theoretical matter, retain the freedom to pursue research topics of their own choosing—either within the SCA or by seeking alternative support for such projects. Factors relevant to this assessment include:
  >
  > (a) the proportion of department/program faculty expected to receive all or most of their funding through the SCA;

(b) the magnitude of any unrestricted funds available within and outside the SCA;

(c) the proportion of department/program physical, administrative, support, and other resources devoted to SCA projects;

(d) the narrowness or breadth of the type of projects fundable through the SCA;

(e) departmental/program commitments to funding diversity of research beyond the SCA;

(f) whether the success of the SCA has been identified as one of the strategic goals of the department, thereby putting undue pressure on faculty to take part in it;

(g) the likely effect of the SCA on projects/programs traditionally conducted in the public interest.[592]

• Finally, in developing SCA agreements, institutions may want to consider tithing, or other fundraising initiatives, to generate income that will support academic work not funded by the SCA.

PRINCIPLE 46: Early Termination of SCA Sponsor Funding

With any large-scale SCA, sponsors may threaten reduction or termination of funding in order to shape the research agenda or to express displeasure with its direction or findings. To reduce this risk, SCA contracts should include legally binding provisions to prohibit early termination of the agreement. If the negotiating process leads to inclusion of an early-termination option, it must prohibit the sponsor from arbitrarily or suddenly terminating the agreement or lowering pledged funding without at least three months advance notification. Salaries and research costs associated with the project must be continued for that period.

PRINCIPLE 47: Independent, Majority Faculty Oversight of the SCA, and Post-Agreement Evaluation

An independent, majority faculty oversight committee consisting of faculty with no direct involvement in the SCA should be established at the start of a new SCA agreement to monitor and at least annually review the SCA and its compliance with university policies and guidelines. A post-agreement evaluation plan should also be included in the SCA contract so the campus can reflect and draw on the experience in organizing future campus-based academy-industry alliances. External evaluation may be appropriate for broad SCAs. Evaluation reports should be public documents.

- The first purpose of independent faculty review committees should be to assess how the SCA is upholding the university's educational, research, and public service missions.

- This committee should also receive and carefully review grievances by faculty, postdoctoral fellows, students, academic professionals, and outside public interest groups;

- Working with the university's standing COI committees, this committee should regularly review and assess FCOI, commercial competition concerns, IP issues, and the overall impact of the SCA on faculty, students, and other campus researchers both inside and outside the collaboration.

- With each review, this faculty committee should propose concrete remedies for any negative impact identified.

- Each independent review should be made available to all members of the university community—the faculty, research staff, and students working on SCA-funded projects, as well as the public.

- After the alliance has terminated, this same faculty committee should perform a final evaluation, summarizing the overall accomplishments of and concerns raised by the SCA. That evaluation should be posted on a public website and distributed to all faculty.

- This principle draws on long-standing AAUP policies, as articulated in the "Statement on Government of Colleges and Universities" and the 1966–67 AAUP "Statement on Corporate Funding of Academic Research" (2004).[593] The latter document reads in part as follows: "Consistent with the principles of sound academic governance, the faculty should have a major role not only in formulating the institution's policy with respect to research undertaken in collaboration with industry, but also in developing the institution's plan for assessing the effectiveness of the policy." The statement goes on to state that the "faculty should call for, and participate in, the periodic review of the impact of industrially sponsored research on the education of students, and on the recruitment and evaluation of researchers (whether or not they hold regular faculty appointments) and postdoctoral fellows."[594]

- We also draw on Cornell University's statement, which recommends that the faculty, through its representatives, should have a central role in the approval, evaluation, and oversight of SCAs, with annual external evaluations and broader evaluations as well.[595]

PRINCIPLE 48: Public Disclosure of SCA Research Contracts and Funding Transparency

No SCA or other industry-, government-, or nonprofit-sponsored contract should restrict faculty, students, postdoctoral fellows, or academic professionals from freely disclosing their funding source. A signed copy of all final research contracts and MOUs formalizing the SCAs and any other types of sponsored research agreements formed on campus should be made freely available to the public—with discrete redactions only to protect valid commercial trade secrets, not for other reasons.

- Public disclosure is the best way to eliminate any possible suspicion that the SCA sponsor may be unduly influencing the university or its researchers. Full transparency also enhances accountability, helping to ensure that both the SCA sponsor and the university investigators uphold their contractual obligations.

- It is highly unusual for private companies to disclose any corporate proprietary trade secrets in a university sponsored research contract, so redactions should not be necessary.

- Due to the university's substantial public funding and public-interest obligations, intellectual property terms should also be considered a matter of public record.

- Some recent government support for graduate students derives from intelligence agency funding and imposes secrecy requirements on recipients. Among other problems, this prevents recipients from telling their major advisers what financial support they have. It also creates a secret cohort of students on campus. These restrictions are incompatible with university traditions. Such secret grad student funding has become a more pressing problem in the post 9/11 years. In 2004, Congress approved section 318 of the Intelligence Authorization Act, which appropriated four million dollars to fund a pilot program known as the Pat Roberts

Intelligence Scholars Program (PRISP). PRISP students are required to participate in closed meetings with other PRISP scholars and people from their administering intelligence agency. PRISP is a decentralized scholarship program administered not only by the CIA, but also through other intelligence agencies like the NSA, MI, and Naval Intelligence. The 2010 federal budget made PRISP a permanent program.[596]

Part VII.
Targeted Principles: Clinical Medicine, Clinical Research, and Industry Sponsorship (49–56)

Why Are Targeted Principles Needed for Clinical Medicine and Clinical Research?

As the Introduction explains, numerous academic and medical groups have warned about FCOI and industry influence in biomedicine. These include the AAU, the AAMC, the Federation of American Societies for Experimental Biology, the latter in both 2006[597] and 2008.[598] All have issued guidelines designed to reign in industry influence and FCOI in both clinical medicine and clinical research.[599]

In 2002, the American Board of Internal Medicine and more than 100 world-wide medical groups endorsed a new "Charter on Medical Professionalism," a comprehensive statement that emphasized both a "commitment to scientific knowledge" and a "commitment to maintaining trust by managing conflicts of interest."[600] The Charter reads in part as follows:

- "Physicians have a duty to uphold scientific standards, to promote research, and to create new knowledge and ensure its appropriate use. The profession is responsible for the integrity of this knowledge, which is based on scientific evidence and physician experience."

- "Medical professionals and their organizations have many opportunities to compromise their professional responsibilities by pursuing private gain or personal advantage. Such compromises are especially threatening in the pursuit of personal or organizational interactions with for-profit industries, including medical equipment manufacturers, insurance companies, and pharmaceutical firms. Physicians have an obligation to recognize, disclose to the general public, and deal with conflicts of interest that arise in the course of their professional duties and activities. Relationships between industry and opinion leaders should be disclosed, especially when the latter determine the criteria for conducting and reporting clinical trials, writing editorials or therapeutic guidelines, or serving as editors of scientific journals."

In 2006, the AAMC announced it was issuing *Principles for Protecting Integrity in the Conduct and Reporting of Clinical Trials* because current levels of "inconsistency in research standards can affront human research ethics, undermine academic integrity, distort public policy and medical practice, and impair public health."[601]

Working with these guidelines, the AAUP offers the following recommendations to safeguard academic medicine, research integrity, and the interests of both research volunteers and patients.

PRINCIPLE 49: Access to Complete Clinical Trial Data and the Performance of Independent Academic Analysis

All the provisions of Principle 5 should apply to clinical trial data as well.

- Principle 49 extends Principle 5 and all its provisions to clinical trial data. It is consistent with recommendations issued by the AAMC (2001),[602] FASEB (2006),[603] ICMJE (2001),[604] and the WAME.[605]

Pharmaceutical companies commonly assert proprietary control over all clinical data associated with a particular drug trial (data often generated from multiple testing sites simultaneously), as well as the corresponding statistical codes required to interpret the data.[606] Often these companies require in-house data analysis by company statisticians and restrict data to company computers. One academic physician calls these industry-controlled drug trials "ghost research" because they effectively permit the sponsor to control both the analysis and final interpretation of all study results, rendering academic authorship essentially meaningless.

The prevalence of this industry practice is impossible to quantify, but reported incidents of industry control over drug trials are pervasive and mounting.[607] Clear evidence that journals considered the problem serious came in 2001, when 13 medical journal editors sounded an alarm in a *New England Journal of Medicine* editorial criticizing excessive drug industry influence over study design, data access, and final interpretive analysis. They announced that ICMJE was issuing new standards for journal submissions designed to enhance research integrity and identified its key principles:

> A submitted manuscript is the intellectual property of its authors, not the study sponsor. We will not review or publish articles based on studies that are conducted under conditions that allow the sponsor to have sole control of the data or to withhold publication. We encourage investigators to use the revised ICMJE requirements on publication ethics to guide the negotiation of research contracts. Those [sponsored research] contracts should give the researchers a

substantial say in trial design, access to the raw data, responsibility for data analysis and interpretation, and the right to publish — the hallmarks of scholarly independence and, ultimately, academic freedom.[608]

The ICMJE's requirements now ask authors to provide full disclosure of the sponsor's role in the research and assurances that the investigators are independent of the sponsor, are fully accountable for the design and conduct of the trial, have independent access to all trial data, and control all editorial and publication decisions.[609] But compliance is voluntary.

In 2001 the AAMC issued COI recommendations that also addressed the dual problems of data access and data analysis. Like the journal editors, the AAMC specifically cited the need to protect data access and independent data analysis in contracts signed with industry:

> The [conflict of interest] policy should affirm an investigator's accountability for the integrity of any publication that bears his or her name. The policy should also affirm the right of a principal investigator to receive, analyze, and interpret all data generated in the research, and to publish the results, independent of the outcome of the research. Institutions should not enter, nor permit a covered individual to enter, research agreements that permit a sponsor or other financially interested company to require more than a reasonable period of pre-publication review, or that interfere with an investigator's access to the data or ability to analyze the data independently.[610]

PRINCIPLE 50: Registry of Academic-Based Clinical Trials in a National Registry

Universities and affiliated academic medical centers should adopt clear, uniform, written policies to require all clinical trials conducted by their academic investigators to be entered into ClinicalTrials.gov (http://www.clinicaltrials.gov/)—the national clinical trial registry maintained by the US National Library of Medicine (NLM) and the National Institutes of Health (NIH). The entry should be made at or before the onset of patient enrollment. Entry in the register will help ward against manipulation of study results, suppression of negative findings, and improper altering of clinical trial protocols after the research has begun.

- The purpose of this principle is to discourage sponsors or academic researchers from altering clinical trial protocols after the research has begun if the aim is to manipulate study results or suppress negative findings. This does not prevent researchers from altering protocol designs when there are valid medical or other reasons for doing so.

- ICMJE (2005),[611] the US Congress, FDA (2007),[612] AAMC (2006),[613] and the IOM have all endorsed or mandated use of publicly accessible online clinical trial registries—such as the *www.ClinicalTrials.gov* registry.[614]

- It is time for universities and academic medical centers to incorporate such registry filings into their sponsored research practices and policies.

- The NLM and the NIH established ClinicalTrials.gov as a publicly accessible online registry in 2000 because sponsors of drug trials were often failing to disclose studies with negative research results or reporting distorted results in the medical literature. The ClinicalTrials.gov registry requires summary information concerning the trial's original design, including measured endpoints; the stage of the clinical trial (i.e., Phase I–IV); criteria for participation; overall outcomes of the study; and a summary of adverse events experienced by participants.[615]

- Two 2009 studies, however, found that fewer than half of published clinical trials are adequately registered on national registries and confirmed that selective publication of clinical trial results remains a serious problem. Even among clinical trials that were registered, fewer than half were published in peer-reviewed journals. Still, without a national registry, knowledge of these human clinical trials, as well as critical data on original study design, protocol and endpoint changes, and research suppression would be difficult if not impossible to obtain. These findings suggest that greater university oversight and faculty compliance is needed.[616]

Registry of clinical trials should curb undue industry-sponsor influence over the conduct and reporting of clinical research trials. According to a 2009 IOM panel on COI in biomedicine:

> The registration of clinical trials and the provision of key details about the trial protocol and the data analysis plan ensure that basic methods for the conduct and analysis of the findings of a study as well as the primary clinical end points to be assessed and reported are specified before the trial begins and before data are analyzed. The substitution of ad hoc or secondary end points for primary end points and other important departures from the protocol can thus be detected in reports of the findings of a trial. Clinical trials registries also allow others to determine whether the results from a trial

have not been presented or reported at all. Researchers carrying out critical literature reviews can then contact the investigators to try to obtain unpublished results.[617]

Registry of clinical trials is important not only to safeguard the scientific and evidentiary foundations of medicine, but also to uphold its ethical under-pinnings. As Robert Steinbrook wrote in a 2005 *NEJM* commentary about industry suppression and distortion of trial results:

> A basic tenet of research ethics is that the data from clinical trials should be fully analyzed and published. If the knowledge gained from trials is not shared, subjects have been exposed to risk needless-ly. Moreover, participants in future studies may be harmed because earlier results were not available. These principles are reflected in fed-eral regulations regarding the protection of human subjects, which define research as "a systematic investigation designed to develop or contribute to generalizable knowledge."[618]

PRINCIPLE 51: Safeguarding the Integrity and Appropriate Conduct of Clinical Trials

All clinical trials affiliated with academic institutions should be required to use independent data safety monitoring boards (DSMBs) and/or publication and analysis committees to protect the integrity and appro-priate conduct of academic-based clinical trial research.

- This principle is consistent with the AAMC's 2006 recommendation in *Principles for Protecting Integrity in the Conduct and Reporting of Clinical Trials,* which asserts that any "multisite clinical trial, at the outset, should establish a publication and analysis (P&A) committee."[619] The recom-mendation continues:

  > It is essential that the P&A committee be independent of the spon-sor's control, have access to the full data set, understand and imple-ment the prespecified analysis plan, and have the resources and skills both to interpret that analysis and perform additional analysis if required. In order to prevent any appearance of undue influence by the sponsor, the P&A committee should contain a majority of partic-ipating, non-sponsor-employed investigators, with appropriate skills in analysis and interpretation of clinical trials. The P&A committee and the steering committee may have the same membership.[620]

- This recommendation is also consistent with a 2001 FDA guidance stating that it is desirable for all DSMBs overseeing a clinical trial to have statistical reports prepared by statisticians who are independent of the trial sponsors and clinical investigators.[621]

- *JAMA* (2008) has also pressed for greater assurances that data has been independently analyzed, insisting that for all industry-funded clinical trials "in which the data analysis is conducted only by statisticians employed by a company sponsoring the research," the *Journal* will require that a statistical analysis also be conducted by an independent statistician at an academic institution, such as a medical school, academic medical center, or government research institute, that has oversight over the person conducting the analysis and that is independent of the commercial sponsor.[622]

PRINCIPLE 52: Patient Notification

No industry-, government-, or nonprofit-sponsored research agreements should restrict faculty or academic professionals from notifying patients about health risks or lack of treatment efficacy when such information emerges and patients' health may be adversely affected.

- Whenever research is connected with a university, an academic medical center, or any of their affiliated teaching hospitals, patients' rights must be protected and treated as sacrosanct.

- This principle reflects recommendations in an October 2001 Canadian Association of University Teachers investigative report about the high-profile academic freedom case of Dr. Nancy Olivieri, a Canadian physician-researcher at the University of Toronto.[623] Legal provisions in Dr. Olivieri's corporate-sponsored research contract sought to prevent her from communicating health risks to the study's patient volunteers. The case is summarized in greater detail in the Introduction. The AAUP endorses the following specific recommendations drawn from *The Olivieri Report*:

- "[Academic contracts signed with an industry sponsor] should expressly provide that the clinical investigators shall not be prevented by the sponsor (or anyone) from informing participants in the study, members of the research group, other physicians administering the treatment, research ethics boards, regulatory agencies, and the scientific community, of risks to participants that the investigators identify during the research. The same provisions should apply to any risks of a treatment identified following the conclusion of a trial in the event there are patients being administered the treatment in a non-trial setting." [624]

- "Certain circumscribed confidentiality restrictions may be appropriate, for example, those pertaining to information on the chemical structure, or synthesis of a drug, or its method of encapsulation. However, restrictions on disclosure of risks to patients are not appropriate, subject only to the condition that the investigator believes there is a reasonable basis for identification of the risk. Under the term 'risk' we include inefficacy of the treatment, as well as direct safety concerns." [625]

PRINCIPLE 53: Undue Commercial Marketing Influence and Control at Academic Medical Centers

Educational programs, academic events, and presentations by faculty, students, postdoctoral fellows, and academic professionals must be free of industry marketing influence and control. Both academics and administrators should be prohibited from participating in industry-led "speakers bureaus" financed by pharmaceutical or other industry groups. Institutions should also establish funding mechanisms for clinical practice guidelines and high-quality accredited continuing medical education (CME) programs free of industry influence.

- The influence of industry marketers is excessive in three central areas for academic medical faculty: Industry-led Speakers Bureaus, Clinical Practice Guidelines, and Continuing Medical Education.

- Medical associations have advocated remedies in all three areas. They have done so because industry influence over educational programs and faculty presentations undermines research integrity and public trust and because this type of corporate marketing influence is often illegal.

According to the IOM (2009), the DOJ as well as state attorneys general have filed charges against a number of pharmaceutical and medical device companies for illegally awarding educational grants to induce use of the company's products (which can be illegal under the Medicare law), as well as industry initiatives to bias the content of educational programs, writings, and presentations, particularly as part of campaigns to promote off-label use of drugs. Drug promotion for purposes not approved by the FDA is also illegal.[626]

The IOM report cited several cases, including a $430 million payment in 2004 by Warner-Lambert to settle DOJ charges that the company promoted off-label uses of the drug Neurontin in violation of the Food, Drug, and Cosmetic Act: "According to DOJ, this illegal and fraudulent promotion scheme corrupted the information process relied upon by doctors in their medical decision making, thereby putting patients at risk." IOM noted the following tactics: promoting "so-called 'consultants meetings' in which physicians received a fee for attending expensive dinners or conferences during which presentations about off-label uses of Neurontin were made . . . [and sponsoring] purportedly 'independent medical education' events on off-label Neurontin uses with extensive input from Warner-Lambert regarding topics, speakers, content, and participants."[627]

The Office of the Inspector General at DHHS also stated that providing educational grants places a company at higher risk for violating federal anti-kickback rules and certain FDA regulations.[628] These compliance guidelines advise manufacturers to separate their [educational] grant making activities from their sales and marketing activities to "help insure that grant funding is not inappropriately influenced by sales or marketing motivations and that the educational purposes of the grant are legitimate."

The next three sections provide recommendations on issues of special concern.

Industry-Led Speakers Bureaus

The AAUP recommends that faculty be restricted from participating in industry-led "speakers bureaus" or other long-term industry-led paid speaking engagements, whether financed by the pharmaceutical industry or other industry groups.

- It is entirely appropriate for faculty to speak to industry groups and deliver presentations related to their research and areas of expertise. Yet when an industry group pays a faculty member to help market its products by delivering positive messages about them, the relationship between the faculty member and the company dishonors academic independence and professional integrity and should be prohibited. This principle is supported by several consensus recommendations. Both the IOM (2009)[629] and the AAMC (2008)[630] strongly discourage faculty from participation industry-led speakers bureaus. In 2006, a group of physicians at IMAP and other academic centers issued a set of detailed recommendations urging that medical faculty should be prohibited from involvement in speakers bureaus.[631] Some leading academic medical institutions (The University of Massachusetts, the Mayo Clinic, Johns

Hopkins, Stanford, and the University of Pittsburgh) have also instituted policy restrictions or outright prohibitions on faculty participation in speakers bureaus. These should be emulated.[632]

Studies suggest academic participation in industry-led speakers bureaus is surprisingly high: a 2007 study of 459 medical school department chairs found that 21 percent of clinical chairs had ongoing corporate speaking relationships.[633] This suggests pharmaceutical firms may target higher level faculty, often referred to in industry circles as "key opinion leaders." The apparent industry preference for recruiting senior faculty raises serious institutional COI concerns for the university. According to the IOM (2009), faculty participation in industry-led speakers bureaus presents a number of problems:

> ongoing company payments for presentations (and travel to attractive locations) create a risk of undue influence. A second concern that is frequently tied to the speakers bureau label is that the company exerts substantial control over the content of a presentation. Industry influence in these arrangements may be direct (e.g., when a talk and slides are largely or entirely prepared by someone else or when speakers are instructed to provide the company-prepared responses to questions and avoid the favorable mention of competing products). Influence may also be less direct (e.g., when a company-trained and company-paid physician modifies talks to fit the objectives of the company).[634]

Clinical Practice Guidelines

The AAUP endorses the following recommendations on Clinical Practice Guidelines originally issued by Institute of Medicine in 2009. These recommendations read as follows:

- Groups that develop clinical practice guidelines should generally exclude panel members with COI and should not accept direct funding for clinical practice guideline development from medical product companies or their foundations.

- Groups should publicly disclose their COI policies and procedures with their guidelines, along with the sources and amounts of indirect or direct funding received for guideline development.

- In the exceptional situation in which avoidance of panel members with COI is impossible because of the critical need for their expertise, groups should:

    (a) publicly document that they made a good-faith effort to find experts without COI by issuing a public call for members and other recruitment measures;

    (b) appoint a chair without a COI;

    (c) limit members with a COI to a distinct minority of the panel;

    (d) exclude individuals who have a fiduciary or promotional relationship with a company making a product that may be affected by the guidelines;

    (e) exclude panel members with conflicts from deliberating, drafting, or voting on specific recommendations; and

    (f) publicly disclose panel members' relevant COI.[635]

The IOM's 2009 COI report offers this explanation for its recommendation:

> Given the important role that clinical practice guidelines play in many aspects of health care, it is important that these guidelines be free of industry influence and be viewed by clinicians, policy makers, patients, and others as objective and trustworthy. . . . On the basis of its judgment and experience (including experience with conflicting guidelines and guidelines not based on formal reviews of the evidence), the committee believes that the risk of undue industry influence on clinical practice guidelines is significant, and that risk justifies that strong steps be taken to strengthen conflict of interest policies governing the development of guidelines.[636]

Studies have found that the process of developing Clinical Practice Guidelines, which physicians routinely use to guide medical practice, is rife with FCOI. One 2002 study by Choudhry et al. found that authors of practice guidelines had widespread financial relationships with the pharmaceutical industry; moreover, of the 44 practice guidelines reviewed, only two disclosed authors' financial relationships. A follow-up survey of 100 authors involved with developing 37 of these guidelines found that 87 percent had some financial relationship with industry, and that 59 percent had relationships with companies whose products were considered in the guideline itself.[637]

According to the IOM, several case studies reveal pervasive FCOI related to specific clinical guideline development programs. In one case from 2006,

"14 of 16 members of a group that worked on the development of guidelines for the treatment of anemia in patients with chronic kidney disease received consultant fees, speaking fees, research funds, or some combination thereof from at least one company that could be affected by the guidelines."[638] The principal guidelines funder was a company that would be affected by the guidelines, and the chair and co-chair of the work group had financial relationships with that company.[639] The development group recommended that the dosage of a drug made by the company be raised, which could have substantially increased profits to the company and costs to the Medicare program. By coincidence, the guidelines were announced at the same time that research was published showing adverse patient outcomes associated with the approach recommended by the guidelines. According to the IOM panel, the lead investigator allegedly informed the guidelines development work group that the study in question had been terminated early due to these adverse patient outcomes, and he advised the group to wait for the results before issuing new guidelines. But the guidelines group chose not to wait."[640]

In another case, Amgen, the manufacturer of epoetin, a drug that increases hemoglobin levels, was the founding and primary sponsor of the Kidney and Dialysis Outcomes Quality Initiative carried out by the National Kidney Foundation.[641] This project issued practice guidelines recommending an increase in the target hemoglobin level for patients with chronic kidney disease, which would entail the use of higher doses of epoetin and increased sales of the sponsor's product.

Continuing Medical Education (CME)

The AAUP endorses the 2009 IOM recommendation that calls for "a broad-based consensus process to develop a new system for funding high-quality accredited continuing medical education that is free of industry influence."[642]

- The AAUP encourages all universities, academic medical centers, and their faculty to develop new policies that preclude faculty from participating in CME programs paid for and influenced by industry.

- Universities and their medical faculty bear significant responsibility for the content and quality of this nation's CME programs, which all medical school graduates are required to take throughout their careers to keep their medical licenses and their medical knowledge up to date.

- In the past, fees paid by attendees covered the majority of the costs associated with the operation of these CME programs. Today, according to the Accreditation Council for Continuing Medical Education, roughly half of all funding for accredited continuing education programs comes from commercial sources.[643] (Although these programs are frequently administered by professional societies, academic medical schools also sponsor CME programs, and academic faculty members are extensively involved in all CME content development and instruction.)

- According to Congressional testimony by Eric Campbell, a member of the 2009 IOM panel that issued the above recommendation on CME: "The members of the IOM generally agreed that accredited continuing medical education has become far too reliant on industry funding and that such support tends to promote a narrow focus on medical products and a neglect of broader education on alternative strategies for preventing and managing health conditions and other important issues."[644]

Some institutions have already successfully limited their reliance on industry funded CME programs. In 2008, Stanford University School of Medicine announced that it would no longer accept direct industry funding for specific accredited CME courses either on or off campus, nor would it accept payments from third parties that have received commercial support.[645] Industry support is, however, permitted, provided it is not tied to a specific subject, course, or program and is provided through a central university office for continuing medical education.

According to the IOM, Memorial Sloan-Kettering Cancer Center went still further: In 2007, it "announced a 6-month trial period during which it would no longer accept industry funding for its continuing medical education programs (industry had provided about 25 percent of their CME funding). To reduce costs, off-site programs were moved on-site, free lunches were eliminated, advertising was cut, and fewer external speakers were used. Although the fees for external participants were raised by 10 to 20 percent, program attendance stayed the same. The ban on industry funding is now permanent."[646] The rationale for a permanent ban is clear: you cannot take the money without also taking on the bias associated with it.

PRINCIPLE 54: Appropriate Use of Facilities and Classrooms at Universities and Academic Medical Centers

Universities, academic medical schools, and affiliated teaching hospitals should have clear and consistent policies and practices barring pharmaceutical, medical device, and biotechnology companies from distributing free meals, gifts, or drug samples on campus and at affiliated academic medical centers, except under the control of central administration offices for use by patients who lack access to medications. As a general principle, academic facilities and classrooms should not be used for commercial marketing and promotion purposes unless advance written permission from academic institutional authorities is explicitly granted and academic supervision ensured. (Commercial marketing of services would, for example, be appropriate at a job fair.) Campus policies should also require all marketing representatives to obtain authorization before site visits. Finally, faculty, physicians, trainees, and students should be prohibited from directly accepting travel funds from industry, other than for legitimate reimbursement of contractual academic services. Direct or indirect industry travel funding for commercial marketing junkets, which may include trips to luxury resorts and expensive dinners, should be prohibited.

- This principle is consistent with recommendations issued by the IOM (2009),[647] AAMC (2008),[648] and IMAP and the ABIM Foundation jointly (2006).[649]

- Many physicians believe industry payments and free gifts do not affect their clinical behavior, but social science and neurobiological research indicates people often cannot assess their own bias accurately even when real bias exists.[650] Studies show that even token gifts create reciprocal expectations and behaviors that can distort research outcomes and professional behavior.

- According to a 2000 *JAMA* research review, industry-physician marketing and financial relationships have several negative consequences[651]:

  - Reduced generic prescribing (leading to higher drug expenditures)

  - Increased overall prescription rates

  - Quick uptake of the newest, most expensive drugs, including those of only marginal benefit over existing options with established safety records

  - Formulary request for drugs with few if any advantages over existing drugs.

Residents and physicians alike admit that without these marketing gifts and meals their interaction with the industry would decline.

The AAUP endorses the following recommendations (with some minor modifications) issued by the AAMC in 2008.[652] They cover four areas of direct relevance to Principle 54—industry distribution of free gifts, meals, and drug samples; marketing by pharmaceutical companies; marketing by device manufacturers; and industry-funded professional travel:

Industry Distribution of Free Gifts, Meals, and Drug Samples

- Academic medical centers should implement policies that prohibit acceptance of any industry gifts by physicians and other faculty, staff, students, and trainees of academic medical centers, whether on-site or off-site. Such standards should encompass gifts from equipment and service providers as well as pharmaceutical and device suppliers.

- With the exception of food provided in connection with ACCME-accredited programming and in compliance with ACCME guidelines, institutions should implement policies that industry-supplied food and meals are considered personal gifts and will not be permitted within academic medical centers. Policies should make clear that the same standard of behavior will be observed off-site.

- The distribution of medications in academic medical centers, including samples (if permitted), should be centrally managed in a manner that ensures timely patient access to optimal therapeutics throughout the health care system.

- If central management is not feasible, or would interfere with patient access to optimal therapeutics, the academic medical center should consider whether or not there are alternative ways to manage pharmaceutical sample distribution that do not carry the risks to professionalism associated with current practices.[653]

Summarizing, both the AAMC (2008) and the IOM (2009) call for stringent restrictions on corporate marketing of free meals, gifts, and drug samples at academic medical centers because research shows that these gifts often subconsciously bias physicians' medical decisions. On-site commercial marketing is pervasive at many academic medical schools and their affiliated teaching hospitals, where pharmaceutical, medical device, and biotechnology companies routinely distribute marketing pens, pads, mugs, free meals, and drug samples as gifts to both physicians and trainees.

The 2009 IOM panel report on COI in biomedicine noted that such restrictions are not intended to discourage "appropriate and productive research collaborations between industry and academic researchers. In addition to promoting scientific progress and the development of useful products, academy-industry collaborations can provide educational benefits to medical students, graduate students, and postdoctoral fellows who are engaged in legitimate collaborative research projects with industry partners under appropriate supervision."[654] However, the AAUP agrees with the IOM, AAMC, IMAP, ABIM, and others who have stated that industry marketing and gift giving must cease if the practice of medicine and teaching are to be free of industry influence and bias.

Marketing by Pharmaceutical Representatives[655]

- To protect patients, patient care areas, and work schedules, access by pharmaceutical representatives to individual physicians should be restricted to nonpatient care areas and nonpublic areas and should take place only by appointment or invitation of the physician.

- Involvement of students and trainees in such individual meetings should occur only for educational purposes and only under the supervision of a faculty member.

- Academic medical centers should develop mechanisms whereby industry representatives who wish to provide educational information on their products may do so by invitation in faculty supervised, structured group settings that provide opportunities for interaction and critical evaluation. Industry representatives with MD, PhD, or PharD degrees are best suited to transmit scientific information in these settings.

Marketing by Medical Device Companies[656]

- Access by device manufacturer representatives to patient care areas should be permitted by academic medical centers only when the representatives are appropriately credentialed by the center and should take place only by appointment or invitation of the physician.

- Representatives should not be allowed to be present during patient care interaction unless there has been prior disclosure to and consent by the patient, and then only to provide in-service training or assistance on devices and equipment.

- Student interaction with representatives should occur only for educational purposes under faculty supervision.

Industry-Funded Travel Expenses[657]

- Academic medical centers should prohibit their physicians, trainees, and students from directly accepting travel funds from industry, other than for legitimate reimbursement or contractual services as described above.

PRINCIPLE 55: Marketing Projects Masquerading as Clinical Research

Faculty, students, postdoctoral fellows, and academic professionals based at academic-affiliated institutions must not participate in marketing studies that masquerade as scientifically-driven clinical trial research. Such thinly disguised marketing studies are frequently referred to as "seeding trials" because they are intended primarily to expose doctors and patients to newer, brand-name drugs, not to uncover medically valuable or scientifically important insights.

- University and academic medical center policies should prohibit faculty and other academic researchers from accepting industry sponsored clinical research trials that have little or no objective scientific value or academic merit; such studies are often intended only to facilitate the marketing goals of the industry sponsor.

- In industry funded seeding trials[658] the sponsor's principle motivation is to change the prescribing habits of participating physicians or promote a new medical intervention.[659] Such a study may also take the form of a clinical trial protocol that is riddled with study design bias; by design, such a study enhances the likelihood of research outcomes that will favor the sponsor's product.

- Prominent academic medical journal editors and others, including former FDA commissioner David Kessler, have written critically of seeding trials and other types of research distortion and have urged academic institutions to decline this type of pseudo-scientific research.[660]

PRINCIPLE 56: Predetermined Research Results

Faculty and other academic investigators should be prohibited from soliciting research funding from outside sponsors with the implied suggestion or promise of predetermined research results.

- Promising a prospective sponsor positive research results before a study has begun is unethical and scientifically unsound. It should be prohibited in university codes of conduct; whenever identified and proven to have occurred, it should be punished.

Ethical research, especially research that involves human subjects, requires doubt about the outcome; this is known as equipoise. It is unethical to use human beings for commercially motivated trials whose findings are predetermined or manipulated to yield predetermined conclusions. Following litigation, several cases have come to light—at Harvard (medicine)[661] and UCLA (tobacco),[662] for example—where university professors pitched research studies to potential corporate sponsors by explicitly suggesting that predetermined research outcomes would favor the corporate sponsors' products or commercial interests. Such practices should be strictly forbidden, with appropriate review procedures, sanctions, and punishment specified for noncompliance.

Appendix A

Faculty Handbook and Collective Bargaining Agreement Versions of the 56 Principles

In a number of cases, translating these principles into handbook language required only adopting declarative in place of imperative language. Thus we replaced "the university should" with "the university will" or "the university should prohibit" with "the university prohibits" when appropriate. We also removed arguments advocating the principles or further explaining them, leaving handbook language to embody only the principles themselves. Some principles, including Principle 1, required more elaborate revision before they were fully consistent with a handbook context, and other principles, including 10 and 22, require a campus to draft its own policies.

On campuses with academic collective bargaining, those of these 56 principles that concern or affect terms and conditions of academic employment should be incorporated directly or by reference into the academic collective bargaining agreements. These provisions might especially include applicable grievance procedures, academic freedom and publication rights, intellectual property policies, and individual conflict of interest reporting obligations. The academic agreement should also ensure that the academic senate has a substantial role in establishing and implementing those of the recommendations that are not incorporated in the collective bargaining agreement.

PART I—GENERAL PRINCIPLES TO GUIDE ACADEMY-INDUSTRY ENGAGEMENT UNIVERSITY-WIDE

HANDBOOK PRINCIPLE 1: Faculty Governance: The university recognizes the primacy of shared academic governance in establishing campuswide policies for planning, developing, implementing, monitoring, and assessing all donor agreements and collaborations, whether with private industry, government, or nonprofit groups. In these areas, there will be meaningful participation of the appropriate faculty governance bodies, and, to the extent that donor agreements and collaborations relate to the academic mission of the university, the administration should concur with the judgment of these governance bodies regarding these donor agreements and collaborations except in rare instances and for compelling reasons that should be stated in detail. Faculty, not outside sponsors, will retain majority control over the campus management of these agreements and collaborations.

HANDBOOK PRINCIPLE 2: Academic Freedom, Autonomy, and Control: The university will protect and preserve its academic autonomy—including the academic freedom rights of faculty, students, postdoctoral fellows, and academic professionals—in all its relationships with industry and other funding sources by maintaining majority academic control over joint academy-industry committees and exclusive academic control over core academic functions (such as faculty research evaluations, faculty hiring and promotion decisions, curriculum development, classroom teaching, and course content).

HANDBOOK PRINCIPLE 3: Academic Publication Rights: Agreements between the university and third parties will fully protect academic publication rights, with only limited delays (a maximum of 30–60 days) to remove corporate proprietary or confidential information or to file for patents or other IP protection prior to publication. The university does not permit either sponsor efforts to obstruct publication or sponsored research agreements that limit or prohibit the free, timely, and open dissemination of research data, codes, reagents, methods, and results. Sponsor attempts to compel a faculty member, student, postdoctoral fellow, or academic professional to edit, revise, withhold, or delete contents of an academic publication (including a master's thesis or doctoral dissertation) or presentation (beyond legally justified claims to protect explicit trade secrets) are prohibited and must be acknowledged in writing as prohibited in all sponsored research contracts. While funders are free to make editorial suggestions, academic researchers are free at all times to accept or reject them.

HANDBOOK PRINCIPLE 4: The Authenticity of Academic Authorship: To protect the authenticity of academic publishing, the university prohibits faculty, students, postdoctoral fellows, medical residents, and other academic professionals from engaging in practices variously described as industry-led "ghostwriting" or "ghost authorship." Ghostwriting or ghost-authorship occurs when a private firm or an industry group initiates the publication of an "academic" article in a science or medical journal in support of its commercial products or interests, without publicly disclosing that the corporate entity has initiated and also often performed the initial drafting of the article, and then recruited an academic researcher (sometimes referred to as an "academic opinion leader") to sign on as the nominal "author" (frequently in exchange for a fee). This practice violates scholarly standards and is unacceptable in any academic setting.

HANDBOOK PRINCIPLE 5: Access to Complete Study Data and Independent Academic Analysis: The university prohibits faculty and others on campus from participating in sponsored research that restricts investigators' ability to gain access to the complete study data related to their sponsored research or that limits investigators' ability to conduct free, unfettered, and independent analyses of complete data to verify the accuracy and validity of final reported results. These basic academic freedom rights will be secured within the legal terms of all sponsored research contracts.

HANDBOOK PRINCIPLE 6: Confidential and Classified Research: The university does not permit classified research to be conducted on campus, and it does not permit confidential corporate, government, or nonprofit research that may not be published. [See the full Principle 6 for further specifications your campus may wish to embody in its handbook.]

HANDBOOK PRINCIPLE 7: Academic Consulting: To address the potential for conflicts of commitment and other financial conflicts of interest, all consulting contracts worth $5,000 or more a year are to be reported to and reviewed and managed by the university's standing conflict of interest committee(s) that are charged with addressing both individual and institutional conflicts of interest. Neither faculty members nor administrators may sign consulting contracts that undercut their professional ability to express their own independent expert opinions, except when consulting with industry, government, or other parties on explicitly classified or proprietary matters. All such consulting agreements are to be secured in writing.

PART II—GENERAL PRINCIPLES FOR ACADEMIC EDUCATION AND TRAINING

HANDBOOK PRINCIPLE 8: Recruiting and Advising Graduate Students, Medical Residents, and Faculty: The admission of graduate students to degree programs and the appointment of medical residents and faculty will be based on their overall qualifications, not on their potential to work under a particular donor agreement or collaborative research alliance, whether commercial, governmental, or nonprofit. A PhD student's main adviser must not have any significant financial interest, including equity, in a company that is funding or stands to profit from the student's thesis or dissertation research. Requests for exceptions will be evaluated with respect to both conflicts of interest and potential conflicts of commitment, all of which should be disclosed orally and in writing to all affected parties and periodically reviewed by [insert name of faculty body].

HANDBOOK PRINCIPLE 9: Impartial Academic Evaluation: Students, postdoctoral fellows, academic professionals, and junior colleagues are entitled to impartial and fair evaluations of their academic performance. Because of the risk of both real and perceived bias, faculty members with a significant personal financial interest in the outcome of their students' research may not have sole responsibility for evaluating student progress toward a degree.

HANDBOOK PRINCIPLE 10: Grievance Procedures: Although collective bargaining contracts often include detailed and exemplary grievance procedures, the AAUP as a whole has not endorsed model grievance procedures that go beyond what is called for in Regulation 16 of the *Recommended Institutional Regulations on Academic Freedom and Tenure:* "If any faculty member alleges cause for grievance in any matter not covered by the procedures described in the foregoing regulations, the faculty member may petition the elected faculty grievance committee [here name the committee] for redress. The petition will set forth in detail the nature of the grievance and will state against whom the grievance is directed. It will contain any factual or other data that the petitioner deems pertinent to the case. Statistical evidence of improper discrimination, including discrimination in salary, may be used in establishing a prima facie case. The committee will decide whether or not the facts merit a detailed investigation; if the faculty member succeeds in establishing a prima facie case, it is incumbent upon those who made the decision to come forward with evidence in support of their decision. Submission of a petition will not automatically entail investigation or detailed consideration thereof. The committee may seek to bring about a settlement of the issue(s) satisfactory to the parties. If in the opinion of the committee such a settlement is not possible or is not appropriate, the committee will report its findings and recommendations to the petitioner and to the appropriate administrative officer and faculty body, and the petitioner will, upon request, be provided an opportunity to present the grievance to them. The grievance committee will consist of three [or some other number] elected members of the faculty. No officer of the administration will serve on the committee." Faculty with financial conflicts related to a grievance filing will recuse themselves from its adjudication in formal proceedings. (See Principle 10 in the main report for specific guarantees that might be included in a handbook or collective bargaining agreement.)

PART III—GENERAL PRINCIPLES FOR MANAGEMENT OF INTELLECTUAL PROPERTY (IP)

HANDBOOK PRINCIPLE 11: Faculty Inventor Rights and IP Management: Faculty members' fundamental rights to direct and control their own research do not terminate when they make a new invention or other research discovery; these rights extend to decisions about their intellectual property—including invention management, IP licensing, commercialization, dissemination, and public use. Faculty assignment of an invention to a management agent, including the university that hosted the underlying research, will be voluntary and negotiated, rather than mandatory, unless federal statutes or previous sponsored research agreements dictate otherwise. Faculty inventors retain a vital interest in the disposition of their research inventions and discoveries and will, therefore, retain rights to negotiate the terms of their disposition. Neither the university nor its management agents will undertake IP decisions or legal actions directly or indirectly affecting a faculty member's research, inventions, instruction, or public service without the faculty member's and the inventor's express consent. Of course, faculty members, like other campus researchers, may voluntarily undertake specific projects as "work for hire" contracts. When such work for hire agreements are truly voluntary and uncoerced, their contracted terms may legitimately narrow faculty IP rights.

HANDBOOK PRINCIPLE 12: Shared Governance and the Management of University Inventions: The faculty senate or an equivalent body will play a primary role in defining the policies and public-interest commitments that will guide university-wide management of inventions and other knowledge assets stemming from campus-based research. University protocols that set the norms, standards, and expectations under which faculty discoveries and inventions will be controlled, distributed, licensed, and commercialized are subject to approval by the faculty senate or an equivalent governance body, as are the policies and public-interest commitments that will guide university-wide management of inventions and other knowledge assets stemming from campus-based research. A standing faculty committee will regularly review the university's invention management practices, ensure compliance with these principles, represent the interests of faculty investigators and inventors to the campus, and make recommendations for reform when necessary.

HANDBOOK PRINCIPLE 13: Adjudicating Disputes Involving Inventor Rights: Just as the right to control research and instruction is integral to academic freedom, so too are faculty members' rights to control the disposition of their research inventions. Inventions made in the context of university work are the results of scholarship. Invention management agents are directed to represent and protect the expressed interests of faculty inventors, along with the interests of the institution and the broader public to the maximum extent possible. Where the interests diverge insurmountably, the faculty senate or an equivalent body will adjudicate the dispute with the aim of recommending a course of action to promote the greatest benefit for the research in question, the broader academic community, and the public good. Student and other academic professional inventors have access to grievance procedures if they believe their inventor or other IP rights have been violated. Students will not be urged or required to surrender their IP rights to the university as a condition of participating in a degree program.

HANDBOOK PRINCIPLE 14: IP Management and Sponsored Research Agreements: In negotiating outside sponsored-research agreements, university administrators will make every effort to inform potentially affected faculty researchers and to involve them meaningfully in early-stage negotiations concerning invention management and IP. In the case of large-scale corporate sponsored research agreements like strategic corporate alliances (SCAs), which can have an impact on large numbers of faculty members, not all of whom may be identifiable in advance, a special faculty committee will be convened to participate in early-stage negotiations, represent collective faculty interests, and ensure compliance with relevant university protocols. Faculty participation in all institutionally negotiated sponsored research agreements will always be voluntary.

HANDBOOK PRINCIPLE 15: Humanitarian Licensing, Access to Medicines: When lifesaving drugs and other critical public-health technologies are developed in academic laboratories with public funding support, the university will make a strong effort to license such inventions in a manner that will ensure broad public access in both the developing and the industrialized world. When issuing an exclusive license to a company for the development of a promising new drug—or any other critical agricultural, health, or environmental safety invention—the university will always seek to include provisions to facilitate distribution of these inventions in developing countries at affordable prices.

HANDBOOK PRINCIPLE 16: Securing Broad Research Use and Distribution Rights: All contracts and agreements relating to university-generated inventions will include an express reservation of rights—often known as a "research exemption"—to allow for academic, nonprofit, and governmental use of academic inventions and associated intellectual property for non-commercial research purposes. Research exemptions will be reserved and well publicized prior to assignment or licensing so that faculty members and other academic researchers can share protected inventions and research results (including related data, reagents, and research tools) with colleagues located at this university or at any other nonprofit or governmental institution. The freedom to share and practice academic discoveries, for educational and research purposes, whether legally protected or not, is vitally important for the advancement of research and scientific inquiry. It also enables investigators to replicate and verify published results, a practice essential to scientific integrity.

HANDBOOK PRINCIPLE 17: Exclusive and Nonexclusive Licensing: The university, its contracted management agents, and faculty will always work to avoid exclusive licensing of patentable inventions, unless such licenses are absolutely necessary to foster follow-on use or to develop an invention that would otherwise languish. Exclusive and other restrictive licensing arrangements will be used sparingly, rather than as a presumptive default. When exclusive licenses are granted, they will have limited terms (preferably less than eight years), include requirements that the inventions be developed, and prohibit "assert licensing," sometimes referred to as "trolling" (aggressively enforcing patents against an alleged infringer, often with no intention of manufacturing or marketing the product yourself). Exclusive licenses made with the intention of permitting broad access through reasonable and nondiscriminatory sublicensing, cross-licensing, and dedication of patents to an open standard should meet public-access expectations. However, the preferred methods for disseminating university research are nonexclusive licensing and open dissemination, to protect the university's public interest mission, open-research culture, and commitment to advancing research and inquiry through broad knowledge sharing. To enhance compliance and public accountability, the university requires all invention-management agents to report publicly and promptly any exclusive licenses issued together with written statements detailing why an exclusive license was necessary and why a nonexclusive one would not suffice. The faculty senate, or another designated governance body, has the authority to review periodically any exclusive licenses and corresponding statements for consistency with the principle.

HANDBOOK PRINCIPLE 18: Upfront Exclusive Licensing Rights for Research Sponsors: The university will refrain from signing sponsored research agreements, especially multi-year, large-scale SCA agreements, granting sponsors broad title, or exclusive commercial rights, to future sponsored research inventions and discoveries unless such arrangements are narrowly defined and agreed to by all faculty members participating in, or foreseeably affected by, the alliance. If this arrangement is not feasible, as in the case of larger SCAs, the faculty senate (or another designated governance body) will review and approve the agreement and confirm its consistency with principles of academic freedom and faculty independence and with the university's public interest missions. Special consideration will be given to the impact exclusive licenses could have on future, as-yet-unimagined uses of technologies. When granted, exclusive rights will be defined as narrowly as possible and restricted to targeted fields of use only, and every effort will be made to safeguard against abuse of the exclusive position.

HANDBOOK PRINCIPLE 19: Research Tools and Upstream Platform Research: The university and its contracted management agents will undertake every effort to make available and broadly disseminate research tools and other upstream platform inventions in which they have acquired an ownership interest. They will avoid assessing fees, beyond those necessary to cover the costs of maintaining the tools and disseminating them, and avoid imposing other constraints that could hamper downstream research and development. No sponsored research agreement will include any contractual obligations that prevent outside investigators from accessing data, tools, inventions, and reports relating to scholarly review of published research, matters of public health and safety, environmental safety, and urgent public policy decisions.

HANDBOOK PRINCIPLE 20: Diverse Licensing Models for Diverse University Inventions: Faculty investigators and inventors and their management agents will work cooperatively to identify effective licensing or distribution models for each invention with the goal of enhancing public availability and use.

HANDBOOK PRINCIPLE 21: Rights to "Background Intellectual Property" (BIP): University administrators and their agents will not act unilaterally when granting sponsors rights to university-managed background intellectual property (BIP) related to a sponsor's proposed research area but developed without the sponsor's funding support. The university will be mindful of how BIP rights will affect faculty inventors and other investigators who are not party to the sponsored research agreement. University administrators and managers will not obligate the BIP of one set of investigators to another's sponsored research project, unless that BIP is already being made available under nonexclusive licensing terms or the affected faculty inventors and investigators have consented.

PART IV—GENERAL PRINCIPLES FOR MANAGEMENT OF CONFLICTS OF INTEREST (COI) AND FINANCIAL CONFLICTS OF INTEREST (FCOI)

HANDBOOK PRINCIPLE 22: [This principle asks that campuses develop their own financial COI policies. We have identified key elements of what such a policy should include, but campus implementation will require integrating the policy with local committee responsibilities and governance structures. However, a policy might begin with COI definitions, as suggested under the full Principle 22 discussion, and proceed to general statements (the university COI policy specifies how FCOI will be reported, reviewed, managed, or eliminated, along with our enforcement policies) before proceeding to details].

HANDBOOK PRINCIPLE 23: Consistent COI Enforcement across Campus: University COI policies apply consistently across the whole institution, including affiliated medical schools, hospitals, institutes, centers, and other facilities; they apply to faculty, students, administrators, and academic professionals.

HANDBOOK PRINCIPLE 24: Standing COI Committees: The COI committee oversees implementation of policies to address individual and institutional COI. At least one member is from outside the institution and has been approved by [insert the name of the appropriate faculty governance body]. Members must be free of conflicts of interest related to their COI oversight functions. After faculty financial COI disclosure statements have been reviewed by an appropriate campus standing committee, they will be made available to the public.

HANDBOOK PRINCIPLE 25: Reporting Individual COI: Faculty members and academic professionals are required to report to the standing campus COI committee all significant outside financial interests relating directly or indirectly to their professional responsibilities (research, teaching, committee work, and other activities), including the dollar amounts involved and the nature of the services compensated—regardless of whether or not they believe their financial interests might reasonably affect their current or anticipated university activities. Faculty members must also report family member patent royalty income and equity holdings related to their own teaching and research areas. All administrators will report similar financial interests both to their superiors and to the standing COI committee. Presidents and chancellors will also report such information to the standing committee.

HANDBOOK PRINCIPLE 26: Inter-office Reporting and Tracking of Institutional COI: To keep track of institutional conflicts of interest, our institutional COI committee has a campuswide reporting system that requires the technology transfer office, the office of sponsored programs, the development office, the grants office, institutional review boards (IRBs), purchasing operations, and corresponding offices at affiliated medical institutions to report, at least quarterly, to the standing COI committee on situations that might give rise to institutional conflicts.

HANDBOOK PRINCIPLE 27: Strategies for Reviewing, Evaluating, and Addressing COI: Our strategies for addressing individual financial COI include divesting troublesome assets, terminating consulting arrangements, resigning corporate board seats, and withdrawing from affected projects. Our methods for addressing institutional financial COI include divesting equity interest in companies doing campus research, placing conflicted equity holdings in independently managed funds with explicit firewalls to separate financial from academic decisions, recusing conflicted senior administrators from knowledge of, or authority over, affected research projects, and requiring outside committee review or oversight. Because of conflicting fiduciary responsibilities, the university prohibits senior administrators from receiving compensation for serving on corporate boards during their time in office.

HANDBOOK PRINCIPLE 28: Developing a Formal, Written COI Management Plan: If the university's standing COI committee finds compelling circumstances for allowing a research project, or other professional activity, to continue in the presence of a significant financial COI—without the elimination of the conflict—the committee will document the circumstances and write a formal management plan for each case. The plan will detail how the university will manage the financial COI and eliminate or reduce risks to its affected constituents (students, collaborating researchers, faculty, patients), its pertinent missions (research integrity, informed consent, and recruitment of research volunteers), and its reputation and public trust.

This policy is consistent with the Department of Health and Human Services (DHHS)-National Institutes of Health (NIH) rules implemented in 2011 to address financial conflicts, requiring all universities that receive DHHS or NIH grants to prepare and enforce such management plans.

HANDBOOK PRINCIPLE 29: Oversight and Enforcement of COI Rules: The university's COI policy details our oversight procedures, as well as our available sanctions for noncompliance. These are essential for ensuring compliance with university rules and maintaining public trust in the university's ability to regulate itself.

HANDBOOK PRINCIPLE 30: University–Vendor Relationships and COI: The university will ensure that vendor evaluation, selection, and contracting for university products and services are consistent with our academic mission and do not jeopardize the best interests of our students. Vendors must not be asked to make, or be coerced into making, financial contributions to the university, either through direct university donations or through the recruitment of other contributing donors, in exchange for winning university contracts. All university bidding for contracts and services related to such areas as banking and student loans will be conducted through a fair, impartial, and competitive selection process.

HANDBOOK PRINCIPLE 31: COI Transparency: Public Disclosure of Financial Interests and COI Management Plans: University COI policy requires faculty, administrators, students, postdoctoral fellows, and academic professionals to disclose to all journal editors all significant personal financial interests that may be directly or indirectly related to the manuscripts they are submitting for consideration. COI disclosure on publications is to summarize funding sources for the last five years, not just for the project at hand. The same COI disclosure requirements apply to oral presentations, including those presented in conferences, courts, and legislative chambers. After the university's standing COI committee reviews faculty COI disclosure statements, they will be posted to a public website, and the information on the website will remain publicly accessible for at least a decade. This measure addresses growing demands from Congress, state governments, journal editors, the media, and public-interest groups for increased reporting and transparency of faculty COI. It is also consistent with DHHS-NIH (2011) rules, which require universities to disclose all significant financial COI (as per the DHHS-NIH definition) related to a faculty member's DHHS-funded research on a public website or to provide the information upon public request within five days. Disclosure of financial COI also extends to affected patients and to volunteers for human subject research projects.

PART V—TARGETED PRINCIPLES: MANAGING COI IN THE CONTEXT OF CLINICAL CARE AND HUMAN SUBJECT RESEARCH

HANDBOOK PRINCIPLE 32: Individual and Institutional COI and Human Subject Research: To maximize patient safety and preserve public trust in the integrity of academic research, the university operates with a strong presumption against permitting financial COI related to clinical medical research and experimental studies involving human subjects. A "rebuttable presumption" against permitting clinical trial research that may be compromised by financial COI will govern decisions about whether financially conflicted researchers or financial conflicts involving the institution will be allowed in pursuing a particular human subject research protocol or project, unless a compelling case can be made to justify an exception.

HANDBOOK PRINCIPLE 33: Institutional Review Boards (IRBs) and COI Management: An institutional review board (IRB) must review all proposed human clinical trial protocols, paying careful consideration to all related financial COI, before research is allowed to proceed. First, financially conflicted IRB members will recuse themselves from deliberations related to studies with which they have a potential conflict. Second, the institution's standing COI committee will prepare summary information about all institutional and individual financial COI related to the research protocol under review. The summary will accompany the protocol when it is presented to the IRB. The IRB will take the COI information into account when determining whether, and under what circumstances, to approve a protocol. Neither the IRB nor the standing COI committee is to reduce the stringency of the other's management requirements. Finally, if a research protocol is allowed to proceed, the IRB will disclose any institutional or investigator financial COI as well as the university's management plans for addressing them to all patient volunteers (in informed consent documents) and all investigators and units involved with the research protocol.

HANDBOOK PRINCIPLE 34: COI, Medical Purchasing, and Clinical Care: The university's COI policy requires all personnel with financial interests in any manufacturer of pharmaceuticals, devices, or equipment, or in any provider of services, to disclose such interests and to recuse themselves from involvement in related purchasing decisions. To the extent an individual's expertise is necessary in evaluating a product or a service, the individual's financial ties will be disclosed to those responsible for purchasing decisions.

HANDBOOK PRINCIPLE 35: COI Transparency in the Context of Medical Care: University policy requires all physicians, dentists, nurses, pharmacists, and other health professionals, as well as investigators, to disclose their financial COI to both patients and the broader public.

PART VI—TARGETED PRINCIPLES: STRATEGIC CORPORATE ALLIANCES (SCAs)

HANDBOOK PRINCIPLE 36: Shared Governance and Strategic Corporate Alliances (SCAs): The planning, negotiation, approval, execution, and ongoing oversight of new SCAs formed on campus require the involvement of the faculty senate. The senate will appoint a committee to review a first draft of a confidential memorandum of understanding (MOU) pertaining to newly proposed SCAs. The direct and indirect financial obligations of all parties will be made clear from the outset. Before a final agreement is reached on a broad SCA, the full faculty senate will review it. Formal approval of broad SCAs must await both stages in this process. All approved SCA agreements will be made available to all faculty and academic professionals as well as to the public. If the SCA designates specific funding for new full-time faculty appointments (FTEs), all normal university and departmental procedures for academic searches and appointments—as well as advancement and promotion decisions—will be followed to honor and protect academic self-governance. Temporary employees may not exclusively staff, administer, or supervise SCAs. Normal grievance procedures and due process will govern complaints regarding interference with academic freedom or other faculty or academic rights that may arise under SCAs.

HANDBOOK PRINCIPLE 37: SCA Governance and Majority Academic Control: The university will retain majority academic control and voting power over internal governance bodies charged with directing or administering SCAs in collaboration with outside corporate sponsors. The SCA's main governance body will include members who are not direct stakeholders of the SCA and are based in academic disciplines and units that do not stand to benefit from the SCA in any way. A joint university-industry SCA governance body may have a role in awarding funding, but it will have no role in such exclusively academic functions as faculty hiring, curriculum design, and course content.

HANDBOOK PRINCIPLE 38: Academic Control over SCA Research Selection (for Broad SCAs): In the case of broad SCAs, university representatives will retain majority representation and voting power on SCA committees charged with evaluating and selecting research proposals or making final research awards. These committees must also employ an independent peer-review process.

HANDBOOK PRINCIPLE 39: Peer Review (for Broad SCAs): Using a standard peer-review process, independent academic experts will evaluate applications and award funding whenever SCAs issue a request for proposals (RFP) in a new grant cycle. Any expert involved in the peer-review and grant-award process should be free of personal financial COI related to the area of research being reviewed to ensure that research selection is scientifically driven, impartial, and fair. Appointees to committees charged with research selection are prohibited from awarding commercial research funding to themselves, their departments, or their labs and should not be past recipients of funding from that SCA.

HANDBOOK PRINCIPLE 40: Transparency regarding the SCA Research Application Process (for Broad SCAs): SCA agreements will clearly and transparently detail their methods and criteria for research selection and will explain how academic researchers may apply for SCA grant funding.

HANDBOOK PRINCIPLE 41: Protection of Publication Rights and Knowledge Sharing in SCA Agreements: All the provisions of Principle 3 apply to strategic corporate alliances as well.

HANDBOOK PRINCIPLE 42: SCA Confidentiality Restrictions: To protect the university's distinctively open academic research environment, restrictions on sharing confidential corporate information and other confidentiality restrictions will be minimized insofar as possible in SCA agreements.

HANDBOOK PRINCIPLE 43: SCA Anti–Competitor Agreements: Restrictions in SCA agreements on faculty, academic professionals, postdoctoral fellows, and students interacting or sharing information and research with private-sector competitors of SCA sponsors, or receiving separate research support from outside firms—often embodied in anti-competitor or noncompete agreements—will be avoided or minimized to the greatest extent possible.

HANDBOOK PRINCIPLE 44: Exclusive Licensing and SCA Agreements: All the provisions of Principles 17 and 18 apply to strategic corporate alliances as well.

HANDBOOK PRINCIPLE 45: Limits on Broader Academic Disruption by SCAs: SCAs can be approved only if faculty members and students within all academic units will, as a practical as well as a theoretical matter, retain the freedom to pursue their chosen research topics, including avenues of inquiry that are outside the purview of, not in conformity with, or even in opposition to the SCA's research agenda. All SCA agreements must strive to limit to the greatest extent possible negative financial, intellectual, or professional impacts on other academic units, colleges, and the university as a whole, as well as on faculty members, academic professionals, postdoctoral fellows, and students engaged in research and activities outside the purview of the collaborative SCA arrangement. No faculty member, postdoctoral fellow, academic professional, or student will be coerced into participating in a sponsored project; all participation will be entirely voluntary.

HANDBOOK PRINCIPLE 46: Early Termination of SCA Sponsor Funding: All SCA legal contracts must include provisions to prohibit sudden, early termination of the agreement. If the negotiating process leads to inclusion of an early-termination option, it must prohibit the sponsor from arbitrarily or suddenly terminating the agreement or decreasing pledged funding prior to the expected term, without at least three months of advance notification. Salaries and research costs associated with the project must be continued for that period.

HANDBOOK PRINCIPLE 47: Independent, Majority Faculty Oversight of the SCA, and Post-Agreement Evaluation: An independent, majority faculty oversight committee consisting of faculty members with no direct involvement in the SCA will be established at the start of a new SCA agreement to monitor and at least annually review the SCA and its compliance with university policies and guidelines. A post-agreement evaluation plan will also be included in the formal SCA contract so the campus can reflect and draw on the experience in organizing future campus-based academy-industry alliances. External evaluation may be appropriate for broad

SCAs and will be initiated as appropriate. Evaluation reports will be public documents.

HANDBOOK PRINCIPLE 48: Public Disclosure of SCA Research Contracts and Funding Transparency: No SCA or other industry-, government-, or nonprofit-sponsored contract may restrict faculty members, students, postdoctoral fellows, or academic professionals from freely disclosing their funding source. A signed copy of all final legal research contracts formalizing an SCA and any other types of sponsored research agreements formed on campus will be made freely available to the public—with discrete redactions only to protect valid commercial trade secrets, not for other reasons.

PART VII—TARGETED PRINCIPLES: CLINICAL MEDICINE, CLINICAL RESEARCH, AND INDUSTRY SPONSORSHIP

HANDBOOK PRINCIPLE 49: Access to Complete Clinical Trial Data and the Performance of Independent Academic Analysis: All the provisions of Principle 5 apply to clinical trial data as well.

HANDBOOK PRINCIPLE 50: Registry of Academic-Based Clinical Trials in a National Registry: All clinical trials conducted by the university's academic investigators will be entered into ClinicalTrials.gov (http://www.clinicaltrials.gov/)—the national clinical trial registry maintained by the US National Library of Medicine and the National Institutes of Health. The entry will be made at or before the onset of patient enrollment.

HANDBOOK PRINCIPLE 51: Safeguarding the Integrity and Appropriate Conduct of Clinical Trials: All clinical trials affiliated with the university are required to use independent data safety monitoring boards (DSMBs) and/or publication and analysis committees to protect the integrity and appropriate conduct of academic-based clinical trial research.

HANDBOOK PRINCIPLE 52: Patient Notification: Industry-, government-, and nonprofit-sponsored research agreements may not restrict faculty members or academic professionals from notifying patients about health risks and/or lack of treatment efficacy when such information emerges and patients' health may be adversely affected.

HANDBOOK PRINCIPLE 53: Undue Commercial Marketing Influence and Control at Academic Medical Centers: Educational programs, academic events, and presentations by faculty members, students, postdoctoral fellows, and academic professionals must be free of industry marketing influence and control. Both academics and administrators are prohibited from participating in industry-led "speakers bureaus" financed by pharmaceutical or other industry groups.

HANDBOOK PRINCIPLE 54: Appropriate Use of Facilities and Classrooms at Universities and Academic Medical Centers: Pharmaceutical, medical-device, and biotechnology companies may not distribute free meals, gifts, or drug samples on campus or at affiliated academic medical centers, except under the control of central administration offices for use by patients who lack access to medications. Academic facilities and classrooms may not be used for commercial marketing and promotion purposes unless advance written permission from academic institutional authorities has been explicitly granted and academic supervision arranged. (Commercial marketing of services would, for example, be appropriate at a job fair.) All marketing representatives are required to obtain advance authorization before site visits. Finally, faculty members, physicians, trainees, and students are prohibited from directly accepting travel funds from industry, other than for legitimate reimbursement of contractual academic services. Direct or indirect industry travel funding for commercial marketing junkets, which may include trips to luxury resorts and expensive dinners, are prohibited.

HANDBOOK PRINCIPLE 55: Marketing Projects Masquerading as Clinical Research: Faculty members, students, postdoctoral fellows, and academic professionals based at our academic-affiliated institutions are prohibited from participating in marketing studies that masquerade as scientifically driven clinical trial research.

HANDBOOK PRINCIPLE 56: Predetermined Research Results: Faculty members and other academic investigators are prohibited from soliciting research funding from outside sponsors with the implied suggestion or promise of predetermined research results.

Appendix B

The Sources of the 56 Principles: A Summary of Which Principles Are New, versus Those Derived from AAUP or Other Professional Groups' Recommendations

Here we review which principles fall into each of three categories and briefly identify their sources. It should be noted that assigning the categories "Closely Drawn from Previous Recommendations," "Adapted," or "New"—to each principle is not an exact science. A rough tally finds:

- 35 of these 56 principles are closely drawn from principles issued by the AAUP or other professional groups.

- 2 of these recommendations are adapted from previous recommendations issued by the AAUP or other groups.

- 21 are new; to our knowledge, they have not been previously endorsed.

PART I. GENERAL PRINCIPLES TO GUIDE ACADEMY-INDUSTRY ENGAGEMENT UNIVERSITY-WIDE (1–7)

- Principles 1–6 are closely drawn from previous recommendations issued by the AAUP and other professional academic groups, including the Association of American Universities (AAU),[663] Association of American Medical Centers (AAMC),[664] AAU and the AAMC jointly,[665] Federation of American Societies for Experimental Biology (FASEB),[666] Institute of Medicine (IOM),[667] International Committee of Medical Journal Editors (ICMJE),[668] and the World Association of Medical Editors (WAME);[669]

- Principle 7 is adapted, primarily from a recommendation issued by the IOM (see the main report for details).[670]

PRINCIPLE 1—Faculty Governance
(closely drawn from previous recommendations):

- Faculty self-governance and academic freedom have been closely linked in AAUP policy since the organization was founded. We have separated them into principles 1 and 2 not only for clarity's sake, but also because the support they require in Industry-Academy agreements necessitates somewhat different statements and guarantees. But we will address their history in AAUP documents in tandem. After reminding us that one of the purposes of the university is "to develop experts for various branches of the public service," the AAUP's 1915 founding "Declaration of Principles on Academic Freedom and Academic Tenure" notably adds the following: "the first condition of progress is complete and unlimited freedom to pursue inquiry and publish its results. Such freedom is the breath in the nostrils of all scientific activity."[671] Years later, the 1966 "Statement on Government of Colleges and Universities," which was jointly formulated by the AAUP, the American Council on Education (ACE), and the Association of Governing Boards of Universities (AGB), emphasized that "the faculty has primary responsibility for such fundamental areas" as instruction and research.[672] The ACE recommended the statement to its members and the AGB formally adopted it. The 1994 statement "On the Relationship of Faculty Governance to Academic Freedom" repeats that principle and adds that in shared governance "the faculty's voice on matters having to do with teaching and research should be given the greatest weight."[673] The 1965 statement "On Preventing Conflicts of Interest in Government-Sponsored Research at Universities" specifies that the "process of disclosure and consultation" in research "must, of course, be carried out in a manner that does not infringe on the legitimate freedoms and flexibility of action of the university and its staff members that have traditionally characterized a university. It is desirable that standards and procedures of the kind discussed be formulated and administered by members of the university community themselves, through their joint initiative and responsibility."[674]

- In 2005, this principle on faculty self governance was reaffirmed by a special Cornell University Faculty Senate Committee charged with developing principles to guide the development of large-scale strategic corporate alliances (SCAs) on that campus.[675]

PRINCIPLE 2—Academic Freedom, Autonomy, and Control (closely drawn from previous recommendations):

- This principle stems from long-standing, broadly supported academic principles endorsed previously by AAUP (see the AAUP statements discussed directly above that apply to both Principles 1 and 2).

- See also the AAUP's "Statement on Conflicts of Interest" (1990), and its statement on "Freedom in the Classroom" (2007), which further touch on these issues of academic freedom and academic autonomy in both teaching and research.[676]

PRINCIPLE 3—Academic Publication Rights (closely drawn from previous recommendations):

- The freedom of faculty to publish their views without restraint is foundational with the AAUP, and has enjoyed widespread endorsement within the university community. The AAUP first affirmed this principle in its 1915 "Declaration of Principles on Academic Freedom and Academic Tenure," where it observed that faculty "freedom of inquiry and research" was already nearly universally accepted. More recently, the AAUP has addressed those rights in the "Statement on Corporate Funding of Academic Research" (2004), affirming as a matter of principle that corporate research "contracts should explicitly provide for the open communication of research results, not subject to the sponsor's permission for publication."[677] Footnote no. 4 of this document elaborates by quoting and summarizing a 1999 National Institutes of Health (NIH) principles and guidelines statement, which states that grant "recipients are expected to avoid signing agreements that unduly limit the freedom of investigators to collaborate and publish" and that they further "have an obligation to preserve research freedom" and "ensure timely disclosure of their scientists' research findings." The note concludes with the following: "excessive publication delays or requirements for editorial control, approval of publication, or withholding of data all undermine the credibility of research results and are unacceptable."[678] The AAUP's "Statement on Conflicts of Interest" (1990) had earlier enunciated similar principles: "faculties should ensure that any cooperative venture between members of the faculty and outside agencies, whether public or private, respects the primacy of the university's principal mission, with regard to the choice of subjects of research and the reaching and publication of results."[679]

- The 30–60 day maximum publication delay, recommended here, has also been adopted by universities and endorsed by the NIH, which considers this to be sufficient time to secure commercial rights to intellectual property through the filing of a provisional patent or other methods.[680]

PRINCIPLE 4—The Authenticity of Academic Authorship (closely drawn from previous recommendations):

- The IOM, the AAMC, and several other groups have also called for unambiguous prohibitions on faculty participation in ghostwriting and other violations of authentic academic authorship.[681] The ICMJE and WAME also have sought to rein in this practice through journal submission policies and signature guarantees from authors.[682]

- This Principle upholds foundational standards of academic integrity that the AAUP has championed in numerous past policy statements. The AAUP's "Statement on Professional Ethics" (1966), for example, points out that faculty must "practice intellectual honesty" and adds that "although professors may follow subsidiary interests, these interests must never seriously hamper or compromise their freedom of inquiry." The statement concludes more broadly: "As citizens engaged in a profession that depends upon freedom for its health and integrity, professors have a particular obligation to promote conditions of free inquiry and to further public understanding of academic freedom."[683] The AAUP's "Statement on Multiple Authorship" (1990) calls for "making plain the actual contribution of each scholar to a collaborative work," and warns that accurate acknowledgment of multiple authorship is essential in establishing "the authority that individual scholars may claim." It further adds that disciplinary practices that obscure authorial responsibility "may give rise to the suspicion, if not the actuality, of questionable ethical practices."[684] The Association's "Statement on Plagiarism" (1990) calls for "any discovery of suspected plagiarism" to be "brought at once to the attention of the affected parties and, as appropriate, to the profession at large."[685]

PRINCIPLE 5—Access to Complete Study Data and Independent Academic Analysis (closely drawn from previous recommendations):

- This principle draws from recent guidelines and recommendations issued by the AAMC, ICMJE, and WAME.[686] See the main report for further details.

PRINCIPLE 6—Confidential and Classified Research (closely drawn from previous recommendations):

- This is a general principle with broad academic endorsement. The AAUP has addressed this issue on numerous occasions, most recently in a 2003 statement entitled, "Academic Freedom and National Security in a Time of Crisis," which addresses the sweeping legal changes that Congress adopted governing intelligence gathering and secrecy after the September 11, 2001, terrorist attacks.[687]

- Many prominent universities have written policies that ban confidential and/or classified research on campus, including Cornell University, the Massachusetts Institute of Technology, and University of California, Berkeley.[688] However, several of these institutions also permit such classified and confidential research in designated facilities off campus (see the main report for more discussion and details). Other universities—such as Alaska, Colorado, Michigan, and Virginia—permit classified research "on a case by case basis." In total, the AAUP estimates there are roughly two dozen universities at which researchers are permitted to take on some classified work.[689]

PRINCIPLE 7—Academic Consulting (adapted):

- Most aspects of this principle have been endorsed by other academic groups, but not in this precise form, which is why we label it "adapted." In 2009, for example, the IOM issued a similar guidance.[690] And in 2008 the AAMC-AAU jointly recommended that particular care and attention be paid to "specific types" of consulting activities (including "Speakers' bureaus or speaking engagements whose primary purpose is product marketing rather than an independent presentation of educational material"; or "Service as an officer, director, member of the scientific advisory board of a company"), as well as particular terms that may surface in consulting agreements that are inconsistent with professional academic duties (such as "non-competition provisions" or "confidentiality").[691]

- Many individual colleges and universities have written policies that address some aspects of academic consulting, however most broadly emphasize that such outside activities must not interfere with university commitments, or compromise the faculty's primary professional obligations, without providing much specificity (see, for example, the University of California system-wide policy).[692] There are significant institutional differences with respect to whether or how much effort employees may devote to consulting outside the institution, and how much oversight and monitoring of these activities the university will perform.[693]

- Finally, the AAUP's recommendation that all faculty consulting income valued at $5,000 or more must be reported to a university's standing COI committee for review is consistent with the rules addressing financial COI issued by the Department of Health and Human Services (DHHS) and the NIH in 2011, which mandate a $5,000 threshold for disclosure and management of a faculty member's financial COI.[694]

PART II. GENERAL PRINCIPLES FOR ACADEMIC EDUCATION AND TRAINING (8–10)

PRINCIPLE 8—Recruiting and Advising Graduate Students, Medical Residents, and Faculty (new):

To the AAUP's knowledge, this principle is new because it has not been officially addressed in previous consensus reports issued by any major professional academic organizations. However, it is influenced and closely drawn from language that appeared in recommendations issued by the University of California, San Diego's Joint Academic Senate-Administration Committee on University Interaction with Industry in 1999.[695] This UCSD committee was charged with addressing the increasingly numerous, varied, and complex interactions between UCSD faculty and private, for-profit companies; it devoted considerable attention to the problems that may surface when a supervisor or mentor has a financial COI related to his or her academic research.

- This principle is also influenced by recommendations issued by the AAMC advising schools to prohibit "agreements with sponsors or financially interested companies that place restrictions on the activities of students or trainees or that bind students or trainees to non-disclosure provisions."[696] And by recommendations, issued by the AAMC, that address the mentoring responsibilities of the faculty, noting that advisers should "recognize the possibility of conflicts between the interests of externally funded research programs and those of the graduate student," and should ensure that those conflicts will not be allowed to interfere with the student's thesis or dissertation research.[697]

PRINCIPLE 9—Impartial Academic Evaluation (adapted):

- The AAUP's "Statement on Graduate Students" (1999) lists a number of principles, including "graduate students have the right to academic freedom," and "they should be able to express their opinions freely about matters of institutional policy, and they should have the same freedom of action in the political domain as faculty members should have." It goes on to say that "graduate students are entitled to the protection of their intellectual property rights," and that "graduate-student employees with grievances, as individuals or as a group, should submit them in a timely fashion and should have access to an impartial faculty committee or, if provided under institutional policy, arbitration."[698] The "Joint Statement on Rights and Freedoms of Students" (1967) affirms that all "students should have protection through orderly procedures against prejudiced or capricious academic evaluation."[699]

- The language in this principle was adapted from the AAMC recommendations cited above under Principle 8, and from an IOM proposal discussed just below. In its 2008 report, the AAMC-AAU cautioned that when a faculty adviser has a related financial conflict of interest, the university should carefully assess whether "the roles of students, trainees, and junior faculty and staff [are] appropriate and free from exploitation," and whether special protections are needed for "vulnerable members" of the research team.[700] In such a scenario, the IOM proposed that "one protection might be to provide such individuals with access to independent senior faculty members for independent review and guidance when questions and concerns arise."[701]

PRINCIPLE 10—Grievance Procedures (new):

- This recommendation is new; however, it draws upon the AAUP's earlier "Recommended Institutional Regulations," known as the RIRs, which contain specific due process and grievance procedures for various claims and for different categories of employees, and from the AAUP policy statement titled "The Assignment of Course Grades and Student Appeals."[702]

PART III. GENERAL PRINCIPLES FOR MANAGEMENT OF INTELLECTUAL PROPERTY (IP) (11–21)

PRINCIPLE 11—Faculty Inventor Rights and IP Management (closely drawn from previous recommendations):

- The academic freedom principles undergirding Principle 11 have been guiding the AAUP since its founding. To the AAUP's knowledge, this Principle has not been endorsed previously by other professional academic groups, however it builds upon several recent policy statements issued by the AAUP relating to faculty generated IP. It is also consistent with long-standing principles of academic freedom, and with US patent and copyright laws pertaining to the ownership rights of inventors.

- As the AAUP's 1999 "Statement on Copyright" observed regarding faculty research and inventions subject to copyright: "the faculty member rather than the institution determines the subject matter, the intellectual approach and direction, and the conclusions"; for the institution to control the "dissemination of the work" would be "deeply inconsistent with fundamental principles of academic freedom." The statement goes on to note: "it has been the prevailing academic practice to treat the faculty member as the copyright owner of works that are created independently and at the faculty member's own initiative for traditional academic purposes."[703]

- In 1998, the AAUP established a Special Committee on Distance Education and Intellectual Property Issues, which released several documents the following year, including one recommending language for campus policies regarding IP rights and management titled "Sample Intellectual Property Policy and Contract Language." This document begins: "the copyright statement takes as its guiding assumption that the faculty member (or members) who create the intellectual property own the intellectual property," adding that "that assumption applies to the patent area as well." It went on to recommend the following language for campus adoption: "Intellectual property created, made, or originated by a faculty member shall be the sole and exclusive property of the faculty, author, or inventor, except as he or she may voluntarily choose to transfer such property, in full or in part."[704] Drawing on a detailed discussion of "work made for hire" in the "Statement on Copyright," the Special Committee endorsed the following: "A work should not be treated as 'made for hire' merely because it is created with the use of university resources, facilities, or materials of the sort traditionally and commonly made available to faculty members." It went on to note: "Funds received by the faculty member from the sale of intellectual property owned by the faculty author or inventor shall be allocated and expended as determined solely by the faculty author or inventor." Recognizing the current trend for universities to assign IP rights to institutions involuntarily, the AAUP "Statement on Copyright" further warns: "If the faculty member is indeed the initial owner of copyright, then a unilateral institutional declaration cannot effect a transfer, nor is it likely that a valid transfer can be effected by the issuance of appointment letters to new faculty members requiring, as a condition of employment, that they abide by a faculty handbook that purports to vest in the institution the ownership of all works created by the faculty member for an indefinite future."[705]

- Principle 11 was additionally influenced by recent media reports about university technology transfer offices abrogating the academic freedom rights of faculty related to IP decisions pertaining to their research (some of these cases are discussed in the main report), and also by a 2010 faculty Advisory Board ruling in an academic freedom case involving a dispute between Stanford University and a Stanford professor (also discussed in the main report).

- The principles expressed here were further affirmed by a US Supreme Court decision handed down in 2011, in *Board of Trustees of Leland Stanford Junior University v. Roche Molecular Systems, Inc. (Stanford v. Roche)*, which served to clarify the rights of faculty inventors under the 1980 Bayh-Dole Act (this legislation and ruling are discussed in greater detail in the Introduction). Here the US Supreme Court affirmed that US patent law has always favored, and should continue to favor, the rights of individual inventors, and that universities seeking to claim rights to inventions must therefore get explicit concurrence from the inventors involved.[706]

PRINCIPLE 12—Shared Governance and the Management of University Inventions (closely drawn from previous recommendations):

- Principle 12 grows directly out of earlier AAUP policy statements on IP-related issues discussed under Principle 11 and here. As noted under Principle 12, the AAUP has already recommended that a campus IP committee "play a role in policy development." The AAUP's 2004

"Statement on Corporate Funding of Academic Research" further observes: "Consistent with principles of sound academic governance, the faculty should have a major role not only in formulating the institution's policy with respect to research undertaken in collaboration with industry, but also in developing the institution's plan for assessing the effectiveness of the policy."[707] The AAUP has long asserted the faculty's primary responsibility for the "subject matter and methods" of research, a principle reaffirmed in the 1966 "Statement on Government of Colleges and Universities."[708]

- Principle 12 also draws on a National Academy of Sciences report titled "Managing University Intellectual Property in the Public Interest," published in 2011, which reads as follows:

> Universities with sizable research portfolios should consider creating a standing advisory committee composed of members of the faculty and administration; representatives of other business development units in or affiliated with the institution such as business incubators, research parks, proof-of-concept centers, and entrepreneurial education programs; members of the relevant business and investment communities; and, if appropriate, local economic development officials. The committee should meet regularly to help the technology licensing unit elaborate practices consistent with the institution's goals and policies, consider how best to exploit inventions where the path to wide availability and broad public benefit is not clear, and identify new opportunities.
>
> A separate committee of faculty, employee, and administration representatives (who may or may not also serve on the advisory committee) should be charged with advising on university policy regarding technology transfer and hearing and helping to resolve disputes between inventors and the technology transfer office with respect to the protection and commercialization of inventions. Both the full advisory committee and the internal committee should make recommendations to the provost or other executives of the university.[709]

PRINCIPLE 13—Adjudicating Disputes Involving Inventor Rights (new):

- Principle 13 is new; however, it grows directly out of earlier AAUP policy statements on IP-related issues discussed under Principle 11, above, as well as here. The AAUP's 1999 "Sample Intellectual Property Policy and Contract Language" takes a parallel approach to the one offered here: "In light of the changing legislative environment, and in view of the evolution of contracts and policies in the intellectual property area AAUP believes that the establishment of an on-going Intellectual Property Committee representing both faculty and administration would serve a useful purpose in both collective bargaining and non-collective bargaining environments. Such a committee could serve a variety of purposes, including keeping faculty and administration apprised of technological changes that will affect the legislative, contract, and policy contexts. Such a committee would play a role in policy development, as well as perform a dispute resolution function. In the absence of such an overall policy committee, a dispute resolution committee with both administrative and faculty representation is essential."[710] Here, we recommend an independent role for a faculty governing body.

PRINCIPLE 14—IP Management and Sponsored Research Agreements (new):

- Principle 14 is new; however, it flows logically from the recommendations contained in Principle 11, which were drawn from earlier AAUP statements relating to faculty rights to own and control their own intellectual property. The purpose of Principle 14 is to extend these faculty rights to both traditional and larger-scale corporate-sponsored research agreements.

PRINCIPLE 15—Humanitarian Licensing, Access to Medicines (closely drawn from previous recommendations):

- This principle is closely drawn from recommendations endorsed by the Association of University Technology Managers (AUTM), the AAMC, and 50 universities in a statement titled "In the Public Interest: Nine Points to Consider in Licensing University Technology."[711]

- In 2003, the University of California, Berkeley, adopted a Socially Responsible IP Licensing and Management Program, which aims to "promote widespread availability of technology and healthcare, including in the developing world." A student-led group called Universities Allied for Essential Medicines (UAEM), which has chapters at Berkeley and numerous other campuses nationwide, was instrumental in moving these policies forward. UC Berkeley has stated that the "opportunity cost of giving away University-generated therapies, diagnostics, and other research technologies for free … is low compared to the societal benefit… . Giving away rights for a 'charitable purpose' in developing countries … usually does not affect commercial markets in developed countries."[712]

- In 2006, UAEM also spearheaded the "Philadelphia Consensus Statement," which advocates three major changes to university policies on health-related innovations: (1) Promote equal access to research; (2) Promote research and development for neglected diseases; and (3) Measure research success according to impact on human welfare. The statement has been signed by over 150 opinion leaders in science, medicine, law, and health policy.[713]

- In 2009, AUTM and its university partners further elaborated on this critical public health goal in their "Statement of Principles and Strategies for the Equitable Dissemination of Medical Technologies," endorsed by many top universities as well as by the NIH and the Centers for Disease Control.[714]

- Finally, Principle 15 is supported by a National Academy of Sciences committee report, titled "Managing University Intellectual Property in the Public Interest," which endorsed the following recommendation: "Universities should try to anticipate which technologies may have applications that address important unmet social needs unlikely to be served by terms appropriate for commercial markets and to structure agreements to allow for these applications. The principal examples are technologies suited to meeting the agricultural, medical, and food needs of developing countries." This same report, much like Principle 15, cautions: "Patenting and licensing practices should not be predicated on the goal of raising significant revenue for the institution. The likelihood of success is small, the probability of disappointed expectations high, and the risk of distorting and narrowing dissemination efforts great. Nonetheless, in the rare case where significant revenue is generated, universities should have a plan in place for handling and distributing such gains."[715]

PRINCIPLE 16—Securing Broad Research Use and Distribution Rights (closely drawn from previous recommendations):

- Principle 16 draws on a virtually identical "research exemption" recommendation endorsed by more than 50 universities (as well as the AAMC and the AUTM) in a consensus statement titled "In the Public Interest:

Nine Points to Consider in Licensing University Technology," which was originally released in 2007.[716]

PRINCIPLE 17—Exclusive and Nonexclusive Licensing (closely drawn from previous recommendations):

- This principle is consistent with a recommendation issued in 2011 by a committee panel convened by the National Academy of Sciences addressing university IP.[717] Principle 17 is also consistent with recommendations endorsed by the AAMC, AUTM, and over 50 universities in a consensus statement titled "In the Public Interest: Nine Points to Consider in Licensing University Technology."[718]

PRINCIPLE 18—Upfront Exclusive Licensing Rights for Research Sponsors (closely drawn from previous recommendations):

- A similar recommendation appears in the consensus statement, titled "In the Public Interest: Nine Points to Consider in Licensing University Technology," endorsed by the AAMC, AUTM, and over 50 universities;[719] and also in a Cornell University faculty senate statement on principles for guiding large-scale university-industry alliances.[720]

PRINCIPLE 19—Research Tools and Upstream Platform Research (closely drawn from previous recommendations):

- The NIH issued a similar recommendation in its 1999 guidance, discussed in the main report.[721] The AAMC, AUTM, and over 50 universities—in their consensus statement titled "In the Public Interest: Nine Points to Consider in Licensing University Technology"—also issued and endorsed a similar recommendation: "Consistent with the NIH Guidelines on Research Tools, principles set forth by various charitable foundations that sponsor academic research programs and by the mission of the typical university to advance scientific research, universities are expected to make research tools as broadly available as possible."[722] A similar recommendation has also been endorsed by a committee of the National Academies of Sciences in its 2011 report titled Managing University Intellectual Property in the Public Interest.[723]

PRINCIPLE 20—Diverse Licensing Models for Diverse University Inventions (new):

- To the AAUP's knowledge this recommendation is new; however, there is broad evidence that university technology licensing operations need to be more careful about not to imposing a "one size fits all" model of licensing on diverse university inventions.[724] The need to better differentiate between biotechnology and information technology (IT) inventions, for example, has been widely documented and discussed by both industry and non-industry experts.[725] UC Berkeley implemented a new policy that encourages greater flexibility in the handling of IT inventions to address this problem.[726]

PRINCIPLE 21—Rights to "Background Intellectual Property" (BIP) (new):

- This recommendation is new; however, it draws heavily from a 2001 report titled "Working Together, Creating Knowledge," based on a two-year assessment of university-industry research collaborations carried out by the University-Industry Research Collaboration Initiative (RCI), a project of the Business–Higher Education Forum.[727] The RCI's members included 37 university presidents, senior officers at major corporations, and heads of major business and educational associations.

- It also draws from an internal UC Berkeley faculty senate committee examination of a ten-year research alliance agreement with BP, UC Berkeley, and two other public research institutions—known as the Energy Biosciences Institute—where the BP terms were extensive and quite unusual (see the main report for further discussion and details).[728]

PART IV. GENERAL PRINCIPLES FOR MANAGEMENT OF CONFLICTS OF INTEREST (COI) AND FINANCIAL CONFLICTS OF INTEREST (FCOI) (22–31)

All the principles under Part IV (except for portions of Principles 27 and 31 addressing public disclosure of COI) are closely drawn from previous recommendations issued and endorsed by the AAU (2001); AAMC (2002); AAMC-AAU (2008); Council on Government Relations (COGR) (2003); DHHS (2004); NIH; Office of Inspector General (OIG); and IOM (2009).

(See the main report, and discussions below, for citations pertaining to each Principle.) Most of these previous professional and other recommendations were drawn up for the purpose of addressing COI problems within the field of academic medicine in particular. In this report, however, the AAUP is recommending that these COI policies be extended to encompass the university as a whole, not just biomedicine.

PRINCIPLE 22—Comprehensive COI Policies (closely drawn from previous recommendations):

- As early as 1915, the AAUP observed that "the university teacher shall be exempt from any pecuniary motive or inducement to hold, or to express, any conclusion which is not the genuine and uncolored product of his own study or that of fellow specialists." It added: "To the degree that professional scholars, in the formation and promulgation of their opinions, are, or by the character of their tenure appear to be, subject to any motive other than their own scientific conscience and a desire for the respect of their fellow experts, to that degree the university teaching profession is corrupted; its proper influence upon public opinion is diminished and vitiated; and society at large fails to get from its scholars, in an unadulterated form, the peculiar and necessary service which it is the office of the professional scholar to furnish."[729]

- In recommending such a comprehensive approach to addressing FCOI on campus, the AAUP has the support of numerous professional academic groups, including the AAU, which has already strongly recommended that university COI policies need to be comprehensive and cover research "across all academic fields, not just biomedical ones."[730] This comprehensive approach also has the endorsement of the AAU-AAMC[731] and a recent IOM panel addressing COI.[732] According to IOM, a 2004 study from the General Accounting Office found that 79 percent of universities responding to their survey said they already had a single conflict of interest policy covering all research.[733]

PRINCIPLE 23—Consistent COI Enforcement across Campus (closely drawn from previous recommendations):

- This recommendation is drawn from the AAMC-AAU report.[734]

PRINCIPLE 24—Standing COI Committees
(closely drawn from previous recommendations):

- This principle is drawn from recommendations issued by the IOM and other professional and academic groups.[735]

PRINCIPLE 25—Reporting Individual COI
(closely drawn from previous recommendations):

- This recommendation is adapted, slightly, from one issued jointly by the AAU and AAMC in 2008.[736] It is also in line with the new COI rules issued by DHHS-NIH (2011), which expand the definition of what financial relationships investigators must report to their university employers.

PRINCIPLE 26—Inter-office Reporting and Tracking
of Institutional COI: (closely drawn from previous
recommendations):

- This recommendation has been endorsed in similar form by the Institute of Medicine, IOM (2009)[737] and by the AAMC/AAU (2008).[738]

PRINCIPLE 27—Strategies for Reviewing, Evaluating, and
Addressing COI (closely drawn from previous recommendations):

- This recommendation is closely drawn from the IOM.[739] See the main report for details.

PRINCIPLE 28—Developing a Formal, Written COI Management
Plan (closely drawn from previous recommendations):

- This recommendation is compatible with the DHHS-NIH rules for managing COI related to universities and other external grantees.[740]

PRINCIPLE 29—Oversight and Enforcement of COI Rules
(closely drawn from previous recommendations):

- This recommendation draws from IOM, DHHS, and COGR.[741]

PRINCIPLE 30—University-Vendor Relationships and COI (closely drawn from previous recommendations):

- This principle draws partly on recommendations issued in 2007 by the AAU in its "Statement of Guiding Principles Regarding Institutional Relationships with Student Loan Providers."[742] It also draws on the "College Loan Code of Conduct" developed by New York Attorney General Andrew Cuomo in 2007;[743] US Department of Education regulations pertaining to federal student loans, issued in November 2007;[744] and various new, state-level consumer protection laws for students and parents addressing financial aid assistance to pay for higher education.[745]

PRINCIPLE 31—COI Transparency: Public Disclosure of Financial Interests and COI Management Plans (closely drawn from previous recommendations):

- This principle is consistent with the standards on author disclosure of financial interests adopted by the ICMJE and the WAME.[746] It is also compatible with the DHHS–NIH COI rules.[747]

PART V: TARGETED PRINCIPLES: MANAGING COI IN THE CONTEXT OF CLINICAL CARE AND HUMAN SUBJECT RESEARCH (32–35)

PRINCIPLE 32—Individual and Institutional COI and Human Subject Research (closely drawn from previous recommendations):

- This principle has been endorsed, in similar form, by the IOM, AAMC, and the AAMC-AAU.[748]

PRINCIPLE 33: Institutional Review Boards (IRBs) and COI Management (closely drawn from previous recommendations):

- This principle is drawn directly from recommendations endorsed by the AAMC- AAU and the AAU.[749]

PRINCIPLE 34—COI, Medical Purchasing, and Clinical Care (closely drawn from previous recommendations):

- This principle is drawn directly from recommendations issued by the AAMC in 2008 and 2010, for addressing management of financial COI in the context of clinical care.[750]

PRINCIPLE 35—COI Transparency in the Context of Medical Care (closely drawn from previous recommendations):

- This principle is closely drawn from one that was issued by the AAMC in 2010.[751]

PART VI: TARGETED PRINCIPLES: STRATEGIC CORPORATE ALLIANCES (SCAs) (36–48)

The SCA principles offered here under Part VI are all new (with the exception of Principle 41 on Publication rights) in the sense that they have not been previously endorsed by the AAUP or other large professional academic groups, however the academic freedom principles undergirding these recommendations are clearly not new, and have been guiding AAUP policy for a long time.

The AAUP recommendations for addressing the management of SCAs are drawn primarily from a detailed, well executed Cornell University academic senate report titled "Faculty Statement of Principles & Best Practices Concerning Strategic Corporate Alliances" (2005), which was conducted by a special committee composed of professors from a broad range of academic disciplines.[752] It also draws from other academic senate reports and faculty reviews performed at UC Berkeley; a commissioned external review of the UC Berkeley-Novartis SCA by researchers at Michigan State University; and the transcripts of a California state senate hearing held at the time of the Novartis deal.[753] Finally, it draws from a detailed analysis of the legal terms and conditions spelled out in ten SCA contracts between US universities and energy-related firms during the period 2002–11, published by the Center for American Progress.[754]

For Principles 36–40 see the source notes directly above:

PRINCIPLE 36—Shared Governance and Strategic Corporate Alliances (SCAs) (new)

PRINCIPLE 37—SCA Governance and Majority Academic Control (new)

PRINCIPLE 38—Academic Control over SCA Research Selection (for broad SCAs) (new)

PRINCIPLE 39—Peer Review (for broad SCAs) (new)

PRINCIPLE 40—Transparency regarding the SCA Research Application Process (new)

PRINCIPLE 41—Protection of Publication Rights and Knowledge Sharing in SCA Agreements: All the provisions of Principle 3, above, should apply to strategic corporate alliances as well (closely drawn from previous recommendations):

- See the source notes for Principle 3, above.

PRINCIPLE 42—SCA Confidentiality Restrictions (new):

- See the source notes directly under Part VI, above.

PRINCIPLE 43—SCA Anti-Competitor Agreements (new):

- See the source notes directly under Part VI, above.

PRINCIPLE 44—Exclusive Licensing and SCA Agreements: (new):

- See the source notes directly under Part VI and for Principles 17 and 18 above.

For Principles 45–48 see the source notes under the discussion for Part VI, above:

PRINCIPLE 45—Limits on Broader Academic Disruption by SCAs (new)

PRINCIPLE 46—Early Termination of SCA Sponsor Funding (new)

PRINCIPLE 47—Independent, Majority Faculty Oversight of the SCA, and Post-Agreement Evaluation (new)

PRINCIPLE 48—Public Disclosure of SCA Research Contracts and Funding Transparency (new)

PART VII: TARGETED PRINCIPLES: CLINICAL MEDICINE, CLINICAL RESEARCH, AND INDUSTRY SPONSORSHIP (49–56)

PRINCIPLE 49—Access to Complete Clinical Trial Data and the Performance of Independent Academic Analysis (closely drawn from previous recommendations):

All the provisions of Principle 5, above, should apply to clinical trial data as well.

This principle in keeping with recommendations issued by the AAMC, FASEB, ICMJE, and WAME.[755]

PRINCIPLE 50—Registry of Academic-Based Clinical Trials in a National Registry (closely drawn from previous recommendations):

- The ICMJE,[756] US Food and Drug Administration (FDA),[757] AAMC,[758] and IOM have all either endorsed, or mandated, use of publicly accessible online clinical trial registries—such as the http://www.clinicaltrials.gov/ registry—to protect the integrity of evidence-based medicine (see the Principles Statement for details).

PRINCIPLE 51—Safeguarding the Integrity and Appropriate Conduct of Clinical Trials
(closely drawn from previous recommendations):

- This principle is fully consistent with a recommendation issued in 2006 by the AAMC in its "Principles for Protecting Integrity in the Conduct and Reporting of Clinical Trials."[759] It is also consistent with FDA guidance issued in 2001, stating that it is desirable for all DSMBs overseeing a clinical trial to have statistical reports prepared by statisticians who are independent of the trial sponsors and clinical investigators.[760]

PRINCIPLE 52—Patient Notification
(closely drawn from previous recommendations):

- This principle is drawn from a recommendation contained in an October 2001 investigative report, commissioned by the Canadian Association of University Teachers, concerning a high-profile academic freedom case involving Canadian researcher Dr. Nancy Olivieri at the University of Toronto.[761]

PRINCIPLE 53—Undue Commercial Marketing Influence and Control at Academic Medical Centers
(closely drawn from previous recommendations):

- This principle concerning speakers bureaus has been endorsed in very similar form by the IOM and also by the AAMC.[762] The Institute on Medicine as a Profession (IMAP) and the American Board of Internal Medicine (ABIM) Foundation have also jointly recommended that medical faculty be "prohibited" from involvement in "speakers bureaus."[763] Some academic and medical institutions (the University of Massachusetts, the Mayo Clinic, Johns Hopkins University) have already instituted policy restrictions or outright prohibitions on faculty participation in "speakers bureaus"; these should be emulated.[764]

The recommendations pertaining to Clinical Practice Guidelines and Continuing Medical Education are both drawn directly from the IOM.[765] Regarding CME, the IOM recommends that a "new system of funding accredited continuing medical education should be developed that is free of industry influence, enhances public trust in the integrity of the system, and provides high-quality education."[766]

PRINCIPLE 54—Appropriate Use of Facilities and Classrooms at Universities and Academic Medical Centers (closely drawn from previous recommendations):

- All the recommendations made in Principle 54 are consistent with ones already issued by prominent medical groups, including the IOM, AAMC, IMAP, and ABIM Foundation.[767]

PRINCIPLE 55—Marketing Projects Masquerading as Clinical Research (new):

- This policy recommendation is new; however, it seeks to address an area of deep and growing concern regarding the performance of industry-marketing research at universities under the guise of genuine science and the publication of that research in prominent academic journals. This practice has been decried by prominent medical journal editors and others, including former FDA commissioner David A. Kessler.[768]

PRINCIPLE 56—Predetermined Research Results (new):

- This principle is new; however, again it seeks to address a growing problem that has been documented with increasingly frequency. Most academics and scientists would firmly agree with the position that ethical research, especially research that involves human subjects, requires doubt about the outcome; this is known as equipoise. It is unethical to use human beings for commercially motivated trials whose findings are predetermined, or manipulated, to come to predetermined conclusions. Following litigation, several cases have come to light—at Harvard (medicine)[769] and UCLA (tobacco),[770] for example—where university professors pitched research studies to potential corporate sponsors by either implicitly or explicitly suggesting that the anticipated and/or predetermined research outcomes would favor the corporate sponsors' products and/or commercial interests. Such practices should be strictly forbidden inside any academic institution.

Endnotes

1. As Wikipedia explains: "A work made for hire (sometimes abbreviated as work for hire or WFH) is a work created by an employee as part of his or her job, or a work created on behalf of a client where all parties agree in writing to the WFH designation. It is an exception to the general rule that the person who actually creates a work is the legally recognized author of that work. According to copyright law in the United States and certain other copyright jurisdictions, if a work is "made for hire", the employer—not the employee—is considered the legal author. In some countries, this is known as corporate authorship. The incorporated entity serving as an employer may be a corporation or other legal entity, an organization, or an individual. The actual creator may or may not be publicly credited for the work, and this credit does not affect its legal status. States that are party to the Berne Convention for the Protection of Literary and Artistic Works recognize separately copyrights and moral rights, with moral rights including the right of the actual creators to publicly identify themselves as such, and to maintain the integrity of their work." Original Source: US Copyright Office, Circular 9: Work-Made-For-Hire Under the 1976 Copy Right Act, available at: http://www.copyright.gov/circs/circ09.pdf

2. American Association of University Professors (AAUP), "1915 Declaration of Principles on Academic Freedom and Academic Tenure," in *Policy Documents and Reports*, 10th ed. (Washington, DC: AAUP; Baltimore: Johns Hopkins University Press, 2006), 297.

3. Ibid.

4. AAUP, "Statement on Corporate Funding of Academic Research," (2004) *Policy Documents and Reports,* 130.

5. AAUP, "Statement on Conflicts of Interest," (1990), *Policy Documents and Reports,* 185.

6. Ibid. One of the more striking examples of an academic program marginalizing or even abandoning its traditional commitments and priorities is embodied in departments that replace their original research with company-directed drug or agricultural product testing. See Cary Nelson, "The Corporate University," in *Academic Keywords: A Devil's Dictionary for Higher Education,* ed. Cary Nelson and Stephen Watt (New York: Routledge, 1999), especially pp. 86–87 for further details.

7. AAUP, "On Preventing Conflicts of Interest in Government-Sponsored Research at Universities" (1965), *Policy Documents and Reports,* 184.

8. AAUP, "Statement on Government of Colleges and Universities" (1966), *Policy Documents and Reports,* 139.

9. AAUP, "On the Relationship of Faculty Governance to Academic Freedom" (1994), *Policy Documents and Reports,* 143.

10. AAUP, "Academic Freedom and Academic Tenure," op. cit. note 2.

11. The University-Industry Demonstration Project (UIDP) describes itself as an organization of universities and companies "committed to increasing the number and breadth of university-industry collaborative partnerships in the US." The UIDP states that it is a

project of the National Academies, carried out in association with the National Academy of Sciences, the National Academy of Engineering, and the Institute of Medicine (IOM), although its recommendations are far less comprehensive and strong than the 2009 IOM recommendations related to conflicts of interest in health research, cited frequently in this AAUP report. In addition to issuing several university-industry guidelines, including "Guiding Principles for University-Industry Endeavors" and "Contract Accords for University Industry Sponsored Agreements," UIDP has put out a software program, called TurboNegotiator, which it says can be used to streamline industry-academy contract negotiations and "reach consensus regarding critical business elements in these agreements, such as intellectual property, indemnification and publication rights." The UIDP's Contract Accords pamphlet admirably lays out the fundamental purposes of university research, and it contains good advice about how to work collaboratively with industry. However, in the AAUP's view, it does not offer guidelines sufficient to protect the distinctive campus "open research environments" it endorses. In what follows, we note agreements and disagreements the AAUP has with the work UIDP has done. *Conflicts of Interest:* The "Contract Accords" statement lists among its principles that "conflicts of interest, real and potential, should be reduced, eliminated, or managed in accordance with university policy and disclosed to the sponsor"(8), but it fails to address our primary concern: conflicts of interest that arise directly from the relationship with the sponsor, which must be disclosed, not only to the sponsor, but to other outside parties as well, including members of the scientific community, journal editors, and the broader public. *Publication:* The "Contract Accords" properly declares that "[publication] delays shouldn't be allowed to jeopardize academic progress of students" (11). It also points out that "publication of research results in a timely and appropriate manner can be beneficial to opening markets and expanding product options" (12). It further notes, "Research conducted by tax-exempt organizations must be performed in the public interest and is expected to lead to information that is published and available to the interested public" (11). It thus concludes that "universities need to be free to publish, present, or otherwise disclose results in a timely manner following review by sponsors," properly suggesting that "the time of publication delay must be specified and specific." However, glaringly absent from the Contract Accords document are any suggested limits to the publication delays that can be negotiated, or any acknowledgement that this "review by sponsors" should be authorized only to protect commercial trade secrets, not to alter or edit reported academic research findings.

12 Nathan Rosenberg and Richard R. Nelson, "American Universities and Technical Advance in Industry," *Research Policy* 23, no. 3 (1994): 323–48; Roberto Mazzoleni and Richard R. Nelson, "The Benefits and Costs of Strong Patent Protection: A Contribution to the Current Debate," *Research Policy* 27, no. 3 (1998): 274–84; David C. Mowery and Nathan Rosenberg, "The US National Innovation System," in *National Innovation Systems: A Comparative Analysis,* ed. Richard R. Nelson (New York: Oxford University Press, 1993); David C. Mowery and Timothy S. Simcoe, "The Origins and Evolution of the Internet," in *Technological Innovation and National Economic Performance,* ed. David G. Victor, Benn Steil, and Richard R. Nelson (Princeton, NJ: Princeton University Press, 2012). See also the Association of University

Technology Manager's *Better World* report series (2006–11), which profiles the many new products and innovative technologies that have stemmed from university-industry research collaborations as well as the activities of the technology licensing officers who are AUTM's core members: AUTM, *Better World Project—Past Reports,* accessed March 19, 2013, available at http://www.betterworldproject.org/Past_Reports.htm.

13   Ibid.

14   Association of American Universities (AAU) Task Force on Research and Accountability, *Report on Individual and Institutional Financial Conflict of Interest,* October 2001, available at http://www.aau.edu/publications/reports.aspx?id=6900.

15   Academic freedom does not embody a principle comparable to the one the US Supreme Court articulated in *Buckley v. Valeo* (1976), in which it ruled that spending money to influence elections is a form of constitutionally protected speech. The ability of universities to set standards for academic research and for the approval of outside funding would be decisively compromised if higher education adopted the notion that the simple availability of outside funding necessarily carries with it the right to spend it in the institution's name. If the power of industry money were to become absolute in academic research, it would also carry the risk that given areas of research could be overwhelmed by resources that competing research agendas and hypotheses could not match. Academic freedom and research integrity would suffer as a result.

16   Robert Gorman, "Report of Committee A, 1991–92," *Academe,* 78, no. 5 (1992):43–50. See section "An Issue of Academic Freedom in Refusing Outside Funding for Faculty Research," 49.

17   Joan Wallach Scott, "Report of Committee A, 2002–03," *Academe,* 90, no. 5 (2003): 77–85. See section "Academic Freedom and Rejection of Research Funds from Tobacco Corporations," 83. This 2003 wording is slightly revised from "An Issue of Academic Freedom in Refusing Outside Funding for Faculty Research." Gorman, "Report of Committee A, 1991–92," op. cit. note 16.

18   Ibid.

19   See the website of the World Health Organization (WHO) Framework Convention on Tobacco Control (http://www.who.int/fctc/en), for a 2010 history of the framework's adoption, the text of the framework itself, and a list of the nations that have signed. The quote about "vested interests" is taken from Article 5.3 of the framework, available at http://who.int/fctc/protocol/guidelines/adopted/article_5_3/en/index.html.

20   National Institute on Drug Abuse (NIDA), "Points to Consider Regarding Tobacco Industry Funding of NIDA Applicants," available http://www.drugabuse.gov/about/organization/nacda/points-to-consider.html.

21   The full final ruling from the US District Court for the District of Columbia in this case, *US Department of Justice v. Philip Morris USA Inc. et al.,* dated September 8, 2006, is available at http://www.justice.gov/civil/cases/tobacco2/amended%20opinion.pdf.

22   NIDA, " Points to Consider Regarding Tobacco Industry Funding of NIDA Applicants," op. cit. note 20.

23 Ibid.

24 For one example, see George F. DeMartino, *The Economist's Oath: On the Need for and Content of Professional Economic Ethics* (New York: Oxford University Press, 2011). DeMartino argues: "Over the long sweep of its history, the American economics profession has been far more ambitious about achieving influence than it has been attentive to the harm that it might do or the ethical questions that might arise were it to achieve the influence it sought" (227). He also observes that "absent careful thinking by the profession, it is not clear that well-meaning economists will recognize when the circumstances in which they find themselves represent a conflict of interest or know what to do about it when they do recognize apparent or real conflicts . . . Conflicts of interest can bleed into outright corruption" (135).

25 For other recent examples of companies and products that have grown out of university-industry research collaborations, see also the Association of University Technology Manager's *Better World* report series (2006–11), which profiles the many new products and innovative technologies that have stemmed from university-industry research collaborations as well as the activities of the technology licensing officers who are AUTM's core members: AUTM, *The Better World Report* series, op. cit. note 12.

26 See the two-year study of academy-industry partnerships: Business-Higher Education Forum (BHEF), *Working Together, Creating Knowledge: The University-Industry Research Collaboration Initiative* (Washington, DC: Business-Higher Education Forum, 2001), 11, available at http://www.bhef.com/solutions/documents/working-together.pdf.

27 Food & Water Watch, *Public Research, Private Gain: Corporate Influence Over University Agricultural Research* (Washington DC: Food & Water Watch, 2012), available at http://documents.foodandwaterwatch.org/doc/PublicResearchPrivateGain.pdf.

28 Ron Nissimov, "Enron, Lay family give to Rice: $8 Million Gift Will Help Research, Technology," *Houston Chronicle*, sec. A, 31, June 24, 2000; Stuart Silverstein and Lianne Hart, "A Fellow May Squirm a Bit in a Chair Endowed by Ken Lay," *Los Angeles Times,* February 24, 2002, available at http://articles.latimes.com/2002/feb/24/news/mn-29608.

29 Nelson, "The Corporate University," 2. The list continues with "the Kmart Professor of Marketing at Wayne State University, the McLamore/Burger King Chair at the University of Miami, the Lego Professor of Learning Research and the Chevron Professor of Chemical Engineering at MIT, the Federal Express Chair of Information Management-Systems at the University of Memphis, the General Mills Chair of Cereal Chemistry and Technology at the University of Minnesota, the Coral Petroleum Industries Chair in Renewable-Energy Resources at the University of Hawaii at Manoa, the LaRoche Industries Chair in Chemical Engineering at the Georgia Institute of Technology" and many others (94–95).

30 "At the University of Illinois National Center for Supercomputing Applications, managers seek corporate partners who gain a degree of exclusivity in a particular research area once a joint contract is signed. The corporations have limited horizons and often want to initiate and complete a project in a year or two. The university's horizon is usually much wider; it wants to develop a research area over time by hiring faculty, admitting graduate students, and making a long-term commitment. But the corporations want rapid results. The university

wants to keep its business partners happy, so it tries to achieve profitable outcomes quickly. That frequently means hiring new graduate assistants or shifting personnel from elsewhere to respond to changing needs for a rapidly developing project. There never seems to be time to renegotiate the contracts fast enough to have the corporations pick up the new unanticipated expenses. So the university puts its own money into the corporation's research," Nelson, "The Corporate University," 88, op. cit. note 6. This information comes from an interview with an administrator at the Supercomputing Center.

31 Rosenberg and Nelson, "American Universities and Technical Advance in Industry," op. cit. note 12; Mazzoleni and Nelson, "The Benefits and Costs of Strong Patent Protection," op. cit. note 12; Mowery and Rosenberg, "The US National Innovation System," op. cit. note 12; Mowery and Simcoe, "The Origins and Evolution of the Internet," op. cit. note 12. For more recent examples, see the Association of University Technology Manager's *Better World* report series (2006–11), which profiles the many new products and innovative technologies that have stemmed from university-industry research collaborations as well as the activities of the technology licensing officers who are AUTM's core members: AUTM, *The Better World Report* series, op. cit. note 12.

32 In 2006, to cite but one example of nondisclosure of financial interests, a scandal erupted in the pages of the *Wall Street Journal over a Journal of the American Medical Association* publication that investigated the pros and cons of antidepressant withdrawal during pregnancy. The paper failed to disclose that the investigators had sixty financial relationships to pharmaceutical companies, and most authors were paid consultants to the makers of antidepressants. David Armstrong, "Financial Ties to Industry Cloud Major Depression Study," *Wall Street Journal,* July 11, 2006, available at http://online.wsj.com/article/SB115257995935002947.html.

33 Center for Science in the Public Interest, "Animal Ag Report Encounters Industry Interference," *Integrity in Science Watch,* May 5, 2008, available at http://www.cspinet.org/integrity/watch/200805051.html#3; Rick Weiss, "Report Targets Costs of Factory Farming," *Washington Post,* April 30, 2008, available at http://www.washingtonpost.com/wp-dyn/content/article/2008/04/29/AR2008042902602.html. The report referenced is the Pew Commission on Industrial Farm Animal Production, *Putting Meat on the Table: Industrial Farm Production in America* (Baltimore: Pew Charitable Trusts and Johns Hopkins Bloomberg School of Public Health, 2008), available at http://www.ncifap.org/bin/e/j/PCIFAPFin.pdf.

34 See, for example, Thomas Bodenheimer, "Uneasy Alliance—Clinical Investigators and the Pharmaceutical Industry," *New England Journal of Medicine,* 342, no. 20 (2000): 1539–44.

35 Joseph S. Ross, Kevin P. Hill, David S. Egilman, and Harlan M. Krumholz, "Guest Authorship and Ghostwriting in Publications Related to Rofecoxib," *Journal of the American Medical Association* 299, no. 15 (2008): 1800–12. See also US Senate Committee on Finance (Sen. Charles E. Grassley, ranking member), *Ghostwriting in Medical Literature,* Minority Staff Report, 111th Congress, June 24, 2010; and Jeffrey R. Lacasse and Jonathan Leo, "Ghostwriting at Elite Academic Medical Centers in the United States," *PLoS Medicine* 7, no. 2 (2010): e1000230, available at http://www.plosmedicine.org/article/info%3Adoi%2F10.1371%2Fjournal.pmed.1000230.

36   Dan Berrett, "Not Just Florida State," *Inside Higher Ed.com,* June 28, 2011, available at http://
      www.insidehighered.com/news/2011/06/28/koch_foundation_gifts_to_colleges_and_
      universities_draw_scrutiny; Kris Hundley, "Billionaire's Role in Hiring Decisions at Florida
      State University Raises Questions," *Tampa Bay Times,* May 9, 2011, available at http://www.
      tampabay.com/news/business/billionaires-role-in-hiring-decisions-at-florida-state-university-
      raises/1168680.

37   For example, the tobacco industry created several organizations, including the Council for
      Tobacco Research and the Center for Indoor Air Research. These were presented to the
      public as independent scientific organizations governed by principles of peer review when,
      in fact, they were covertly managed by cigarette company executives and lawyers to serve
      political, legal, and public relations purposes. This "myth of independent science" was a
      key element of a federal court ruling finding that the companies had constituted an illegal
      "racketeering enterprise" for the purpose of defrauding the American public under the
      Racketeer Influenced and Corrupt Organizations (RICO) Act. The full RICO ruling, a
      seventeen-hundred-page document by District Court Judge Gladys Kessler, is available at
      http://www.justice.gov/civil/cases/tobacco2/amended%20opinion.pdf.

38   Matthew Keenan, "CEOs Pushing Ayn Rand Studies Use Money to Overcome Resistance,"
      Bloomberg.net, April 11, 2008, available at http://www.bloomberg.com/apps/news?pid=newsa
      rchive&sid=as6BR0QV4KE8.

39   Anne Marie Chaker, "Companies Design, Fund Curricula at Universities," *Wall Street Journal,*
      September 11, 2006, available at http://www.post-gazette.com/stories/business/news/
      companies-design-fund-curricula-at-universities-449866/.

40   Institute of Medicine (IOM), "Conflicts of Interest," in *Conflict of Interest in Medical Research,
      Education, and Practice,* ed. Bernard Lo and Marilyn J. Field (Washington, DC: National
      Academies Press, 2009), 189–215.

41   Marcia Angell, *The Truth about the Drug Companies: How They Deceive Us and What to Do
      about It* (London: Random House, 2005); Derek Bok, *Universities in the Marketplace: The
      Commercialization of Higher Education* (Princeton, NJ: Princeton University Press, 2000);
      Daniel s. Greenberg, *Science for Sale: The Perils, Rewards, and Delusions of Campus Capitalism*
      (Chicago: University of Chicago Press, 2007); Jerome P. Kassirer, *On the Take: How Medicine's
      Complicity with Big Business Can Endanger Your Health* (New York: Oxford University Press,
      2004); Sheldon Krimsky, *Science in the Private Interest: Has the Lure of Profits Corrupted Biomedical
      Research?* (Lanham, MD: Rowman and Littlefield, 2003); David Michaels, *Doubt Is Their
      Product* (New York: Oxford University Press, 2008); Thomas O. McGarity and Wendy E.
      Wagner, *Bending Science: How Special Interests Corrupt Public Health Research* (Cambridge, MA:
      Harvard University Press, 2008); Jennifer Washburn, *University Inc.: The Corporate Corruption of
      Higher Education* (New York: Basic Books, 2005).

42   Bronwyn H. Hall, "University-Industry Research Partnerships in the United States," in
      *Rethinking Science Systems and Innovation Policies, Proceedings of the 6th International Conference on
      Technology Policy and Innovation,* ed. Jean-Pierre Contzen, David Gibson, and Manuel V. Heitor
      (West Lafayette, IN: Purdue University Press, 2004). (An earlier version of this paper was

presented at the 6th International Conference on Technology Policy and Innovation, Kansai, Japan, August 2002, available here: http://elsa.berkeley.edu/~bhhall/papers/BHH04_Kansai. pdf.) See Table 1.

43   There thus continues to be some variation here between the amounts received by private and public institutions. According to the National Science Foundation, "In FY 2008, the federal government provided 72% of the R&D funds spent by private institutions, compared with 55% for public institutions. Conversely, public institutions received approximately 9% of their $35.3 billion in R&D expenditures from state and local governments, compared with 2% of private institutions' $16.6 billion." National Science Board (NSB), "Academic Research and Development," *Science and Engineering Indicators* (Arlington, VA: National Science Foundation, 2010), available at http://www.nsf.gov/statistics/seind10/c5/c5h.htm. The new data for 2012 is available at http://www.nsf.gov/statistics/seind12/pdf/c05.pdf.

44   "Industrial support accounts for the smallest share of academic R&D funding (6%), and support of academia has never been a major component of industry-funded R&D. After a three-year decline between 2001 and 2004, industry funding of academic R&D increased for the fourth year in a row, to $2.9 billion in FY 2008." NSB, "Academic Research and Development," 2008, 5–14. op cit. note 43. (See appendix table 4-5 for time-series data on industry-reported R&D funding.)

45   "Universities are increasingly subsidizing grants from their own funds (see [paragraph] 'Footing the US research bill'). Between 1969 and 2009, the proportion of research funding supported by institutional money rose from 10% to 20%, according to the US National Science Foundation. Public universities and all but the wealthiest private ones are increasingly taking that money from tuition fees." Eugenie Samuel Reich, "Thrift in Store for US Research," *Nature* 476, (August 25, 2011): 385, available at http://www.nature.com/news/2011/110824/full/476385a.html.

46   National Center for Science and Engineering Statistics, "Detailed Statistical Tables NSF 11-313," in *Academic Research and Development Expenditures: Fiscal Year 2009* (Arlington, VA: National Science Foundation, 2011), available at http://www.nsf.gov/statistics/nsf11313/.

47   Food & Water Watch, *Public Research, Private Gain,* op. cit. note 27.

48   Ibid.

49   Ibid. The graph that follows is from page 6 of the report.

50   Quoted in IOM, "Conflicts of Interest," 101, op. cit. note 40. Original sources: J. Leighton Read, and Paul M. Campbell, "Health Care Innovation: A Progress Report," *Health Affairs* 7, no. 3 (1988): 174–85; and J. Leighton Read, and Kenneth B. Lee, Jr., "Health Care Innovation: Progress Report and Focus on Biotechnology," *Health Affairs* 13, no. 3 (1994): 215–25.

51   Quoted in IOM, "Conflicts of Interest," 101, op. cit. note 40. Original sources: Hamilton Moses , E. Ray Dorsey, David H. M. Matheson, and Samuel O. Their, "Financial Anatomy of Biomedical Research," *Journal of the American Medical Association* 294, no. 11 (2005): 1333–42; Lindsay A. Hampson, Justin E. Bekelman, and Cary P. Gross, "Empirical Data on Conflicts of Interest," in *The Oxford Textbook of Clinical Research Ethics,* ed. Ezekiel J. Emanuel, Christine

Grady, Robert A. Crouch, Reidar K. Lie, Franklin G. Miller, and David Wendler (New York: Oxford University Press, 2008).

52 Eric G. Campbell, Joel S. Weissman, Susan Ehringhaus, Sowmya R. Rao, Beverly Moy, Sandra Feibelmann, and Susan Dorr Goold, "Institutional Academy-Industry Relationships," *Journal of the American Medical Association* 298, no. 15 (2007): 1779–86.

53 NSB, "Academic Research and Development," op. cit. note 43.

54 Campbell Zinner, "Participation of Academic Scientists in Relationships with Industry," *Health Affairs* 28, no. 6 (2009): 1820. Among those in clinical departments, the percentage decreased from 36 percent to 23 percent; in nonclinical departments the percentage decreased from 21 percent to 9 percent.

55 David C. Mowery, Richard R. Nelson, Bhaven N. Sampat, and Arvids A. Ziedonis, *Ivory Tower and Industrial Innovation: University-Industry Technology Transfer before and after the Bayh-Dole Act* (Stanford, CA: Stanford Business Books, 2004).

56 Gerald Epstein, Jessica Carrick-Hagenbarth, "Financial Economists, Financial Interests and Dark Corners of the Meltdown: It's Time to Set Ethical Standards for the Economics Profession," in *Working Paper Series, No. 239* (Amherst, MA: Political Economy Research Institute, November 2010), available at http://www.peri.umass.edu/fileadmin/pdf/working_papers/working_papers_201-250/WP239_revised.pdf.

57 Charles H. Ferguson, *Predator Nation: Corporate Criminals, Political Corruption, and the Hijacking of America* (NY: Crown Business, 2012), 253–56. Also see the discussions of Summers (248–53), Tyson (258), and Feldstein (259–60). Consult the index to the book for other references.

58 See, for example, Kaustuv Basu, "Fracking Open," *Inside Higher Education,* July 6, 2012, available at http://www.insidehighered.com/news/2012/07/06/gas-drilling-research-stirs-controversies-universities; Kevin Begos, "Critics question shale gas researcher, schools," *Wall Street Journal,* May 25, 2012; Nick DeSantis, "U. of Texas Will Review Fracking Study for Potential Conflict of Interest," *Chronicle of Higher Education,* July 26, 2012, available at http://chronicle.com/blogs/ticker/u-of-texas-will-review-fracking-study-for-potential-conflict-of-interest/46; Jim Efstathiou Jr., "Frackers Fund University Research That Proves Their Case," *Bloomberg News,* July 23, 2012, available at http://www.bloomberg.com/news/2012-07-23/frackers-fund-university-research-that-proves-their-case.html; Brantley Hargrove, "Lead Researcher of UT Fracking Report Has Substantial Ties to Industry," *Dallas Observer,* July 24, 2012, available at http://blogs.dallasobserver.com/unfairpark/2012/07/lead_researcher_of_ut_fracking.php; Mireya Navarro, "Fracking Research and the Money That Flows To It," *The New York Times,* June 11, 2012.

59 "A Letter from UB President Satish K. Tripathi," SUNY University at Buffalo press release, November 19, 2012, available at http://www.buffalo.edu/news/news-releases.host.html/content/shared/www/news/private/2012/11/13820.html. Reports from Public Accountability Initiative are available on the the "reports" section of their web site: public-accountability.org/research/reports. They include "The UB Shale Play: Distorting the Facts about Fracking—A Review of the University at Buffalo Shale Resources and Society

Institute's Report on 'Environmental Impacts During Marcellus Shale Gas Drilling'" (May 2012), ""Contaminated Inquiry: How a University of Texas Fracking Study Led by a Gas Industry Insider Spun the Facts and Misled the Public" (July 2012), "Fracking and the Revolving Door in Pennsylvania: Natural gas industry ties among Pennsylvania's regulartors and public officials" (February 2013), and "Industry Partner or Industry Puppet?: How MIT's influential study of fracking was authored, funded, and released by oil and gas industry insiders" (March 2013).

60 See Terrence Henry, "Review of UT Fracking Study Finds Failure to Disclose Conflict of Interest (Updated)," *State Impact,* December 6, 2012, available at http://stateimpact.npr.org/texas/2012/12/06/review-of-ut-fracking-study-finds-failure-to-disclose-conflict-of-interest/.

61 For a popular review of environmental and social consequences of fracking by way of a case study of fracking in North Dakota, see Dobb, Edwin, "The New Oil Landscape: The Fracking Frenzy in North Dakota has Boosted the US Fuel Supply—But at What Cost?" *National Geographic,* March 2013, 28–59.

62 Patent and Trademark Amendments of 1980 (P.L. 96-517), known as the Bayh-Dole Act.

63 Economic Recovery Tax Act of 1981 (1981 ERTA, §221(d)); Tax Reform Act of 1986 (1986 TRA, §231(a)). The Economic Recovery Tax Act of 1981 (P.L. 97-34) provides a 25 percent tax credit for 65 percent of private investments in universities for basic research. This tax credit substantially reduces the cost of industrial R&D; IOM, "Conflicts of Interest," 36, op. cit. note 40.

64 The widespread perception in the 1980s that US technological leadership was slipping led policymakers to conclude that existing US antitrust laws and penalties were too restrictive and were possibly impeding the ability of US companies to compete in global markets. The passage of the National Cooperative Research Act (NCRA) in 1984 encouraged US firms to collaborate on generic, precompetitive research. To gain protection from antitrust litigation, NCRA required firms engaging in research joint ventures to register them with the US Department of Justice. By the end of 1996 more than 665 research joint ventures had been registered. In 1993, Congress again relaxed restrictions—this time on cooperative production activities—by passing the National Cooperative Research and Production Act, which enables participants to work together to apply technologies developed by their research joint ventures. SEMATECH has perhaps been the most significant private R&D consortium formed since the US Congress passed the National Cooperative Research Act of 1984. See Albert L. Link, "Research Joint Ventures: Patterns from Federal Register Filings," *Review of Industrial Organization* 11.5 (October 1996): 617–28.

65 The complete US Supreme Court decision in *Board of Trustees of Leland Stanford Junior University v. Roche Molecular Systems* (2011) is available at http://www.supremecourt.gov/opinions/10pdf/09-1159.pdf.

66 Maddy F. Baer, Stephanie Lollo Donahue and Rebecca J. Cantor, *"Stanford v. Roche:* Confirming The Basic Patent Law Principle That Inventors Ultimately Have Rights In Their Inventions," *les Nouvelles* (March 2012): 12–23, available at http://www.velaw.com/uploadedFiles/VEsite/Resources/TheBasicPatentLawPrinciple.pdf

67 Lisa Lapin, "Stanford 'Disappointed' In Supreme Court Ruling In Roche Case," Stanford University News Press Release, June 7, 2011, available at: http://news.stanford.edu/news/2011/june/court-roche-ruling-060711.html.

68 This section draws from written comments from Gerald Barnett, PhD, Director, Research Technology Enterprise Initiative, to the American Association of University Professors (AAUP), April 30, 2012: "Under Bayh-Dole's primary standard patent rights clause, the university contractor is to designate personnel responsible for the administration of patent matters (37 CFR 401.14(a)(f)(2)). The primary duties of those personnel under the standard patent rights clause are very limited: receive reports of invention, send those reports on to the federal sponsors, and notify the federal sponsors if the university obtains title to a federally supported invention and elects to retain that title. These and other duties are essentially paperwork notifications" (Title 37, "Patents, Trademarks, and Copyrights," Chapter IV, Part 401, Rights to inventions made by nonprofit organizations and small business firms under government grants, contracts, and cooperative agreements," Government Printing Office, available at http://www.gpo.gov/fdsys/pkg/CFR-2002-title37-vol1/content-detail.html

69 Kathi Wescott, "Faculty Ownership of Research Affirmed," *Academe,* 97, no. 5 (2011), available at http://www.aaup.org/AAUP/pubsres/academe/2011/SO/nb/patentlaw.htm.

70 AAUP, "1915 Declaration of Principles," op. cit. note 2.

71 See Matt Jones, "Supreme Court Rules for Roche, Clarifies Bayh-Dole," *GenomeWeb Daily News* (June 6, 2011): "The most likely effect of the ruling will be that universities will begin making sure that their employees sign assignation agreements that make it clear if they expect to own the rights to the patents their employees generate, Steve Chang, an attorney with the IP firm Banner and Witcoff, told *GenomeWeb Daily News* Monday." For an example of a comprehensive claim of IP ownership by a universssity see the University of Washington's "Patent and Invention Policy" at www.washington.edu/admin/rules/policies/PO/E36.html

72 The University of California's letter of assignment that all faculty are required to sign reads, in part, in "consideration of my employment, and of wages and/or salary to be paid to me during any period of my employment, by University, and/or my utilization of University research facilities and/or my receipt of gift, grant, or contract research funds through the University . . . I acknowledge my obligation to assign, and do hereby assign, inventions and patents that I conceive or develop 1) within the course and scope of my University employment while employed by the University, 2) during the course of my utilization of any University research facilities, or 3) through any connection with my use of gift, grant, or contract research funds received through the University." The full policy is available at www.ucop.edu/ucophome/policies/bfb/upay585.pdf

73 Beth Cate, David Drooz, Pierre Hohenberg, and Kathy Schulz, "Creating Intellectual Property Policies and Current Issues in Administering Online Courses," a paper presented at The National Association of College and University Attorneys (NACUA), San Diego, CA, November 7–9, 2007. See also: Cary Nelson, "Whose Intellectual Property?," Opinion Editorial, *Inside Higher Ed.com,* June 21, 2012, available at http://www.insidehighered.com/views/2012/06/21/essay-faculty-members-and-intellectual-property-rights. Because the Cate

et al. paper is posted on its member's only website, NACUA permitted *Inside Higher Ed.com* to post a link on its own website, noting that while the paper reflected the authors' views at the time, some issues and some of their thinking may have changed since then: http://www. insidehighered.com/views/2012/06/21/essay-faculty-members-and-intellectual-property-rights

74   Ibid., 6.

75   Ibid., 6.

76   Jerry G. Thursby, Richard Jensen, Marie C. Thursby, "Objectives, Characteristics and Outcomes of University Licensing: A Survey of Major US Universities," *The Journal of Technology Transfer,* 26, no. 1/2 (2001), 59–72.

77   Archie M. Palmer, *Survey of University Patent Policies: Preliminary Report* (Washington, DC: National Research Council, 1948), Appendix, with reprints of 37 university patent policies. The policies for the Universities of Arizona, California, Cincinnati, Rutgers, and Texas apppear, respectively, on pages 122, 126–27, 130, 157, and 162. Columbia is on page 132 and Princeton is on page 155. Also see Archie M. Palmer, *University Research and Patent Policies, Practices, and Procedures* (Washington, DC: National Academy of Science-National Research Council, 1962) for a more extensive list of patent policies. For comments on the history of university faculty inventorship policy, see Barnett, Gerald, "Blasts from the Past," Blog Post, May 12, 2012, available at http://rtei.org/blog/2012/05/12/blasts-from-the-past/

78   National Research Council, *Managing University Intellectual Property in the Public Interest,* (Washington, DC: The National Academies Press, 2010), available at http://www.nap.edu/catalog.php?record_id=13001. See Recommendations 1 and 2, quote on p. 4 and p. 66.

79   Robert E. Litan, Lesa Mitchell, E.J. Reedy, "Commercializing University Innovations: A Better Way," working paper 449, Regulation2point0, available at http://regulation2point0.org/wp-content/uploads/downloads/2010/04/RP07-16_topost.pdf.

80   Wayne Johnson (Vice President, University Relations, Hewlett-Packard), "Bayh-Dole—The next 25 years," Testimony before House Committee on Science & Technology, Subcommittee on Technology and Innovation, July 17, 2007; Kramer, David. "Universities and industry find roadblocks to R&D partnering," *Physics Today* 61, no. 5 (2008): 20–22.

81   Thursby et al., "Objectives, Characteristics and Outcomes of University Licensing," op. cit. note 76.

82   Wesley M. Cohen, Richard R. Nelson, and John P. Walsh, "Links and Impacts: The Influence of Public Research on Industrial R&D," *Management Science,* 48, no. 1 (2002): 1–23; and Ajay Agrawal and Rebecca Henderson, "Putting Patents in Context: Exploring Knowledge Transfer from MIT," *Management Science* 48, no. 1 (2002): 44–60.

83   Alfonso Gambardella, *Science and Innovation* (Cambridge: Cambridge University Press, 1995).

84   Kenneth J. Arrow, "Economic Welfare and the Allocation of Resources for Invention," in *Science Bought and Sold: Essays in the Economics of Science,* ed. Philip Mirowski and Esther-Mirjam Sent (1962; reprint, Chicago: University of Chicago Press, 2002), 165–81; Richard R. Nelson, "The Simple Economics of Basic Research," in *Science Bought and Sold: Essays in the Economics of Science,* ed. Philip Mirowski and Esther-Mirjam Sent (1959; reprint, Chicago: University of Chicago Press, 2002), 151–64.

85   Thursby et al., "Objectives, Characteristics and Outcomes of University Licensing," op. cit. note 76.

86   Jerry G. Thursby and Marie C. Thursby, "Industry perspectives on licensing university technologies: Sources and problems," *Industry and Higher Education,* 15, no. 4, (2001): 289–94.

87   Christina Jansen and Harrison F. Dillon, "Where do the Leads for Licences Come From? Source Data from Six Institutions," *The Journal of the Association of University Technology Managers,* 11 (1999).

88   Thursby et al., "Objectives, Characteristics and Outcomes of University Licensing," op. cit. note 76.

89   Wesley M. Cohen, and John P. Walsh, "Real Impediments to Academic Biomedical Research," in *Innovation Policy and the Economy,* 8 (2008): 1–30, available at http://www.nber. org/~marschke/mice/Papers/cohenwalsh.pdf.

90   All original statistics on university and hospital patenting and licensing come from Licensing Activity Surveys coordinated by the Association of University Technology Managers (AUTM). However these figures were extracted from: Cohen and Walsh, "Real Impediments to Academic Biomedical Research" op. cit. note 89; and also from Anthony D. So, Bhaven N. Sampat, Arti K. Rai, Robert Cook-Deegan, Jerome H. Reichman, Robert Weissman and Amy Kapczynski, "Is Bayh-Dole Good for Developing Countries? Lessons from the US Experience," *PLoS Biology,* 6, no. 10 (2008): e262, available at http://www.plosbiology.org/ article/info:doi/10.1371/journal.pbio.0060262.

91   AUTM, *FY 2007 Licensing Activity Survey Full Report,* ed. Robert Tieckelmann, Richard Kordal, Sean Flanigan, Tanya Glavicic-Théberge, and Dana Bostrom (2007).

92   So et al., "Is Bayh-Dole Good for Developing Countries?" op. cit. note 90. Original sources: AUTM, *FY2006 US Licensing Activity Survey* (2006); David C. Mowery, Richard R. Nelson, Bhaven N. Sampat, and Arvids A. Ziedonis, "The growth of patenting and licensing by US universities: An assessment of the effects of the Bayh-Dole Act of 1980," *Research Policy,* 30, no. 1(2001): 99–119.

93   Harun Bulut and Giancarlo Moschini, "US Universities' Net Returns from Patenting and Licensing: A Quantile Regression Analysis," Center for Agricultural and Rural Development at Iowa State University Working Paper 06-WP 432 (2006), available at http://www.card. iastate.edu/publications/dbs/pdffiles/06wp432.pdf

94   Lita Nelsen, "The Rise of Intellectual Property Protection in the American University," *Science* 279, no. 5356 (1998): 1460–61.

95   Mowery et al., *Ivory Tower and Industrial Innovation,* 241, op. cit. note 55.

96   Jeanette Colyvas, Michael Crow, Annetine Gelijns et al., "How Do University Inventions Get into Practice?," *Management Science* 48, no. 1 (2002): 61–72.

97   The landmark 1980 *Diamond v. Chakrabarty* US Supreme Court decision, for example, and the 1985 ex parte *Hibbard et al.* opinion made it possible to patent live artificially engineered organisms, including plants and animals. For a deeper discussion of this expansion of patent eligibility, see Dan L. Burk and Mark A. Lemley, *The Patent Crisis and How the Courts Can Solve It* (Chicago: University of Chicago Press, 2009). Regarding medical process patents, see

Aaron Kesselheim and Michelle Mello, "Medical-Process Patents: Monopolizing the Delivery of Health Care," *New England Journal of Medicine,* 355, no. 19 (2006): 2036–41.

98 Hall, "University-Industry Research Partnerships in the United States," op. cit. note 42. See also Hank Chesbrough, "Is the Central R&D Lab Obsolete?," *MIT Technology Review,* April 24, 2001, available at http://www.technologyreview.com/business/12357/.

99 Hall, "University-Industry Research Partnerships in the United States," op. cit. note 42.

100 NSB, "Academic Research and Development," op. cit. note 43.

101 Ibid.: "The share of support provided by institutional (university) funds increased steadily between 1972 (12%) and 1991 (19%) but since then has remained fairly stable at roughly one-fifth of total funding. After a 3-year decline between 2001 and 2004 (low of $2.1 billion), industry funding of academic R&D increased for the fourth year in a row, to $2.9 billion in 2008."

102 BHEF, *Working Together, Creating Knowledge,* 3, op. cit. note 26.

103 National Research Council (NRC), *Government-Industry Partnerships for the Development of New Technologies* (Washington, DC: National Academies Press, 2003).

104 Denis O. Gray, Mark Lindblad, and Joseph Rudolph, "Industry-University Research Centers: A Multivariate Analysis of Member Retention," *Journal of Technology Transfer* 26, no. 3 (2001): 247–54. The authors write: "According to research by Cohen and his colleagues (1994), industry-university research centers in the US had research expenditures of $2.53 billion, accounting for roughly 15 percent of university research funding. Add to this support for traditional cooperative activities like consulting and contract research and industry-sponsored and industry-leveraged government research probably accounts for 20 percent to 25 percent of university R&D," 247.

105 Phone interview with Jilda D. Garton, associate vice provost for research at Georgia Institute of Technology, and Jennifer Washburn, October 18, 2007, published in Jennifer Washburn, *Big Oil Goes to College* (Washington, DC: Center for American Progress, October 2010), 46, available at http://www.americanprogress.org/issues/2010/10/big_oil.html

106 Historically, according to a 2003 National Science Board survey, the National Institutes of Health (NIH) did not provide grants to industry. However, in 1998–99, NIH had 166 CRADAs providing access to government resources and supporting public-private research partnerships, and its SBIR program issued more than $300 million to small companies. That same year, the Department of Energy (DOE) operated 700 CRADAs. Source: NRC, *Government-Industry Partnerships,* op. cit. note 103. See also: Greg Linden, David Mowery, and Rosemarie Ziedonis, "National Technology Policy in Global Markets," in *Innovation Policy in the Knowledge-Based Economy,* ed. Albert Link and Maryann Feldman (Boston: Kluwer Academic, 2001), 312; and Leon Rosenberg, "Partnerships in the Biotechnology Enterprise," *Capitalizing on New Needs and New Opportunities: Government-Industry Partnerships in Biotechnology and Information Technologies* (Washington, DC: National Academy of Sciences, 2001).

107 Phone interview with Doug Hooker, division director for Renewable Energy Projects Division, Department of Energy (DOE) Golden Field Office, and Jennifer Washburn,

January 22, 2008, published in Washburn, *Big Oil Goes to College,* op. cit. note 105. According the DOE's website, "The mission of the Golden Field Office is to support DOE's Office of Energy Efficiency and Renewable Energy through R&D partnerships, outreach to stakeholders nationwide to further the use of energy efficiency and renewable energy technologies, and laboratory contract administration" (www.eere.energy.gov/golden/About_The_Office.aspx).

108 Hall, "University-Industry Research Partnerships in the United States," op. cit. note 42. An earlier version was presented at the Sixth International Conference on Technology Policy and Innovation, Kansai, Japan, August 2002 (6).

109 Eric G. Campbell and David Blumenthal, "Industrialization of Academic Science and Threats to Scientific Integrity," in *The Oxford Textbook of Clinical Ethics,* ed. Ezekiel J. Emanuel, Christine Grady, et al. (Oxford: Oxford University Press, 2008), 780–86; see Table 71.1, "Conceptualization of AIRs," 781.

110 Adapted from ibid., 781.

111 For a detailed analysis of these types of centers, see Wesley M. Cohen, Richard L. Florida, and Richard Goe, *University-Industry Research Centers in the United States* (Pittsburgh: Carnegie Mellon University Press, 1994). See also Hall, "University-Industry Research Partnerships in the United States," op. cit. note 42.

112 Adapted from Campbell and Blumenthal, "Industrialization of Academic Science and Threats to Scientific Integrity" 781, op. cit. note 109.

113 Adapted from Campbell and Blumenthal, "Industrialization of Academic Science and Threats to Scientific Integrity" 781, op. cit. note 109.

114 See, e.g., Cornell University, "Faculty Statement of Principles and Best Practices Concerning Strategic Corporate Alliances," Fall 2005, final document, available at http://www.theuniversityfaculty.cornell.edu/forums/forums_main.html, 9; Lawrence Busch, Richard Allison, Craig Harris, et al., *External Review of the Collaborative Research Agreement between Novartis Agricultural Discovery Institute, Inc. and the Regents of California* (East Lansing: Michigan State University, Institute for Food and Agricultural Standards, July 13, 2004): 13, 152, available at http://berkeley.edu/news/media/releases/2004/07/external_novartis_review.pdf; and UC Berkeley Academic Senate, Task Force on University-Industry Partnerships, "Principles and Guidelines for Large-Scale Collaborations between the University and Industry, Government, and Foundations," final, n.d., 12–13, available at http://academic-senate.berkeley.edu/sites/default/files/recommendations-reports/tf_uip_report-final1.pdf.

115 Busch et al., *External Review of the Collaborative Research Agreement,* op. cit. note 114.

116 Cornell University, "Faculty Statement of Principles and Best Practices," 9, op. cit. note 114.

117 Quoted in BHEF, *Working Together, Creating Knowledge,* 22, op. cit. note 26. See also Industrial Research Institute, *A Report on Enhancing Industry-University Cooperative Research Agreements* (Washington, DC, 1995), 1.

118 Ibid., 22.

119 Ibid., 74.

120 David Blumenthal, Eric G. Campbell, Nancyanne Causino, and Karen Seashore Louis,

"Participation of Life-Science Faculty in Research Relationships with Industry," *New England Journal of Medicine* 335, no. 23 (1996): 1734–39.

121 IOM, "Conflicts of Interest," 102, op. cit. note 40.

122 BHEF, *Working Together, Creating Knowledge,* 23, op. cit. note 26.

123 Zinner, "Participation of Academic Scientists in Relationships with Industry," 1818, op. cit. note 54.

124 Research by Diana Hicks and Kimberly Hamilton (CHI Research Inc., Haddon Heights, NJ) found that, between 1981 and 1992, 3.3 of every one thousand papers published by university-industry collaborations were among the one thousand most cited in other scientific publications over the next four years. By contrast, 2.2 of every one thousand multiuniversity papers, and only 1.7 of every one thousand single-university papers, landed among the top-cited publications. Diana Hicks and Kimberly Hamilton, "Does University-Industry Collaboration Adversely Affect University Research?," *Issues in Science and Technology* 15, no. 4 (1999), 74–75.

125 Zinner, "Participation of Academic Scientists in Relationships with Industry," 1818, op. cit. note 54; Blumenthal et al., "Participation of Life-Science Faculty in Research Relationships with Industry." op. cit. note 120.

126 Pierre Azoulay, Ryan Michigan, and Bhaven N. Sampat, "The Anatomy of Medical School Patenting," *New England Journal of Medicine* 20, no. 357 (2007): 2049–56.

127 BHEF, *Working Together, Creating Knowledge,* 27–28, op. cit. note 26. Studies by Diane Rahm and Robert Morgan at Washington University in St. Louis did find a small association between greater faculty involvement with industry and more applied research. However, statistics from the National Science Foundation show that the amount of basic research performed in academia has remained relatively stable since 1980. Diana Hicks and Kimberly Hamilton of CHI Research also categorized research according to the journal in which it appeared and found that the percentage of basic research being performed in universities was unchanged from 1981 to 1995. Richard Florida, "The Role of the University: Leveraging Talent, Not Technology," *Issues in Science and Technology* 15, no. 4 (1999), available at http://www.issues.org/15.4/florida.htm; Hicks and Hamilton, "Does University-Industry Collaboration Adversely Affect University Research?" op. cit. note 124.

128 There is widespread recognition that a large amount of scientific research involves methods that both seek fundamental understanding of scientific problems, and, at the same time, seek to be eventually beneficial to society, thus blurring the popular distiction often made between basic and applied science. Louis Pasteur's research is thought to exemplify this type of method. The term was introduced by Donald Stokes in 1997: Donald E. Stokes, *Pasteur's Quadrant: Basic Science and Technological Innovation* (Washington, DC: Brookings Institution Press, 1997).

129 Nancy Olivieri appealed to the Canadian Association of University Teachers (CAUT) for assistance in November 1998. CAUT subsequently intervened in several matters on her behalf, but the situation remained unresolved. Following a procedure used by CAUT in other unresolved cases, CAUT decided in 1999 to set up a formal Committee of Inquiry. For the committee's final report on her case, see Jon Thompson, Patricia Baird and Jocelyn Downie,

The Olivieri Report: The Complete Text of the Report of the Independent Inquiry Commissioned by the Canadian Association of University Teachers (Toronto: James Lorimer, 2001).

130 For further background on Olivieri's case, see Miriam Shuchman, *The Drug Trial: Nancy Olivieri and the Science Scandal That Rocked the Hospital for Sick Children* (Toronto: Random House, 2005); Jon Thompson, Patricia A. Baird, and Jocelyn Downie, "The Olivieri Case: Context and Significance," *Ecclectica,* December 2005, available at http://www.ecclectica. ca/issues/2005/3/index.asp?Article=2; and Miriam Shuchman, "Legal Issues Surrounding Privately Funded Research Cause Furore in Toronto," *Canadian Medical Association Journal* 159 (1998): 983–86.

131 Ralph T. King Jr., "Bitter Pill: How A Drug Firm Paid for University Study, Then Undermined It," *Wall Street Journal,* April 25, 1996.

132 Betty J. Dong, Walter W. Hauck, John G. Gambertoglio, et al., "Bioequivalence of Generic and Brand-Name Levothyroxine Products in the Treatment of Hypothyroidism," *Journal of the American Medical Association* 277, no. 15 (1997): 1205–13.

133 David Shenk, "Money and Science = Ethics Problems on Campus," *The Nation,* May 12, 1999, 11–18.

134 Dong et al., "Bioequivalence of Generic and Brand-Name Levothyroxine Products," op. cit. note 132.

135 Richard Saltus, "AIDS Drug Researchers Say Firm Pressured Them: Findings Published, but Fight Goes to Court," *Boston Globe,* November 1, 2000.

136 Phillip J. Hilts, "Drug Firm, Scientists Clash over HIV Study," *Chicago Tribune,* November 1, 2000.

137 James O. Kahn, Deborah Weng Cherng, Kenneth Mayer, et al., "Evaluation of HIV-1 Immunogen, an Immunologic Modifier, Administered to Patients Infected with HIV Having 300 to 549x106/L CD4 Cell Counts: A Randomized Controlled Trial," *Journal of the American Medical Association* 284, no. 17 (2000): 2193–2202. (Erratum, *Journal of the American Medical Association* 285, no. 17 (2001): 2197.)

138 Natash Lee, "UCSF, Immune Response Drop Countersuits," *San Diego Business Journal* 22, no. 39 (2001): 14. A study including the disputed data was published in April 2001, concluding that Remune was beneficial for certain patients. J. Turner et al., "The effects of an HIV-1 Immunogen (Remune) on viral load, CD4 counts and HIV-specific immunity in a double-blind, randomized, adjuvant-controlled subset study in HIV infected subjects regardless of concomitant antiviral drugs," *HIV Medicine* 2[2]:68–77, 2001. Today Remune continues to be explored in clinical trials and is considered potentially useful in conjunction with retroviral medications.

139 This section draws heavily from Washburn, *University Inc.,* chap. 1, op. cit. note 41. We also draw on more recent studies and news reports: Charles Duhigg, "Debating How Much Weed Killer Is Safe in Your Water Glass," *New York Times,* August 22, 2009, available at www.nytimes. com/2009/08/23/us/23water.html?_r=1&hp=pagewanted=all; "How the EPA is Ignoring Atrazine Contamination in Sueface and Drinking Water in the Central United States," *New York Times,* August 2009, available at http://graphics8.nytimes.com/packages/pdf/us/NRDC-

Atrazine-report.pdf?scp=2&sq=atrazine&st=cse; Laura E. Beane Freeman, Atrazine and Cancer Incidence Among Pesticide Applicators in the Agricultural Health Study(1994–2007), 2011, available at http:ehp03.niehs.nih.gov/article/fetchArticle.action;jsessionid=16CAE F820312206AF426693F83851464?articleURI=info;doi/10.1289/ehp.1103561; "Interim Reregistration Eligibility Decision for Atrazine," EPA, January 2003, available at http://www. epa.gov/pesticides/reregistration/atrazine/atrazine_update.htm#cancer.

140 Glennda Chui, "Study: Herbicide Wrecks Frog Sex Organs; Report May Explain Population Decline among Amphibians," *San Jose Mercury News,* April 16, 2002.

141 Jennifer Lee, "Popular Pesticide Faulted for Frogs' Sexual Abnormalities," *New York Times,* June 19, 2003.

142 Robert Sanders, "Popular Weed Killer Demasculinizes Frogs, Disrupts Their Sexual Development, UC Berkeley Study Shows," *Berkeleyan* (UC Berkeley press release), April 4, 2002.

143 Ecorisk Press Release, "Frog Research on Atrazine Casts Doubt on Earlier Studies," *PR Newswire,* June 20, 2002.

144 Goldie Blumenstyk, "The Price of Research," *Chronicle of Higher Education,* October 31, 2003.

145 Tyrone Hayes, Kelly Haston, Mable Tsui, et al., "Atrazine-Induced Hermaphroditism at 0.1 PPB in American Leopard Frogs (Rana Pipiens): Laboratory and Field Evidence," *Environmental Health Perspectives* 111, no. 4 (2003): 568–75.

146 Lee, "Popular Pesticide Faulted for Frogs' Sexual Abnormalities," op. cit. note 141.

147 Alison Pierce, "Bioscience Warfare," *SF (CA) Weekly,* June 2, 2004.

148 Jennifer Washburn, "Academic Freedom and the Corporate University," *Academe* 97, no. 1 (2011), available at http://www.aaup.org/AAUP/pubsres/academe/2011/JF/Feat/wash.htm.

149 All documentary records provided by Kern are available, in electronic form, from Jennifer Washburn.

150 "Report: Investigation of Alleged Interference with the Academic Freedom of David Kern, M.D.," Brown University, May 6, 1997, prepared by a "Committee of Inquiry" formed by Donald J. Marsh, then dean of the Brown Medical School, which was composed of deans Lois Montero, Peter Shank, and Peder Estrup.

151 David G. Kern, "The Unexpected Result of an Investigation of an Outbreak of Occupational Lung Disease," *International Journal of Occupational and Environmental Health* 4, no. 1(1998): 19–32.

152 Microfibres Confidentiality agreement for the initial air testing visit, signed by Dr. Kern's research associate, Kate Durand, December 2, 1994, available at http://www.thejabberwock. org/blog/2/kern2.pdf. (The other Memorial Hospital contract you see at this website page is one Dr. Kern drew up himself, and attempted to present to Microfibres during his second consulting health investigation. However the company never signed it.)

153 Letter from Peter Shank, Brown University's associate dean of medicine and biomedical research to David Kern, November 18, 1996, available at http://scientific-misconduct. blogspot.com/2007/04/dr-david-kerns-dilemma-learning-from.html.

154 Memorandum from Francis R. Dietz, President of Memorial Hospital, to David Kern, December 23, 1996, available from Jennifer Washburn.

155 Letter from Donald J. Marsh, Dean of the Brown Medical School, to Frank Dietz, President of Memorial Hospital, April 30, 1997, available from Jennifer Washburn.

156 Kern and his colleagues published their study as David G. Kern, Robert S. Crausman, Kate T. H. Durand, et al., "Flock Worker's Lung: Chronic Interstitial Lung Disease in the Nylon Flocking Industry," *Annals of Internal Medicine* 129, no. 4 (1998): 261–72.

157 Brown University News Bureau, "Brown University Supports the Academic Freedom of Dr. David Kern," May 21, 1997, available at http://brown.edu/Administration/News_Bureau/1996-97/96-133.html.

158 Kern et al., "Flock Worker's Lung," op. cit. note 156.

159 David G. Kern, Eli Kern, Robert S. Crausman, and Richard W. Clapp, "A Retrospective Cohort Study of Lung Cancer Incidence in Nylon Flock Workers, 1998–2008," *International Journal of Occupational and Environmental Health* 17, no. 4 (2011): 345–51.

160 Busch et al., *External Review of the Collaborative Research Agreement*, 41–43, op. cit. note 114. Busch is also quoted in the media saying that the agreement "played a very clear role and an unsatisfactory role in the tenure process" of Chapela; see Goldie Blumenstyk, "Peer Reviewers Give Thumbs Down to Berkeley-Novartis Deal," *Chronicle of Higher Education,* July 30, 2004.

161 David Quist and Ignacio Chapela, "Transgenic DNA Introgressed into Traditional Maize Landraces in Oaxaca, Mexico," *Nature* 414, (November 29, 2001): 541–43.

162 Marc Kaufman, "The Biotech Corn Debate Grows Hot in Mexico," *Washington Post,* March 25, 2002.

163 This AgBioWorld listserver circulated a petition calling on *Nature* and Chapela to retract the study. George Monbiot, a reporter with the *Guardian,* found a number of suspicious connections between the critics who posted messages on this site and a PR firm called the Bivings Group, which specializes in Internet viral lobbying. According to Monbiot, an article on the PR firm's website, titled "Viral Marketing: How to Infect the World," warns that "there are some campaigns where it would be undesirable or even disastrous to let the audience know that your organisation is directly involved. . . . it simply is not an intelligent PR move. In cases such as this, it is important to first 'listen' to what is being said online. . . . Once you are plugged into this world, it is possible to make postings to these outlets that present your position as an uninvolved third party. . . . Perhaps the greatest advantage of viral marketing is that your message is placed into a context where it is more likely to be considered seriously." Monbiot, George, "The Fake Persuaders," *Guardian* (London), May 14, 2002, available at http://artsci.wustl.edu/~anthro/bnc/readings/Monbiot%20The%20fake%20persuaders.htm.

164 When John E. Losey of Cornell University, for example, published a study showing that Monarch butterfly caterpillars exposed to pollen from GM cotton became sick and died in lab studies, his research was roundly attacked by industry-funded scientists, and an aggressive public relations campaign was launched against him. John E. Losey, Linda S. Rayor, and Maureen E. Carter, "Transgenic Pollen Harms Monarch Larvae," *Nature* 399, (May 20, 1999): 214. For a discussion of Losey's and other similar cases, see "The Pulse of Scientific Freedom in the Age of the Biotech Industry," a public conversation sponsored by the Knight Center for

Science and Environmental Journalism at the UC Berkeley School of Journalism, Berkeley, CA, December 10, 2003, available at http://nature.berkeley.edu/pulseofscience.

165   Matthew Metz and Johannes Fütterer, Suspect Evidence of Transgenic Contamination, *Nature* 416 (April 11, 2002): 600–01; Nick Kaplinsky, David Braun, Damon Lisch, et al., "Biodiversity (Communications arising): Maize Transgene Results in Mexico Are Artefacts," *Nature* 416 (April 11, 2002): 600–01. All the above authors except Fütterer are or were working in UC Berkeley's Department of Plant and Microbiology.

166   Ayala Ochert, "Food Fight," *California Monthly,* June 2002.

167   Charles C. Mann, "Has GM Corn 'Invaded' Mexico?," *Science* 295, no. 5560 (March 1, 2002): 1617–19; Kaufman, "The Biotech Corn Debate Grows Hot in Mexico," op. cit. note 162.

168   Carol Kaesuk Yoon, "Journal Raises Doubts on Biotech Study," *New York Times,* April 5, 2002; Russell Schoch, "Novartis: Gone but Not Forgotten," *California Monthly,* April 13, 2004.

169   Washburn, *University Inc.,"* 14–17, op. cit. note 41.

170   Busch et al., *External Review of the Collaborative Research Agreement,* 143, op. cit. note 114.

171   Barry Bergman, "Prof. Ignacio Chapela Granted Tenure," news bulletin, College of Natural Resources, UC Berkeley, May 21, 2005, available at http://cnr.berkeley.edu/blogs/news/2005/05/prof_ignacio_chapela_granted_t.php.

172   Patricia Baird, "Getting It Right: Industry Sponsorship and Medical Research," *Canadian Medical Association Journal,* 168, no. 10 (2003): 1267–69.

173   Food & Water Watch, *Public Research, Private Gain,* op. cit. note 27. See p. 12, in particular, where the report explains: "In 2009, SDSU [South Dakota State University] filed suit against South Dakota farmers for the first time, alleging illegal use of SDSU-controlled seeds. One accused farmer called the lawsuit a "rotten scam" in which SDSU purportedly entrapped him to violate university patents by running a fake "seed wanted" ad in a newspaper. He and four other farmers settled the 2009 cases for more than $100,000. In 2011, SDSU settled another lawsuit against a farmer for $75,000. Farmers not only paid damages but also consented to allow SDSU inspect their farms, facilities, business records and telephone records for up to five years. SDSU is not alone in suing farmers over seed patents. Texas A&M, Kansas State University and Colorado State University have pursued similar lawsuits against farmers."

174   Ibid.

175   Andrew Pollock, "Crop Scientists Say Biotechnology Seed Companies Are Thwarting Research," *New York Times,* February 20, 2009.

176   Food & Water Watch, *Public Research, Private Gain,* op. cit. note 27.

177   Ibid.

178   Rex Dalton, "Superweed study falters as seed firms deny access to transgene," *Nature* 419 (October 17, 2002): 655.

179   Emily Waltz, "Under Wraps," *Nature Biotechnology* 27 (October 2009): 880–82.

180   Food & Water Watch, *Public Research, Private Gain,* op. cit. note 27. Original Source: Goldberger, Jessica, Jeremy Foltz, Bradford Barham and Timo Goeshl, "Modern Agricultural Science in Transition: A Survey of US Land grant Agricultural and Life Scientists," PATS Research Report no. 14 (October, 2005), available at http://www.pats.wisc.edu/pubs/32.

181 Food & Water Watch, *Public Research, Private Gain,* op. cit. note 27. Original Source: University of Georgia Center for Food Safety, "Industry Membership, Invitation from the Center Director," archived on January 3, 2011 at http://web.archive.org/web/20120121150758/http://www.ugacfs.org/industry.html >>

182 Food & Water Watch, *Public Research, Private Gain,* op. cit. note 27. Original Source: Purdue University. College of Agriculture, Food Science, "Involvement with Industry," archived on January 3, 2011 at <<http://web.archive.org/web/20110103064247/http://www.ag.purdue.edu/foodsci/Pages/industry.aspx>>.

183 Melanie Brandert. "Relationship Between Monsanto , SDSU President Questioned," *Argus Leader,* May 7, 2009.

184 Food & Water Watch, *Public Research, Private Gain,* op. cit. note 27. In endnote 143, the authors of the Food & Water Watch report explain: "It is unknown how much money public and private sources have contributed to wheat breeding at SDSU. SDSU refused to honor an open-records request from Food & Water Watch without agreeing to an estimated payment of $629. Food & Water Watch refused this payment on the grounds that research grant information is public information and should be freely disseminated."

185 IOM, "Conflicts of Interest," 103–4, op. cit. note 40. See Claire Bombardier, Loren Laine, Alise Reicin, et al., "Comparison of Upper Gastrointestinal Toxicity of Rofecoxib and Naproxen in Patients with Rheumatoid Arthritis," *New England Journal of Medicine* 343, no. 21 (2000): 1520–28, two pages following 1528; Fred W. Silverstein, Gerald Faich, Jay L. Goldstein, et al., "Gastrointestinal Toxicity with Celecoxib vs. Nonsteroidal Anti-inflammatory Drugs for Osteoarthritis and Rheumatoid Arthritis: The CLASS Study—A Randomized Controlled Trial, Celecoxib Long-Term Arthritis Safety Study," *Journal of the American Medical Association* 284, no. 10 (2000): 1247–55; and Gregory D. Curfman, Stephen Morrissey, and Jeffrey M. Drazen, "Expression of Concern: Bombardier et al., 'Comparison of Upper Gastrointestinal Toxicity of Rofecoxib and Naproxen in Patients with Rheumatoid Arthritis,'" *New England Journal of Medicine* 353, no. 26 (2005): 2813–14.

186 Bodenheimer, "Uneasy Alliance," op. cit. note 34.

187 Ibid.

188 Silverstein, et al., "Gastrointestinal Toxicity with Celecoxib vs. Nonsteroidal Anti-inflammatory Drugs," 1247–55, op. cit. note 185.

189 Jennifer Berg Hrachovec and Marc Mora, "Reporting of Six-Month vs. Twelve-Month Data in a Clinical Trial of Celecoxib," *Journal of the American Medical Association* 286, no. 19 (2001): 2398; author reply, 2399–2400.

190 James M. Wright, Thomas L. Perry, Ken L. Bassett, and G. Keith Chambers, "Reporting of Six-Month vs. Twelve-Month Data in a Clinical Trial of Celecoxib," *Journal of the American Medical Association* 286, no. 19 (2001): 2398–2400.

191 Susan Okie, "Missing Data on Celebrex: Full Study Altered Picture of Drug," *Washington Post,* August 5, 2001.

192 Ibid.

193 Frank Davidoff, Catherine D. DeAngelis, Jeffrey M. Drazen, et al., "Sponsorship, Authorship,

and Accountability," *New England Journal of Medicine* 345 no. 11 (2001): 825–27; International Committee of Medical Journal Editors (ICMJE), "Uniform Requirements for Manuscripts Submitted to Biomedical Journals," available at http://www.icmje.org.

194 ICMJE, "Uniform Requirements for Manuscripts," op. cit. note. 193.

195 Kevin A. Schulman, Damon M. Seils, Justin W. Timbie, et al., "Provisions in Clinical-Trial Agreements," *New England Journal of Medicine* 347, no. 17 (October 24, 2002): 1335–41.

196 Bodenheimer, "Uneasy Alliance," op. cit. note 34.

197 Aubrey Blumsohn, "Authorship, Ghost-Science, Access to Data and Control of the Pharmaceutical Scientific Literature: Who Stands Behind the Word?," *Professional Ethics Report* 19, no. 3 (2006): 1–8, published by the American Association for the Advancement of Science (AAAS), Scientific Freedom, Responsibility, and Law Program, and available at http://www. aaas.org/spp/sfrl/per/per46.pdf.

198 Robert Steinbrook, "Gag Clauses in Clinical Trial Agreements," *New England Journal of Medicine* 352, no. 21 (2005): 2160–62.

199 Discussed in IOM, "Conflicts of Interest," 47, op. cit. note 40. For original sources, see David Healy, "Did Regulators Fail over Selective Serotonin Reuptake Inhibitors?," *British Medical Journal* 333 (July 6, 2006): 92–95; Erick H. Turner, Annette M. Matthews, Eftihia Linardatos, Robert A. Tell, and Robert Rosenthal, "Selective Publication of Antidepressant Trials and Its Influence on Apparent Efficacy," *New England Journal of Medicine* 358, no. 3 (2008): 252–60. See also Jonathan Leo, "The SSRI Trials in Children: Disturbing Implications for Academic Medicine," *Ethical Human Psychology and Psychiatry* 8, no. 1 (2006): 29–41.

200 Quoted in Leo, "The SSRI Trials in Children," op. cit. note. 199. See also David Healy, "Suicidal Evidence Not Addressed by FDA," (2004) (Letter from David Healy to Peter J. Pitts, associate commissioner for external relations, Food and Drug Administration), unpublished manuscript, available at http://www.ahrp.org/risks/healy/FDA0204.php.

201 American College of Neuropsychopharmacology (ACN), "Executive Summary," in *Preliminary Report of the Task Force on SSRIs and Suicidal Behavior in Youth* (Nashville, TN: CAN, 2004), available at http://www.acnp.org/asset.axd?id=aad01592-01b2-4672-ad28-119537460ffa.

202 Craig J. Whittington, Tim Kendall, Peter Fonagy, David Cottrell, Andrew Cotgrove, and Ellen Boddington, "Selective Serotonin Reuptake Inhibitors in Childhood Depression: Systematic Review of Published versus Unpublished Data," *Lancet* 363, no. 9418 (2004): 1341–45.

203 IOM, "Conflicts of Interest," 24, op. cit. note 40.

204 Barry Meier, "Contracts Keep Drug Research out of Reach," *New York Times,* November 29, 2004; Steinbrook, "Gag Clauses in Clinical Trial Agreements," op. cit. note 198.

205 Leo, "The SSRI Trials in Children," op. cit. note 199.

206 Editors, "Depressing Research," *Lancet* 363, no. 9418 (2004): 1335.

207 Carl Elliot, "Making a Killing: Clinical Trials Have Become Marketing Exercises for Big Pharma—and Cash-Strapped Universities Are Helping Make the Sale. Too Bad for Dan Markingson," *Mother Jones,* September–October 2010, 58.

208 Peter Jüni, Linda Nartey, Stephan Reichenbach, Rebekka Sterchi, Paul A. Dieppe, and

Matthias Egger, "Risk of Cardiovascular Events and Rofecoxib: Cumulative Meta-analysis," *Lancet* 364, no. 9450 (2004): 2021–29; Curfman et al., "Expression of Concern," op. cit. note 185; Gregory D. Curfman, Stephen Morrissey, and Jeffrey M. Drazen, "Expression of Concern Reaffirmed," *New England Journal of Medicine* 354, no. 11 (2006):1193. See also Anne Wilde Matthews and Barbara Martinez, "Emails Suggest Merck Knew Vioxx's Dangers at Early Stage," *Wall Street Journal,* November 1, 2004.

209 David J. Graham, "COX-2 Inhibitors, Other NSAIDs, and Cardiovascular Risk: The Seduction of Common Sense," *Journal of the American Medical Association* 296, no. 13 (2006): 1653–56; Harlan M. Krumholz, Harold H. Hines, Joseph S. Ross, Amos H. Presler, and David S. Egilman, "What have we learnt from Vioxx?" *British Medical Journal* 334, no. 7585 (2007): 120–23.

210 Ross et al., "Guest Authorship and Ghostwriting in Publications Related to Rofecoxib," op. cit. note 35; see also US Senate Committee on Finance (Sen. Charles E. Grassley, ranking member), *Ghostwriting in Medical Literature,* Minority Staff Report, 111th Congress, June 24, 2010.

211 Alex Berenson, "Evidence in Vioxx Suits Shows Intervention by Merck Officials," *New York Times,* April 24, 2005.

212 Robert Steinbrook and Jerome P. Kassirer, "Analysis: Data Availability for Industry Sponsored Trials: What Should Medical Journals Require?," *British Medical Journal* 341 (October 12, 2010): c5391.

213 Gardiner Harris, "Caustic Government Report Deals Blow to Diabetes Drug," *New York Times,* July 9, 2010.

214 Gardiner Harris, "F.D.A. to Restrict Avandia, Citing Heart Risk," *New York Times,* September 23, 2010.

215 Jennifer Washburn, "Science's Worst Enemy: Corporate Funding," *Discover,* October 11, 2007.

216 Steven E. Nissen and Kathy Wolski, "Effect of Rosiglitazone on the Risk of Myocardial Infarction and Death from Cardiovascular Causes," *New England Journal of Medicine* 356, no. 24 (2007): 2457–71.

217 Washburn, "Science's Worst Enemy," op. cit. note 215.

218 Gardiner Harris, "Diabetes Drug Maker Hid Test Data, Files Indicate," *New York Times,* July 13, 2010, available at http://www.nytimes.com/2010/07/13/health/policy/13avandia.html.

219 Committee on Finance, US Senate, *Staff Report on GlaxoSmithKline and the Diabetes Drug Avandia,* January 2010, available at http://finance.senate.gov/newsroom/chairman/release/?id=bc56b552-efc5-4706-968d-f7032d5cd2e4. For more background on US Congressional hearings and reports by Grassley, Baucus, and Rosa DeLauro, see "Grassley, DeLauro Comment on JAMA Reports re: Diabetes Drug Avandia," press release, June 28, 2010, available at http://grassley.senate.gov/news/Article.cfm?customel_dataPageID_1502=27286.

220 Committee of Finance, *Staff Report on GlaxoSmithKline and the Diabetes Drug Avandia,* 1–2, op. cit. note 219

221 Gardiner Harris, "Diabetes Drug Linked to Higher Heart Risk," *New York Times,* June 28,

2010. See also David J. Graham, Rita Ouellet-Hellstrom, Thomas E. MaCurdy, Farzana Ali, Christopher Sholley, Christopher Worrall, and Jeffrey A. Kelman, "Risk of Acute Myocardial Infarction, Stroke, Heart Failure, and Death in Elderly Medicare Patients Treated with Rosiglitazone or Pioglitazone," *Journal of the American Medical Association* 304, no. 4 (2010): 411–18.

222 See Robert K. Merton, "Priorities in Scientific Discovery," *American Sociological Review* 22, no. 6 (1957): 635–59; Robert K. Merton, *The Sociology of Science* (Chicago: University of Chicago Press, 1973). Also see more recent writings on the economics of science, including Partha S. Dasgupta and Paul Allan David, "Information Disclosure and the Economics of Science and Tech," in *Arrow and the Ascent of Modern Economics Theory,* ed. George R. Feiwel (New York: New York University Press, 1987), 519–42; Partha S. Dasgupta and Paul Allan David, "Toward a New Economics of Science," *Research Policy* 23, no. 5 (1994): 487–521; and Paula E. Stephan, "The Economics of Science," *Journal of Economic Literature* 34, no. 3 (1996): 1199–1235. In "Priorities in Scientific Discovery," Merton states, "Once he has made his contribution, the scientist no longer has exclusive rights of access to it. It becomes part of the public domain of science. Nor has he the right of regulating its use by others by withholding it unless it is acknowledged as his. In short, property rights in science become whittled down to just this one: the recognition by others of the scientist's distinctive part in having brought the result into being" (640).

223 Bodenheimer, "Uneasy Alliance," op. cit. note 34. See also IOM, "Conflicts of Interest," Box 4-1, 107, op. cit. note 40. This IOM study reports the following cases, among others: The manufacturer of aprotinin, an antifibrinolytic drug used in cardiac surgery to decrease bleeding, withheld data that use of the drug increased the risk of renal failure, heart attack, and congestive heart failure (Jerry Avorn, "Dangerous Deception—Hiding the Evidence of Adverse Drug Effects," *New England Journal of Medicine* 355, no. 21, (2006): 2169–71.) The results of a clinical trial that compared the use of ezetimibe plus a statin with the use of a statin alone in individuals with elevated cholesterol levels were not published until two years after the conclusion of the trial. The results showed no difference in carotid artery wall thickness in the two groups (John J. Kastelein, Fatima Akdim, Erik S. G. Stroes, Aeilko H. Zwinderman, Michiel L. Bots, Anton F. Stalenhoef, Frank L. J. Visseren, et al., "Simvastatin With or Without Ezetimibe in Familial Hypercholester-olemia," *New England Journal of Medicine* 358, no.14 (2008): 1431–43.). The results of a pivotal clinical trial of a blood substitute (PolyHeme) in patients undergoing elective vascular surgery were not released for five years after the trial was stopped by the sponsor. The trial showed significant increases in the rates of mortality and heart attacks in the group receiving the experimental intervention (Thomas M. Burton, "Amid Alarm Bells, A Blood Substitute Keeps Pumping," *Wall Street Journal,* February 22, 2006, A1, A12; Northfield Laboratories, Northfield Laboratories Releases Summary Observations from Its Elective Surgery Trial, 2006, available at http://phx. corporate-ir.net/phoenix.zhtml?c=91374&p=irol-newsArticle&ID=833808&highlight). The manufacturer of an implantable cardioverter-defibrillator allegedly failed to report critical, potentially fatal design defects for more than three years (Robert G. Hauser, and Barry J.

Maron, "Lessons From the Failure and Recall of An Implantable Cardioverter-Defibrillator," *Circulation* 112, no. 13, (2006): 2040–42.).

224 IOM, "Conflicts of Interest," 107, box 4-1, op. cit. note 40: "Examples of Biased Reporting in Clinical Research." For more details on this case see Liza Gibson, "GlaxoSmithKline to Publish Clinical Trials after US Lawsuit," *British Medical Journal* 328, no. 7455 (2004): 1513.

225 Cohen and Walsh, "Real Impediments to Academic Biomedical Research," 15–16, op. cit. note 89. John P. Walsh, Mujuan Jiang, and Wesley M. Cohen, "Publication in the Entrepreneurial University," paper presented at the American Sociological Association annual meeting, August 12, 2007, New York. Here Walsh et al. find that publication delay is associated with commercial activity and ties to small and medium enterprises (SMEs) and that excluding information from publications is associated with industry funding. See also Justin E. Bekelman, Yan Li, and Cary P. Gross, "Scope and Impact of Financial Conflicts of Interest in Biomedical Research," *Journal of the American Medical Association* 289, no. 4 (2003): 454–65; David Blumenthal, Eric G. Campbell, Melissa S. Anderson, Nancyanne Causino, and Karen Seashore Louis, "Withholding Research Results in Academic Life Science: Evidence from a National Survey of Faculty," *Journal of the American Medical Association* 277, no. 17 (1997): 1224–28; Eric G. Campbell, Brian R. Clarridge, Manjusha Gokhale, Lauren Birenbaum, Stephen Hilgartner, Neil A. Holtzman, and David Blumenthal, "Data Withholding in Academic Genetics," *Journal of the American Medical Association* 287, no. 4 (2002): 473–80; Cohen et al., *University-Industry Research Centers in the United States,* op. cit. note 111; Wesley M. Cohen, Richard Florida, Lucien Randazzese, and John Walsh. "Industry and the Academy: Uneasy Partners in the Cause of Technological Advance," in *Challenges to Research Universities,* ed. Roger G. Noll (Washington, DC: Brookings Institute, 1998), 171–99.

226 Cohen and Walsh, "Real Impediments to Academic Biomedical Research," op. cit. note 89.

227 David Blumenthal, Nancyanne Causino, Eric Campbell, and Karen Seashore Louis, "Relationships between Academic Institutions and Industry in the Life Sciences: An Industry Survey," *New England Journal of Medicine* 334, no. 6 (1996): 368–74.

228 Cohen et al., *University-Industry Research Centers in the United States,* op. cit. note 111. See also a discussion in Florida, "The Role of the University," op. cit. note 127.

229 For details on BP restrictions on academic scientists after the Gulf oil spill, see Russ Lea, "BP, Corporate R&D, and the University," *Academe* 96, no. 6 (2010), available at http://www.aaup.org/AAUP/pubsres/academe/2010/ND/feat/lea.htm. (This website also provides Internet links to a draft research-contract and a retention agreement between BP and the University of South Alabama.) For observations on the conjunction between industry and government restrictions on Gulf oil spill research, see Linda Hooper-Bui, "The Oil's Stain on Science," *Scientist,* August 5, 2010, available at http://classic.the-scientist.com/news/display/57610/; and Robert B. Gagosian and Christopher D'Elia, "Gulf Oil Spill Research Can't Wait," *Washington Post,* July 27, 2010.

230 Gerald Markowitz and David Rosner, *Deceit and Denial: The Deadly Politics of Industrial Pollution* (Berkeley: University of California Press, 2002). See www.deceitanddenial.org for documents and a timeline related to the industry's response to their book.

231 Jon Wiener, "Cancer, Chemicals, and History," *The Nation,* February 7, 2005, available at http://www.thenation.com/article/cancer-chemicals-and-history

232 Ibid.

233 Peter Schmidt, "Scholar's Right to Keep Unpublished Work Private Is at Issue in Lawsuit," *Chronicle of Higher Education,* October 12, 2009, available at http://chronicle.com/article/Scholars-Right-to-Kep/48792.

234 Jon Wiener, "Big Tobacco and the Historians," *The Nation,* February 25, 2010, available at http://www.thenation.com/article/big-tobacco-and-historians

235 Anne Landman and Stanton A. Glantz, "Tobacco Industry Efforts to Undermine Policy-Relevant Research," *American Journal of Public Health* 99, no. 1 (2009): 45–58. For Phillip Morris's "Action Plan: Scientists," see 49; for a reproduction of the referenced display ads, and a list of all known tobacco industry consultants and associates, including faculty members, who publicly criticized Glantz from 1990 to 1997, see 50 and 52.

236 See Richard R. Nelson, "The Market Economy and the Scientific Commons," *Research Policy* 33, no. 3 (2004): 455–71; Richard R. Nelson, "Reflections on 'The Simple Economics of Basic Scientific Research': Looking Back and Looking Forward," *Industrial and Corporate Change* 15, no. 6 (2006): 903–17; Dasgupta and David, "Toward a New Economics of Science," op. cit. note 222; Mowery et al., *Ivory Tower and Industrial Innovation,* op. cit. note 55; and Rebecca S. Eisenberg, "Patent Swords and Shields," *Science* 299, no. 5609 (2003): 1018–19; among others.

237 Nelson, "The Market Economy and the Scientific Commons," 456, op. cit. note 236.

238 Lori Andrews, Jordan Paradise, Timothy Holbrook and Danielle Bochneak, "When Patents Threaten Science," *Science* 314, no. 5804 (2006): 1395–96; Michael A. Heller and Rebecca S. Eisenberg, "Can Patents Deter Innovation? The Anticommons in Biomedical Research," *Science* 280, no. 5364 (1998): 698–701.

239 Mowery et al., "The Growth of Patenting and Licensing by US Universities," op. cit. note 92.

240 So, et al., "Is Bayh-Dole Good for Developing Countries?" op. cit. note 90. Original Sources: US Supreme Court, *Gottschalk v. Benson* (1972), 409 US 63, No. 71-485, available at http://www.altlaw.org/v1/ cases/398051; and Jerome H. Reichman and Rochelle Cooper Dreyfuss, (2007) "Harmonization without Consensus: Critical Reflections on Drafting a Substantive Patent Law Treaty," *Duke Law Journal* 57, no. 1 (2007): 85–130.

241 In 2010, a lawsuit challenging these breast cancer gene patents went before a US District Court judge, who invalidated seven patents filed on two human genes whose mutations are associated with breast cancer; John Schwartz and Andrew Pollack, "Judge Invalidates Human Gene Patent," *New York Times,* March 29, 2010, available at http://www.nytimes.com/2010/03/30/business/30gene.html. Later, in July 2011, the Court of Appeals for the Federal Circuit reversed that lower court decision, declaring the patents once again legally valid; Andrew Pollack, "Ruling Upholds Gene Patent in Cancer Test," *New York Times,* July 29, 2011. Finally, in March 2012, the US Supreme Court weighed in on the matter, calling on the appeals court to reconsider its decision, throwing the validity of the gene patents once again into question; Andrew Pollack, "Justices Send Back Gene Case," *New York Times,* March 26,

2012, available at http://www.nytimes.com/2012/03/27/business/high-court-orders-new-look-at-gene-patents.html.

242 James A. Thomson, inventor; Wisconsin Alumni Research Foundation, assignee, Primate Embryonic Stem Cells, US Patent 5,843,780 (1998); Primate Embryonic Stem Cells, US Patent 6,200,806 (2001); Primate Embryonic Stem Cells, US Patent 7,029,913 (2006); Constance Holden, "US Patent office casts doubt on Wisconsin stem cell patents," *Science* 316, no. 5822 (2007): 182.

243 Holden, "US Patent office casts doubt on Wisconsin stem cell patents," 182.

244 Quoted from So, et al., "Is Bayh-Dole Good for Developing Countries?" op. cit. note 90. See also Arti K. Rai and Rebecca S. Eisenberg, "Bayh-Dole Reform and the Progress of Biomedicine," *Law and Contemporary Problems* 66, no. 1/2 (2003): 289–314.

245 Department of Health and Human Services (DHHS), National Institutes of Health (NIH), "Principles and Guidelines for Recipients of NIH Research Grants and Contracts on Obtaining and Disseminating Biomedical Research Resources: Final Notice," *Federal Register* 64, no. 246 (1999): 72090–96, available at http://www.ott.nih.gov/policy/rt_guide_final.html.

246 DHHS, NIH, "Best Practices for the Licensing of Genomic Inventions: Final Notice," *Federal Register* 70, no. 68 (2005): 18413–15, available at http://www.ott.nih.gov/policy/lic_gen.html.

247 Maria Freire, presentation to NIH Advisory Committee to the Director, December 7, 2000.

248 Stanton A. Glantz, John Slade, Lisa A. Bero and Peter Hanauer, *The Cigarette Papers,* (Berkeley, Los Angeles: University of California Press, 1996); Allan M. Brandt, *The Cigarette Century: The Rise, Fall, and Deadly Persistence of the Product That Defined America,* (New York, Basic Books, 2007); David Michaels, *Doubt Is Their Product,* (New York, Oxford: Oxford University Press, 2008); Robert N. Proctor, *The Golden Holocaust: Origins of the Cigarette Catastrophe and the Case for Abolition,* (Berkeley, Los Angeles: University of California Press, 2011).

249 The full final ruling from the US District Court for the District of Columbia in the case, *US Department of Justice v. Philip Morris USA Inc. et al.,* dated September 8, 2006, is available online at http://www.justice.gov/civil/cases/tobacco2/amended%20opinion.pdf.

250 Allan M. Brandt, "Inventing Conflicts of Interest," *American Journal of Public Health* 102, no. 1 (2012): 63–71, esp. 63–64; Brandt, *The Cigarette Century,* 165–207, op. cit. note. 248; Glantz et al. *The Cigarette Papers,* 32–46, op. cit. note 248; Michaels, *Doubt Is Their Product,* 3–11, op. cit. note 248; and Proctor, *The Golden Holocaust,* 257–88, op. cit. note 248. A passage from the US District Court judge's 2006 ruling in the Racketeer Influenced Corrupt Organizations (RICO) case against the tobacco companies suggests what the fruits of this meeting were: "Finally, a word must be said about the role of lawyers in this fifty-year history of deceiving smokers, potential smokers, and the American public about the hazards of smoking and second hand smoke, and the addictiveness of nicotine. At every stage, lawyers played an absolutely central role in the creation and perpetuation of the Enterprise and the implementation of its fraudulent schemes. They devised and coordinated both national and international strategy; they directed scientists as to what research they should and should not undertake; they vetted scientific research papers and reports as well as public relations materials to ensure that the interests of the Enterprise would be protected; they identified

'friendly' scientific witnesses, subsidized them with grants from the Center for Tobacco Research and the Center for Indoor Air Research, paid them enormous fees, and often hid the relationship between those witnesses and the industry; and they devised and carried out document destruction policies and took shelter behind baseless assertions of the attorney client privilege." *US Department of Justice v. Philip Morris USA Inc. et al.,* September 8, 2006, 4, available online at http://www.justice.gov/civil/cases/tobacco2/amended%20opinion.pdf.

251 Michaels, *Doubt Is Their Product,* 11, op. cit. note 248.

252 Ibid., 4. Michaels details the use of the "tobacco strategy" on behalf of multiple products and contaminants. For a time, the PR firm Hill and Knowlton benefited from providing its services to other companies marketing toxic products. As Michaels documents, the PR firm used the tobacco strategy to defend asbestos (18), vinyl chloride (36–37), and lead (42). Eventually Hill and Knowlton would be superceded: "As the product defense work has gotten more and more specialized, the makeup of the business has changed: generic public relations operations like Hill and Knowlton have been eclipsed by product defense firms, specialty boutiques run by scientists" (46).

253 The Legacy Tobacco Documents Library archive is available at http://legacy.library. ucsf.edu. It became fully text searchable as a digital archive only in 2007, which enabled Robert N. Proctor, a historian based at Stanford, to compile and publish representative lists of thousands of faculty (including historians, scientists, statisticians, and others) who had testified for Big Tobacco, or served as industry consultants without testifying. In his book *The Golden Holocaust,* Proctor also offers a case study of the risks to research integrity, public understanding, and public health that resulted as an outgrowth of these pervasive financial relationships between the Medical College of Virginia (MCV, later renamed Virginia Commonwealth University [VCU]) and a rogue industry. Commenting on the MCV/VCU's seventy-year entanglement with the tobacco industry, Proctor wrote: "It would be a mistake to characterize this interpenetration of tobacco and academia as merely a 'conflict of interest;' the relationship has been far more symbiotic. We are really talking about a confluence of interests, and sometimes even a virtual identity of interests" (Proctor, *The Golden Holocaust,* 190, op. cit. note 248). For Proctor's list of academic statisticians who have testified for tobacco companies, see 439–41; for his list of historians who have testified as witnesses on behalf of tobacco companies, see 460–63; for his list of historians who served as tobacco industry consultants without testifying, see 464.

254 Discussed in IOM, "Conflicts of Interest," 217, Box 8-1: "Cases and Controversies Involving Institutional Conflicts of Interest," op. cit. note 40; David Armstrong, "Surgery Journal Threatens Ban for Authors' Hidden Conflicts," *Wall Street Journal,* December 28, 2005.

255 This is adapted from the IOM, "Conflicts of Interest," 46, op. cit. note 40; and Dennis F. Thompson, "Understanding Financial Conflicts of Interest," *New England Journal of Medicine* 329, no. 8 (1993): 573–76.

256 Association of American Medical Colleges and Association of American Universities (AAMC-AAU), *Protecting Patients, Preserving Integrity, Advancing Health: Accelerating the Implementation of COI Policies in Human Subjects Research—Report of the AAMC-AAU Advisory Committee on*

Financial Conflicts of Interest in Human Subjects Research (Washington, DC: AAMC, 2008), 36, available at https://services.aamc.org/Publications/showfile.cfm?file=version107.pdf&prd_id=220&prv_id=268&pdf_id=107. The IOM offers this definition: "Institutional conflicts of interest arise when an institution's own financial interests, or those of its senior officials, pose risks of undue influence on decisions involving the institution's primary interests." "Conflicts of Interest," 218, op. cit. note 40.

257 IOM, "Conflicts of Interest," 61, op. cit. note 40.

258 Association of American Medical Colleges (AAMC), *Protecting Subjects, Preserving Trust, Promoting Progress: Policy and Guidelines for the Oversight of Individual Financial Interests in Human Subjects Research* (Washington, DC: AAMC, 2001), 3, available at http://www.aamc.org/research/coi/firstreport.pdf.

259 The PLoS Medicine Editors, "Does Conflict of Interest Disclosure Worsen Bias?," *PLoS Medicine,* 9, no. 10, (2012): e1001210, available at http://www.plosmedicine.org/article/info%3Adoi%2F10.1371%2Fjournal.pmed.1001210. This editorial is responding in part to: Lisa Cosgrove, Sheldon Krimsky, "A Comparison of *DSM*-IV and *DSM*-5 Panel Members' Financial Associations with Industry: A Pernicious Problem Persists," *PLoS Medicine* 9, no. 3 (2012): e1001190, available at http://www.plosmedicine.org/article/info%3Adoi%2F10.1371%2Fjournal.pmed.1001190.

260 See, e.g., Deborah E. Barnes and Lisa A. Bero, "Why Review Articles on the Health Effects of Passive Smoking Reach Different Conclusions," *Journal of the American Medical Association* 279, no. 19 (1998): 1566–70; M. Scollo, A. Lal, A. Hyland and S. Glantz, "Review of the Quality of Studies on the Economic Effects of Smoke-Free Policies on the Hospitality Industry," *Tobacco Control* 12, no. 1 (2003): 13–20; and Janine K. Cataldo, Judith J. Prochaska, and Stanton A. Glantz, "Cigarette Smoking Is a Risk Factor for Alzheimer's Disease: An Analysis Controlling for Tobacco Industry Affiliation," *Journal of Alzheimer's Disease* 19, no. 2 (2010): 465–80.

261 Association of American Medical Colleges (AAMC), *In the Interest of Patients: Recommendations for Physician Financial Relationships and Clinical Decision Making: Report of the Task Force on Financial Conflicts of Interest in Clinical Care* (Washington, DC: AAMC, June 2010), 6–7.

262 Ibid., 5. For references to specific research studies, see James P. Orlowski and Leon Wateska, "The Effects of Pharmaceutical Firm Enticements on Physician Prescribing Patterns: There's No Such Thing as a Free Lunch," *Chest* 102, no. 1 (1992): 270–73; Mary-Margaret Chren and C. Seth Landefeld, "Physicians' Behavior and Their Interactions with Drug Companies: A Controlled Study of Physicians Who Requested Additions to a Hospital Drug Formulary," *Journal of the American Medical Association* 271, no. 9 (1994): 684–89; Lisa D. Chew, Theresa S. O'Young, Thomas K. Hazlet, et al., "A Physician Survey of the Effect of Drug Sample Availability on Physicians' Behavior," *Journal of General Internal Medicine* 15, no. 7 (2000): 478–83; Barbara Symm, Michael Averitt, Samuel N. Forjuoh and Cheryl Preece, "Effects of Using Free Sample Medications on the Prescribing Practices of Family Physicians," *Journal of the American Board of Family Medicine* 19, no. 5 (2006): 443–49; Richard F. Adair and Leah R. Holmgren, "Do Drug Samples Influence Resident Prescribing Behavior? A Randomized Trial," *American Journal of Medicine* 118, no. 8 (2005): 881–84; and John M. Boltri, Elizabeth R.

Gordon, and Robert L. Vogel, "Effect of Antihypertensive Samples on Physician Prescribing Patterns," *Family Medicine* 34, no. 10 (2002): 729–31.

263 Chren and Landefeld, "Physicians' Behavior and Their Interactions with Drug Companies," op. cit. note 262.

264 Nicole Lurie, Eugene C. Rich, Deborah E. Simpson, et al., "Pharmaceutical Representatives in Academic Medical Centers," *Journal of General Internal Medicine* 5, no. 3 (1990): 240–43.

265 Orlowski and Wateska, "The Effects of Pharmaceutical Firm Enticements on Physician Prescribing Patterns," op. cit. note 262.

266 Marilyn Y. Peay and Edmund R. Peay, "The Role of Commercial Sources in the Adoption of a New Drug," *Social Science and Medicine* 26, no. 12 (1988): 1183–89; John D. Cleary, "Impact of Pharmaceutical Sales Representatives on Physician Antibiotic Prescribing," *Journal of Pharmacy Technology* 8, no. 1 (1992): 27–29.

267 Warren S. Sandberg, Ruth Carlos, Elisabeth H. Sandberg, and Michael F. Roizen, "The Effect of Educational Gifts from Pharmaceutical Firms on Medical Students' Recall of Company Names of Products," *Academic Medicine* 72, no. 10 (1997): 916–18; Gregory L. Brotzman and David H. Mark, "Policies Regulating the Activities of Pharmaceutical Representatives in Residency Programs," *Journal of Family Practice* 34, no. 1 (1992): 54–57.

268 Ashley Wazana, "Physicians and the Pharmaceutical Industry: Is a Gift Ever Just a Gift?," *Journal of the American Medical Association* 283, no. 3 (2000): 373–80.

269 Association of American Medical Colleges and Baylor College of Medicine, Department of Neuroscience and Computational Psychiatry Unit, *The Scientific Basis of Influence and Reciprocity: A Symposium* (Washington, DC: Association of American Medical Colleges, 2007), available at www.aamc.org/reciprocity. See also Jason Dana and George Loewenstein, "A Social Science Perspective on Gifts to Physicians from Industry," *Journal of the American Medical Association* 290, no. 2 (2003): 252–55.

270 IOM, "Conflicts of Interest," Appendix D: Jason Dana, "How Psychological Research Can Inform Policies for Dealing with Conflict of Interest in Medicine," 358–74, op. cit. note 40.

271 IOM, "Conflicts of Interest," 110, op. cit. note 40.

272 IOM, "Conflicts of Interest," 36, op. cit. note 40. The California Political Reform Act maybe be accessed here: http://www.fppc.ca.gov/Act/2007Act.pdf

273 US Public Health Service Commissioned Corps (USPHS), "Objectivity in Research: Final Rule," *Federal Register* 60, no. 132 (1995): 35810–19; 42 CFR 50.601.

274 Anthony Mazzaschi, "NIH and ADAMHA's Conflict-of-Interest Guidelines Withdrawn," *FASEB Journal* 4, no. 2 (1990): 137–38. "On September 15, 1989, the National Institutes of Health and the Alcohol, Drug Abuse, and Mental Health Administration jointly published draft conflict-of-interest guidelines. By the end of the 90-day comment period, the agencies had received more than 700 letters of comment, most opposing the guidelines as drafted. In addition to FASEB comments, many of the Federation's constituent Societies submitted comments on the proposal" (137).

275 AAUP, "Statement on Conflicts of Interest," op. cit. note 5.

276 USPHS, "Objectivity in Research," op. cit. note 273.

277 See IOM, "Conflicts of Interest," table 1-1: "Timeline of Selected Events Relevant to the
     Evolution of Conflict of Interest Principles, Policies, and Practices," 36–38, op. cit. note
     40. In 1994, the National Science Foundation (NSF) issued a new Investigator Financial
     Disclosure Policy "to help ensure the appropriate management of actual or potential conflicts"
     (effective 1995). In 1998, the Food and Drug Administration (FDA) followed suit, publishing
     regulations (63 FR 5233) requiring disclosure by clinical investigators of certain financial
     relationships. As the Association of American Universities notes, FDA regulations are largely
     directed at drug companies, not universities: "they require companies filing a New Drug
     Application to certify that no financial arrangements with an investigator have been made
     where study outcomes could affect compensation, and to disclose to the FDA any pertinent
     investigator financial arrangements and the steps taken to minimize the potential for bias."
     AAU, *Report on Individual and Institutional Financial Conflict of Interest,* 3, op. cit. note 14.

278 S. Van McCrary, Cheryl B. Anderson, Jalena Jakovljevic, et al., "A National Survey of Policies
     on Disclosure of Conflicts of Interest in Biomedical Research," *New England Journal of
     Medicine* 343, no. 22 (2000): 1621; Mildred K. Cho, Ryo Shohare, Anna Schissel, and
     Drummond Rennie, "Policies on Faculty Conflicts of Interest at US Universities," *Journal
     of the American Medical Association* 284, no. 17 (2000): 2203–08; Bernard Lo, Leslie E. Wolf,
     and Abiona Berkeley, "Conflict-of-Interest Policies for Investigators in Clinical Trials," *New
     England Journal of Medicine* 343, no. 22 (2000): 1616.

279 IOM, "Conflicts of Interest," 217, op. cit. note 40. See also Robert Steinbrook, "The Gelsinger
     Case," in *The Oxford Textbook of Clinical Research Ethics,* ed. Ezekiel J. Emanuel, Christine
     Grady, Robert A. Crouch, Reidar Lie, Franklin Miller, and David Wendler (New York: Oxford
     University Press, 2008); and Sheryl Gay Stolberg, "The Biotech Death of Jesse Gelsinger,"
     New York Times Magazine, November 28, 1999, 136–40, 149–50.

280 National Institutes of Health (NIH), Department of Health and Human Services (DHHS),
     Food and Drug Administration (FDA), Centers for Disease Control (CDC), "Human Subject
     Protection and Financial Conflicts of Interest Conference," Washington, DC, agenda and
     speakers list available at http://www.hhs.gov/ohrp/archive/coi/agenda.htm; Donna Shalala,
     "Protecting Research Subjects: What Must Be Done," *New England Journal of Medicine* 343,
     no. 11 (2000): 808–10; DHHS Office of Inspector General, "Protecting Human Research
     Subjects: Status of Recommendations," Department of Health and Human Services, OEI-01-
     97-00197, 22, 3; General Accounting Office (GAO), "Biomedical Research: HHS Direction
     Needed to Address Financial Conflicts of Interest," November 2001, GAO-02-89: In this
     2001 report to Congress, the GAO called upon the US Department of Health and Human
     Services to promulgate new regulations or to issue guidance to address institutional conflicts
     of interest, noting that equity ownership or other investment in a research sponsor "may color
     [an institution's] review, approval, or monitoring of research conducted under its auspices or
     its allocation of equipment, facilities, and staff for research."

281 DHHS, "Financial Relationships in Clinical Research: Draft Interim Guidance," January 10,
     2001, available at http://ohrp.osophs.dhhs.gov/humansubjects/finreltn/finguid.html.

282 See Washburn, *University Inc.,* 134, which references Letters of Comment to the Office of

Human Research Protections from major university consortiums, including the Association of American Medical Colleges, the Association of American Universities, the Council on Government Relations, and the National Association of State Universities and Land Grant Colleges, all demanding that the 2001 HHS proposed guidelines be withdrawn, op. cit. note 41.

283 Davidoff et al., "Sponsorship, Authorship, and Accountability," op. cit. note 193; ICMJE, "Uniform Requirements for Manuscripts Submitted to Biomedical Journals," op. cit. note 193.

284 Davidoff et al., "Sponsorship, Authorship, and Accountability," op. cit. note 193.

285 Starting in 2005, the Senate Committee on Finance (Committee) initiated an inquiry into educational grants for continuing medical education (CME) programs. This inquiry began after reports that drug companies were using the grants to promote off-label uses of their drugs, i.e., uses that had not been approved by the Food and Drug Administration. The findings of that inquiry were released in a committee staff report in April 2007. See Committee Staff Report to the Chairman and Ranking Member, "Use of Educational Grants by Pharmaceutical Manufacturers," S. Prt. 110–21, April 2007, available at http://finance. senate.gov/newsroom/chairman/release/?id=af4af834-3fab-4293-be6d-ca7f1246484f. In 2008, Grassley also started to investigate university researchers' financial conflicts of interest; Charles Grassley, "Payment to Physicians," *Congressional Record—Senate,* 2008, S5030, available at http://frwebgate.access.gpo.gov/cgi-bin/getpage.cgi?dbname=2008_record&page=S5030 &position=all.

286 Charles Grassley, "Grassley Works to Disclose Financial Ties between Drug Companies and Doctors," press release, January 22, 2009, available at http://grassley.senate.gov/news/Article. cfm?customel_dataPageID_1502=18901; Charles Grassley, "Grassley Seeks Information about Medical School Policies for Disclosure of Financial Ties," June 29, 2009, available at http:// grassley.senate.gov/news/Article.cfm?customel_dataPageID_1502=21465.

287 IOM, "Conflicts of Interest," 74, op. cit. note 40.

288 Gardiner Harris, "Top Psychiatrist Didn't Report Drug Makers' Pay," *New York Times,* October 3, 2008, available at http://www.nytimes.com/2008/10/04/health/policy/04drug. html?fta=y&pagewanted=all.

289 Stacy Shelton, "Emory Will Punish Psychiatrist Nemeroff: Chairmanship Taken Away, Outside Income to Be Vetted," *Atlanta Journal-Constitution,* December 23, 2008.

290 Jocelyn Kaiser, "Conflicts Investigation Turns to Stanford," *ScienceNOW,* June 24, 2008, available at http://news.sciencemag.org/sciencenow/2008/06/24-01.html.

291 Paul Thacker, "The Ugly Underbelly of Medical Research," Project on Government Oversight, blog post with internal NIH—Stanford University e-mail correspondence, January 13, 2011, available at http://pogoblog.typepad.com/pogo/nih-emails-mifepristone-20080515. html.

292 Banerjee, Devin, "Conflict forces professor to quit grant post; Under Senate investigation, Schatzberg temporarily resigns," *Stanford Daily,* September 22, 2008, available at: http://www. stanforddaily.com/2008/09/22/conflict-forces-professor-to-quit-grant-post/ This story originally ran Aug. 14, 2008.

293 Gardiner Harris and Benedict Carey, "Researchers Fail to Reveal Full Drug Pay," *New York Times,* June 8, 2008.

294 Ed Silverman, "Harvard Docs Disciplined for Conflicts of Interest," *Pharmalot,* July 2, 2011, available at http://www.pharmalive.com/harvard-docs-disciplined-conflicts-interest.

295 David Armstrong, "Protocol Breach Reported in Biederman Study of Preschoolers," *Wall Street Journal,* March 20, 2009.

296 Liz Kowalczyk, "Senator Broadens Inquiry into Psychiatrist; Suggests MGH Doctor Was Biased in Research," *Boston Globe,* March 21, 2009; Gardiner Harris, "Drug Maker Told Studies Would Aid It, Papers Say," *New York Times,* March 19, 2009.

297 Office of the Inspector General (OIG), National Institutes of Health, *Conflicts of Interest in Extramural Research,* (Washington, DC: US Department of Health and Human Services, 2008), available at http://oig.hhs.gov/oei/reports/oei-03-06-00460.pdf.

298 Physician Payments Sunshine Act (S.301). For details see "Pew Prescription Project Fact Sheet: The Physician Payment Sunshine Act, 2009," available at http://www.prescriptionproject.org/tools/sunshine_docs/files/0001.pdf.

299 According to the IOM, "Conflicts of Interest," "District of Columbia, Maine, Massachusetts, Minnesota, Vermont, and West Virginia require pharmaceutical manufacturers to report their financial relationships with physicians; and a number of other states are considering such requirements (Wallack, 2008; Lopes, 2009; MedPAC, 2009). Minnesota and Massachusetts make the information public. Vermont requires the state's attorney general to make an annual public report based on the information that the pharmaceutical manufacturers have disclosed" (71). On the industry side, according to the IOM, "Conflicts of Interest," "Eli Lilly announced that it would create a publicly accessible registry of its payments to physicians beginning in 2009 (Lilly, 2008). Pfizer has released information about its grants and educational awards to medical, scientific, and patient organizations and has announced that it is eliminating grants to commercial providers of continuing medial education (Pfizer, 2008)" (180–81), op. cit. note 40.

300 Department of Health and Human Services (DHHS) 42 CFR Part 50, 45 CFR Part 94, "Responsibility of Applicants for Promoting Objectivity in Research for which Public Health Service Funding is Sought and Responsible Prospective Contractors," *Federal Register,* vol. 76, no. 165, August 25, 2011, available at: http://www.gpo.gov/fdsys/pkg/FR-2011-08-25/pdf/2011-21633.pdf

301 Quote from IOM, "Conflicts of Interest," 88, op. cit. note 40.

302 See discussion in IOM, "Conflicts of Interest," 110, op. cit. note 305. This 2003 AAMC survey is S. Ehringhaus and D. Korn, *US Medical School Policies on Individual Financial Conflicts of Interest: Results of an AAMC Survey* (Washington, DC: Association of American Medical Colleges, 2004), available at http://www.aamc.org/research/coi/coiresults2003.pdf.

303 IOM, "Conflicts of Interest," 68, op. cit. note 40. K. P. Weinfurt, M. A. Dinan, J. S. Allsbrook, J. Y. Friedman, M. A. Hall, K. A. Schulman, and J. Sugarman, "Policies of Academic Medical Centers for Disclosing Financial Conflicts of Interest to Potential Research Participants," *Academic Medicine* 81.2 (2006b): 113–18.

304 Discussed in IOM, "Conflicts of Interest," 221–22, op. cit. note 40. The survey cited here is S. Ehringhaus, J. S. Weissman, J. L. Sears, S. D. Goold, S. Feibelmann, and E. G. Campbell, "Responses of Medical Schools to Institutional Conflicts of Interest," *Journal of the American Medical Association* 299.6 (2008): 665–71. This study concludes as follows: "Despite strong national recommendations from 2 prominent higher education organizations, adoption of ICOI [Institutional Conflict of Interest] policies by US medical schools is far from complete. . . . wider adoption of ICOI policies covering these interests is imperative in light of the compelling interests of research integrity, protection of human subjects, and preservation of public trust."

305 Department of Health and Human Services (DHHS), Office of the Inspector General (OIG), "How Grantees Manage Financial Conflicts of Interest in Research Funded by the National Institutes of Health," OEI-03-07-00700, November 2009, 12, available at http://oig.hhs.gov/ oei/reports/oei-03-07-00700.pdf.

306 Ibid.

307 IOM, "Conflicts of Interest," op. cit. note 40: "One analysis of cases in which researchers disclosed their financial relationships found that university conflict of interest committees determined that 26 percent of the cases reviewed involved conflicts of interest that needed management [Boyd, E. A., S. Lipton, and L. A. Bero, "Implementation of Financial Disclosure Policies to Manage Conflicts of Interest," *Health Affairs* 23, 2 (2004): 206–14]. The three most commonly applied management strategies were requiring disclosure in publications and presentations (40 percent of the managed cases), appointing an oversight committee to protect the interests of students involved in the project (21 percent of the managed cases), and eliminating the relationship during the period of the project (22 percent of managed cases). The least common management approach was eliminating the conflict of interest or prohibiting the research" (84).

308 DHHS, OIG, "How Grantees Manage Financial Conflicts of Interest in Research Funded by the National Institutes of Health," , op. cit. note 40: "The most common type of conflict among researchers was equity ownership (including stocks and stock options) in companies in which the researchers' financial interests could significantly affect the grant research. One-hundred eleven researchers owned equity in companies ranging from publicly traded companies to small, privately held companies. Of these 111 researchers, 44 (39 percent) were founding members of the companies" (8).

309 Ibid., iii, 19.

310 General Accounting Office (GAO), "University Research: Most Federal Agencies Need to Better Protect against Financial Conflicts of Interest," November 2003, GAO-04-31, available at http://www.gao.gov/new.items/d0431.pdf.

311 Sally J. Rockey and Francis S. Collins, "Managing Financial Conflict of Interest in Biomedical Research," *Journal of the American Medical Association* 303, no. 23 (2010): 2400–02.

312 Davidoff et al., "Sponsorship, Authorship, and Accountability," op. cit. note 193; ICMJE, "Uniform Requirements for Manuscripts Submitted to Biomedical Journals," op. cit. note 193.

313 Schulman et al., "Provisions in Clinical-Trial Agreements." op. cit. note 195.

314 Ibid.

315 Jeffrey M. Drazen, "Institutions, Contracts, and Academic Freedom," *New England Journal of Medicine* 347, no. 17 (October 24, 2002), 1362–63.

316 Michelle M. Mello, Brian R. Clarridge, and David M. Studdert, "Academic Medical Centers' Standards for Clinical-Trial Agreements with Industry," *New England Journal of Medicine* 352, no. 21 (2005): 2202–10.

317 Troyen A. Brennan, David J. Rothman, Linda Blank, et al., "Health Industry Practices That Create Conflicts of Interest: A Policy Proposal for Academic Medical Centers," *Journal of the American Medical Association* 295, no. 4 (2006): 429–33; David J. Rothman and Susan Chimonas, "New Developments in Managing Physician-Industry Relationships," *Journal of the American Medical Association* 300, no. 9 (2008): 1067–69.

318 Association of American Medical Colleges (AAMC), *Industry Funding of Medical Education: Report of an AAMC Task Force* (Washington, DC: AAMC, June 2008), available at https://services.aamc.org/Publications/showfile.cfm?file=version114.pdf&prd_id=232.

319 IOM, "Conflicts of Interest," op. cit. note 40.

320 Susan Chimonas, Lisa Patterson, Victoria H. Raveis, and David J. Rothman, "Managing Conflicts of Interest in Clinical Care: A National Survey of Policies at US Medical Schools," *Academic Medicine* 86, no. 3 (March 2011): 293–99.

321 Robert Berdahl (UC Berkeley), *Proceedings of "A Dialog on University Stewardship: New Responsibilities and Opportunities, Government-University-Industry Research Roundtable,"* (Washington, DC: National Academy Press, 1999), 24.

322 For a discussion of this skirting of faculty governance and review, see the discussion of a major strategic alliance agreement signed by UC Berkeley and BP in Washburn, *Big Oil Goes to College,* e.g., 85–94, esp. 91, op. cit. note 105. On November 9, 2007, UC Berkeley (Regents of University of California) signed a $500 million strategic alliance agreement with BP Technology Ventures Inc. to launch the Energy Biosciences Institute (also in partnership with Lawrence Berkeley National Laboratory and the University of Illinois at Urbana-Champagne). A copy of the final EBI agreement is available at http://www.energybiosciencesinstitute.org/images/stories/pressroom/FINAL_EXECUTED_11-14.pdf.

323 Donald L. Lemish, *Establishing a University Foundation,* (Washington, DC, American Association of State Colleges and Universities, 1989).

324 Student Press Law Center (SPLC), "SPLC Tip Sheet: Access to University Foundation Records," 2010, available at http://www.splc.org/knowyourrights/legalresearch.asp?id=110. See also SPLC, "Crumbling Foundations: Records of University Fundraising Entities May Be Open under State Laws," *Legal Analysis* 26, no. 2 (Spring 2005): 34, available at http://www.splc.org/news/report_detail.asp?id=1194&edition=36.

325 Bill Roberts, "Multiple Civil Suits End with $8.3 Million Settlement," *Idaho Statesman,* October 13, 2006; "Former Official at U. of Idaho Pleads Guilty over Failed Development Project," *Chronicle of Higher Education,* November 22, 2006.

326 "It's Higher Learning, Not Learning for Hire: Corporate Cash Compromises the Public

Purpose of the University System of Georgia Foundation," *Atlanta Journal-Constitution,* January 2, 2005.

327 Sean Hill, SPLC, "Iowa District Court Orders ISU Foundation to Release Documents; Decision Is in Line with Iowa Supreme Court's February Ruling That Foundation Is Public," June 22, 2005, available at http://www.splc.org/news/newsflash.asp?id=1038; Liz Allen, "ISU Foundation Audit Includes Walden's Pay," *Ames (Iowa) Tribune,* March 6, 2001.

328 Fred Grimm, "Catanese Affair Suggests a New FAU Nickname," *Miami Herald,* September 30, 2003.

329 AAUP, "Statement on Corporate Funding of Academic Research," op. cit. note 4. This report was prepared by a subcommittee of the Association's Committee A on Academic Freedom and Tenure. It was approved by Committee A and adopted by the Association's Council in November 2004. Its first two recommendations are "1. Consistent with principles of sound academic governance, the faculty should have a major role not only in formulating the institution's policy with respect to research undertaken in collaboration with industry, but also in developing the institution's plan for assessing the effectiveness of the policy. The policy and the plan should be distributed regularly to all faculty, who should inform students and staff members associated with them of their contents" (6). See AAUP, "Statement on Government of Colleges and Universities," 135–40, op. cit. note 8: "2. The faculty should work to ensure that the university's plan for monitoring the institution's conflict-of-interest policy is consistent with the principles of academic freedom. There should be emphasis on ensuring that the source and purpose of all corporate-funded research contracts can be publicly disclosed. Such contracts should explicitly provide for the open communication of research results, not subject to the sponsor's permission for publication."

330 AAUP, "Statement on Conflicts of Interest," 185, op. cit. note 5.

331 AAUP, "Freedom in the Classroom," (2007), available at http://www.aaup.org/AAUP/comm/rep/A/class.htm.

332 In 2011, it came to light that two leading German universities, Humboldt University and the Technical University of Berlin, signed an agreement with Deutsche Bank to sponsor a joint institute for applied mathematical research, known as the Quantitative Products Laboratory. Under the terms of the 2007 contract—worth $17 million over four years—Deutsche Bank was given a say in the hiring of both of the two endowed professorships, one at each university. Deutsche Bank was also granted the right to have bank employees designated as adjunct professors, who were allowed to grade student work. Under the contract, appropriate *topics for research and research strategy were decided by a steering committee made up of two academics and two bank employees, with the managing director, a bank employee, casting the deciding vote in the event of a tie.* Finally, Deutsche Bank was granted permission to review all academic work sixty days before it was published, and could *withhold permission for publication for as long as two years.* The agreement further specified that the laboratory would be located "in close proximity to the Deutsche Bank" headquarters in Berlin. Finally, the whole agreement was to be secret. The contract only became public after Peter Grottian, a political scientist and emeritus professor at Humboldt, became a shareholder and obtained a copy, resulting in huge

headlines in the German news media. "You cannot avoid the impression that science is for sale," Michael Hartmer, director of the German Association of University Professors, told *Der Spiegel*. Donald D. Guttenplan, "Cash Tempts the Ivory Tower's Guardians," *New York Times,* July 17, 2011.

333 "Colleges and Universities with Programs Supported by the Charles Koch Foundation," February 2013, available at http://www.kochfamilyfoundations.org/pdfs/ CKFUniversityPrograms.pdf.

334 Berrett, "Not Just Florida State," op. cit. note 36; Hundley, "Billionaire's Role in Hiring Decisions at Florida State University Raises Questions," op. cit. note 36.

335 Chaker, "Companies Design, Fund Curricula at Universities," op. cit. note 39.

336 Keenan, "CEOs Pushing Ayn Rand Studies Use Money to Overcome Resistance," op. cit. note 38.

337 DHHS, NIH, "Principles and Guidelines for Recipiets of NIH Research Grants and Contracts," 72093, op. cit. note 245. Under the heading "Prompt Publication," this NIH guidance reads in part as follows: "Agreements to acquire materials for use in NIH-funded research are expected to address the timely dissemination of research results. Recipients should not agree to significant publication delays, any interference with the full disclosure of research findings, or any undue influence on the objective reporting of research results. A delay of thirty to sixty days to allow for patent filing or review for confidential proprietary information is generally viewed as reasonable."

338 IOM, "Conflicts of Interest," op. cit. note 40.

339 Susan Ehringhaus and David Korn, *Principles for Protecting Integrity in the Conduct and Reporting of Clinical Trials* (Washington, DC: AAMC, January 2006), partially reprinted in David Korn and Susan Ehringhaus, "Principles for Strengthening the Integrity of Clinical Research," *PLoS Clinical Trials* 1, no. 1 (2006): e1, available at http://clinicaltrials.ploshubs.org/article/ info:doi/10.1371/journal.pctr.0010001. See Principle 16: "Ghost or guest authorship is unacceptable. Authorship implies independent, substantial, and fully disclosed participation in the study and in the preparation of the manuscript." The full *Principles for Protecting Integrity in the Conduct and Reporting of Clinical Trials* is available at https://www.aamc.org/ download/49882/data/clinical_trials_reporting.pdf.

340 AAMC, *Industry Funding of Medical Education,* op. cit. note 318. In this report the AAMC recommends that "[a]cademic medical centers should prohibit physicians, trainees, and students from allowing their professional presentations of any kind, oral or written, to be ghostwritten by any party, industry or otherwise" (22). It also notes that properly acknowledged collaborations with industry personnel or medical writers is not ghostwriting.

341 Davidoff et al., "Sponsorship, Authorship, and Accountability," op. cit. note 193; ICMJE, "Uniform Requirements for Manuscripts Submitted to Biomedical Journals," op. cit. note 193. For World Association of Medical Editors (WAME) sources, see WAME, "Publication Ethics Policies for Medical Journals," available at http://www.wame.org/resources/publication-ethics-policies-for-medical-journals. See also WAME, "Policy Statements: Ghost Writing Initiated by Commercial Companies," available at http://www.wame.org/resources/policies#ghost .

342   See "Harvard University Policy on Individual Financial Conflicts of Interest For Persons Holding Faculty and Teaching Appointments," amended as of May 23, 2012, available at www.provost.harvard.edu/policies_guidelines/Harvard_University_fCOI_policy.pdf.

343   Lacasse and Leo, "Ghostwriting at Elite Academic Medical Centers in the United States," op. cit. note 35.

344   IOM, "Conflicts of Interest," 153, op. cit. note 40.

345   Barton Moffatt and Carl Elliott, "Ghost Marketing: Pharmaceutical Companies and Ghostwritten Journal Articles," *Perspectives in Biology and Medicine* 50, no. 1 (2007): 18–31.

346   David Healy and Dinah Cattell, "Interface between Authorship, Industry and Science in the Domain of Therapeutics," *British Journal of Psychiatry* 183 (July, 2003): 22–27.

347   Elizabeth Lopatto, Jef Feeley, and Margaret Cronin Fisk, "Eli Lilly 'Ghostwrote' Articles to Market Zyprexa, Files Show," *Bloomberg.com,* June 12, 2009, available at http://www.bloomberg.com/apps/news?pid=newsarchive&sid=aVvfe.v1k_VY.

348   Michael A. Steinman, Lisa A. Bero, Mary-Margaret Chren, and C. Seth Landefeld, "Narrative Review: The Promotion of Gabapentin: An Analysis of Internal Industry Documents," *Annals of Internal Medicine* 145, no. 4 (2006): 284–93.

349   Natasha Singer, "Medical Papers by Ghostwriters Pushed Therapy," *New York Times,* August 5, 2009.

350   Ross et al., "Guest Authorship and Ghostwriting in Publications Related to Rofecoxib," op. cit. note 35.

351   Leemon B. McHenry and Jon J. Jureidini, "Industry-Sponsored Ghostwriting in Clinical Trial Reporting: A Case Study," *Accountability in Research* 15, no. 3 (2008): 152–67; Leemon B. McHenry, "On the Origin of Great Ideas: Science in the Age of Big Pharma," *Hastings Center Report* 35, no. 6 (2005): 17–19.

352   Melody Petersen, "Madison Ave. Has Growing Role in the Business of Drug Research," *New York Times,* November 22, 2002.

353   David Healy, *Let Them Eat Prozac* (New York: New York University Press, 2004).

354   Howard Brody, *Hooked: Ethics, the Medical Profession, and the Pharmaceutical Industry* (Lanham, MD: Rowman and Littlefield, 2007).

355   Carl Lemmens, "Pharma Goes to the Laundry: Public Relations and the Business of Medical Education," *Hastings Center Report* 34, no. 5 (2004): 18–23.

356   Annette Flanagin, Lisa A. Carey, Phil B. Fontanarosa, et al. "Prevalence of Articles with Honorary Authors and Ghost Authors in Peer-Reviewed Medical Journals," *Journal of the American Medical Association* 280, no. 3 (1998): 222–24, quoted in IOM, "Conflicts of Interest," 153, op. cit. note 40.

357   Peter C. Gøtzsche, Asbjørn Hróbjartsson, Helle Krogh Johansen, et al., "Ghost Authorship in Industry-Initiated Randomised Trials," *PloS Medicine* 4, no. 1 (2007): e19, available at http://www.plosmedicine.org/article/info:doi/10.1371/journal.pmed.0040019; Sergio Sismondo, "Ghosts in the Machine: Publication Planning in the Medical Sciences," *Social Studies of Science* 39, no. 2 (2009): 171–98; House of Commons Health Committee, *The Influence of the Pharmaceutical Industry,* vol. 1 (London: Stationary Office, 2005), 53.

358 Elisa K. Tong, Lucinda England, and Stanton A. Glantz, "Changing Conclusions on Secondhand Smoke in a Sudden Infant Death Syndrome Review Funded by the Tobacco Industry," *Pediatrics* 115, no. 3 (2005): e356–66; Elisa K. Tong and Stanton A. Glantz, "Tobacco Industry Efforts Undermining Evidence Linking Secondhand Smoke with Cardiovascular Disease," *Circulation* 116, no. 16 (2007): 1845–54; Anne Landman, Daniel K. Cortese, and Stanton Glantz, "Tobacco Industry Sociological Programs to Influence Public Beliefs about Smoking," *Social Science and Medicine* 66, no. 4 (2008): 970–81; Lisa A. Bero, Stanton Glantz, and Mi-Kyung Hong, "The Limits of Competing Interest Disclosures," *Tobacco Control* 14, no. 2 (2005): 118–26; Mark D. Neuman Asaf Bitton, and Stanton A. Glantz, "Tobacco Industry Influence on the Definition of Tobacco Related Disorders by the American Psychiatric Association," *Tobacco Control* 14, no, 5 (2005): 328–37; Asaf Bitton, Mark D. Neuman, Joaquin Barnoya, and Stanton A. Glantz, "The p53 Pumour Suppressor Gene and the Tobacco Industry: Research, Debate, and Conflict of Interest," *Lancet* 365, no. 9458 (2005): 531–40; Richard L. Barnes and Stanton A. Glantz, "Endotoxins in Tobacco Smoke: Shifting Tobacco Industry Positions," *Nicotine and Tobacco Research* 9, no. 10 (2007): 995–1004; Richard L. Barnes, S. Katherine Hammond, and Stanton A. Glantz, "The Tobacco Industry's Role in the Sixteen Cities Study of Secondhand Tobacco Smoke: Do the Data Support the Stated Conclusions?," *Environmental Health Perspectives* 114, no. 12 (2006): 1890–97.

359 Duff Wilson and Natasha Singer, "Ghostwriting Is Called Rife in Medical Journals," *New York Times,* September 11, 2009.

360 US Senate Committee on Finance (Sen. Charles E. Grassley, ranking member), *Ghostwriting in Medical Literature,* Minority Staff Report, 111th Congress, June 24, 2010.

361 Lacasse and Leo, "Ghostwriting at Elite Academic Medical Centers in the United States," op. cit. note 35. Here is a list of original references 1–10 for quotations and references used in this original quote: (1) Moffatt and Elliott, "Ghost Marketing," op. cit. note 345; (2) Ross et al., "Guest Authorship and Ghostwriting in Publications Related to Rofecoxib," op. cit. note 35; (3) *PLoS Medicine* Editors, "Ghostwriting: The Dirty Little Secret of Medical Publishing That Just Got Bigger," *PLoS Medicine* 6, no. 9 (2009): e1000156; (4) McHenry and Jureidini, "Industry-Sponsored Ghostwriting in Clinical Trial Reporting. op cit. note 351."; (5) SmithKline Beecham, "Adolescent Depression—Study 329: Proposal for a Journal Article" (2009), available at http://www.webcitation.org/5mOJ8CJuz; (6) SmithKline Beecham, Keller et al., "Draft I Dated 12/18/1998, Prepared by Sally Laden of Scientific Therapeutics Information" (1998), available at http://www.webcitation.org/5mOJGmrM0; (7) Jon Jureidini, "Comparison of First to Final Draft [Study 329]" (2007), available at http://www.webcitation. org/5mOJMHUhX; (8) Martin B. Keller, Neal D. Ryan, Michael Strober, et al., "Efficacy of Paroxetine in the Treatment of Adolescent Major Depression: A Randomized, Controlled Trial," *Journal of the American Academy of Child and Adolescent Psychiatry* 40, no. 7 (2001): 762–72; (9) Jon J. Jureidini, Leemon B. McHenry, and Peter R. Mansfield, "Clinical Trials and Drug Promotion: Selective Reporting of Study 329," *International Journal of Risk and Safety in Medicine* 20, no. 1–2 (2008): 73–81; (10) Sergio Sismondo and Mathieu Doucet, "Publication Ethics and the Ghost Management of Medical Publication," *Bioethics* 24, no.6 (2009).

362   AAMC, *Protecting Subjects, Preserving Trust, Promoting Progress,* op. cit. note 258.

363   Ehringhaus and Korn, *Principles for Protecting Integrity in the Conduct and Reporting of Clinical Trials,* op. cit. note 339. See Principle 10, "Publication and Analysis Committee," which reads in part: "It is essential that the P&A committee be independent of the sponsor's control, have access to the full data set, understand and implement the prespecified analysis plan, and have the resources and skills both to interpret that analysis and perform additional analysis if required."

364   Davidoff et al., "Sponsorship, Authorship, and Accountability," op. cit. note 193; ICMJE, "Uniform Requirements for Manuscripts Submitted to Biomedical Journals," op. cit. note 193. See also ICMJE, "Ethical Considerations in the Conduct and Reporting of Research: Authorship and Contributorship," available at http://www.icmje.org/ethical_1author.html.

365   For World Association of Medical Editors sources, see WAME, "Publication Ethics Policies for Medical Journals," op. cit. note 341 See also WAME, "Policy Statements: Ghost Writing Initiated by Commercial Companies," op. cit. note 341.

366   AAMC, "Protecting Subjects, Preserving Trust, Promoting Progress," 19, op. cit. note 258.

367   Drazen, "Institutions, Contracts, and Academic Freedom," op. cit. note 315.

368   Mello, Clarridge, and Studdert, "Academic Medical Centers' Standards for Clinical-Trial Agreements with Industry," op. cit. note. 316; Michelle M. Mello, Brian R. Clarridge, and David M. Studdert, "Researchers' Views of the Acceptability of Restrictive Provisions in Clinical Trial Agreements with Industry Sponsors," *Accountability in Research* 12, no. 3 (2005): 163–91.

369   Bodenheimer, "Uneasy Alliance," op. cit. note 34; Blumsohn, "Authorship, Ghost-Science, Access to Data, and Control of the Pharmaceutical Scientific Literature." op. cit. note 197.

370   Blumsohn, "Authorship, Ghost-Science, Access to Data, and Control of the Pharmaceutical Scientific Literature," op. cit. note 197.

371   Quoted in ibid. See also collated media reports on the Blumsohn case at http://www.thejabberwock.org/presshw.htm and http://www.doctorsintegrity.org/blumsohn.htm.

372   Davidoff et al., "Sponsorship, Authorship, and Accountability," op. cit. note 193; ICMJE, "Uniform Requirements for Manuscripts Submitted to Biomedical Journals," op. cit. note 193.

373   According to the IOM, "Conflicts of Interest," op. cit. note 40, a study by Jessica S. Ancker and Annette Flanagin was able to locate online conflict of interest policies for only 33 percent of 84 "high-impact, peer-reviewed" journals in twelve scientific disciplines, but a subsequent survey found that 80 percent of the forty-nine responding journals reported that they had policies in place. Journals vary in whether they give specific guidance to authors regarding what financial relationships or conflicts of interest must be disclosed. IOM, "Conflicts of Interest," op. cit. note 40; see also Jessica S. Ancker and Annette Flanagin, "A Comparison of Conflict of Interest Policies at Peer-Reviewed Journals in Different Scientific Disciplines," *Science and Engineering Ethics* 13, no. 2 (2007): 147–57.

374   *AAUP Bulletin* 53 (1967): 134.

375   AAUP, "Academic Freedom and National Security in a Time of Crisis," 2003, available

at http://www.aaup.org/AAUP/comm/rep/crisistime.htm. Also published in *Academe,* November–December 2003, see 37–38, available at http://www.aaup.org/AAUP/pubsres/academe/2003/ND/Col/fte.htm.

376 Robert A. Rosenbaum et al., "The Enlargement of the Classified Information System," *Academe* 69, no. 1 (1983): 9a.

377 Ibid., 11a.

378 Cornell University, *Guidelines on Sensitive and Proprietary Research,* adopted by the Cornell Research Council on May 20, 1985, reproduced in *Faculty Handbook* at 91.

379 Massachusetts Institute of Technology (MIT), *Policies and Procedures: A Guide for Faculty and Students,* Section 14.2: "Open Research and Free Interchange of Information," available at http://web.mit.edu/policies/14/14.2.html. This policy reads in part as follows: "The profound merits of a policy of open research and free interchange of information among scholars is essential to MIT's institutional responsibility and to the interests of the nation as a whole. Openness requires that as a general policy MIT not undertake, on the campus, classified research or research whose results may not be published without prior permission—for example, without permission of governmental or industrial research sponsors. Openness also requires that, once they are at MIT, foreign faculty, students, and scholars not be singled out for restriction in their access to MIT's educational and research activities. The vast majority of on-campus research projects can be conducted in a manner fully consistent with the principles of freedom of inquiry and open exchange of knowledge. MIT, however, is an institution that plays a unique role in important areas of science and technology that are of great concern to the nation. It recognizes that in a very few cases the pursuit of knowledge may involve critically important but sensitive areas of technology where the immediate distribution of research results would not be in the best interests of society. In such cases, exceptions to these policies regarding publication, classification, and access by foreign students and scholars may be made, but only in those very rare instances where the area of work is crucially important to MIT's educational mission and the exception is demonstrably necessary for the national good. If these conditions are not met, MIT will decline or discontinue the activity and, if appropriate, propose it for consideration off-campus or elsewhere. Since the implementation of classified or otherwise restricted research on campus would drastically change the academic environment of the Institute, it is essential that each project be reviewed and acted upon in light of its impact on the Institute as a whole."

380 Massachusetts Institute of Technology (MIT), "MIT Panel Urges Off-Campus Sites for Classified Research; Reaffirms Openness on MIT Campus," press release, June 12, 2002, available at http://web.mit.edu/newsoffice/2002/publicinterest.html.

381 University of California at Berkeley, "Policy Guidelines Governing Openness and Freedom to Publish," issued by Joseph Cerny, UC Berkeley provost of research to all deans, directors, department chairs, and administrative officers on May 6, 1991, available at http://research.chance.berkeley.edu/page.cfm?id=171#cerny.

382 Ibid. This policy further states: "The principal reasons that classified projects are unacceptable are (1) the resultant requirement for a campus facility clearance and (2) the inherent

publication restrictions. In general, classified projects are not consistent with the teaching, research, and public service missions of the Berkeley campus."

383 The Recitals section of the final EBI Master Agreement asserts: "the Proprietary Component [of the EBI] . . . will conduct private, confidential and proprietary research, the product of which will be the sole property of BP" (4).

384 Washburn, *Big Oil Goes to College,* op. cit. note 105.

385 Regarding the external public criticism this provision elicited, see "UC and the Perils of Partnership," *San Francisco Chronicle,* April 1, 2007, available at http://www.sfgate.com/cgi-bin/article.cgi?file=/chronicle/archive/2007/04/01/EDG5GOTV2L1.DTL. See also Jennifer Washburn, "Big Oil Buys Berkeley," *Los Angeles Times,* March 24, 2007, available at http://www.latimes.com/news/opinion/la-oe-washburn-24mar24,0,4865913.story?coll=la-opinion-center. In UC Berkeley's original draft EBI proposal to BP (dated November 2006), this language granting BP the right to perform confidential, nonpublishable research on campus was expressed even more baldly: "BP personnel will engage in proprietary research in the leased space and will have no obligation to publish research performed in the leased space." See UC Berkeley EBI Draft Proposal to BP, dated November 2006, Section II, Intellectual Property, 73.

386 AAMC-AAU, *Protecting Patients, Preserving Integrity, Advancing Health,* 8, op. cit. note 256.

387 IOM, "Conflicts of Interest," 158, op. cit. note 40.

388 Corporate officers and board of directors, for example, owe a "fiduciary duty of loyalty" to the corporation, which includes a duty to act solely in the best interest of the corporation.

389 For details on BP restrictions on academic scientists after the Gulf oil spill, see Lea, "BP, Corporate R&D, and the University," op. cit. note 229. For observations on the conjunction between industry and government restrictions on Gulf oil spill research, see Hooper-Bui, "The Oil's Stain on Science"; and Gagosian and D'Elia, "Gulf Oil Spill Research Can't Wait."

390 "BP Buys Up Gulf Scientists for Legal Defense, Roiling Academic Community," *Mobile Press-Register,* July 16, 2010; "BP Accused of 'Buying Academic Silence," *BBC News,* July 22, 2010; "BP Tries to Limit Release of Oil Spill Research," Associated Press, July 23, 2010.

391 Amanda Mascarelli, "Freedom of Spill Research Threatened: Scientists Call for Impartial Funding and Open Data as BP and Government Agencies Contract Researchers," *Nature News,* July 28, 2010, available at http://www.nature.com/news/2010/100728/full/466538a.html.

392 Marc Lipsitch, "The Risk to Academic Freedom That Lurks in Corporate Consulting Contracts," *Chronicle of Higher Education,* June 27, 2010.

393 Ibid.

394 This discussion draws from Association of American Medical Colleges (AAMC), *Compact between Biomedical Graduate Students and Their Research Advisors* (Washington, DC: AAMC, 2008), available at https://services.aamc.org/Publications/showfile.cfm?file= version127.pdf; and AAMC-AAU, *Protecting Patients, Preserving Integrity, Advancing Health,* op. cit. note 256.

395 IOM, "Conflicts of Interest," 109, op. cit. note 40.

396 DHHS, "Responsibility of Applicants for Promoting Objectivity in Research," op. cit. note

300, quotes on pp. 53283–84. The DHHS rule defines a "significant" financial conflict of interest as follows:

"Financial conflict of interest (FCOI) means a significant financial interest that could directly and significantly affect the design, conduct, or reporting of PHS-funded research… Significant financial interest means:

(1) A financial interest consisting of one or more of the following interests of the Investigator (and those of the Investigator's spouse and dependent children) that reasonably appears to be related to the Investigator's institutional responsibilities:

(i) With regard to any publicly traded entity, a significant financial interest exists if the value of any remuneration received from the entity in the twelve months preceding the disclosure and the value of any equity interest in the entity as of the date of disclosure, when aggregated, exceeds $5,000. For purposes of this definition, remuneration includes salary and any payment for services not otherwise identified as salary (e.g., consulting fees, honoraria, paid authorship); equity interest includes any stock, stock option, or other ownership interest, as determined through reference to public prices or other reasonable measures of fair market value;

(ii) With regard to any non-publicly traded entity, a significant financial interest exists if the value of any remuneration received from the entity in the twelve months preceding the disclosure, when aggregated, exceeds $5,000, or when the Investigator (or the Investigator's spouse or dependent children) holds any equity interest (e.g., stock, stock option, or other ownership interest); or

(iii) Intellectual property rights and interests (e.g., patents, copyrights), upon receipt of income related to such rights and interests.

(2) Investigators also must disclose the occurrence of any reimbursed or sponsored travel (i.e., that which is paid on behalf of the Investigator and not reimbursed to the Investigator so that the exact monetary value may not be readily available), related to their institutional responsibilities; provided, however, that this disclosure requirement does not apply to travel that is reimbursed or sponsored by a Federal, state, or local government agency, an Institution of higher education as defined at 20 U.S.C. 1001(a), an academic teaching hospital, a medical center, or a research institute that is affiliated with an Institution of higher education. The Institution's FCOI policy will specify the details of this disclosure, which will include, at a minimum, the purpose of the trip, the identity of the sponsor/organizer, the destination, and the duration. In accordance with the Institution's FCOI policy, the institutional official(s) will determine if further information is needed, including a determination or disclosure of monetary value, in order to determine whether the travel constitutes an FCOI with the PHS-funded research.

(3) The term significant financial interest does not include the following types of financial interests: salary, royalties, or other remuneration paid by the Institution to the Investigator if the Investigator is currently employed or otherwise appointed by the Institution, including intellectual property rights assigned to the Institution and agreements to share in royalties related to such rights; any ownership interest in the Institution held by the Investigator, if the Institution is a commercial or for-profit organization; income from investment vehicles, such

as mutual funds and retirement accounts, as long as the Investigator does not directly control the investment decisions made in these vehicles; income from seminars, lectures, or teaching engagements sponsored by a Federal, state, or local government agency, an Institution of higher education as defined at 20 U.S.C. 1001(a), an academic teaching hospital, a medical center, or a research institute that is affiliated with an Institution of higher education; or income from service on advisory committees or review panels for a Federal, state, or local government agency, an Institution of higher education as defined at 20 U.S.C. 1001(a), an academic teaching hospital, a medical center, or a research institute that is affiliated with an Institution of higher education." [Emphasis added]

397 "Report of Joint Academic Senate-Administration Committee on University Interaction with Industry," University of California, San Diego, dated July 1999, available at http://research.ucsd.edu/industry/report/index.htm.

398 AAMC, *Protecting Subjects, Preserving Trust, Promoting Progress,* op. cit. note 258.

399 AAMC, *Compact between Biomedical Graduate Students and Their Research Advisors,* 6, op. cit. note 394.

400 This recommendation is compatible with one recently made in a draft report issued by the MIT Ad Hoc Faculty Committee, *A Shared Responsibility: Report of the Committee on Managing Potential Conflicts of Interest in Research,* April 21, 2010, available at http://web.mit.edu/provost/coi/index.html.

401 Washburn, *University Inc.,* 86–97, op. cit. note 41; Greenberg, *Science for Sale,* op. cit. note 41. See also Chris MacDonald and Bryn Williams-Jones, "Supervisor-Student Relations: Examining the Spectrum of Conflicts of Interest in Bioscience Laboratories," *Accountability in Research: Policies and Quality Assurance* 16, no. 2 (2009), available at http://www.ncbi.nlm.nih.gov/pmc/articles/PMC2876133/#R23; Adil E. Shamoo and David B. Resnik, "Mentoring and Collaboration," in *Responsible Conduct of Research,* ed. Adil E. Shamoo and David B. Resnik (Oxford: Oxford University Press, 2009).

402 BHEF, *Working Together, Creating Knowledge,* op. cit. note 26.

403 Ibid., 28–29. Pramod Khargonekar, University of Michigan, interview by Beth Starbuck, Calyx Inc., Case Study Final Report, September 7, 2000, 36; Robert L. Carman, interview by Beth Starbuck, Calyx Inc., Case Study Final Report, September 7, 2000, 19.

404 The AAUP defines a financial interest to be "significant" if it is valued at or above $5,000 per year, and it is not controlled and/or managed by an independent entity, such as a mutual or pension fund. This is consistent with the definitions and de minimis threshold for financial disclosure established by the US Department of Health and Human Services under its 2011 conflict of interest disclosure rules. DHHS, "Responsibility of Applicants for Promoting Objectivity in Research," op. cit. note 300.

405 AAMC, *Protecting Subjects, Preserving Trust, Promoting Progress,* op. cit. note 258; AAMC-AAU, *Protecting Patients, Preserving Integrity, Advancing Health,* 20, op. cit. note 256.

406 AAMC, Compact between Biomedical Graduate Students and Their Research Advisors, 6, op. cit. note 394.

407 AAMC, *Protecting Subjects, Preserving Trust, Promoting Progress,* 25, 28, op. cit. note 258.

408   IOM, "Conflicts of Interest," 116, op. cit. note 40.

409   Trade secrets, which are information with economic value not generally known to the public and subject to reasonable controls on disclosure, are sometimes, but not always, included in discussions of intellectual property.

410   Mark A. Lemley, "Are Universities Patent Trolls?," *Fordham Intellectual Property, Media & Entertainment Law Journal* 18, no. 3 (2008).

411   Siddhartha Mukherjee, *The Emperor of All Maladies: A Biography of Cancer* (New York: Scribner, 2010), 434.

412   Ibid., 440.

413   Annalee Newitz, "Genome Liberation: The Information That Details Who We Are Is Too Important to Be Privately Owned," *Salon.com*, February 26, 2002, available at http://www.salon.com/2002/02/26/biopunk/.

414   Dr. Robert Shafer discusses the details of his own case, and provides substantial documentation, at http://harmfulpatents.org/blog/.

415   Stanford Advisory Board, April 20, 2010, quoted 'at http://harmfulpatents.org/blog/. For more background on the Shafer case, see Joe Mullin, "The Fight of His Life," *IP Law and Business,* May 1, 2009, available at http://www.law.com/jsp/iplawandbusiness/PubArticleFriendlyIPLB.jsp?id=1202430332016.

416   AUTM, "Nine Points to Consider in Licensing University Technology," March 6, 2007, available at http://www.autm.net/Nine_Points_to_Consider1.htm.

417   Association of University Technology Managers (AUTM) Board of Trustees, "Statement of Principles and Strategies for the Equitable Dissemination of Medical Technologies" (SPS), November 9, 2009, available at http://www.autm.net/source/Endorsement/endorsement.cfm?section=endorsement. These principles were developed by a team comprised of AUTM leaders, including Jon Soderstrom, AUTM immediate past president, of Yale University; and Ashley J. Stevens, AUTM president-elect, of Boston University. These guidelines discuss best practices for universities when considering the equitable dissemination of medical technologies. For universities that have endorsed this statement see the link above.

418   Bhaven N. Sampat and Frank Lichtenberg, "What Are the Respective Roles of the Public and Private Sectors in Pharmaceutical Innovation?," *Health Affairs* 30.2 (2011): 332–39.

419   The antiretroviral HIV drug Stavudine (Zerit) was originally developed by researchers at Yale University with extensive federal government funding. Yale licensed this drug compound to Bristol-Myers-Squibb, in exchange for a share of the royalty income. The cost of the drug was $10,439 per patient for a year in 2002. For individuals who live on just a few dollars per day, this expense was prohibitive and barred millions of dying HIV patients in the developing world from accessing this key component of the "triple-drug AIDS cocktail" that was then rapidly saving lives in the industrialized world. Student activists and the humanitarian organization Médecins Sans Frontières successfully pressured Yale University and Bristol-Myers Squibb (the patent holder and license partner) to allow generic production of Stavudine. The generic price of Stavudine in the developing world then dropped more than a hundredfold, to $87 per patient per year. Today, a new student organization, which grew

out of the Yale campaign—Universities Allied for Essential Medicines—is working to expand generic production as one key way of address the global crisis of access to medicines.

420   Universities Allied for Essential Medicines, http://essentialmedicine.org/projects/university-technology-transfer.

421   The Uniform Administrative Requirements for Grants and Contracts with Institutions of Higher Education, Hospitals, and Other Non-Profit Organizations is available at http://www.law.cornell.edu/cfr/text/10/600/subpart-B.

422   AUTM, "Nine Points to Consider in Licensing University Technology," op. cit. note 416.

423   Washburn, *Big Oil Goes to College,* op. cit. note 105.

424   The full decision issued by the US Court of Appeals for the Federal Circuit in the *Madey v. Duke University* (2002) case is available at http://cyber.law.harvard.edu/people/tfisher/2002Madeyedit.html. For a detailed discussion of this decision and its significance, see Eisenberg, "Patent Swords and Shields."

425   NRC, Managing University Intellectual Property, op. cit. note 78. See Recommendation 5 (71).

426   AUTM, "Nine Points to Consider in Licensing University Technology," op. cit. note 416.

427   When Cornell University's faculty senate appointed a special faculty committee to review large-scale, multi-year industrial research alliances, known as strategic corporate alliances (SCA), its final consensus report advised that the university show a preference for nonexclusive licensing: "Licensing of inventions derived from SCA-funded work should, whenever possible, take the form of non-exclusive licenses to the corporate partner to use university-owned patents. By giving the licensor a monopoly over use of the patented invention, exclusive licensing inevitably interferes with full and open sharing of the results of academic research. Moreover, unless circumstances are very carefully assessed, it may allow the principal beneficiary of the patent right to become the private, rather than the public, interest." Cornell University, "Faculty Statement of Principles and Best Practices," 16, op. cit. note 114.

428   Ibid. The Nine Points statement reads in part as follows: "Special consideration should be given to the impact of an exclusive license on uses of a technology that may not be appreciated at the time of initial licensing. A license grant that encompasses all fields of use for the life of the licensed patent(s) may have negative consequences if the subject technology is found to have unanticipated utility. This possibility is particularly troublesome if the licensee is not able or willing to develop the technology in fields outside of its core business. Universities are encouraged to use approaches that balance a licensee's legitimate commercial needs against the university's goal (based on its educational and charitable mission and the public interest) of ensuring broad practical application of the fruits of its research programs. There are many alternatives to strict exclusive licensing, several of which are described in the Appendix." AUTM, "Nine Points to Consider in Licensing University Technology," 2, op. cit. note 416.

429   See IRS, Rev Proc 2007-47, July 16, 2007, available at http://www.irs.gov/irb/2007-29_IRB/ar12.html. 2007-47 concerns the interpretation of the Tax Reform Act of 1986. The section in question has to do with qualified users of facilities built with tax-free bonds.

The guidance concerns a safe harbor for what constitutes private use that might otherwise jeopardize the tax-free status of a bond issue. Noteworthy is that under the original Rev Proc, 97-14, the US government was construed as a "private user" of such facilities if it had a license interest in inventions made in the facility. The Rev Proc stipulates that the financial terms have to be established at the time that the "resulting technology is available for use" (see 6.02).

430   DHHS, NIH, "Principles and Guidelines for Recipients of NIH Research Grants and Contracts," op. cit. note 245.

431   AUTM, "Nine Points to Consider in Licensing University Technology," op. cit. note 416.

432   The Uniform Administrative Requirements for Grants and Contracts with Institutions of Higher Education, Hospitals, and Other Non-Profit Organizations is available at http://www.law.cornell.edu/cfr/text/10/600/subpart-B.

433   Michael A. Heller and Rebecca S. Eisenberg, "Can Patents Deter Innovation? The Anticommons in Biomedical Research," *Science* 280, no. 5364 (1998): 698–701. See also, Washburn, *University Inc.,* op. cit. note 41. especially pp. 149–70.

434   BHEF, *Working Together, Creating Knowledge,* op. cit. note 26.

435   Wayne Johnson, "Bayh-Dole: The Next Twenty-Five Years," testimony before the Committee on Science and Technology, Subcommittee on Technology and Innovation (July 17, 2007), available at http:// science.house.gov/publications/Testimony.aspx?TID=7129; Robert E. Litan, Lesa Mitchell, and E. J. Reedy "Commercializing University Innovations: A Better Way," National Bureau of Economic Research working paper, 2007, available at http://www.brookings.edu/papers/2007/05_innovations_litan.aspx?rssid=education

436   For details on the Cohen-Boyer invention and the licensing strategy employed, see Maryann P. Feldman, Alessandra Caolaianni, and Connie Kang Liu, "Lessons from the Commercialization of the Cohen-Boyer Patents: The Stanford University Licensing Program" in *Intellectual Property Management in Health and Agricultral Innovation: A Handbook of Best Practices,* ed. Anatole Krattiger, Richard T. Mahoney, Lita Nelsen, et al., (MIHR and PIPRA, 2007), available at http://www.iphandbook.org/handbook/chPDFs/ch17/ipHandbook-Ch%2017%2022%20Feldman-Colaianni0Liu%20Cohen-Boyer%20Patents%20and%20Licenses.pdf.

437   For details on the Axel patent and the licensing strategy employed, see http://www.ncbi.nlm.nih.gov/pmc/articles/PMC2750841/.

438   For a good discussion of the Hall invention and how it was managed, see http://www.wrfseattle.org/about/WRF_2007_Annual_Report.pdf (5–7). Also see the following interview: http://www.cbiz.com/eflassociates/pdfs/HallInterview.pdf. At the time of this interview, the Hall invention had generated roughly $400 million in royalties—since then it has generated at least another $100 million, with two years left on the patents.

439   See sources listed under e392, directly above.

440   University of California Office of the President, "Electrical Engineering and Computer Science Intellectual Property Pilot Program Office of Technology Transfer," No. 2000 02, August 30, 2000: "Recently PEAC (President's Engineering Advisory Council) reviewed the

matter of how engineering industry sponsors access University intellectual property resulting from extramural sponsored research. It was observed that the rapid rate of technological change in the engineering fields of electronics, communications technology, [and] computer hardware and software results in new products with a typical lifetime of a few years or less. Competitive success rarely is based upon the statutory protection of intellectual property as requirements for conformance with industry wide standards reduce the value of proprietary technology. Rapid product development and early market entry with innovative products are the keys to market leadership and successful products."

441 *BHEF, Working Together, Creating Knowledge,* op. cit. note 26.

442 Ibid., 60–61.

443 Ibid., 59–60.

444 Master Agreement, BP Technology Ventures Inc. and Regents of the University of California, November 9, 2007, available at http://www.energybiosciencesinstitute.org/images/stories/pressroom/FINAL_Execution_11-9.pdf.

445 University of California at Berkeley Academic Senate Committee letter addressed to Professor William Drummond, Chair of the Berkeley Division of the Academic Senate, November 2, 2007, 3. In this letter, a Senate subcommittee made up of five faculty (Ellwood, Hesse, Kutz, Villas Boas, and Moore), informally known as the "Gang of Four-plus," reported back to Drummond regarding eight stated areas of Academic Senate concern regarding the BP-funded Energy Biosciences Institute.

446 AAUP, *Policy Documents and Reports,* 10th ed. (Washington, DC: AAUP; Baltimore: Johns Hopkins University Press, 2006), 184.

447 DHHS, "Responsibility of Applicants for Promoting Objectivity in Research," op. cit. note 300; DHHS, OIG, "How Grantees Manage Financial Conflicts of Interest in Research Funded by the National Institutes of Health," 53258. op. cit. note 305

448 DHHS, "Responsibility of Applicants for Promoting Objectivity in Research," op. cit. note 300. The quote, cited here, is contained in this full passage: "*The 1995 regulations were aimed at preventing bias in PHS-funded research, and as such, were intended to be proactive rather than reactive to specific evidence of bias.* Nonetheless, over the past few years, there have been several specific allegations of bias among PHS-funded researchers reported in the press. This has led to increased public concern, as evidenced by statements and correspondence from members of Congress and the language in the Department of Health and Human Services Appropriations Act, 2010, to amend the 1995 regulations 'for the purpose of strengthening Federal and institutional oversight and identifying enhancements.' And as mentioned above, the 2009 OIG report found that 'vulnerabilities exist in grantee Institutions' identification, management, and oversight of financial conflicts of interest.' It is vital that the public have confidence in the objectivity of PHS-funded research. The revised regulations, with their emphasis on increasing transparency and accountability, as well as providing additional information to the PHS Awarding Component, are aimed at doing just that" [Emphasis added] (53258).

449 IOM, "Conflicts of Interest," Executive Summary, 2, op. cit. note 40.

450 AAU, *Report on Individual and Institutional Financial Conflict of Interest,* op. cit. note 14: "*Conflict*

of interest will be considered across all academic fields, not just biomedical ones (though biomedical conflicts have some unique aspects and invoke a special intensity and interest)" [Emphasis added] (2). According to the IOM, "Conflicts of Interest," op. cit. note 40, in 2004 the Government Accountability Office reported that 79 percent of universities responding to its survey said that they had a single conflict of interest policy covering all research. IOM, "Conflicts of Interest," 68, op. cit. note 40.

451 AAMC-AAU, *Protecting Patients, Preserving Integrity, Advancing Health,* op. cit. note 256: "Although this report focuses on those conflicts that arise in the context of human subjects research conducted primarily within or under the supervision of medical schools and teaching hospitals or by their personnel, *institutions should strongly consider making the principles and processes recommended in this report applicable to all research. Protection of integrity and public trust are indeed values that underpin all academic research, irrespective of whether the particular challenges associated with human subjects research are present"* [Emphasis added] (4). Later this report reads: "The Committee recognizes that institutional COIs can arise in non-human subjects research, clinical care, and education, as well as in purchasing and other university business transactions and *the Committee strongly recommends that institutions implement comprehensive institutional COI policies that embrace the full spectrum of the institution's activities"* [Emphasis added] (36).

452 IOM, "Conflicts of Interest," op. cit. note 40: *"No matter the type or stage of research, certain fundamentals still apply. All researchers should be subject to an institution's disclosure policies,* as described in Chapter 3, and the institution's conflict of interest committee or its equivalent should be notified when investigators have financial stakes in the outcomes of their research. Similarly, following the conceptual framework presented in Chapter 2, once a financial relationship or interest has been disclosed, it should be evaluated for determination of the likelihood that it will have an undue influence that will lead to bias or a loss of trust. If a risk is judged to exist, a conflict of interest committee might conclude that the implementation of safeguards is necessary. Such safeguards could consist of a management plan that includes the involvement of a researcher without a conflict of interest in certain aspects of the research and disclosure of the conflict to coinvestigators and in presentations and publications" [Emphasis added] (119).

453 AAMC-AAU, *Protecting Patients, Preserving Integrity, Advancing Health,* op. cit. note 256: "The Committee recognizes that institutional COIs can arise in non-human subjects research, clinical care, and education, as well as in purchasing and other university business transactions and the Committee strongly recommends that institutions implement comprehensive institutional COI policies that embrace the full spectrum of the institution's activities" (36).

454 IOM, "Conflicts of Interest," op. cit. note 40., 221: "The guidance on financial relationships in research with human participants published by the US Department of Health and Human Services discusses the identification and management of institutional as well as individual financial interests (HHS, 2004)" (221).

455 Department of Health and Human Services (DHHS), Office of the Inspector General (OIG), "Institutional Conflicts of Interest at NIH Grantees," Daniel R. Levinson, Inspector General, January 2011, OEI-03-09-00480: "We recommend that NIH: Promulgate regulations

that address institutional financial conflicts of interest. Until regulations are promulgated, NIH should encourage grantee institutions to develop policies and procedures regarding institutional financial interests and conflicts." See also DHHS, OIG, "How NIH Grantees Manage Financial Conflicts of Interest," OEI-03-07-00700, November 2009: "Develop Regulations That Address Institutional Financial Conflicts of Interest. Institutional financial conflicts of interest are not addressed by Federal regulations. Because there is the potential for grantee institutions to have financial conflicts of interest related to grant research, NIH should develop regulations that address these interests. In developing regulations NIH should address: the definition of an institutional financial conflict of interest; the elements required in a grantee institution's policy regarding institutional financial conflicts of interest; how institutional financial conflicts of interest are reported to NIH; and how institutional financial conflicts of interest are managed, reduced, or eliminated" (22).

456 IOM, "Conflicts of Interest," op. cit. note 40. Recommendation 8.1: "The boards of trustees or the equivalent governing bodies of institutions engaged in medical research, medical education, patient care, or practice guideline development should establish their own standing committees on institutional conflicts of interest. These standing committees should have no members who themselves have conflicts of interest relevant to the activities of the institution; include at least one member who is not a member of the board or an employee or officer of the institution and who has some relevant expertise; create, as needed, administrative arrangements for the day-to-day oversight and management of institutional conflicts of interest, including those involving senior officials; and submit an annual report to the full board, which should be made public but in which the necessary modifications have been made to protect confidential information. Recommendation 8.2: The National Institutes of Health should develop rules governing institutional conflicts of interest for research institutions covered by current US Public Health Service regulations. The rules should require the reporting of identified institutional conflicts of interest and the steps that have been taken to eliminate or manage such conflicts" (21–22).

457 AAU, *Report on Individual and Institutional Financial Conflict of Interest*, 5, op. cit. note 14: "Disclosure of financial interests related to non-federally sponsored research (which is not subject to regulation) ensures that all potential conflicts of interest are identified and handled similarly, instead of having an extensive process for some potential conflicts but not for others".

458 AAMC-AAU, *Protecting Patients, Preserving Integrity, Advancing Health,* op. cit. note 256: "Although this report focuses on those conflicts that arise in the context of human subjects research conducted primarily within or under the supervision of medical schools and teaching hospitals or by their personnel, *institutions should strongly consider making the principles and processes recommended in this report applicable to all research. Protection of integrity and public trust are indeed values that underpin all academic research, irrespective of whether the particular challenges associated with human subjects research are present"* (4; emphasis added).

459 See DHHS, "Responsibility of Applicants for Promoting Objectivity in Research," op. cit. note 300. The new DHHS rules require investigators to report not just how their financial

interests might affect a particular federally funded project or grant, but how these financial interests might affect *all their "institutional responsibilities," including research, consulting, teaching, membership on university committees,* etc., thus significantly broadening what needs to be reported as a possible financial conflict of interest. The new PHS rules also now require disclosure of all *nonprofit income* (from seminars, lectures, educational events, etc.), because it is increasingly common for nonprofits to receive substantial financial support from industry. As the PHS explains: "We proposed this change due to the growth of non-profit entities that sponsor such activities since the 1995 regulations were promulgated. Some of these non-profit entities receive funding from for-profit entities that may have an interest in the outcome of the Investigators' research (e.g., foundations supported by pharmaceutical companies)" (53265). In part, these new rules grew out of a 2009 NIH Office of Inspector General report that made the following recommendation: "Require Grantee Institutions to Collect Information on All Significant Financial Interests Held by Researchers and Not Just Those Deemed by Researchers to Be Reasonably Affected by the Research. . . . Full and complete disclosure ensures that the determination of whether a significant financial interest relates to the research rests with the grantee institution and not with the researcher. To maintain consistency across grantee institutions and researchers, we recommend that NIH amend 45 CFR § 50.604(c)(1) to require researchers to report all significant financial interests to the grantee institutions"; DHHS, OIG, "How NIH Grantees Manage Financial Conflicts of Interest."

460 AAU, *Report on Individual and Institutional Financial Conflict of Interest,* 2, op. cit. note 14.

461 NIH, DHHS, FDA, CDC, "Human Subject Protection and Financial Conflicts of Interest Conference," op. cit. note 280; Shalala, "Protecting Research Subjects: What Must Be Done," op. cit. note 280; DHHS Office of Inspector General, "Protecting Human Research Subjects: Status of Recommendations," op. cit. note 280; GAO, "Biomedical Research: HHS Direction Needed to Address Financial Conflicts of Interest," op. cit. note 280. In this 2001 report to Congress, the GAO called on the US Department of Health and Human Services to promulgate new regulations or to issue guidance to address institutional conflicts of interest, noting that equity ownership or other investment in a research sponsor "may color [an institution's] review, approval, or monitoring of research conducted under its auspices or its allocation of equipment, facilities, and staff for research." See also: Grassley, "Payment to Physicians," op. cit. note 285; Grassley, "Grassley Works to Disclose Financial Ties between Drug Companies and Doctors," op. cit. note 286; Grassley, "Grassley Seeks Information about Medical School Policies for Disclosure of Financial Ties," op. cit. note 268.

462 For a listings of these academic associations' reports on conflicts of interest, see IOM, "Conflicts of Interest," 41, op. cit. note 40: Table 1-2: "Selected Reports on Conflict of Interest Released since 2000."

463 Quote from IOM, "Conflicts of Interest," 88, op. cit. note 40.

464 Ibid., 189–215, 46.

465 The first definition comes from AAU, *Report on Individual and Institutional Financial Conflict of Interest,* 2, op. cit. note 14. The second definition is taken from "Harvard University Policy

on Individual Financial Conflicts of Interest for Persons Holding Faculty and Teaching Appointments," 3, op. cit. note 342.

466 AAMC-AAU, *Protecting Patients, Preserving Integrity, Advancing Health,* 36, op. cit. note 256.

467 AAMC, *Protecting Subjects, Preserving Trust, Promoting Progress,* 16, op. cit. note 258; AAU, *Report on Individual and Institutional Financial Conflict of Interest,* 7–8, op. cit. note 14.

468 The Physician Payment Sunshine provisions were included in the Patient Protection and Affordable Care Act of 2009 (H.R. 3590, section 6002), which was signed into law on March 23, 2010. The act requires manufacturers of drugs and biologic and medical devices to report certain gifts and payments ("transfers of value") made to physicians. The information will be registered in a national and publicly accessible online database. Companies failing to report incur financial penalties. For more information, see "Pew Prescription Project Fact Sheet."

469 For details on various state-level physician payment disclosure laws, see ibid. Such laws, sometimes referred to as "sunshine laws," now exist in the District of Columbia, Minnesota, Vermont, Maine, West Virginia, and Massachusetts. Numerous other states, including New York, are considering similar legislation.

470 In the next few years, universities will have far more capacity—and, indeed, greater public pressure imposed on them—to verify the accuracy of faculty self-reporting concerning their financial interests. In the field of medicine, for example, universities can now check their faculty's reported financial interests against pharmaceutical industry reporting to the federal government under the Physician Payments Sunshine Act. The Physician Payment Sunshine provisions were included in the Patient Protection and Affordable Care Act of 2009 (H.R. 3590, section 6002), which was signed into law on March 23, 2010. The act requires all pharmaceutical and medical device makers to report payments to physicians through a publicly accessible database. Many states have also implemented similar disclosure and reporting rules.

471 IOM, "Conflicts of Interest," 72, op. cit. note 40.

472 Ibid., 31. A similar quote may also be found in AAMC, *Protecting Subjects, Preserving Trust, Promoting Progress II: Principles and Recommendations for Oversight of an Institution's Financial Interests in Human Subjects Research* (Washington, DC: AAMC, 2002), 240, available at http://www.aamc.org/research/coi/2002coireport.pdf

473 IOM, "Conflicts of Interest," 216, op. cit. note 40.

474 AAMC-AAU, Protecting Patients, Preserving Integrity, Advancing Health, op. cit. note 256: "A. Development and Adoption of Policies. Although the Advisory Committee was charged with examining institutional conflicts of interest specifically in the context of human subjects research, the Committee urged AAU and AAMC member institutions to commit themselves to develop and implement comprehensive institutional conflicts of interest policies that govern all operational aspects of a university or an academic medical center" [Emphasis added] (xi). The report reiterates this point later: "Institutions should assure in policy and practice that institutional COIs will be addressed consistently throughout the institution, such that those subject to institutional financial conflict of interest policies, specifically officials of the institution and the institutions themselves, are subject to substantive reporting, disclosure,

and management of their financial interests to protect the integrity of human subjects research and the subjects who participate in it, as well as institutional values and decision-making" (15). Similar consistency of implementation is required for individual COI rules as well, of course, and is addressed elsewhere by these organizations.

475 See, e.g., IOM, "Conflicts of Interest," op. cit. note 40: "To manage identified conflicts of interest and to monitor the implementation of management recommendations, institutions should create a conflict of interest committee. That committee should use a full range of management tools, as appropriate, including elimination of the conflicting financial interest, prohibition or restriction of involvement of the individual with a conflict of interest in the activity related to the conflict, and providing additional disclosures of the conflict of interest. A conflict of interest committee should bring experience and consistency to evaluations of financial relationships with industry and decisions about those relationships, although the specific details (e.g., how risks and potential benefits are assessed and what management options are considered) may vary, depending on the activity in question" (89–90). The report further notes that these standing committees should have no members who themselves have conflicts of interest relevant to their COI oversight functions (226–27).

476 According to IOM, "Conflicts of Interest," op. cit. note 40: "Standing Committees will ensure that policies are applied fairly across the institution" (60). Under "Fairness," the IOM report continues: "The formal principle of fairness requires similar treatment for those in relevantly similar situations and different treatment for those in relevantly different situations. This principle has at least two implications for the application of conflict of interest policies. First, these policies should apply to all employees or members of an institution who make significant decisions for the institution or who have substantial influence over these decisions. . . . Second, fairness requires that individuals in different institutions who are in situations that are similar in all ethically relevant ways be treated similarly. Otherwise, the ethical basis for policies may be called into question and conflict of interest policies and decisions may be regarded as arbitrary" (ibid.).

477 This is consistent with a recommendation made in AAU, *Report on Individual and Institutional Financial Conflict of Interest,* 7, op. cit. note 14.

478 IOM, "Conflicts of Interest," 224–25, op. cit. note 40.

479 This recommendation is a slightly adapted version of one issued in AAMC-AAU, *Protecting Patients, Preserving Integrity, Advancing Health,* viii, op. cit. note 256.

480 Doug Lederman, "Revised Rules on Financial Conflicts," *Inside Higher Ed.com,* August 24, 2011. Quotes from "Proposed Rules, Department of Health and Human Services," 42 CFR Part 50 and 45 CFR Part 94, *Federal Register* 75, no. 98 (2010), available at http://www.gpo.gov/fdsys/pkg/FR-2010-05-21/pdf/2010-11885.pdf.

481 "Harvard University Policy on Individual Financial Conflicts of Interest," 4, op. cit. note 342.

482 DHHS, "Responsibility of Applicants for Promoting Objectivity in Research," op. cit. note 300. This section reads as follows: "With regard to 'paid authorship,' although it should be clear that receipt of payment from an entity in exchange for drafting a publication constitutes payment for services, we believe it is important to reference this form of payment specifically

in the regulations. *We are particularly concerned about situations in which Investigators may have accepted payment from private entities, in return for allowing their names to be used as authors on publications for which they had very limited input. This practice has come under increasing scrutiny in recent years and we wish to make it clear to Institutions and Investigators that such activity may be subject to the disclosure and reporting requirements depending on the circumstances of a given case, such as the amount of payment"* [Emphasis Added] (53264).

483   Under the new PHS rules, income from seminars, lectures, advisory committees, review panels, and teaching engagements, if sponsored by a federal, state, or local government agency, or an institution of higher education as defined at 20 U.S.C. 1001(a), are exempted from federal reporting requirements. However, if such income stems from another type of nonprofit, it is not. DHHS, "Responsibility of Applicants for Promoting Objectivity in Research," op. cit. note 300.

In comments, the PHS explains: "We proposed this change due to the growth of non-profit entities that sponsor such activities since the 1995 regulations were promulgated. Some of these non-profit entities receive funding from for-profit entities that may have an interest in the outcome of the Investigators' research (e.g., foundations supported by pharmaceutical companies)" (53265).

484   David J. Rothman, Walter J. McDonald, Carol D. Berkowitz, et al., "Professional Medical Associations and Their Relationships with Industry: A Proposal for Controlling Conflict of Interest," *Journal of the American Medical Association* 301, no. 13 (2009): 1367–72.

485   IOM, "Conflicts of Interest," 220, op. cit. note 40; Nada Stotland, "APA Responds to Sen. Grassley," *Psychiatric News* 43, no. 17 (2008): 3; Matthew Perrone, 2009. "Drugmakers' Push Boosts 'Murky' Ailment," Associated Press, February 8, 2009, available at http://abcnews. go.com/Business/WireStory?id=6831203&page=3.

486   It has become quite common for corporations to fund seemingly independent nonprofit groups, and/or to create new nonprofits with beneficent-sounding names and seemingly objective programs, to advance their corporate sponsors' commercial and public relations interests. For a review these seemingly independent industry-funded groups, including professional associations, charities, and nonprofit industry-created front groups, and their sources of funding see: Center for Science in the Public Interest (CSPI), *Lifting the Veil of Secrecy,* Washington DC, July 2003, available at http://www.cspinet.org/new/200307092. html The main research and data component of this report is available at http://cspinet. org/new/pdf/lift_the_veil_guts_fnl.pdf. Some examples cited include: the Foundation for Clean Air Progress (funded by petroleum, trucking, and chemical companies), the Coalition for Animal Health (funded by cattle, hog, and agribusiness concerns), and the Center for Consumer Freedom (originally funded by Philip Morris, and later funded by chain restaurants and bars). Another example cited here is the Air Quality Standards Coalition. According to the *Washington Post,* this is a "coalition of more than 500 businesses and trade groups… Created specifically to battle the clean air proposals, the coalition operates out of the offices of the National Association of Manufacturers, a Washington-based trade group. Its leadership includes top managers of petroleum, automotive and utility companies." Another example

cited is the Center for Indoor Air Research. According to *US Newswire* ("Statement by Matthew L. Myers, Campaign for Tobacco Free Kids," *US Newswire,* National Desk, May 15, 2003), "the Center for Indoor Air Research (CIAR) was . . . shut down by the state attorneys general as part of the 1998 state tobacco settlement. [On] January 29, 2003, court filings to support its racketeering lawsuit against the tobacco industry, the US Department of Justice stated, 'CIAR was officially created . . . to act as a coordinating organization for Defendants' efforts to fraudulently mislead the American public about the health effects of ETS [environmental tobacco smoke] exposure.' The Justice Department also stated that CIAR 'was not only used for litigation and public relations, but it was [*sic*] also funded research designed not to find answers to health questions, but solely to attack legislative initiatives related to ETS exposure. Lawyers specifically engineered and constructed scientific studies to get results that would be useful for public relations, litigation, and legislative battles, as opposed to results that would assist the scientific community in further understanding the health effects of ETS exposure.'" With respect to university research in particular, CSPI's *Lifting the Veil of Secrecy* report also identifies more than thirty university-based research centers that draw substantial financial support from companies or corporate trade associations. Among these are several university centers on forestry funded by timber or paper industries, and several centers on nutrition funded by food and agribusiness companies. According to CSPI, "All such centers let corporations put an academic sheen on industry-funded research."

487 "Harvard University Policy on Individual Financial Conflicts of Interest," 5–6, op. cit. note 342.

488 IOM, "Conflicts of Interest," 222, op. cit. note 40.

489 "Separation of Administrative Responsibility," in AAMC-AAU, *Protecting Patients, Preserving Integrity, Advancing Health,* xi–xii, op. cit. note 256.

490 This discussion is drawn from AAU, *Report on Individual and Institutional Financial Conflict of Interest,* 11, op. cit. note 14.

491 Hamilton Moses III and Joseph B. Martin, "Academic Relationships with Industry: A New Model for Biomedical Research," *Journal of the American Medical Association* 285, no. 7 (2001): 933–35.

492 This is adapted from AAU, *Report on Individual and Institutional Financial Conflict of Interest,* 13–14, op. cit. note 14.; and IOM, "Conflicts of Interest," 64, op. cit. note 40.

493 DHHS, "Responsibility of Applicants for Promoting Objectivity in Research," 53291, 53292, op. cit. note 300.

494 Council on Governmental Relations (COGR), *Recognizing and Managing Personal Financial Conflicts of Interest* (Washington, DC: COGR, 2002), available at http://www.cogr.edu/docs/COIFinal.pdf; quoted in IOM, "Conflicts of Interest," 76, op. cit. note 40.

495 Charles Grassley, "Grassley Works to Protect Medicare Dollars, Empower Patients with Information," press release, July 25, 2008, available at http://www.senate.gov/~finance/press/Gpress/2008/prg072508.pdf; Grassley, "Payment to Physicians," op. cit. note 285; Grassley, "Grassley Works to Disclose Financial Ties between Drug Companies and Doctors," op. cit. note 286.

496   Quoted in IOM, "Conflicts of Interest," 76, op. cit. note 40; American Medical Student
      Association (AMSA), *PharmFree Scorecard,* 2008 (Reston, VA: AMSA: 2008), available at http://
      amsascorecard.org/. According to the IOM report, AMSA's methodology for conducting
      these policy reviews involved two independent, trained reviewers who read the policies
      that the medical schools submitted (without identifying information) and then rated
      them according to specified criteria. For the administration and oversight categories, the
      reviewers gave "Yes" or "No" answers to these two questions: Is it clear that there is a party
      responsible for general oversight to ensure compliance? Is it clear that there are sanctions for
      noncompliance? See IOM, "Conflicts of Interest," op. cit. note 40.

497   IOM, "Conflicts of Interest," 75, op. cit. note 40.

498   American Association of Universities (AAU), "Statement of Guiding Principles Regarding
      Institutional Relationships with Student Loan Providers," April 26, 2007, available at http://
      www.aau.edu/policy/student_loans.aspx?id=8406. For a general review of student debt issues
      see Jeffrey J. Williams, "Academic Freedom and Indentured Students," *Academe,* January–
      February 2012, available at www.aaup.org/article/academic-freedom-and-indentured-
      students#UyqK1JxrbOc.

499   New York State Office of Attorney General Andrew M. Cuomo, "College Loan Code of
      Conduct," available at http://www.ag.ny.gov/sites/default/files/press-releases/archived/
      College%20Code%20of%20Conduct.pdf. See also US House Education and Labor
      Committee, "Student Loan Industry; Testimony by Andrew M. Cuomo, Attorney General,"
      CQ Congressional Testimony, *Congressional Quarterly,* April 25, 2007. This "Code of Conduct"
      prohibits revenue sharing and kickbacks in other forms, as well as lender financing of gifts
      and trips for institutions' financial aid employees. The code further prohibits lender-staffed call
      centers and lays out strong guidelines concerning, among other things, preferred lender lists,
      advisory board compensation, and loan resale.

500   *Federal Register* 72, no. 211 (November 1, 2007): 61,959–62,011. These DOE rules, attached
      to eligibility for federal student aid, require colleges to include at least three lenders on
      a preferred lender list, restrict lender gifts to colleges in exchange for business, prohibit
      payments to college financial aid employees, and encourage loan counseling.

501   Many of these state-level laws are reviewed in California Research Bureau, "Student Loans for
      Higher Education," January 2008, CRB 08-002.

502   The Board of Governors of the Federal Reserve system was mandated, in accordance with
      Section 305 of the Credit Card Accountability Responsibility and Disclosure Act of 2009,
      Pub. L. No. 111–24, 123 Stat. 1734 (2009), to make these annual reports to Congress. In 2011,
      pursuant to Title X of the Dodd-Frank Wall Street Reform and Consumer Protection Act
      of 2010, responsibility for preparing these annual reports transferred to the newly established
      Bureau of Consumer Financial Protection.

503   Information included in this report is also available on the board's public website at www.
      federalreserve.gov/collegecreditcardagreements. In addition, under Section 304 of the Credit
      CARD Act and the Board's implementing regulations, 12 C.F.R. § 226.57(b), the public
      can obtain college credit card agreements between a card issuer and an institution of higher

education directly from the institution.

504 Nancy Zuckerbrod, "Education Dept. Places Official on Leave," *AP Education Writer,* April 6, 2007:

> A Department of Education official who oversaw the student loan industry and owned at least $100,000 worth of stock in a student loan company has been placed on leave, a department spokeswoman said Friday.
>
> Matteo Fontana, who keeps an eye on lenders and guarantee agencies that participate in the Federal Family Education Loan Program, was placed on leave with pay a day after his ownership of stock in Education Lending Group Inc. was disclosed by Higher Ed Watch, part of the New America Foundation, a nonpartisan think tank.
>
> The case has been referred to the department's inspector general. . . . At issue is whether Fontana violated department conflict of interest rules.

505 New York Attorney General Andrew Cuomo, "Letter to College Presidents," March 2007, document no longer available online, formerly accessed at http://www.oag.state.ny.us/press/2007/mar/OAG%20Letter%20to%20Colleges.pdf.

506 Karen Arenson and Diana Jean Schemo, "Report Details Deals in Student Loan Industry," *New York Times,* June 15, 2007; Doug Lederman, "Two More Aid Directors Fall," *Inside Higher Ed,* May 22, 2007, available at http://www.insidehighered.com/news/2007/05/22/loans#ixzz1p2g2KsZw; Jon Marcus, "Fury over Kickback Allegation," *Times Higher Education,* May 11, 2007.

507 US House Education and Labor Committee, "Student Loan Industry; Testimony by Andrew M. Cuomo, Attorney General," CQ Congressional Testimony, *Congressional Quarterly,* April 25, 2007, available at http://www.ag.ny.gov/sites/default/files/pdfs/bureaus/legislative/other_documents/House_Testimony.pdf.

508 US Senate Health, Education, Labor, and Pensions Committee, *Report on Marketing Practices in the Federal Family Education Loan Program,* July 2007; and US Senate Health, Education, Labor and Pensions Committee, *Second Report on Marketing Practices in the Federal Family Education Loan Program,* September 4, 2007. See also Marcus, "Fury over Kickback Allegation," op. cit. note 506.

509 Marcus, "Fury over Kickback Allegation," op. cit. note 506.

510 See California Research Bureau, "Student Loans for Higher Education," op. cit. note 501, which reports the following university settlement payments: Columbia University—$1.1 million; New York University—$1,394,563.75 covering students who received loans issued over a five-year period; St. John's University—$80,553.00 for loans issued over a one-year period; Syracuse University—$164,084.74 for loans issued over a two-year period; Fordham University—$13,840.00 for loans issued over a one-year period; University of Pennsylvania—$1,617,580.00 for loans issued over a two-year period; and Long Island University—$2,435.41 for loans issued over a one-year period.

511 Jonathan Glater and Karen Arenson, "Lenders Sought Edge against US in Student Loans," *New York Times,* April 15, 2007.

512 Paul Basken, "Colleges Are Again Asked about Lender Dealings," *Chronicle of Higher Education,*

November 9, 2007, 25.

513 US Senate Health, Education, Labor, and Pensions Committee, *Report on Marketing Practices in the Federal Family Education Loan Program,* July 2007; and US Senate Health, Education, Labor, and Pensions Committee, *Second Report on Marketing Practices in the Federal Family Education Loan Program,* op. cit. note 511.

514 Quoted in Elizabeth Redden, "A 'Systemic' Scandal," *Inside Higher Ed.,* June 15, 2007. See also Government Accountability Office (GAO), "Federal Family Education Loan Program," GAO-07-750, July 2007, 10, citing 20 U.S.C. § 1085(d)(5)(A) and C.F.R. § 682.603(e)(3), which reads in part as follows: "The Higher Education Act of 1965 prohibits lenders from offering 'points, premiums, payments, or other inducements' to individuals or institutions 'in order to secure [student loan] applicants,' and prohibits schools from engaging 'in any pattern or practice that results in a denial of the borrower's access to FFEL loans . . because of . . . selection of a particular lender.'"

515 GAO, "Federal Family Education Loan Program," 8, op. cit. note 514.

516 See, e.g., Laurel Rosenhall, "CSUS, UC Davis Strike Deals to Let IDs Be ATM Cards," *Sacramento Bee,* August 12, 2010, which reports the following: "The photo ID cards issued to UC Davis students this fall will have a new feature: a built-in connection to a bank that wants their business. The cards students use to borrow books from the library and work out in the campus gym will now double as ATM debit cards—if they sign up for a US Bank account. California State University, Sacramento, has a similar arrangement with Wells Fargo. New students going through orientation this week stopped in a campus office to have their pictures taken, then proceeded to a tent where Wells Fargo employees offered free iPod speakers to those linking their ID cards to a new Wells Fargo account."

517 New America Foundation, Higher Ed Watch blog post, "Selling Out Students When State Support Drops," April 15, 2008, available at http://higheredwatch.newamerica.net/blogposts/2008/selling_out_students_when_state_support_drops-19351.

518 Ibid.

519 Paul Basken, "Iowa Lawmakers Shine Spotlight on Lending Abuses," *Chronicle of Higher Education,* November 9, 2007, 22.

520 New America Foundation, Higher Ed Watch blog post, "Selling Out Students When State Support Drops," op. cit. note 517.

521 Federal Reserve Board of Governors, *Report to the Congress on College Credit Card Agreements,* October 2010, available at http://www.federalreserve.gov/boarddocs/rptcongress/creditcard/2010/downloads/CCAP_October_web.pdf.

522 California Research Bureau, "Student Loans for Higher Education." op. cit. 501.

523 Nellie Mae Corporation, *Graduate Students and Credit Cards,* Fall 2006, accessed at http://www.nelliemae.com/pdf/ccstudy_2006.pdf.

524 DHHS, "Responsibility of Applicants for Promoting Objectivity in Research," op. cit. note 300.

525 Davidoff et al., "Sponsorship, Authorship, and Accountability," op. cit. note 193; ICMJE, "Uniform Requirements for Manuscripts Submitted to Biomedical Journals," op. cit. note 193; WAME, "Recommendations on Publication Ethics Policies for Medical Journals," op. cit.

note 341.

526   DHHS, "Responsibility of Applicants for Promoting Objectivity in Research," op. cit. note
300. For details on the DHHS's new requirements for public disclosure of significant faculty
COI related to DHHS funded research, and the development of detailed COI "management
plans," see 53287–88. The section on public disclosure reads as follows:

> (5)(i) Prior to the Institution's expenditure of any funds under a PHS-funded research
> project, the Institution shall ensure public accessibility, via a publicly accessible Web site
> or written response to any requestor within five business days of a request, of information
> concerning any significant financial interest disclosed to the Institution that meets the
> following three criteria:
>
>> (A) The significant financial interest was disclosed and is still held by the senior/key
>> personnel as defined by this subpart;
>> (B) The Institution determines that the significant financial interest is related to the
>> PHS-funded research; and
>> (C) The Institution determines that the significant financial interest is a financial
>> conflict of interest.
>
> (ii) The information that the Institution makes available via a publicly accessible Web site
> or written response to any requestor within five business days of a request, shall include,
> at a minimum, the following: the Investigator's name; the Investigator's title and role with
> respect to the research project; the name of the entity in which the significant financial
> interest is held; the nature of the significant financial interest; and the approximate dollar
> value of the significant financial interest (dollar ranges are permissible: $0–$4,999; $5,000–
> $9,999; $10,000–$19,999; amounts between $20,000–$100,000 by increments of $20,000;
> amounts above $100,000 by increments of $50,000), or a statement that the interest is one
> whose value cannot be readily determined through reference to public prices or other
> reasonable measures of fair market value.
>
> (iii) If the Institution uses a publicly accessible Web site for the purposes of this
> subsection, the information that the Institution posts shall be updated at least annually.
> In addition, the Institution shall update the Web site within sixty days of the Institution's
> receipt or identification of information concerning any additional significant financial
> interest of the senior/key personnel for the PHS-funded research project that was not
> previously disclosed, or upon the disclosure of a significant financial interest of senior/
> key personnel new to the PHS-funded research project, if the Institution determines that
> the significant financial interest is related to the PHS-funded research and is a financial
> conflict of interest. The Web site shall note that the information provided is current as
> of the date listed and is subject to updates, on at least an annual basis and within 60 days
> of the Institution's identification of a new financial conflict of interest. If the Institution
> responds to written requests for the purposes of this subsection, the Institution will note
> in its written response that the information provided is current as of the date of the
> correspondence and is subject to updates, on at least an annual basis and within 60 days
> of the Institution's identification of a new financial conflict of interest, which should be

requested subsequently by the requestor.

(iv) Information concerning the significant financial interests of an individual subject to paragraph (a)(5) of this section shall remain available, for responses to written requests or for posting via the Institution's publicly accessible Web site for at least three years from the date that the information was most recently updated.

527 AAMC-AAU, *Protecting Patients, Preserving Integrity, Advancing Health*, op. cit. note 256.: "D. Pre-Clinical Research. The Advisory Committee believed that certain pre-clinical research may warrant special attention where there is a reasonable anticipation of follow-on human subjects research in the immediate future. Recommendation: With respect to pre-clinical research, institutions should consider requiring covered individuals to indicate if their current non-human subjects research that is linked to any of their reportable financial interests is reasonably anticipated (1) to be a component of an IND submission or (2) to progress to research involving human subjects within the coming 12 months. In such circumstances, the institution's conflicts of interest committee should have the authority to decide whether any of the policy stipulations that apply to human subjects research should apply to this 'pre-clinical' stage of the individual's research" (viii).

528 AAMC, *In the Interest of Patients*, 5–6, op. cit. note 261. The AAMC offers this definition of a COI in area of clinical practice: "A clinical practice conflict of interest . . . occurs when a secondary financial interest creates the risk that the primary duty to the patient and the delivery of optimal care will be unduly influenced by personal financial interests of the care provider or care provider institution. Institutional financial conflicts of interest similarly should not interfere with the delivery of the most appropriate care and best use of patient care resources" (9).

529 "Medical Professionalism in the New Millennium: A Physician Charter" (American Board of Internal Medicine, American College of Physicians Foundation, and European Federation of Internal Medicine, 2002), available at http://www.abimfoundation.org/Professionalism/%7E/media/F8B71F15DE8B486599F13E662603F25D.ashx.

530 IOM, "Conflicts of Interest," chap. 6: "Conflicts of Interest and Medical Practice," 166–88, op. cit. note 40.

531 AAMC-AAU, *Protecting Patients, Preserving Integrity, Advancing Health,* op. cit. note 256. The AAMC-AAU notes the following: "Conflicts of Interest in Clinical Practice: The Advisory Committee, while respectful of its circumscribed charge with respect to conflicts of interest in human subjects research, recognizes that many scientists who engage in human subjects research and have related significant financial interests also have active clinical practices in which those financial interests may be problematic and warrant institutional oversight. The Committee also recognizes that oversight and management of such conflicting financial interests of physician faculty in clinical practice settings is warranted. Recommendation: Institutions should adopt policies and establish standards that minimize bias in the practice of medicine due to real or perceived conflicts of interest of their medical faculty" (11).

532 See "Harvard University Policy on Individual Financial Conflicts of Interest," 17–18, op. cit. note 342.

533   AAMC, *In the Interest of Patients,* 5–6, op. cit. note 261.

534   Eric G. Campbell, "Conflict of Interest in Medical Research, Education, and Practice,"
      Statement before the Special Committee on Aging, US Senate, July 29, 2009, available at
      http://aging.senate.gov/events/hr214ec.pdf.

535   This AAUP recommendation was adapted only slightly from one issued in IOM, "Conflicts of
      Interest," 117–18, op. cit. note 40: see Recommendation 4.1. In its "Report Brief," the IOM
      summarizes its position as follows: "Although the committee recognizes that collaborations
      with industry can be beneficial, the committee recommends, as a general rule, that researchers
      should not conduct research involving human participants if they have a financial interest
      in the outcome of the research, for example, if they hold a patent on an intervention being
      tested in a clinical trial. The only exceptions should be if an individual's participation is judged
      to be essential for the safe and appropriate conduct of the research" (2).

536   AAMC, *Protecting Subjects, Preserving Trust, Promoting Progress,* op. cit. note 258; AAMC, *Protecting
      Subjects, Preserving Trust, Promoting Progress II,* op.cit. note 472; AAMC-AAU, *Protecting Patients,
      Preserving Integrity, Advancing Health,* op. cit. note 256. Here is how the AAMC's *Protecting
      Patients* report expresses this recommendation: "Decisions about whether or not to pursue
      a particular human subjects research project in the presence of an institutional conflict of
      interest should be governed by a 'rebuttable presumption' against doing the research at or
      under the auspices of the conflicted institution" (15) unless a compelling case can be made to
      justify an exception.

537   IOM, "Conflicts of Interest," 80, op. cit. note 40.

538   AAMC-AAU, *Protecting Patients, Preserving Integrity, Advancing Health,* 38–39, op. cit. note 256.

539   IOM, "Conflicts of Interest," 118, op. cit. note 40.

540   AAMC-AAU, *Protecting Patients, Preserving Integrity, Advancing Health,* op. cit. note 256. This
      recommendation reads in part as follows: "Institutions should have clear policies, compliant
      with applicable federal regulations that address the reporting and management of conflicts of
      interest of IRB members. The provisions should require reporting of all financial interests (no
      de minimis threshold) by IRB members . . . upon their initial appointment to the IRB, with
      updating annually and more often when circumstances change. The provisions should specify
      how the IRB Chair and/or the Administrator of the IRB will identify and evaluate potential
      conflicts of interest of IRB members and make clear that any conflicted IRB member must
      be recused from any deliberations relating to studies with which that IRB member has a
      potential conflict of interest."

541   AAU, *Report on Individual and Institutional Financial Conflict of Interest,* op. cit. note 14.

542   See, e.g., Eric C. Campbell, Joel S. Weissman, et al., "Characteristics of Medical School Faculty
      Members Serving on Institutional Review Boards: Results of a National Survey," *Academic
      Medicine* 78, no. 8 (2003): 831–36. Also, a 2002 Inspector General's report estimated that about
      25 percent of IRBs in the department's study were taking action to recognize and manage
      conflicts of interest among members. DHHS Office of Inspector General, "Protecting Human
      Research Subjects: Status of Recommendations," op. cit. note 280.

543   Department of Health and Human Services, Office of Inspector General (OIG), "Institutional

Review Boards: A Time for Reform," June 1998, OEI-01-97-00193, available online at
http://oig.hhs.gov/oei/reports/oei-01-97-00193.pdf; Department of Health and Human
Services, Office of Inspector General (OIG), "Institutional Conflicts at NIH Grantees,"
January 2011, OEI-03-09-00480, available at http://oig.hhs.gov/oei/reports/oei-03-09-
00480.pdf. See also Adil E. Shamoo, "Institutional Review Boards (IRBs) and Conflict of
Interest," *Accountability in Research: Policies and Quality Assurance* 7, no. 2–4 (1999) 201–212,
available at http://www.tandfonline.com/doi/abs/10.1080/08989629908573952.

544 AAU, *Report on Individual and Institutional Financial Conflict of Interest,* 6, op. cit. note 14. This
section reads in part as follows: "One effective way to integrate [IRB and standing COI
committee] processes is for [the standing] conflict of interest committees or officials to try
to review financial interest disclosures regarding human subject protocols before protocols
are submitted to the IRB (however the timing works out, the idea is for the conflict of
interest review to take place in time to affect any informed consent). The conflict of interest
committee or official can then determine whether a conflict exists, and if so, how it should
best be managed, if it should be (see guideline above indicating that such conflicts should
generally not be allowable), or can be. This determination, and summary information about
the financial interests, can then accompany a protocol when it is presented to the IRB. The
IRB could then take this information into account when determining whether and under
what circumstances to approve a given protocol. Universities should consider designing
systems so that an IRB also may determine if there is a financial conflict of interest that needs
to be managed, or if a Management Plan implemented by the conflict of interest committee
or official should be made more stringent. In such a system, neither the IRB nor the conflict
of interest committee would be able to override the other's management requirements if
the result would be to lessen the stringency of the management requirements. Either one
could prohibit the research from proceeding, unless the financial conflict was removed or
mitigated. Such a double-protection system would be consistent with the two sets of federal
regulations governing clinical research, and provide the additional safeguards that research
involving human participants demands. In whatever way a campus's conflict of interest and
human participant protection systems are designed, the focus should be on coordination and
communication of the two systems."

545 For a transcript of the *60 Minutes* report "Deception at Duke: Fraud in Cancer Care?"
broadcast by CBS News on February 12, 2012, see www.cbsnews.com/8301-18560_162-
57376073/deception-at-duke-fraud-in-cancer-care/. The report alleges that the faculty
members conducting the research and testing a particular treatment had a strong financial
interest in choosing that treatment over others. The program quotes other researchers
stating that the faculty members stood to make a "fortune" and that the data supporting the
treatment plan they started had been "fabricated."

546 IOM, "Conflicts of Interest," 69, op. cit. note 40; Weinfurt et al., "Policies of Academic
Medical Centers for Disclosing Financial Conflicts of Interest to Potential Research
Participants," op. cit. note 303.

547 This recommendation is drawn from AAMC, *Industry Funding of Medical Education,* op. cit.

note 318; see recommendations on "Purchasing," ix.

548   AAMC, *In the Interest of Patients,* 23, op. cit. note 261.

549   Ibid., 24.

550   On July 30, 2003, Cornell University's administration completed the Cornell University
      Strategic Corporate Alliance Plan ("the Plan"), the objective of which was "to leverage access
      to Cornell University intellectual capital, including faculty research, into major corporate
      alliances leading to competitive opportunities for select companies and financial support for
      faculty research and related infrastructure." The Plan defines a strategic corporate alliance
      (SCA) as a comprehensive, formally managed company-university agreement centered around
      a major, multi-year financial commitment involving research, programmatic interactions,
      intellectual property licensing, and other services. The initial companies targeted were in the
      life sciences sector, but the Plan contemplated "expand[ing] the alliance concept to other
      industries beyond the scope of the New Life Sciences." Cornell Strategic Alliance Plan (July
      30 version) at 1, 4 [Appendix A]. This version of the Plan superseded an earlier draft.

551   Cornell University, "Faculty Statement of Principles and Best Practices," 5, op. cit. note 114.

552   Rebecca Knight, "Big Pharma Gravitates to the Academe," *Financial Times,* September 2, 2008.

553   GlaxoSmithKline and Harvard Stem Cell Institute Announce Major Collaboration
      Agreement, *HarvardScience,* press release, July 24, 2008, available at http://news.harvard.edu/
      gazette/story/2008/07/glaxosmithkline-and-harvard-stem-cell-institute-announce-major-
      collaboration-agreement/. See also Center for Science in the Public Interest, "Integrity
      in Science Watch, Week of 09/08/2008," available at http://www.cspinet.org/integrity/
      watch/200809081.html.

554   Arlene Weintraub, "Big Drug R&D on Campus: With Pipelines Drying up, Drugmakers Are
      Enlisting Universities to Help Create New Treatments," *BusinessWeek,* May 8, 2008.

555   Bernadette Tansey, "UCSF, Pfizer Sign Collaborative Research Deal," *San Francisco Chronicle,*
      June 10, 2008.

556   Knight, "Big Pharma Gravitates to the Academe," op. cit. note 552.

557   Cornell University, "Faculty Statement of Principles and Best Practices," 16, op. cit. note 114.

558   Ibid., 16.

559   Ibid.; UC Berkeley Academic Senate Committee, letter to Prof. William Drummond, op. cit.
      note 445. UC Berkeley Academic Senate Task Force on University-Industry Partnerships,
      "Principles and Guidelines for Large-Scale Collaborations between the University and
      Industry, Government, and Foundations," e79, 1–23.

560   Busch et al., *External Review of the Collaborative Research Agreement,* 41–43, op. cit. note 114.

561   California State Legislature, Senate, "Impacts of Genetic Engineering on California's
      Environment: Examining the Role of Research at Public Universities (Novartis/UC Berkeley
      Agreement)," Joint Hearing, Committee on Natural Resources and Wildlife, Senate Select
      Committee on Higher Education, California State Legislature, Sacramento, May 15, 2000.

562   Washburn, *Big Oil Goes to College,* op. cit. note 105.

563   Ibid.; see Summary of Findings, 52–59, questions 10 and 11.

564   Ibid.; see discussion on 22, 60, and 64–65. This reads in part as follows: After the BP-funded

Energy Biosciences Institute deal was finalized at the end of 2007, "U.C. Berkeley's press office announced that the executive committee charged with evaluating faculty research projects for possible BP funding would have strong majority academic representation. And when the first formal executive committee convened in 2008 it had eight members, seven of whom were academics and one of whom was a representative from BP. But when this report's author probed a bit deeper, she soon found that seven of these eight committee members had significant potential conflicts of interest, including all but one of the academics. Two of the eight executive committee members, including the EBI's Academic Director and the lone BP representative, had financial ties to firms that could stand to profit from the EBI's academic research. And five of the other committee members had a different potential conflict: All were listed on the EBI website, in the spring of 2008, as 'primary investigators' on research projects funded by BP-EBI. What this strongly suggests is that all five could award BP research grant money to themselves and their labs. At the very least, the application and receipt of BP-EBI funding calls into question whether these faculty members were capable of fairly and impartially evaluating other faculty research proposals. More recently, these potential conflicts of interest on the EBI's executive committee seem to have only worsened. As of September 2010, the EBI listed a total of 13 executive committee members: 11 academics and two representatives from BP. Yet 10 of these academics are also listed as primary EBI investigators or heads of projects supported with BP-EBI funding, and one, EBI Director Chris Somerville, continues to have personal financial interests in an outside firm partnering with BP on research that is similar to that of EBI. That means three of the executive committee's 13 members have financial ties to firms that could profit from EBI research, and the other 10 are academic researchers who have vested research and financial interests with the EBI that could compromise their ability to evaluate incoming faculty research in an impartial and disinterested manner, based on scientific merit" (22).

565   The author obtained ten large-scale SCA contracts between universities and energy industry sponsors from direct requests to universities, and through public record requests. The author generated a list of twenty-seven questions addressing a range of issues from voting authority on the SCA's governance bodies and peer review, to intellectual property provisions and delays on publication. The author then commissioned outside, independent legal experts to analyze each of the ten contracts by applying this common set of twenty-seven questions. Washburn, *Big Oil Goes to College,* op. cit. note 105. See Methodology Box (15), a chart of ten contracts reviewed (13–14), and a Summary of Findings in response to all twenty-seven contract review questions for each of the ten contracts (52–59).

566   Busch et al., *External Review of the Collaborative Research Agreement,* 41–43, op. cit. note 114. The report reads: "Regardless of whether [Prof. Ignacio] Chapela's denial of tenure was justified, there is little doubt that the UCB-N agreement played a role in it. First, the very existence of UCB-N changed the rules of the game. Certain faculty were denied participation in the process because of the agreement. Second, while the administration saw fit to avoid conflict of interest (COI) among faculty, they ignored the potential for COI among administrators. Thus, regardless of its validity, the decision of top administrators to

accept the decision of the Budget Committee was seen by many as a COI" (42–43).

567 Regarding UC Berkeley-BP see UC Berkeley Academic Senate, Task Force on University-Industry Partnerships, "Principles and Guidelines for Large-Scale Collaborations between the University and Industry, Government, and Foundations," e79, 12–13; regarding UC Berkeley-Novartis/Syngenta, see Busch et al., *External Review of the Collaborative Research Agreement,* op. cit. note 114, which reads in part as follows: "The third structural component of the agreement that caused consternation among the campus community and others was the possibility Novartis scientists would be given adjunct status. While the agreement does not preclude the possibility for adjunct status for NADI employees, it never materialized. Several interviewees noted that this is most likely because of strong opposition from faculty outside of PMB. This position is supported by the second survey conducted by the ExCom of CNR. Few respondents to the survey thought adjunct status was appropriate for industry scientists from a firm that was either providing funding to CNR or one of its departments. In interviews, a number of faculty argued that granting Novartis scientists adjunct status would have bypassed the established governance procedures and stringent standards that are normally required for adjunct status. Many critics of the agreement also felt that the offer of adjunct status was a way for Novartis to buy its way into the UCB campus. However, some of those involved in the negotiation of the agreement argued that adjunct status for NADI employees was proposed by PMB as a way to facilitate closer interaction" (49–50).

568 Cornell University, "Faculty Statement of Principles and Best Practices," 9, op. cit. note 114.

569 Busch et al., *External Review of the Collaborative Research Agreement,* op. cit. note 114.

570 See, e.g., California State Legislature, Senate, "Impacts of Genetic Engineering on California's Environment," op. cit. note 561; Busch et al., *External Review of the Collaborative Research Agreement,* op. cit. note 114.; and Cornell University, "Faculty Statement of Principles and Best Practices," op. cit. note 114.

571 Busch et al., *External Review of the Collaborative Research Agreement,* 143, op. cit. note 114.

572 Cornell University, "Faculty Statement of Principles and Best Practices," 9, op. cit. note 114.

573 Ibid.

574 Washburn, *Big Oil Goes to College,* op. cit. note 105.

575 Elizabeth D. Earle, plant breeding and genetics; John M. Guckenheimer, mathematics (joining in this statement except for Section D); Anthony R. Ingraffea, civil and environmental engineering; David A. Levitsky, nutritional science; Risa L. Lieberwitz, industrial and labor relations; David L. Pelletier, nutritional science; Peter C. Stein, physics; Steven A. Wolf, natural resources; Elaine Wethington, human development; Cynthia R. Farina, associate dean of the faculty, chair (nonvoting); Charles Walcott, dean of the faculty, ex officio.

576 Risa L. Lieberwitz, "Faculty in the Corporate University: Professional Identity, Law, and Collective Action," *Cornell Journal of Law and Public Policy* 16 (2007): 263–330, see 310–18. According to Lieberwitz, a professor at the Cornell University School of Industrial and Labor Relations who sat on the Cornell faculty senate committee charged with reviewing strategic corporate alliance (SCA) agreements on campus, there were three central areas of debate among the faculty on this committee: "The most contentious issues concerned the extent of

the corporate funder's role in the university's decisions relating to research funding, the scope of SCAs subject to the principles recommended in the report, and the corporate sponsor's access to research results through 'first look' and exclusive licensing rights. The primary disagreement focused on corporate funders' participation in decisions over funding awards. The Spring 2004 version of the report had restricted corporate funders to participation in the call for research funding proposals (RFPs). In helping to draft the RFPs, the corporate funders could express their research priorities. After this point, however, faculty would have complete control over the funding award decisions. The Cornell administration took the position that excluding the corporate funder from decisions about awarding research proposals and from exclusive licensing would be 'deal killers' in negotiations to enter a SCA. The Spring 2005 version compromised by giving the corporate funders a role in awards decisions, but limited corporate representation to one-third of the members on the selection committee. The Faculty Senate debate of this provision revealed the likelihood that a majority of the Senate would vote to remove this cap. The final version of the report, therefore, eliminated the one-third corporate membership restriction. The final report, which was endorsed by the Faculty Senate in Fall 2005, gives the corporate sponsor the general right to participate in awarding funds to faculty research proposals. The report does emphasize, however, that 'this process should be led by Cornell faculty.' Each draft of the report recommended the use of a peer review process of research proposals submitted by faculty seeking SCA funds. The peer reviews by panels of 'disinterested scholars' at Cornell would provide input to the selection committee on the merit of the research proposals. The final report, however, limits peer review to 'broad SCAs,' defined as corporate funding of 'a potentially large group of faculty.' 'Narrow SCAs,' involving 'a small number of specific faculty . . . identified in advance as the relevant researchers,' would not use either RFPs for funding distribution or peer review to evaluate the merit of proposals. A third area of controversy concerned the scope of corporate funders' 'first-look' and exclusive licensing rights. Each version of the report incorporated the existing Cornell policy that restricted corporate funders to a maximum 90-day pre-publication period of first-look rights. This 90-day period would enable the corporate sponsor to review the research to determine if it contained confidential corporate information that would need to be eliminated. This time also provides a period for the university to file patent applications and for the corporate sponsor to negotiate exclusive licensing rights to future patents. Although the report does not challenge these practices, it does urge the use of non-exclusive licenses, whenever possible. It further recommends that SCA agreements provide for Cornell's right to freely distribute all research methods and results to researchers in any academic setting" (311–13).

577   For one researcher's experience, see Washburn, *Big Oil Goes to College,* op. cit. note 105: "Out of a total of 35 requests for specific university-industry alliance agreements, the author issued 24 as formal 'public record act' (PRA) filings, citing the actual public record laws applicable in each state. State-funded universities are normally subject to public record act laws, due to their receipt of substantial state funding. (The author made the remainder of our requests more informally via phone and email, often in conjunction with scheduled phone interviews

with university staff and administrators.) *State universities failed to fulfill or outright ignored more than half of these 24 legal public record act requests. Often documents were released only after substantial delays. In two instances, both the University of Houston and Texas A&M University forwarded our public record act requests (related to major academy-industry research alliances with General Motors and Chevron, respectively) all the way up to the Texas Attorney General's office. In both cases, the Texas AG's office required the universities to make those requested documents public; however, this resulted in roughly two- and four-month-long delays, respectively.* Sources: Email correspondence between the author and officials at the University of Houston and Texas A&M University, pertaining to public record act requests that the author filed on November 9, 2007 and November 12, 2007 respectively" (11n34).

578 AAUP, "Statement on Government of Colleges and Universities," op. cit. note 8.

579 AAUP, "Statement on Corporate Funding of Academic Research," 132, op. cit. note 4.

580 Cornell University, "Faculty Statement of Principles and Best Practices," 19–20, op. cit. note 114.

581 Ibid., 20.

582 Ibid., 21.

583 Washburn, *Big Oil Goes to College,* 64–65, op. cit. note 105.

584 Michaels, *Doubt Is Their Product,* 53, op. cit. note 248.

585 Cornell University, "Faculty Statement of Principles and Best Practices," 18, op. cit. note 114.

586 BHEF, *Working Together, Creating Knowledge,* 13, 51, op. cit. note 26.

587 Ibid., 51.

588 Cornell University, "Faculty Statement of Principles and Best Practices," 13, op. cit. note 114.

589 Ibid., 14.

590 Ibid., 12.

591 AAUP, "Statement on Conflicts of Interest," op. cit. note 5.

592 Cornell University, "Faculty Statement of Principles and Best Practices," 12, op. cit. note 114.

593 AAUP, "Statement on Government of Colleges and Universities," op. cit. note 8.

594 AAUP, "Statement on Corporate Funding of Academic Research," op. cit. note 4.

595 Cornell University, "Faculty Statement of Principles and Best Practices," section E, 22–26, op. cit. note 114. In addition to annual external faculty evaluations of the SCA, the statement also recommends: "A more comprehensive longitudinal study of the SCA experience should be initiated to examine broader issues related to potential crowding-out of public research, effect on the nature and extent of intellectual interchange among participating and non-participating faculty and students, displacement of funding from other sources, disproportionate growth across unit, impact on external relations, and other issues. The dearth of empirical information on these matters is one of the factors impeding informed and reasoned discussion of SCAs at Cornell and elsewhere, and this study can become a resource for Cornell and the larger set of organizations interested in evolving public-private relations in the production and control of knowledge. According [sic], this study and the other activities noted above should be funded as a charge to overhead of SCAs" (25–26).

596 See David Glenn, "Cloak and Classroom," *Chronicle of Higher Education,* March 25, 2005,

available at www.chronicle.com/article/CloakClassroom/16948, and David H. Price, *Weaponizing Anthropology* (Oakland CA: AK Press, 2011), especially Chapter Two, "The CIA's University Spies."

597 Federation of American Societies for Experimental Biology (FASEB), *Shared Responsibility, Individual Integrity: Scientists Addressing Conflicts of Interest in Biomedical Research,* March 13, 2006, available at http://www.faseb.org/portals/0/pdfs/opa/faseb_coi_paper.pdf.

598 FASEB, *COI Toolkit: Recommendations, Tools, and Resources for the Conduct and Management of Financial Relationships between Academia and Industry in Biomedical Research* (Bethesda, MD: FASEB, 2006), available at http://opa.faseb.org/pages/Advocacy/coi/Toolkit.htm.

599 AAMC, *In the Interest of Patients,* op. cit. note 261: "The Advisory Committee, while respectful of its circumscribed charge with respect to conflicts of interest in human subjects research, recognizes that many scientists who engage in human subjects research and have related significant financial interests also have active clinical practices in which those financial interests may be problematic and warrant institutional oversight. . . . *Recommendation:* Institutions should adopt policies and establish standards that minimize bias in the practice of medicine due to real or perceived conflicts of interest of their medical faculty."

600 ABIM Foundation, American Board of Internal Medicine; ACP-ASIM Foundation, American College of Physicians-American Society of Internal Medicine; European Federation of Internal Medicine, "Medical Professionalism in the New Millennium: A Physician Charter," *Annals of Internal Medicine* 136, no. 3 (2002): 243–46; ABIM Foundation, "Medical Professionalism in the New Millennium: A Physician Charter," American Board of Internal Medicine website, http://www.abimfoundation.org/Professionalism/Physician-Charter.aspx.

601 Ehringhaus and Korn, *Principles for Protecting Integrity in the Conduct and Reporting of Clinical Trials,* op. cit. note 351.

602 AAMC, *Protecting Subjects, Preserving Trust, Promoting Progress,* op. cit. note 258.

603 FASEB, *Shared Responsibility, Individual Integrity,* op. cit. note 596: "Guiding principle 6: Investigators shall have access to, and be involved in the analysis and/or interpretation of all data generated in the research."

604 Davidoff et al., "Sponsorship, Authorship, and Accountability," op. cit. note 193; ICMJE, "Uniform Requirements for Manuscripts Submitted to Biomedical Journals," op. cit. note 193. These standards were originally issued in 2001 in connection with the *New England Journal of Medicine* article cited above.

605 WAME, available at http://www.wame.org/conflict-of-interest-in-peer-reviewed-medical-journals. In its guidelines, under "Authors," WAME states: "All authors should be asked to report their financial COI related to the research and written presentation of their work and any other relevant competing interests. Journals should publish all COI (or their absence) reported by authors that are relevant to the manuscript being considered. In additional to financial COI, policies for authors should be extended to other types of competing interests that might affect (or be seen to affect) the conduct or reporting of the work. Journals should disclose all COIs that they themselves thought were important during the review process. *Declarations should require authors to explicitly state funding sources and whether the organization that*

funded the research participated in the collection and analyses of data and interpretation and reporting of results" [Emphasis added].

606 Pharmaceutical Research and Manufacturers of America (PHARMA), "Principles on Conduct of Clinical Trials and Communication of Clinical Trial Results," revised April 2009, available at http://www.phrma.org/sites/default/files/105/042009_clinical_trial_principles_final.pdf. According this PHARMA statement: "As sponsors, we are responsible for receipt and verification of data from all research sites for the studies we conduct; we ensure the accuracy and integrity of the entire study database, which is owned by the sponsor." However, many research experts now question whether this corporate ownership and tight proprietary control of data is compatible with preserving the integrity and objectivity of medical research, see Steinbrook and Kassirer, "Analysis: Data Availability for Industry Sponsored Trials," , 5391, op. cit. note 212.

607 See the Introduction to this AAUP report. See also Bodenheimer, "Uneasy Alliance," op. cit. note 34.

608 Davidoff et al., "Sponsorship, Authorship, and Accountability," op. cit. note 193

609 ICMJE, "Uniform Requirements for Manuscripts Submitted to Biomedical Journals," op. cit. note 193. See specifically ICMJE, "Ethical Considerations in the Conduct and Reporting of Research," op. cit. note 364.

610 AAMC, *Protecting Subjects, Preserving Trust, Promoting Progress,* op. cit. note 258.

611 In 2005, the International Committee of Medical Journal Editors (ICMJE) instructed its researchers to deposit data into registries, such as ClinicalTrials.gov *as a precondition for publication,* hoping to discourage tampering with trial protocols and final data analysis. Catherine D. DeAngelis, Jeffrey M. Drazen, Frank A. Frizelle, et al., "Is This Clinical Trial Fully Registered? A Statement from the International Committee of Medical Journal Editors," *Journal of the American Medical Association* 293, no. 23 (2005): 2927–29; C. DeAngelis, J. M. Drazen, F. A. Frizelle, C. Haug, J. Hoey, et al. , "Clinical Trial Registration: A Statement from the International Committee of Medical Journal Editors," *New England Journal of Medicine* 351 (2004): 1250–51, available at http://www.icmje.org/clin_trial.pdf. This statement reads in part as follows: "The ICMJE member journals will require, as a condition of consideration for publication, registration in a public trials registry. Trials must register at or before the onset of patient enrollment. This policy applies to any clinical trial starting enrollment after July 1, 2005. For trials that began enrollment prior to this date, the ICMJE member journals will require registration by September 13, 2005, before considering the trial for publication."

612 In 2007, Congress passed the US Food and Drug Administration Amendments Act, which mandated that clinical trials related to all FDA-regulated products, or products seeking regulation, must be registered at ClinicalTrials.gov. The law also imposes penalties for noncompliance. US Public Law 110-85 (Food and Drug Administration Amendments Act of 2007 [FDAAA]), Title VIII, Section 801, mandates that a "responsible party" (i.e., the sponsor or designated principal investigator) register and report results of certain "applicable clinical trials"; see http://prsinfo.clinicaltrials.gov/fdaaa.html. For an overview discussion of the FDAAA, see Elie Dolgin, "Publication Bias Continues despite Clinical-Trial Registration,"

Nature News, September 11, 2009.

613 In 2006, the Association of American Medical Colleges (AAMC) endorsed and finalized a set of recommended *"Principles for Protecting Integrity in the Conduct and Reporting of Clinical Trials,"* which recommends that all clinical trials and their protocols be registered on a publicly accessible database. (These principles were developed in collaboration with the Centers for Education and Research in Therapeutics and the BlueCross BlueShield Association.) The AAMC wrote that it developed these principles to address the "inconsistency in research standards" at academic medical centers, which "can affront human research ethics, undermine academic integrity, distort public policy and medical practice, and impair public health." Ehringhaus and Korn, *Principles for Protecting Integrity in the Conduct and Reporting of Clinical Trials,* op. cit. note 351. See Principles 6, 7, and 8, which recommend regstration of clinical trials within twenty-one days of initiating enrollment of research participants, and in a manner "fully pursuant to the ICMJE requirements" (cited above).

614 ClinicalTrials.gov fact sheet, available at http://www.nlm.nih.gov/pubs/factsheets/clintrial. html. For ClinicalTrials.gov's main website, go to http://clinicaltrials.gov/.

615 Ibid. The ClinicalTrials.gov fact sheet specifies that, "Consistent with the default adverse events reporting provisions of section 801(a) of the FDA Amendments Act of 2007 (FDAAA) [as it amends 42 U.S.C. 28 2(j)(3)(I)(ii)–(iii)], starting on September 27, 2009, Responsible Parties are expected to submit summary adverse event information when providing study results to ClinicalTrials.gov."

616 S. Mathieu, I. Boutron, D. Moher, D. G. Altman, and P. Ravaud, "Comparison of Registered and Published Primary Outcomes in Randomized Controlled Trials," *Journal of the American Medical Association* 302 (2009): 977–84; Joseph S. Ross, Gregory K. Mulvey, Elizabeth M. Hines, et al., "Trial Publication after Registration in ClinicalTrials.gov: A Cross-sectional Analysis," *PLoS Medicine* 6 (2009): e1000144. Here is a summary of both trials taken from Dolgin, "Publication Bias Continues despite Clinical-Trial Registration," op. cit. note 612: "The first study, . . . led by Philippe Ravaud, an epidemiologist at Paris Diderot University, reviewed 323 studies relating to three medical areas—cardiology, rheumatology and gastroenterology—published in high-impact journals [in 2008]. The [study] found that just 46% of the trials had been correctly registered with clearly stated goals before publication. . . . Even among the articles that were properly registered, nearly 1 in 3 studies switched the stated goals in the final publication, [said] Ravaud's team." In the Ross study, "researchers analysed 677 trials at phases II–IV," which were registered at ClinicalTrials.gov and completed before 2006, "and found that only 46% had been published. Of those, fewer than a third had cited their ClinicalTrials.gov record of the trial. Studies primarily sponsored by industry had the worst publication record, with only 40% appearing in medical journals, and NIH-sponsored trials were not much better, at 47%."

617 Quoted from IOM, "Conflicts of Interest," 112, op. cit. note 40.

618 Steinbrook, "Gag Clauses in Clinical Trial Agreements," op. cit. note 198.

619 Ehringhaus and Korn, *Principles for Protecting Integrity in the Conduct and Reporting of Clinical trials,* op. cit. note 351. See Principles 10–14.

620   Ibid.

621   FDA, *Guidance: Financial Disclosure by Clinical Investigators* (Silver Spring, MD: FDA, 2001), available at http://www.fda.gov/oc/guidance/financialdis.html.

622   Phil B. Fontanarosa and Catherine D. DeAngelis, "Publication of Clinical Trials in *JAMA*: Information for Authors," *Journal of the American Medical Association* 299, no. 1 (2008): 95–96.

623   Thompson et al., *The Olivieri Report,* op. cit. note 129.

624   Ibid.

625   Ibid.

626   IOM, "Conflicts of Interest," 149, op. cit. note 40.

627   Cited in IOM, "Conflicts of Interest," 149, op. cit. note 40, see Box 5-3. Direct quotes from US Department of Justice, "Warner-Lambert to Pay $430 Million to Resolve Criminal and Civil Health Care Liability Relating to Off-Label Promotion," press release, May 13, 2004, available at http://www.usdoj.gov/opa/pr/2004/May/04_civ_322.htm.

628   DHHS, OIG, *Compliance Program Guidance for Pharmaceutical Manufacturers* (Washington, DC: DHHS, 2003), available at http://www.oig.hhs.gov/fraud/docs/complianceguidance/042803 pharmacymfgnonfr.pdf.

629   IOM, "Conflicts of Interest," op. cit. note 40: "Faculty should not participate in speakers bureaus and similar promotional activities in which they either present content directly controlled by industry or formulate their remarks to win favor and continued speaking fees" (158).

630   Association of American Medical Colleges (AAMC), *Implementing the Recommendations of the AAMC Task Force on Industry Funding of Medical Education: A Selected Policy Language Compendium* (Washington, DC: AAMC, 2008):

    F. Participation in Industry-Sponsored Programs.

    Recommendations:

        •With the exception of settings in which academic investigators are presenting results of their industry-sponsored studies to peers and there is opportunity for critical exchange, academic medical centers should strongly discourage participation by their faculty in industry-sponsored speakers bureaus.

        • To the extent that academic medical centers choose to allow participation of their faculty and staff in industry-sponsored, FDA-regulated programs, they should develop standards that define appropriate and acceptable involvement.

            1. Academic medical centers should require full transparency and disclosure by their personnel to the centers and when participating in such programs; and

            2. Academic medical centers should require that payments to academic personnel be only at fair market value.

      • Academic medical centers should prohibit their faculty, students, and trainees from:

            1. Attending non-ACCME-accredited industry events billed as continuing medical education;

            2. Accepting payment for attendance at industry-sponsored meetings; and

            3. Accepting personal gifts from industry at such events. (5)

631   Brennan et al., "Health Industry Practices That Create Conflicts of Interest," op. cit. note 317.

632 For a sampling of some of this policy language on speakers bureaus, see AAMC, *Implementing the Recommendations of the AAMC Task,* 33–42. op cit. note 629; and *Ghostwriting and Speakers Bureaus: A Toolkit for Academic Medical Centers* (Prescription Project [created with The Pew Charitable Trusts in partnership with the Institute on Medicine as a Profession], April 2008), available at http://www.prescriptionproject.org/tools/initiatives_resources/files/0013.pdf.

633 Eric G. Campbell, Joel S. Weissman, Susan Ehringhaus, et al., "Institutional Academic-Industry Relationships," *Journal of the American Medical Association* 298, no. 15 (2007): 1779–86.

634 IOM, "Conflicts of Interest," 153–54, op. cit. note 40. Carl Elliott, "The Drug Pushers," *Atlantic Magazine,* April 2006, available at http://www.theatlantic.com/ doc/200604/drug-reps/3; Daniel Carlat, "Dr. Drug Rep," *New York Times Magazine,* November 25, 2007.

635 IOM, "Conflicts of Interest," 20–21, 189–215, op. cit. note 40.

636 Ibid., 210–11.

637 Niteesh K. Choudhry, Henry T. Stelfox, and Allan S. Detsky, "Relationships between Authors of Clinical Practice Guidelines and the Pharmaceutical Industry," *Journal of the American Medical Association* 287, no. 5 (2002): 612–17. The most frequent relationship with companies involved honoraria for speaking (64 percent of the respondents, who reported an average of 7.3 companies as sources of the honoraria). Thirty-eight percent of the authors had an employee or consultant relationship with one or more companies. The majority of the authors surveyed reported no discussion of financial relationships during the guideline development process.

638 IOM, "Conflicts of Interest," 204, op. cit. note 40; D. W. Coyne, "Influence of Industry on Renal Guideline Development," *Clinical Journal of the American Society of Nephrology* 2, no. 1 (2007): 3–7; discussion 13–14.

639 IOM, "Conflicts of Interest," 204, op. cit. note 40; Kidney Disease Outcomes Quality Initiative (KDOQI), "KDOQI Clinical Practice Guideline and Clinical Practice Recommendations for Anemia in Chronic Kidney Disease: 2007 Update of Hemoglobin Target," *American Journal of Kidney Diseases* 50, no. 3 (2007): 471–530.

640 IOM, "Conflicts of Interest," 204, op. cit. note 40.

641 Ibid. 214; Coyne, "Influence of Industry on Renal Guideline Development," op. cit. note 638.

642 For more details on this proposal, see IOM, "Conflicts of Interest," op. cit. note 40: "RECOMMENDATION 5.3. A new system of funding accredited continuing medical education should be developed that is free of industry influence, enhances public trust in the integrity of the system, and provides high-quality education. A consensus development process that includes representatives of the member organizations that created the accrediting body for continuing medical education, members of the public, and representatives of organizations such as certification boards that rely on continuing medical education should be convened to propose within 24 months of the publication of this report a funding system that will meet these goals" (161).

According to the IOM report, 2009, 151, a similar conclusion regarding continuing medical education programs was reached by the Mayo Clinic in a 2008 consensus conference report noting that continuing medical education requires a "strategic management process that focuses on the integrity of an enterprise" and that deals "in a convincing, transparent and accountable manner with issues such as commercial interest influence, conflicts of interest, bias, sources of evidence and the quality of product, process and delivery." (The original Mayo Clinic source is: Gabrielle M. Kane, "Conference Proceedings, Mayo CME Consensus Conference, Rochester, MN, September 25–26, 2008," Rochester, MN: Mayo Clinic, 2008, available at http://www.sacme.org/site/sacme/ assets/pdf/Mayo_CME_Consensus_Conf_ Proceedings_1-20-09.pdf).

643 IOM, "Conflicts of Interest," 34, op. cit. note 40. Accreditation Council for Continuing Medical Education (ACCME), *ACCME Annual Report Data, 2007* (Chicago: ACCME, 2008), available at http://www.accme.org/dir_docs/doc_upload/207fa8e2-bdbe-47f8-9b65-52477f9faade_uploaddocu-ment.pdf. According to this ACCME report, between 1998 and 2007, the share of continuing medical education provider income accounted for by commercial sources, excluding advertising and exhibits, grew from 34 percent to 48 percent, with higher rates for some providers, such as for-profit education and communication companies and medical schools.

644 Campbell, "Conflict of Interest in Medical Research, Education, and Practice," op. cit. note 534.

645 Stanford University School of Medicine, *Continuing Medical Education (CME) Commercial Support Policy* (2008), available at http://cme.stanford.edu/documents/cme_commercial_ support_policy.pdf.

646 IOM, "Conflicts of Interest," 152, op. cit. note 40; Dave Kovaleski, "No Pharma Funding," *MeetingsNet,* January 1, 2008, available at http://meetingsnet.com/cmepharma/cme/no_ pharma_funding_012808/index.html.

647 Strangely, however, the IOM addressed its recommendation in this area to the companies (asking them to adopt policies that prohibit distribution of gifts, free meals, and drug samples), even though this marketing takes place at facilities under the control of academic institutions: "Recommendation 6.2: Pharmaceutical, medical device, and bio-technology companies and their company foundations should have policies and practices against providing physicians with gifts, meals, drug samples (except for use by patients who lack financial access to medications), or other similar items of material value and against asking physicians to be authors of ghostwritten materials. Consulting arrangements should be for necessary services, documented in written contracts, and paid for at fair market value. Companies should not involve physicians and patients in marketing projects that are presented as clinical research." IOM, "Conflicts of Interest," 187, op. cit. note 40.

648 AAMC, *Implementing the Recommendations of the AAMC Task Force,* op. cit. note 630.

649 In January 2006, the Institute on Medicine as a Profession (IMAP) and the American Board of Internal Medicine (ABIM) Foundation, publishing in the *Journal of the American Medical Association,* urged academic medical centers (AMCs) to lead the profession in eliminating undue industry influence in clinical care. Rothman and Chimonas, "New Developments in Managing Physician-Industry Relationships," op. cit. note 317.

650 Dana and Loewenstein, "A Social Science Perspective on Gifts to Physicians from Industry,"

op. cit. note 269; Michael J. Oldani, "Thick Prescriptions: Toward an Interpretation of Pharmaceutical Sales," *Medical Anthropology Quarterly* 18, no. 3 (2004): 328–56.

651 Wazana, *Physicians and the Pharmaceutical Industry,* op. cit. note 268.

652 AAMC, *Implementing the Recommendations of the AAMC Task Force,* op. cit. note 630.

653 Ibid.

654 IOM, "Conflicts of Interest," 158, op. cit. note 40.

655 AAMC, *Implementing the Recommendations of the AAMC Task,* op. cit. note 630.

656 Ibid.

657 Ibid.

658 Harold C. Sox and Drummond Rennie, "Seeding Trials: Just Say 'No,'" *Annals of Internal Medicine* 149, no. 4 (2008): 279–80; David Malakoff, "Clinical Trials and Tribulations: Allegations of Waste: The 'Seeding' Study," *Science* 322, no. 5899 (October 2008): 213.

659 Carl Elliott, "Useless Studies, Real Harm," opinion editorial, *New York Times,* July 28, 2011, available at http://www.nytimes.com/2011/07/29/opinion/useless-pharmaceutical-studies-real-harm.html. See also Samuel D. Krumholz, David S. Egilman, and Joseph S. Ross, "Study of Neurontin: Titrate to Effect, Profile of Safety (STEPS) Trial: A Narrative Account of a Gabapentin Seeding Trial," *Archives of Internal Medicine* 171, no. 12 (2011): 1100–07.

660 David A. Kessler, Janet L. Rose, Robert J. Temple, et al., "Therapeutic-Class Wars: Drug Promotion in a Competitive Marketplace," *New England Journal of Medicine* 331, no. 20 (November 1994): 1350–53; Kenneth A. Katz, "Time to Nip 'Seeding Trials' in the Bud," *Archives of Dermatology* 144, no. 3 (March 2008): 403–04; Sox and Rennie, "Seeding Trials: Just Say 'No.'" op. cit. note 658.

661 Harris, "Drug Maker Told Studies Would Aid It, Papers Say," op. cit. note 296: In this article, the *New York Times* reported the following: On February 26, 2009, Dr. Joseph Biederman, who was director of the Johnson & Johnson Center for Pediatric Psychopathology Research at Harvard's Mass General Hospital, was deposed by attorneys involved in a series of lawsuits against antipsychotic drug manufacturers. An earlier 2008 inquiry by Senator Charles E. Grassley, Republican of Iowa, revealed that Dr. Biederman earned at least $1.6 million in consulting fees from drug makers from 2000 to 2007 but failed to report all but about $200,000 of this income to university officials. A series of unsealed court documents have since shown that Biederman outlined plans to test Johnson & Johnson drugs in presentations to the company's executives. Many of Biederman's slides, presented to company officials, promised to deliver commercially useful, positive results to his prospective corporate sponsors even before commencing his research. All of the slides were prepared by Dr. Biederman, according to his sworn statement. This *New York Times* article goes on to discuss three specific clinical drug trials, which Biederman successfully pitched to drug manufacturers in this manner, each of which was later published in an academic journal with conclusions that matched the predetermined outcomes discussed. After reviewing these legal documents, Grassley wrote a letter asking the presidents of Harvard hospitals and Mass General to explain why these slides suggest an expectation of positive outcomes for the drugs prior to the commencement of the clinical trials. He noted that when he asked an independent

physician researcher to review Biederman's slides, the doctor stated "it appeared that the slides discussed in this letter were nothing more than marketing tools, as opposed to discussions of independent scientific research." Grassley's letter to Drew Gilpin Faust, president of Harvard University Hospital (Partners Healthcare) and Peter L. Slavin, president of Massachusetts General, may be accessed at http://s.wsj.net/public/resources/documents/WSJ-Major_ Protocol_Violation_Letters032009.pdf. In July 2011, Biederman and two other Harvard colleagues were sanctioned for violations of both university and hospital policy.

662 Bero et al., "The Limits of Competing Interest Disclosures," 118–26. op cit. note 358:
"In January 1997, [UCLA Professor James] Enstrom submitted a research proposal to the Philip Morris Research Center, where it was reviewed by the Scientific Research Review Committee (SRRC), a committee whose purpose was to 'ensure that all scientific research, related to tobacco or smoking, conducted or funded by Philip Morris, . . . serves relevant business needs.' The proposal, 'Relationship of low levels of active smoking to mortality,' sought to analyse data from four epidemiological cohorts. . . . In his cover letter to Richard Carchman, Director of Scientific Affairs, Philip Morris, Enstrom stated: 'These data are highly relevant to the ETS issue... level of trust must be developed based on my past research on passive smoking and epidemiology in general in order to work out the best way for me to conduct this research. A substantial research commitment on your part is necessary in order for me to effectively compete against the large mountain of epidemiologic data and opinions that already exist regarding the health effects of ETS and active smoking.' . . . The proposal [Enstrom submitted] stated: 'an unrestricted gift to James E. Enstrom/UCLA with mutual understanding/trust would minimize university restrictions and eliminate overhead costs.' . . . Philip Morris funded the project in April 1997 for $150 000 to be paid in two installments." (121).

663 AAU, Report on Individual and Institutional Financial Conflict of Interest, op. cit. note 14.

664 AAMC, Protecting Subjects, Preserving Trust, Promoting Progress, op. cit. note 258; AAMC, Protecting Subjects, Preserving Trust, Promoting Progress II, op.cit. note 472; Ehringhaus and Korn, Principles for Protecting Integrity, op. cit. note 351; AAMC, Compact between Biomedical Graduate Students and Their Research Advisors, op. cit. note 394.

665 AAMC-AAU, Protecting Patients, Preserving Integrity, Advancing Health, 36, op. cit. note 256.

666 FASEB, Shared Responsibility, Individual Integrity, op. cit. note 596; FASEB, COI Toolkit, op. cit. note 597.

667 IOM, "Conflicts of Interest," op. cit. note 40.

668 Davidoff et al., "Sponsorship, Authorship, and Accountability," op. cit. note 193; ICMJE, "Uniform Requirements for Manuscripts," op. cit. note 193; ICMJE, "Ethical Considerations in the Conduct and Reporting of Research," op. cit. note 364.

669 WAME, "Publication Ethics Policies for Medical Journals," op. cit. note 341; WAME, "Policy Statements: Ghost Writing Initiated by Commercial Companies," op. cit. note 341.

670 IOM, "Conflicts of Interest," op. cit. note 40.

671 AAUP, "1915 Declaration of Principles," 295, op. cit. note 2.

672 AAUP, "Statement on Government of Colleges and Universities," 139, op. cit. note 8.

673　AAUP, "On the Relationship of Faculty Governance to Academic Freedom," in *Policy Documents and Reports,* 141.

674　AAUP, "On Preventing Conflicts of Interest in Government-Sponsored Research at Universities," in *Policy Documents and Reports,* 184.

675　Cornell University, "Faculty Statement of Principles and Best Practices," 9, op. cit. note 114.

676　AAUP, "Statement on Conflicts of Interest," 185, op. cit. note 5: "Because the central business of the university remains teaching and research unfettered by extra-university dictates, faculties should ensure that any cooperative venture between members of the faculty and outside agencies, whether public or private, respects the primacy of the university's principal mission, with regard to the choice of subjects of research and the reaching and publication of results"; AAUP, "Freedom in the Classroom," op. cit. note 331, which notes that academic institutions surrender their autonomy and authority—and diverge with the principles of academic freedom—when they accept outside funding that is "conditioned on a requirement to assign specific course material that the faculty would not otherwise assign."

677　AAUP, "Statement on Corporate Funding of Academic Research," 132, op. cit. note 4.

678　DHHS, NIH, "Principles and Guidelines for Recipients," 72093, op. cit. note 245. These quoted sections of the NIH principles and guidelines are reprinted in AAUP, "Statement on Corporate Funding of Academic Research," 132n4, op. cit. note 4.

679　AAUP, "Statement on Conflicts of Interest," 185, op. cit. note 5.

680　DHHS, NIH, "Principles and Guidelines for Recipients," op. cit. note 245. Under the heading "Prompt Publication," this NIH guidance reads in part as follows: "Agreements to acquire materials for use in NIH-funded research are expected to address the timely dissemination of research results. Recipients should not agree to significant publication delays, any interference with the full disclosure of research findings, or any undue influence on the objective reporting of research results. A delay of 30–60 days to allow for patent filing or review for confidential proprietary information is generally viewed as reasonable."

681　IOM, "Conflicts of Interest," op. cit. note 40; Ehringhaus and Korn, *Principles for Protecting Integrity,* 5, op. cit. note 351, principle 16: "Ghost or guest authorship is unacceptable. Authorship implies independent, substantial, and fully disclosed participation in the study and in the preparation of the manuscript"; AAMC, *Industry Funding of Medical Education,* op. cit. note 318. In this report the AAMC recommends that "[a]cademic medical centers should prohibit physicians, trainees, and students from allowing their professional presentations of any kind, oral or written, to be ghostwritten by any party, industry or otherwise." It also notes that properly acknowledged collaborations with industry personnel or medical writers is not ghostwriting.

682　Davidoff et al., "Sponsorship, Authorship, and Accountability," op. cit. note 193; ICMJE, "Uniform Requirements for Manuscripts," op. cit. note 193; WAME, "Publication Ethics Policies for Medical Journals," op. cit. note 341.

683　AAUP, "Statement on Professional Ethics," in *Policy Documents and Reports,* 10th ed. (Washington, DC: AAUP; Baltimore: Johns Hopkins University Press, 2006), 171–72.

684　AAUP, "Statement on Multiple Authorship," in *Policy Documents and Reports,* 10th ed.

(Washington, DC: AAUP; Baltimore: Johns Hopkins University Press, 2006), 187.

685 AAUP, "Statement on Plagiarism," in *Policy Documents and Reports,* 10th ed. (Washington, DC: AAUP; Baltimore: Johns Hopkins University Press, 2006), 176.

686 AAMC, *Protecting Subjects, Preserving Trust, Promoting Progress,* op. cit. note 258; Ehringhaus and Korn, *Principles for Protecting Integrity,* op. cit. note 351, principle 10: "Publication and Analysis Committee," which reads in part: "It is essential that the P&A committee be independent of the sponsor's control, have access to the full data set, understand and implement the prespecified analysis plan, and have the resources and skills both to interpret that analysis and perform additional analysis if required…"; Davidoff et al., "Sponsorship, Authorship, and Accountability," op. cit. note 193; ICMJE, "Uniform Requirements for Manuscripts," op. cit. note 193; ICMJE, "Ethical Considerations in the Conduct and Reporting of Research," op. cit. note 364; WAME, "Policy Statements: Ghost Writing Initiated by Commercial Companies," op. cit. note 341.

687 AAUP, "Academic Freedom and National Security in a Time of Crisis." op. cit. note 375. This statement discusses the history of classified research on campus, and also puts forward the guiding principles. For direct quotes and discussion, please see the main report.

688 Cornell University, *Guidelines on Sensitive and Proprietary Research,* 104–06, op. cit. note 378; MIT, *Policies and Procedures: A Guide for Faculty and Students.* op. cit. note 379. See note 379 for more detail; UC Berkeley, "Policy Guidelines Governing Openness and Freedom to Publish," op. cit. note 381, which states that "classified projects are not consistent with the teaching, research, and public service missions of the Berkeley campus." It goes on to explain: "The principal reasons that classified projects are unacceptable are (1) the resultant requirement for a campus facility clearance and (2) the inherent publication restrictions. In general, classified projects are not consistent with the teaching, research, and public service missions of the Berkeley campus."

689 AAUP, "Academic Freedom and National Security in a Time of Crisis," op. cit. note 375.

690 IOM, "Conflicts of Interest," 158, op. cit. note 40: "Faculty should engage only in bona fide consulting arrangements that require their expertise, that are based on written contracts with specific tasks and deliverables, and that are paid for at fair market value. As part of their administration of conflict of interest policies, university review of faculty consulting and other contracts is prudent and desirable."

691 AAMC-AAU, *Protecting Patients, Preserving Integrity, Advancing Health,* 68, op. cit. note 256.

692 C. Judson King, Provost, and Joseph Mullinix, Senior Vice President, UC Berkeley, "Guidance for Faculty and Other Academic Employees on Issues related to Intellectual Property and Consulting," March 3, 2003, http://www.ucop.edu/ott/pdf/consult.pdf. This policy reads in part: "Regulation 4, Special Services by Members of the Faculty (APM 020): Members of the faculty may render professional or scholarly services for compensation, unless they are prohibited by the terms of their appointment from accepting such compensation; but in no case may such employment be solicited or interfere with regular University duties." The Principles Underlying Regulation 4 continues, "… such service may be justified if it does not interfere with University commitments and if 1) it gives the individual experience

and knowledge of value to his teaching or research; 2) it is suitable research through which the individual may make worthy contributions to knowledge; or 3) it is appropriate public service."

693 AAMC-AAU, *Protecting Patients, Preserving Integrity, Advancing Health,* 34, op. cit. note 256.

694 DHHS, "Responsibility of Applicants for Promoting Objectivity in Research," op. cit. note 300. This rule expands the definition of what financial relationships investigators must report to their university employers, noting that all federal grant recipients must report not just how their financial interests (in a company, or other entity) might affect a particular federal project or grant, but how they might affect all of their other "institutional responsibilities," including research, consulting, teaching, and membership on university committees. According to DHHS, this rule change is designed to "provide institutions with a better understanding of the totality of an investigator's interests."

695 UC San Diego, Report of Joint Academic Senate-Administration Committee, op. cit. note 397.

696 AAMC, Protecting Subjects, Preserving Trust, Promoting Progress, 20, op. cit. note 258.

697 AAMC, Compact between Biomedical Graduate Students, 6, op. cit. note 394.

698 AAUP, "Statement on Graduate Students," in *Policy Documents and Reports,* 10th ed. (Washington, DC: AAUP; Baltimore: Johns Hopkins University Press, 2006), 280–81.

699 AAUP, "Joint Statement on Rights and Freedoms of Students," in *Policy Documents and Reports,* 10th ed. (Washington, DC: AAUP; Baltimore: Johns Hopkins University Press, 2006), 274.

700 AAMC-AAU, *Protecting Patients, Preserving Integrity, Advancing Health,* 25, op. cit. note 256.

701 IOM, "Conflicts of Interest," 116, op. cit. note 40.

702 The AAUP RIRs are available at http://www.aaup.org/AAUP/pubsres/policydocs/contents/RIR.htm. AAUP, "The Assignment of Course Grades and Student Appeals," in *Policy Documents and Reports,* 10th ed. (Washington, DC: AAUP; Baltimore: Johns Hopkins University Press, 2006), 127–28.

703 AAUP, "Statement on Copyright," in *Policy Documents and Reports,* 10th ed. (Washington, DC: AAUP; Baltimore: Johns Hopkins University Press, 2006), 214–15.

704 AAUP Special Committee on Distance Education and Intellectual Property Issues, "Sample Intellectual Property Policy and Contract Language," accessed June 3, 2012, http://www.aaup.org/AAUP/issues/DE/sampleIP.htm.

705 AAUP, "Statement on Copyright," 214, op. cit. note 703.

706 Westcott, Kathi, "Faculty Ownership of Research Affirmed," *Academe* 97, no. 5 (2011), 7, available at http://www.aaup.org/AAUP/pubsres/academe/2011/SO/nb/patentlaw.htm. The complete US Supreme Court decision from 2011 in *Board of Trustees of Leland Stanford Junior University v. Roche Molecular Systems* is available at http://www.supremecourt.gov/opinions/10pdf/09-1159.pdf.

707 AAUP, "Statement on Corporate Funding of Academic Research," 132, op. cit. note 4.

708 AAUP, "Statement on Government of Colleges and Universities," 139, op. cit. note 8.

709 NRC, Managing University Intellectual Property, op. cit. note 78.

710 AAUP, "Sample Intellectual Property Policy," op. cit. note 704.

711 AUTM, "Nine Points to Consider in Licensing University Technology," op. cit. note 416, a consensus statement signed by over 50 universities and endorsed by the AAMC and the Association of University Technology Managers (AUTM). The list of signatories is available at http://www.autm.net/source/NinePoints/ninepoints_endorsement.cfm.

712 Universities Allied for Essential Medicines (UAEM), "UC Berkeley," accessed June 6, 2012, available at http://essentialmedicine.org/our-work/successes/uc-berkeley/; University of California, Berkeley, Office of Intellectual Property and Industry Research Alliances, "Socially Responsible Licensing at U.C. Berkeley: An IP Management Strategy to Stimulate Research Support & Maximize Societal Impact," accessed June 6, 2012, available at http://ipira. berkeley.edu/sites/default/files/shared/doc/SRLP_Highlights_100910.pdf.

713 UAEM, "Philadelphia Consensus Statement," accessed June 3, 2012, available at http:// essentialmedicine.org/cs.

714 AUTM, "Statement of Principles and Strategies for the Equitable Dissemination of Medical Technologies," op. cit. note 417. See note 417 for more details.

715 NRC, Managing University Intellectual Property, 4, op. cit. note 78.

716 AUTM, "Nine Points to Consider in Licensing University Technology," op. cit. note 416.

717 "Exclusive licenses generally should be reserved for technologies that require significant follow-on investment to achieve commercialization, or where exclusivity is needed to confer a competitive advantage (so-called rival-in-use technologies). For technologies that are not rival-in-use or require little or no follow-on investment, nonexclusive licenses are generally warranted." NRC, *Managing University Intellectual Property,* 71, op. cit. note 78.

718 "When significant investment of time and resources in a technology are needed in order to achieve its broad implementation, an exclusive license often is necessary and appropriate. However, it is important that technology transfer offices be aware of the potential impact that the exclusive license might have on further research, unanticipated uses, future commercialization efforts and markets. Universities need to be mindful of the impact of granting overly broad exclusive rights and should strive to grant just those rights necessary to encourage development of the technology." AUTM, "Nine Points to Consider in Licensing University Technology," 2, op. cit. note 416.

719 "Special consideration should be given to the impact of an exclusive license on uses of a technology that may not be appreciated at the time of initial licensing. A license grant that encompasses all fields of use for the life of the licensed patent(s) may have negative consequences if the subject technology is found to have unanticipated utility. This possibility is particularly troublesome if the licensee is not able or willing to develop the technology in fields outside of its core business. Universities are encouraged to use approaches that balance a licensee's legitimate commercial needs against the university's goal (based on its educational and charitable mission and the public interest) of ensuring broad practical application of the fruits of its research programs. There are many alternatives to strict exclusive licensing, several of which are described in the Appendix." AUTM, "Nine Points to Consider in Licensing University Technology," 2, op. cit. note 416.

720 When Cornell University's Faculty Senate appointed a special faculty committee to review

large-scale, multi-year industrial research alliances, known as strategic corporate alliances (SCAs), its final consensus report advised that the university show a preference for non-exclusive licensing: "[L]icensing of inventions derived from SCA-funded work should, whenever possible, take the form of non-exclusive licenses to the corporate partner to use university-owned patents. By giving the licensor a monopoly over use of the patented invention, exclusive licensing inevitably interferes with full and open sharing of the results of academic research. Moreover, unless circumstances are very carefully assessed, it may allow the principal beneficiary of the patent right to become the private, rather than the public, interest." Cornell University, "Faculty Statement of Principles," 16, op. cit. note 114.

721 DHHS, NIH, "Principles and Guidelines for Recipients," op. cit. note 245.

722 AUTM, "Nine Points to Consider in Licensing University Technology," 5, op. cit. note 416.

723 "Many or most research tools, for example, should be managed in a fashion that is consistent with the broadest possible use and access, for example, by royalty-free licenses or royalties limited to recouping university direct expenses in acquiring patents and managing the licensing process. There may be several reasons for patenting a technology that is made available without a fee or only a modest fee, including an important one being 'defensive,' that is, to preclude patenting by another party that would restrict the availability of the technology. Nevertheless, such inventions are also candidates for deposit into the public domain, and the decision whether to patent or not patent should be carefully considered." NRC, *Managing University Intellectual Property,* 71–72, op. cit. note 78.

724 "The problems that BD [the Bayh-Dole Act] has raised for the biopharmaceutical industry are dwarfed by the problems it has raised for information technology. Universities may too often take a 'one size fits all' approach to patenting research results, notwithstanding the evidence that patents and exclusive licensing play a much more limited role in the development of information technology than they do in the pharmaceutical sector." Anthony D. So et al., "Is Bayh-Dole Good for Developing Countries? Lessons from the US Experience," *PLoS Biology* 6, no. 10 (October 2008). In congressional testimony in 2007, one prominent information technology executive from Hewlett-Packard complained that aggressive university patenting, overvaluing of intellectual assets, and hence unrealistic licensing terms impeded both product development and university-industry collaboration, encouraging companies to find other research partners, including offshore; see *The Bayh-Dole Act—The Next 25 Years, Hearing Before the House Subcomm. on Technology and Innovation, Comm. on Science and Technology,* 110th Cong. (July 17, 2007) (statement of Wayne C. Johnson, vice president, Worldwide University Relations, Hewlett-Packard Company), http://www.hp.com/hpinfo/abouthp/government/us/pdf/johnsontestimonybio.pdf. Similar complaints have surfaced periodically, with some firms stating that they prefer foreign to domestic university partnerships because academic institutions abroad are less insistent upon IP ownership and agreements are more quickly negotiated; see David Kramer, "Universities and Industry Find Roadblocks to R&D Partnering," *Physics Today* 61, no. 5 (2008): 20–22.

725 *The Role of Federally-Funded University Research in the Patent System, Hearing Before the Senate Comm. on the Judiciary,* 110th Cong. (October 24, 2007) (statement by Arti K. Rai, professor of

law, Duke University School of Law), http://www.law.duke.edu/news/pdf/rai_testimony.pdf; Arti K. Rai, John R. Allison, Bhaven N. Sampat, and Colin Crossman, "University Software Ownership and Litigation: A First Examination," *North Carolina Law Review* 87 (2009): 1519–70, available at http://scholarship.law.duke.edu/faculty_scholarship/1629; Robert E. Litan, Lesa Mitchell, and E. J. Reedy, "Commercializing University Innovations: A Better Way" (working paper, National Bureau of Economic Research, May 2007), available at http://www. brookings.edu/~/media/research/files/papers/2007/5/innovations%20litan/05_innovations_ litan.pdf; J. Strother Moore, Lawrence Snyder, and Philip A. Bernstein, "University-Industry Sponsored Research Agreements" (best practices memo, Computing Research Association, July 2003), available at http://www.cra.org/uploads/documents/resources/bpmemos/ University-Industry_Sponsored_Research_Agreements.pdf; J. Strother Moore, University of Texas at Austin, "Model Language for Patent and Licensing Agreements for Industrially Sponsored University Research in Information Technology," memorandum, June 25, 2003, available at http://www.cs.utexas.edu/~moore/publications/ip-memo-3.pdf.

726 University of California Office of the President, Office of Technology Transfer, "Electrical Engineering and Computer Science Intellectual Property Pilot Program," memorandum, August 30, 2000, available at http://patron.ucop.edu/ottmemos/docs/ott00-02.html.

727 BHEF, *Working Together, Creating Knowledge,* 60–62, op. cit. note 26.

728 UC Berkeley Academic Senate Committee, letter to Prof. William Drummond, op. cit. note 445. See note 445 for more detail.

729 AAUP, "1915 Declaration of Principles," 294–95, op. cit. note 2.

730 "Conflict of interest will be considered across all academic fields, not just biomedical ones (though biomedical conflicts have some unique aspects and invoke a special intensity and interest)." AAU, *Report on Individual and Institutional Financial Conflict of Interest,* 2, op. cit. note 14.

731 "Although this report focuses on those conflicts that arise in the context of human subjects research conducted primarily within or under the supervision of medical schools and teaching hospitals or by their personnel, institutions should strongly consider making the principles and processes recommended in this report applicable to all research. Protection of integrity and public trust are indeed values that underpin all academic research, irrespective of whether the particular challenges associated with human subjects research are present." AAMC-AAU, *Protecting Patients, Preserving Integrity, Advancing Health,* 4, op. cit. note 256. In addition, "The Committee recognizes that institutional COIs can arise in non-human subjects research, clinical care, and education, as well as in purchasing and other university business transactions and the Committee strongly recommends that institutions implement comprehensive institutional COI policies that embrace the full spectrum of the institution's activities," 36.

732 "No matter the type or stage of research, certain fundamentals still apply. All researchers should be subject to an institution's disclosure policies, as described in Chapter 3, and the institution's conflict of interest committee or its equivalent should be notified when investigators have financial stakes in the outcomes of their research. Similarly, following the

conceptual framework presented in Chapter 2, once a financial relationship or interest has been disclosed, it should be evaluated for determination of the likelihood that it will have an undue influence that will lead to bias or a loss of trust. If a risk is judged to exist, a conflict of interest committee might conclude that the implementation of safeguards is necessary. Such safeguards could consist of a management plan that includes the involvement of a researcher without a conflict of interest in certain aspects of the research and disclosure of the conflict to coinvestigators and in presentations and publications." IOM, "Conflicts of Interest," 119, op. cit. note 40.

733 IOM, "Conflicts of Interest," 68, op. cit. note 40

734 "A. Development and Adoption of Policies. Although the Advisory Committee was charged with examining institutional conflicts of interest specifically in the context of human subjects research, *the Committee urged AAU and AAMC member institutions to commit themselves to develop and implement comprehensive institutional conflicts of interest policies that govern all operational aspects of a university or an academic medical center…*" [emphasis added]. AAMC-AAU, *Protecting Patients, Preserving Integrity, Advancing Health,* xi, op. cit. note 256. This point is reiterated later: "Institutions should assure in policy and practice that institutional COIs will be addressed consistently throughout the institution, such that those subject to institutional financial conflict of interest policies, specifically officials of the institution and the institutions themselves, are subject to substantive reporting, disclosure, and management of their financial interests to protect the integrity of human subjects research and the subjects who participate in it, as well as institutional values and decision-making," 15. Similar consistency regarding implementation is required for individual COI rules as well, of course, and is addressed elsewhere by these organizations.

735 For example, "To manage identified conflicts of interest and to monitor the implementation of management recommendations, institutions should create a conflict of interest committee. That committee should use a full range of management tools, as appropriate, including elimination of the conflicting financial interest, prohibition or restriction of involvement of the individual with a conflict of interest in the activity related to the conflict, and providing additional disclosures of the conflict of interest. A conflict of interest committee should bring experience and consistency to evaluations of financial relationships with industry and decisions about those relationships, although the specific details (e.g., how risks and potential benefits are assessed and what management options are considered) may vary, depending on the activity in question." IOM, "Conflicts of Interest," 89–90, op. cit. note 40. The IOM further notes that these standing committees should have no members who themselves have conflicts of interest relevant to their COI oversight functions, 226–27.

736 This recommendation is a slightly adapted version of one issued by the AAMC-AAU, *Protecting Patients, Preserving Integrity, Advancing Health,* viii, op. cit. note 256.

737 IOM, "Conflicts of Interest," 222, op. cit. note 40.

738 "Separation of Administrative Responsibility," in AAMC-AAU, *Protecting Patients, Preserving Integrity, Advancing Health,* xi–xii, op. cit. note 256.

739 IOM, "Conflicts of Interest," op. cit. note 40: 65, box 3-1 and 83, box 3-2.

740 DHHS, "Responsibility of Applicants for Promoting Objectivity in Research," 53291–92, op. cit. note 300.

741 IOM, "Conflicts of Interest," 75, op. cit. note 40; DHHS, OIG, "How Grantees Manage Financial Conflicts of Interest," op. cit. note 305; COGR, *Recognizing and Managing Personal Financial Conflicts of Interest,* op. cit. note 494.

742 AAU, "Statement of Guiding Principles Regarding Institutional Relationships with Student Loan Providers," op. cit. note 498.

743 Cuomo, "College Loan Code of Conduct," op. cit. note 499. See also *Examining Unethical Practices in the Student Loan Industry, Hearing Before the House Comm. on Education and Labor,* 110th Cong. (April 25, 2007) (testimony by Andrew M. Cuomo, Attorney General, State of New York), http://www.ag.ny.gov/sites/default/files/pdfs/bureaus/student_loan/House%20 Testimony.pdf. See note 499 for more detail.

744 Department of Education (DOE), "Federal Perkins Loan Program, Federal Family Education Loan Program, and William D. Ford Federal Direct Loan Program," *Federal Register* 72, no. 211 (2007), 61959–62011. These DOE rules, attached to eligibility for federal student aid, require colleges to include at least three lenders on a preferred lender list, restrict lender gifts to colleges in exchange for business, prohibit payments to college financial aid employees, and encourage loan counseling.

745 Many of these state-level laws are reviewed in California Research Bureau, "Student Loans for Higher Education," op. cit. note 501.

746 Davidoff et al., "Sponsorship, Authorship, and Accountability," op. cit. note 193; ICMJE, "Uniform Requirements for Manuscripts," op. cit. note 193; WAME, "Recommendations on Publication Ethics Policies for Medical Journals," op. cit. note 341.

747 DHHS, "Responsibility of Applicants for Promoting Objectivity in Research," op. cit. note 300. For details on the DHHS's new requirements for public disclosure of significant faculty COI related to DHHS funded research, and the development of detailed COI "management plans," see 53287–88. The section on public disclosure reads as follows:

> (5)(i) Prior to the Institution's expenditure of any funds under a PHS- funded research project, the Institution shall ensure public accessibility, via a publicly accessible Web site or written response to any requestor within five business days of a request, of information concerning any significant financial interest disclosed to the Institution that meets the following three criteria:
>
> (A) The significant financial interest was disclosed and is still held by the senior/key personnel as defined by this subpart;
>
> (B) The Institution determines that the significant financial interest is related to the PHS-funded research; and
>
> (C) The Institution determines that the significant financial interest is a financial conflict of interest.
>
> (ii) The information that the Institution makes available via a publicly accessible Web site or written response to any requestor within five business days of a request, shall include, at a minimum, the following: the Investigator's name; the Investigator's title and role with

respect to the research project; the name of the entity in which the significant financial interest is held; the nature of the significant financial interest; and the approximate dollar value of the significant financial interest (dollar ranges are permissible: $0–$4,999; $5,000–$9,999; $10,000–$19,999; amounts between $20,000–$100,000 by increments of $20,000; amounts above $100,000 by increments of $50,000), or a statement that the interest is one whose value cannot be readily determined through reference to public prices or other reasonable measures of fair market value.

(iii) If the Institution uses a publicly accessible Web site for the purposes of this subsection, the information that the Institution posts shall be updated at least annually. In addition, the Institution shall update the Web site within sixty days of the Institution's receipt or identification of information concerning any additional significant financial interest of the senior/key personnel for the PHS-funded research project that was not previously disclosed, or upon the disclosure of a significant financial interest of senior/ key personnel new to the PHS-funded research project, if the Institution determines that the significant financial interest is related to the PHS-funded research and is a financial conflict of interest. The Web site shall note that the information provided is current as of the date listed and is subject to updates, on at least an annual basis and within 60 days of the Institution's identification of a new financial conflict of interest. If the Institution responds to written requests for the purposes of this subsection, the Institution will note in its written response that the information provided is current as of the date of the correspondence and is subject to updates, on at least an annual basis and within 60 days of the Institution's identification of a new financial conflict of interest, which should be requested subsequently by the requestor.

(iv) Information concerning the significant financial interests of an individual subject to paragraph (a)(5) of this section shall remain available, for responses to written requests or for posting via the Institution's publicly accessible Web site for at least three years from the date that the information was most recently updated.

748 IOM, "Conflicts of Interest," 117–18, op. cit. note 40, recommendation 4.1; see also p. 2, "Although the committee recognizes that collaborations with industry can be beneficial, the committee recommends, as a general rule, that researchers should not conduct research involving human participants if they have a financial interest in the outcome of the research, for example, if they hold a patent on an intervention being tested in a clinical trial. The only exceptions should be if an individual's participation is judged to be essential for the safe and appropriate conduct of the research"; AAMC, *Protecting Subjects, Preserving Trust, Promoting Progress,* op. cit. note 258; AAMC, *Protecting Subjects, Preserving Trust, Promoting Progress II,* op. cit. note 472; and AAMC-AAU, *Protecting Patients, Preserving Integrity, Advancing Health,* xii, op. cit. note 256, which states, "Decisions about whether or not to pursue a particular human subjects research project in the presence of an institutional conflict of interest should be governed by a 'rebuttable presumption' against doing the research at or under the auspices of the conflicted institution" unless a compelling case can be made to justify an exception.

749 AAMC-AAU, *Protecting Patients, Preserving Integrity, Advancing Health,* 11, op. cit. note 256,

which reads in part: "Institutions should have clear policies, compliant with applicable federal regulations that address the reporting and management of conflicts of interest of IRB members. The provisions should require reporting of all financial interests (no de minimis threshold) by IRB members ... upon their initial appointment to the IRB, with updating annually and more often when circumstances change. The provisions should specify how the IRB Chair and/or the Administrator of the IRB will identify and evaluate potential conflicts of interest of IRB members and make clear that any conflicted IRB member must be recused from any deliberations relating to studies with which that IRB member has a potential conflict of interest"; AAU, *Report on Individual and Institutional Financial Conflict of Interest,* op. cit. note 14.

750 This recommendation is drawn from AAMC, *Industry Funding of Medical Education,* ix, op. cit. note 318; AAMC, *In the Interest of Patients,* 23, op. cit. note 261.

751 AAMC, *In the Interest of Patients,* 24, op. cit. note 261.

752 Cornell University, "Faculty Statement of Principles," 9, op. cit. note 114.

753 Cornell University, "Faculty Statement of Principles," 16, op. cit. note 114; UC Berkeley Academic Senate Committee, letter to Prof. William Drummond, op. cit. note 445; UC Berkeley Academic Senate Task Force on University-Industry Partnerships, "Principles and Guidelines for Large-Scale Collaborations between the University and Industry, Government, and Foundations," accessed June 6, 2012, available at http://academic-senate.berkeley.edu/sites/default/files/recommendations-reports/tf_uip_report-final1.pdf; Busch et al., "External Review of the Collaborative Research Agreement," 41–43, op. cit. note 114; California State Legislature, Senate, "Impacts of Genetic Engineering on California's Environment," op. cit. note 561.

754 Washburn, *Big Oil Goes to College,* op. cit. note 105.

755 AAMC, *Protecting Subjects, Preserving Trust, Promoting Progress,* op. cit. note 258; FASEB, *Shared Responsibility, Individual Integrity,* op. cit. note 596: "Guiding principle 6: Investigators shall have access to, and be involved in the analysis and/or interpretation of all data generated in the research"; Davidoff et al., "Sponsorship, Authorship, and Accountability," op. cit. note 193; ICMJE, "Uniform Requirements for Manuscripts," op. cit. note 193; WAME, "Publication Ethics Policies for Medical Journals," op. cit. note 341: "All authors must take responsibility in writing for the accuracy of the manuscript, and one author must be the guarantor and take responsibility for the work as a whole. A growing trend among journals is to also require that for reports containing original data, at least one author (e.g., the principal investigator) should indicate that she or he had full access to all the data in the study and takes responsibility for the integrity of the data and the accuracy of the data analysis. This helps assure that authors, and not funding sources, have final say over the analysis and reporting of their results."

756 In 2005, the ICMJE instructed its researchers to deposit data into registries, such as http://www.clinicaltrials.gov/, as a precondition for publication, hoping to discourage tampering with trial protocols and final data analysis. See De Angelis et al., "Is This Clinical Trial Fully Registered?" op. cit. note 611; De Angelis et al., "Clinical Trial Registration," op. cit. note 611, which reads in part: "The ICMJE member journals will require, as a condition of

consideration for publication, registration in a public trials registry. Trials must register at or before the onset of patient enrollment. This policy applies to any clinical trial starting enrollment after July 1, 2005. For trials that began enrollment prior to this date, the ICMJE member journals will require registration by September 13, 2005, before considering the trial for publication."

757 In 2007, Congress passed the Food and Drug Administration Amendments Act, which mandated that clinical trials related to all FDA-regulated products, or products seeking regulation, must be registered at http://www.clinicaltrials.gov/. The law also imposes penalties for noncompliance. Food and Drug Administration Amendments Act of 2007, Pub. L. 110-85, 121 Stat. 823 (2007). Title VIII, Section 801 mandates that a "responsible party" (i.e., the sponsor or designated principal investigator) register and report results of certain "applicable clinical trials"; see http://prsinfo.clinicaltrials.gov/fdaaa.html. For an overview discussion of the FDAAA, see Dolgin, "Publication Bias Continues Despite Clinical-Trial Registration," op. cit. note 612.

758 In 2006, the AAMC endorsed and finalized a set of recommended *Principles for Protecting Integrity in the Conduct and Reporting of Clinical Trials,* which recommends that all clinical trials and their protocols be registered on a publicly accessible database. (These principles were developed in collaboration with the Centers for Education and Research in Therapeutics and the BlueCross BlueShield Association.) The AAMC wrote that it developed these principles to address the "inconsistency in research standards" at academic medical centers, which "can affront human research ethics, undermine academic integrity, distort public policy and medical practice, and impair public health." Ehringhaus and Korn, *Principles for Protecting Integrity,* op. cit. note 351. See Principles 6–8, which recommend registration of clinical trials within 21 days of initiating enrollment of research participants, and in a manner "fully pursuant to the ICMJE requirements."

759 Ibid. See Principles 10–14, which read in part: "[Any] multisite clinical trial, at the outset, should establish a publication and analysis committee [hereinafter P&A committee]. It is essential that the P&A committee be independent of the sponsor's control, have access to the full data set, understand and implement the prespecified analysis plan, and have the resources and skills both to interpret that analysis and perform additional analysis if required. In order to prevent any appearance of undue influence by the sponsor, the P&A committee should contain a majority of participating, non-sponsor-employed investigators, with appropriate skills in analysis and interpretation of clinical trials. The P&A committee and the steering committee may have the same membership."

760 FDA, "Financial Disclosure by Clinical Investigators."

761 Jon Thompson, Patricia Baird, and Jocelyn Downie, *Report of the Committee of Inquiry on the Case Involving Dr. Nancy Olivieri, the Hospital for Sick Children, the University of Toronto, and Apotex Inc.* (Toronto: James Lorimer and Co., 2001), available at http://www.caut.ca/uploads/OlivieriInquiryReport.pdf.

762 IOM, "Conflicts of Interest," 158, op. cit. note 40, 158, which reads in part: "[F]aculty should not participate in speakers bureaus and similar promotional activities in which they either

present content directly controlled by industry or formulate their remarks to win favor and continued speaking fees"; AAMC, *Implementing the Recommendations of the AAMC Task Force : A Selected Policy Language Compendium* (Washington, DC: AAMC, 2008), available at https://www.aamc.org/download/49708/data/compendium2008.pdf.

763 Brennan, et al., "Health Industry Practices That Create Conflicts of Interest," op. cit. note 317; Rothman and Chimonas, "New Developments in Managing Physician-Industry Relationships," op. cit. note 317.

764 "For example, the University of Massachusetts views speakers bureaus as an 'extension of the marketing process' and forbids faculty participation in them. The Mayo Clinic has long prohibited faculty from speaking on behalf of industry, and its current policy prohibits participation in the speakers bureaus of commercial firms because the linkage would imply endorsement by the Mayo Clinic ... . A policy recently adopted by the Johns Hopkins University School of Medicine (2009) states that faculty may not participate on-site or off-site in 'activities with any of the following characteristics ... a company has the contractual right to dictate what the faculty member says; a company (not the faculty member) creates the slide set (or other presentation materials) and has the final approval of all content and edits; the faculty member receives compensation from the company and acts as the company's employee or spokesperson for the purposes of dissemination of company-generated presentation materials or promotion of company products; and/or a company controls the publicity related to the event'. . . . The policy notes that some of these activities occur in the context of speakers bureaus but it is the conditions of an activity that determine whether it is permissible." IOM, "Conflicts of Interest," 156, op. cit. note 40. Other schools, such as the University of Pittsburgh Medical Center, have implemented new institutional oversight policies that seek to ensure editorial independence and financial propriety; see "Policy on Conflicts of Interest and Interactions between Representatives of Certain Industries and Faculty, Staff and Students of the Schools of the Health Sciences and Personnel Employed by UPMC at all Domestic Locations," issued November 12, 2007, http://www.coi.pitt.edu/IndustryRelationships/policy.htm.

765 IOM, "Conflicts of Interest," 20–21, 189–215, op. cit. note 40.

766 "RECOMMENDATION 5.3. A new system of funding accredited continuing medical education should be developed that is free of industry influence, enhances public trust in the integrity of the system, and provides high-quality education. A consensus development process that includes representatives of the member organizations that created the accrediting body for continuing medical education, members of the public, and representatives of organizations such as certification boards that rely on continuing medical education should be convened to propose within 24 months of the publication of this report a funding system that will meet these goals." IOM, "Conflicts of Interest," 161–162, op. cit. note 40.

A similar conclusion regarding continuing medical education programs was reached in the summary of a 2008 consensus conference, held at the Mayo Clinic, which noted that "continuing medical education requires a 'strategic management process that focuses on the integrity of an enterprise' and that deals 'in a convincing, transparent and accountable manner with issues such as commercial interest influence, conflicts of interest, bias, sources of evidence and the quality of product, process and delivery.'" IOM, "Conflicts of Interest," 151, op. cit. note 40, citing Kane, *Conference Proceedings,* op. cit. note 642.

767 Somewhat strangely, the IOM addressed its recommendations in this particular arena of marketing to the biomedical companies (asking them to adopt policies that prohibit distribution of gifts, free meals, and drug samples), even though this marketing takes place at facilities which are under the control of academic and academic-affiliated institutions; *Implementing the Recommendations of the AAMC Task Force,* op. cit. note 630; Rothman and Chimonas, "New Developments in Managing Physician-Industry Relationships," op. cit. note 317, which details the January 2006 recommendations of the IMAP and ABIM Foundation that academic medical centers should lead the profession in eliminating undue industry influence in clinical care.

768 Sox and Rennie, "Seeding Trials: Just Say 'No.'" op. cit. note 658.; Malakoff, "Clinical Trials and Tribulations," op. cit. note 658; Elliott, "Useless Studies, Real Harm," op. cit. note 659; Krumholz, et al. "Study of Neurontin," op. cit. note 659; Kessler, et al., "Therapeutic-Class Wars," op. cit. note 660; Katz, "Time to Nip 'Seeding Trials' in the Bud," op. cit. note 660.

769 "An influential Harvard child psychiatrist told the drug giant Johnson & Johnson that planned studies of its medicines in children would yield results benefiting the company, according to court documents dating over several years that the psychiatrist wants sealed. The psychiatrist, Dr. Joseph Biederman, outlined plans to test Johnson & Johnson's drugs in presentations to company executives. ... An inquiry by Senator Charles E. Grassley, Republican of Iowa, revealed last year that Dr. Biederman earned at least $1.6 million in consulting fees from drug makers from 2000 to 2007 but failed to report all but about $200,000 of this income to university officials." Harris, "Drug Maker Told Studies Would Aid It, Papers Say," op. cit. note 296. This article goes on to discuss three specific clinical drug trials, which Biederman successfully pitched to drug manufacturers and then later published with conclusions that matched those predetermined outcomes. After reviewing these legal documents, Sen. Grassley wrote a letter asking the presidents of Harvard University and Massachusetts General Hospital to explain why these slides suggest an expectation of positive outcomes for the drugs prior to the commencement of the clinical trials. He noted that when he asked a physician researcher to independently review the slides, the doctor said that "it appeared that the slides discussed in this letter were nothing more than marketing tools, as opposed to discussions of independent scientific research." Sen. Charles E. Grassley, letter to Dr. Drew Gilpin Faust and Dr. Peter L. Slavin, March 20, 2009, available at http://s.wsj.net/public/resources/documents/WSJ-Major_Protocol_Violation_Letters032009.pdf.

770 "In January 1997, [UCLA Professor James] Enstrom submitted a research proposal to the Philip Morris Research Center, where it was reviewed by the Scientific Research Review Committee (SRRC), a committee whose purpose was to 'ensure that all scientific research, related to tobacco or smoking, conducted or funded by Philip Morris, ... serves relevant business needs.' The proposal, 'Relationship of low levels of active smoking to mortality,' sought to analyse data from four epidemiological cohorts ... . In his cover letter to Richard

Carchman, Director of Scientific Affairs, Philip Morris, Enstrom stated: 'These data are highly relevant to the ETS issue ... A level of trust must be developed based on my past research on passive smoking and epidemiology in general in order to work out the best way for me to conduct this research. A substantial research commitment on your part is necessary in order for me to effectively compete against the large mountain of epidemiologic data and opinions that already exist regarding the health effects of ETS and active smoking.' ... The proposal [Enstrom submitted] stated: 'an unrestricted gift to James E. Enstrom / UCLA with mutual understanding/trust would minimize university restrictions and eliminate overhead costs.' ... Philip Morris funded the project in April 1997 for $150 000 to be paid in two instalments." Bero et al., "The Limits of Competing Interest Disclosures," 118–26. Op Cit. Note 358.